The

_Spiritual Traveler

∽

BOSTON AND
NEW ENGLAND

A GUIDE TO SACRED SITES AND
PEACEFUL PLACES

JANA RIESS

In Association with Historic Boston Incorporated

HiddenSpring

The Spiritual Traveler series editor: Jan-Erik Guerth

The cover image shows the Portland Head Lighthouse in Portland, Maine. Digital Imagery © 2001 PhotoDisc, Inc. Cover photo by Glen Allison.

Cover design by Alexandra Lord Gatje
Book design by Saija Autrand, Faces Type & Design
Maps by John Riess

Library of Congress Cataloging-in-Publication Data

Riess, Jana.
    The spiritual traveler : Boston and New England : a guide to sacred sites and peaceful places / Jana Riess.
        p. cm.
    Includes bibliographical references and index.
    ISBN 1-58768-008-4
    1. Boston Region (Mass.)—Guidebooks.   2. New England—Guidebooks.
3. Sacred space—Massachusetts—Boston Region—Guidebooks.   4. Sacred space—New England—Guidebooks. 5. Religious institutions—Massachusetts—Boston Region—Guidebooks. 6. Religious institutions—New England—Guidebooks. 7. Boston Region (Mass.)—Religion.   8. New England—Religion.
I. Title.

F73.18 .R54 2002
917.44'610444—dc21

                                                                    2002002874

Published by
HiddenSpring
An imprint of Paulist Press
997 Macarthur Boulevard
Mahwah, New Jersey 07430

www.hiddenspringbooks.com

Printed and bound in the
United States of America

Contents

ABOUT THE AUTHOR

Jana Riess is the religion book review editor for *Publishers Weekly*. She holds a Ph.D. in American religious history from Columbia University and an M.Div. from Princeton Theological Seminary. She did her undergraduate work at Wellesley College in Massachusetts, and has lived in various places throughout New England.

ACKNOWLEDGMENTS

The author would like to acknowledge the kind assistance and support of the following individuals: Edward Bergman, Marilyn Chiat, Susan Elia, Julie Gamponia, Tona Hangen, Tania Rands Lyon, Lillian Miao, Phyllis Riess, John Riess, Linda Roghaar, Karen Glasser Scandrett, Sara Skaldini, Philip and Nelda Smith, Blair Tingley, and Brad Verter. Special thanks are due to the Theologiggle Reunion crew of Rienstras and Burnetts. I hereby present my mudpie.

I wish to also thank those teachers who shared with me their love for American religious history: Randall Balmer, Claudia Bushman, Richard Bushman, Edwin Gaustad, Stephen Marini, James Moorhead, Albert Raboteau, Leigh Schmidt, and especially Judith Weisenfeld.

I owe a special debt to my editor, Jan-Erik Guerth, whose suggestions have made this a better book.

This book is dedicated to my husband Phil, my favorite companion in all travels of the spirit.

The
$\mathcal{S}$piritual Traveler

·························· ∾ ··························

Sacred journeys and sacred sites have been at the center of humankind's spiritual life from the very beginning. The Spiritual Traveler invites seekers of every faith and none to discover and connect with these ancient traditions and to find—either for the first time or anew—unique ways of pilgrimage in today's world.

PLEASE BE IN TOUCH

We have worked very hard to make this edition of The Spiritual Traveler as accurate and up to date as possible. However, any travel information could change at any time. If you think you have come across errors or omissions, please let us know. In addition, we would love to hear about your spiritual discoveries—any sacred sites or peaceful places that you have found along the way, but not in this book. We will try to include them in upcoming editions. You can reach us at:

thespiritualtraveler@hiddenspringbooks.com.

LAST, BUT NOT LEAST

Please understand that the author, editors, and publisher cannot accept responsibility for any errors in this book or adverse experiences you might encounter while traveling. We encourage you to stay alert and be aware of your environment while on your spiritual journey.

"I have seen many things in my travels, and I understand more than I can express."—Sirach (Ecclesiasticus) 34:11, 12

A NOTE TO THE READER

"... none by traveling over known lands can find out the unknown."
—William Blake,
Principle Four of "All Religions are One" (1795)

Why spiritual travel?

As William Blake so aptly put it more than two centuries ago, traveling only known lands cannot teach us the unknown. Conversely, new lands—which we can access through spiritual travel—promise to help us discover new truths. Even known lands can become new when we encounter them as spiritual travelers. Perhaps this is why contemporary Americans, like the pilgrims of old, are demonstrating such an upsurge of interest in spiritual travel.

In a transient society where individuals are constantly in motion, it is no surprise that Americans have, in the words of sociologist Robert Wuthnow, gone from a spirituality of "dwelling" to one of "seeking." According to Wuthnow, spirituality was once defined by membership in a synagogue, church, or mosque; it was tied to a physical place. Now, however, spirituality is often defined by the process of seeking—the journey itself. Spiritual travel, which is all about journeys (both physical and metaphorical), meets the needs of a culture of spiritual seekers. It transforms the journeys themselves into spiritual destinations; peace and lasting joy can be found in the process.

This book is for readers standing anywhere on the spectrum of spiritual travel—from the basic tourist who is interested in visiting houses of worship to the dedicated pilgrim. A pilgrimage is any consciously undertaken spiritual journey, whether physical or simply of the soul. The pilgrim seeks to grow, to learn, to be changed by an experience of the sacred. So whether you are bringing this book along with you on a vacation to New England or simply letting your imagination roam while sitting at home, it is my hope that your travels bring you deeper wisdom and an appreciation for our nation's rich spiritual heritage. As we tour the spiritual sites in this book, we will encounter, time and again, the age-old questions: What constitutes a sacred space? Why have human beings constantly felt the need to construct spiritual sites, whether they be composed of a few benches in a maple grove or a soaring cathedral in the commercial center of a city? How should we approach a house of worship of another religious tradition?

I am a religious historian, and I never tire of the subject. But I realize that history is not enough to understand a spiritual destination. It's not sufficient to merely know the past of a place; the present and the future also make a spot holy. Such sacred spaces are consecrated and reconsecrated by people of faith. What makes history come alive are the stories, not only the stories from the past but also the tales of present-day transformations and future growth. This spirit is embodied in the beautiful frieze that runs around the perimeter of Trinity Church in Boston. If you follow its trajectory you will discover that it stops, quite suddenly, almost in artistic midsentence. What appears, at first glance, to be an architectural mistake (did they run out of money before the project was completed? many visitors wonder) was actually done intentionally. The sudden termination of the frieze represents the sacred history that has yet to be written for that house of worship.

This is a multifaith guidebook. The authors in the Spiritual Traveler series make every effort to include spiritual sites and peaceful places from a broad variety of religious traditions, reflecting the tremendous diversity of faith groups today. Although New England is the clear epicenter of all things Puritan, it is also home to a host of other traditions—Sufism and Mormonism, Judaism and Wicca, just to name a few. Entries from all of these traditions, and many more, are present in this book.

BEYOND HOUSES OF WORSHIP

Many, but not all, of the entries in this guidebook feature houses of worship—churches, mosques, synagogues, temples and the like. But since "the Spirit bloweth where it listeth" (John 3:8), houses of worship comprise only one part of the story. Spiritual sites can also include lovely spots in nature, as with Walden Pond and Bash Bish Falls in Massachusetts, the Spirit in Nature walking trails in Vermont, or Maine's spectacular national park, Acadia. As New England poet Henry Wadsworth Longfellow (1807–82) put it in 1871, "Wondrous truths, and manifold as wondrous, God has written in those stars above; But not less in the bright flowerets under us stands the revelation of his love."

In this book, "peaceful places" in nature are indicated with a and include parks, mountains, waterfalls, seashores, and other natural wonders. Sites for the spiritual traveler also encompass the homes of some of New England's literary greats, from poets Robert Frost and Emily Dickinson to Transcendentalist writers Louisa May Alcott and Henry David Thoreau. Many of these masters of the written word tackled profound spiritual themes in their writing, and their words have offered great wisdom to many.

This book also presents sidebars and entries on human-made peaceful places, such as the covered bridges of Vermont, the rock walls of New Hampshire, or the lighthouses of the Massachusetts shore. Such historic sites, which are often located in rural communities, beckon to the spiritual traveler as vibrant efforts to harness the powers of nature. Finally, numerous cemeteries and gardens are profiled in this book. From the centuries-old crypt in the undercroft of Center Church on the Green in New Haven, Connecticut, to the nineteenth-century "rural cemetery movement" that spawned Mount Auburn and Forest Hills Cemeteries in the Boston area, burying grounds have long been a natural meeting place of the human and the divine. And in their gardens, New Englanders have attempted to beautify their world with flowers and shrubs even as they—in that ever-practical New England mentality—raised their vegetables and crops. Flower lovers will thrill at the roses at the Elizabeth Park Rose Garden in West Hartford, Connecticut, or the dazzling rhododendrons at Heritage Plantation in Sandwich, Massachusetts. Modern-day dryads will likewise enjoy the thousands of trees in Boston's Arnold Arboretum, and history buffs will appreciate the re-created "period gardens" of Strawbery Banke Museum in Portsmouth, New Hampshire, and the Gertrude Jekyll Garden at the Glebe House Museum in Woodbury, Connecticut.

Even with its specialized focus, this book cannot hope to provide a detailed overview of every spiritual site in New England. For example, dozens of New England churches have bells that were cast by Paul Revere; due to space limitations, it is not possible to include them all. This book offers entries on sites that are open to the public—entirely cloistered monastic communities or historic buildings that are not open for visitors have not been included.

A final word on planning your visit: Many of these sites are closed from November to mid-May, so be sure to confirm availability ahead of time if you plan an off-season visit.

CHAPTER ONE

···················· ❧ ····················

*I*ntroduction:
The Story of Spiritual Life
in New England

THE HISTORY OF NEW ENGLAND'S spiritual life is one
of change and of encounter. The first, and potentially most disastrous, of
these encounters came in the early seventeenth century, when English
settlers arrived in New England with the intent of claiming the land. Their
settlement parties—which landed in Plymouth in 1620 and Shawmut
(now Boston) in 1630—came on the heels of decades of incursions by
Spanish conquistadores and French merchants, all intent upon building
personal fortunes and extending national interests. Was it exploration or
exploitation? This question has been argued endlessly and remains unre-
solved. As we continue the debate, we often forget that alongside political
and economic motives, Europe's colonizing nations had religious goals as
well—to convert the "heathen" indigenous population and establish
whichever church the head of state happened to believe was the true,
right, and divinely ordained one. In England, this changed several times in
the sixteenth and seventeenth centuries, as the nation swung between
Catholic and Protestant rulership.

In New England, the Wampanoag, Narragansett, and Pequot nations
paid a heavy price for English settlement. Although the story of English
contact with Native Americans is not entirely unscrupulous—some individuals treated the Indians as fairly as they knew how, given the context
of the time period—in general, the English behaved cruelly. Some did not

even believe that Native Americans ("savages" or "heathens," in their words) were human. Others, such as the Puritan missionary John Eliot (1604–90), believed the Native Americans had souls that desperately needed saving. (The first Bible to be printed in New England, in 1661, was in the Algonquin language. Eliot used it as a missionary tool.) Within a generation of European settlement, the populations of New England's tribes had been severely diminished by wars with the English, wars with other native tribes that were friends of the English, and new diseases such as smallpox. By the end of the seventeenth century, the English had taken most native lands for their own use, usually without purchase or permission.

PURITAN HERITAGE AND COLONIAL NEW ENGLAND

New England became, for better or for worse, a land of Puritan heritage. From the landing of the first Pilgrims in Plymouth in 1620 through subsequent decades of English migration, the "Puritan Way" defined seventeenth- and eighteenth-century life for most New Englanders. Puritan theology exerted a deep influence on the founding of New England's colonies. In the Puritan mentality, salvation was entirely the result of God's grace and foreordained election, and not due to human merit. In other words, good works alone could not guarantee a person's entry into God's kingdom. However, this "election" theology never resulted in a free-for-all, where individuals abandoned good works as meaningless, because Puritans believed that good works—and to a certain extent, material success—were evidence that God had already bestowed his blessing upon the Puritan experiment. Their achievements and good works were therefore signs of God's election.

Puritan religious practices were quite strict; Sabbath observance was mandated for all Massachusetts residents until the late eighteenth century. On Sundays, the Puritans would not travel, conduct business, go visiting, or engage in pleasurable diversions. In Massachusetts today, vestiges of these restrictions still exist in "blue laws" that prevent, for example, the sale of liquor on Sundays in some communities.

The "Puritan experiment" was particularly entrenched in the colonies of Massachusetts and Connecticut. (Rhode Island, as we shall see, was created to be a colony that practiced religious tolerance, while the northern colonies of Vermont, New Hampshire, and Maine always had a rather stubborn independent streak.) Connecticut disestablished its Congregational Church (the institutional legacy of Puritanism) in 1818, while in Massachusetts, the Congregational Church was the official state religion until 1833, almost a full half-century after the nation's Bill of Rights had declared freedom of religion for all citizens. Disestablishment ended the practice of public funding for Congregational ministers and parishes through the taxes that each resident had been required to pay.

New England, then, and particularly southern New England, is closely intertwined with the legacy of Puritanism. In a curious twist of fate, the popular imagination has conflated the Puritans' endurance of religious persecution in England with the idea that they ardently wished to make New England a land that would promote religious freedom. It is certainly true that the Puritans craved religious freedom for *themselves*, but it is far too generous to claim that they were willing to extend religious freedom to anyone who dissented from their covenant. In this book we will meet dissenters such as Roger Williams (1603–83), who was banished from Massachusetts because he rejected certain elements of Puritan theocracy (religiously directed civil government) and because he believed that the church and the state should be entirely separate entities. Williams (see page 14) went on to found the colony of Rhode Island, where he made religious freedom a primary concern. He opened the colony to non-Puritans, like Quakers and Huguenots, and granted asylum to ex-Puritan refugees like the feisty Anne Hutchinson (1591–1643). Excommunicated from the Puritan church and banished from Massachusetts in 1638 for claiming to have received "immediate revelation" from God himself, Hutchinson found a sympathetic new home in Rhode Island (see page 257). Williams even opened the colony to non-Christians, a daring step for the time period. Newport, Rhode Island, became the home of New England's first Jewish synagogue in 1658 (see page 245).

Northern New England, too, had an independent temperament when it came to religion. Certainly, most towns in Maine, New Hampshire, and Vermont were modeled in the Puritan way, with a Congregational meetinghouse at the center of town. But perhaps because these areas were settled decades later, when Massachusetts's ironfisted control of both religion and government had begun to relax somewhat, the northern colonies never experienced the close fusion of church and state that flourished in Massachusetts and Connecticut. (Even Maine, which was officially part of Massachusetts until it joined the Union as an independent state in 1820, did not wholly follow Massachusetts's pattern of fusing religion and government.) Congregationalism was very successful in northern New England, but so were other Christian groups, such as the Shakers, who by the end of the eighteenth century had four thriving communities in New Hampshire and Maine (see pages 319, 325, 347, and 364). The Quakers also found a solid home there, particularly in seafaring communities such as Portsmouth, New Hampshire, and Portland, Maine. Other groups that historian Steve Marini has called "radical sects" prospered in northern New England, including the Freewill Baptists (who denied the Calvinist doctrine of election, believing that everyone had the opportunity to claim salvation; see page 331) and the Universalists (who took that theology a step further by teaching that all people, not just Christians, would be saved by a loving and benevolent God; see page 27).

THE NINETEENTH CENTURY

At the beginning of the nineteenth century, one observer of American religion said he expected that the Presbyterians, Episcopalians (see page 12), and Congregationalists (see page 16) would continue to dominate American life. However, this remark pointed only to a larger truth: that the one constant feature of American religion is its capacity for rapid and dramatic change. Although those three denominations had indeed commanded American religious life in the eighteenth century, the landscape would experience a sea change in the nineteenth.

Within American Protestantism, the primary story of the period revolves around two upstart sects that began to gain ground after the American Revolution. Whereas spiritual life under the "great trio" of Congregationalists, Presbyterians, and Episcopalians emphasized conformance to creed, the Baptists (see page 13) and Methodists (see page 18) stressed an emotional and personal conversion experience. While the colonial churches required clergy to be highly educated, the Baptists and Methodists welcomed to their clergy ranks men armed only with an ardent desire to serve Jesus and to carry the gospel message forward. And these new denominations went straight to the people: to tiny frontier communities, to isolated outposts in the countryside, and to taverns and harbor docks in the cities. They preached in revivals and "camp meetings" and wherever local churches would grant them a pulpit for the night. Moreover, the Baptists and Methodists brought their message to African Americans, who took to their churches more readily than to the more established and scholarly traditions of Congregationalism, Presbyterianism, and Episcopalianism. In the early nineteenth century, several African American Baptist and Methodist congregations were founded in the

Northeast, including the African meetinghouses in Boston and on Nantucket (both Baptist; see pages 82 and 215).

Meanwhile, New England's Congregational and Episcopal churches suffered, at the turn of the nineteenth century, from the Unitarian controversy (see page 27). Beginning with King's Chapel in 1786 (see page 77), many of Boston's Congregational and Episcopal churches began to embrace the more liberal, loving tones of Unitarianism. Unitarianism argued for God as one being (and not three-in-one as Father, Son, and Holy Spirit, the traditional Trinitarian position) and based its claims on the supremacy of human reason. By the end of the nineteenth century, the Unitarian schism had affected most of the Congregational churches in Massachusetts and northern New England; some remained stubbornly Trinitarian and Calvinist, while others discarded much of Puritan theology by turning Unitarian. Unitarianism was most prominent in Boston and the larger towns of Maine and New Hampshire; in the south, Connecticut's Congregationalist churches remained largely unmoved by it.

Beyond the Protestant world, the most important story of nineteenth-century Christian growth in the United States is the tremendous rise of Roman Catholicism. As detailed below (see page 24), changing immigration patterns in the mid– and late–nineteenth century brought millions of Catholic immigrants from Ireland, Italy, Germany, and eastern Europe. They were not always welcomed by the Protestants who had previously enjoyed majority status in New England and elsewhere. Anti-Catholic prejudice ran high, and it was decades before Roman Catholics achieved anything approximating equal status.

The nineteenth century was also an age of spiritual seeking. Some New Englanders looked beyond the usual options of Protestant and Catholic Christianity, and to the East, for spiritual inspiration. Transcendentalism (see page 139) drew from Indian religions such as Buddhism and Hinduism, as well as the romantic poets, to create a new spiritual movement. Initially embraced only by a small circle of poets and philosophers in Concord, Massachusetts, Transcendentalism spread throughout New England in the late 1830s and 1840s, spawning its own literary magazine and intellectual heroes.

At the very end of the nineteenth century, New England began to experience a taste of the religious diversity that would define the region more fully a century later. From roughly 1880 until 1920, eastern European immigration brought millions of Jews to America. Many of them settled in New England, particularly in and around Boston, though they were often not welcome (see page 81). The same boats brought tens of thousands of Eastern Orthodox Christians. There were also tiny communities of Baha'is, Muslims, and Hindus. In short, during the nineteenth century New England had gone from being a Puritan stronghold to an area that was home to many different Christian traditions, to a region of several world faiths.

THE TWENTIETH CENTURY

At the threshold of the twenty-first century, the key word to describe religion in America is *diversity*. This has not always been the case. In 1924, the United States Congress passed the Johnson-Reed Act, ushering in the most isolationist phase of American history. This legislation severely restricted foreign immigration to the United States and ended the nation's four-decade span of rapid immigration. From 1880 to 1924, nine million immigrants had come to the United States from northern and western Europe, 8.2 million from eastern Europe, and 5.3 million from southern Europe. There were also 650,000 Asian immigrants; their numbers were significantly smaller because of an 1882 Chinese Exclusion Act that had limited Chinese, Japanese, Korean, and "Asiatic" immigration. The Johnson-Reed Act of 1924 effectively slammed the door on nonwhite immigrants and prevented most Asian residents from becoming American citizens. The restriction on Asian immigration halted the spread of Asian religions such as Buddhism, Sikhism, and Hinduism, which had all been present in the United States in small numbers since the nineteenth century.

This situation changed, rather dramatically, with the 1965 Immigration and Naturalization Act, in which the U.S. government reversed this longstanding anti-immigration policy. In particular, the new legislation opened the door for immigrants from Asia and the Middle East; in the three decades from 1960 to 1990, more than a third of the fifteen million immigrants to America were Asian. They have brought their religions with them, making the United States a country that Harvard University professor Diana Eck calls "the most religiously diverse nation on earth."

The Immigration and Naturalization Act is one reason why religions of all types have recently flourished in the United States. Another is the simple fact that the Constitution has permitted them to do so. "America's rich religious pluralism today is a direct result of our commitment to religious freedom," writes Eck in *A New Religious America*. Drawing on the examples of colonial Rhode Island and Pennsylvania, Thomas Jefferson saw to it that the Virginia Statute for Religious Freedom granted an explicit freedom of religion in 1786. Five years later, the Bill of Rights legislated this same freedom throughout the nation, setting the stage for America's future religious diversity.

Then, too, the proliferation of faith groups in the United States has resulted in no small part from a peculiarly American predilection for schism. Around the world, theological distinctions are rarely made among different groups of Jews, save the ultra-Orthodox. But in America, several divisions within Judaism have developed since the early nineteenth century. Within Protestantism, this tendency toward fragmentation has resulted in literally hundreds of denominations of varying sizes. Perhaps a legacy of spiritual dissent has been passed down from the very Puritans who landed on New England's shores in search of religious freedom. Or perhaps the capitalistic "religious market" has helped to spawn so many denominations and sects: In the absence of a state-supported religion, all religious groups have had to compete with one another for adherents.

Whatever the reasons, the statistics on the nation's religious diversity since 1965 are truly stunning. While the majority of people in the United States remain Christian, other faiths are growing rapidly. There are now nearly seven million Muslims, six million Jews, and four million Buddhists in the nation. As *Time* magazine declared in 1993, "The world has never seen a nation as religiously diverse as the United States."

Brief Histories of New England's Faith Groups

Mutual respect is born of greater understanding. A major goal of this book is to underscore the importance of respect for all religious traditions by offering accurate and impartial information about each. In the pages that follow, you will find brief histories of New England's most prominent faith groups (those that have long histories in the region or are numerically significant). Obviously, these short entries cannot delve into the complexity that exists in nearly every religious tradition; they can offer only highlights. The entries also point to some of the New England sites that pertain to specific religions in the hope that spiritual travelers can learn more about the faith tradition by visiting those sites. Some of the groups profiled below have been present in New England for hundreds of years; others are ancient faiths that are relatively new to New England. They are described below in alphabetical order, with the entry on Christianity subdivided into denominational categories.

BAHA'I FAITH

The Baha'i Faith emerged out of Shi'ite Islam in nineteenth-century Iran and is founded on the teachings of the Baha'u'llah (1817–92), a prophet who Baha'is believe culminated the great spiritual traditions founded by Jesus, Buddha, Muhammad, and others. The three central tenets of the faith are the oneness of God, the oneness of humanity, and the oneness of all religions. The movement has been racially integrated since its inception and emphasizes the equality of all people. Baha'is have been at the forefront of movements for world peace and improved race relations.

The Baha'i Faith in the United States is still relatively small, with approximately 110,000 members (including children), but it is growing at the modest rate of 2 to 4 percent a year. It is most heavily concentrated in southern California, Arizona, Florida, and South Carolina, though it has pockets of believers in other regions as well. Its spectacular temple in Wilmette, Illinois, is a well-known architectural landmark. In New England, the Baha'i community dates to 1899, when Abdu'l Baha, the son of the Baha'u'llah, visited Boston. The Baha'i Community of Greater Boston is the largest center in New England (see page 106), with other gatherings throughout the region.

BUDDHISM

As a perusal of any bookstore will tell you, Buddhism is now ubiquitous in the United States, its presence felt in such bestsellers as *Zen and the Art of Motorcycle Maintenance* and a celebrity roster that reads like a "who's who" of Hollywood. But despite the recent high-profile attention paid to Buddhism and the fact that there are as many as four million Buddhists in the United States, many Americans know little about the tradition—particularly about how diverse it is. Buddhism is based on the teachings of Siddhartha Gautama (ca. 563–483 B.C.E.), a prince from what is now Nepal. Disenchanted with royal life, he left his family and comfortable station in search of enlightenment. After six years of study and practice, he achieved enlightenment while meditating under a tree. He became the

Buddha, or "awakened one," and began teaching others the path to nirvana. The religion we now call Buddhism is based on the Four Noble Truths: (1) life is suffering; (2) the source of suffering is desire; (3) quenching desire is the way to end suffering; and (4) release can be had by following an eightfold path of right understanding, right thought, right speech, right action, right livelihood, right effort, right mindfulness, and right concentration. As a religion, Buddhism is essentially nontheistic (without a belief in God), although some Buddhist traditions do profess a pantheon of enlightened beings. All Buddhists "take refuge" in (entrust themselves to) the Three Jewels: the Buddha, the Dharma (teachings), and the Sangha (the Buddhist community).

The existence of Buddhism in America goes back more than a century. Buddhism was present in the first half of the nineteenth century in the territories that became Hawaii and California, via a substantial Japanese immigrant community; it was also practiced among Chinese workers who extended the railroad throughout the American West. Not until the twentieth century, however, did Buddhism achieve a significant following in this country. In the 1950s Americans began evincing a definite interest in Buddhism, one that was probably furthered by the Beat poets' presentation of the faith as countercultural. Although "Beat Zen" was criticized by some Zen teachers for its neglect of disciplined meditation techniques, it had the desired effect of increasing Americans' awareness of, and interest in, Buddhism. As immigration from Asia swelled after 1965, new Buddhist traditions were added to the mix already present in the United States.

A tremendous amount of spiritual and ethnic diversity exists in Buddhism. As the religion spread from India to nations such as China, Japan, Korea, Vietnam, Cambodia, Nepal, Tibet, and Thailand, it was intermingled with local folk and ethnic traditions and became subtly different in each region. There are two major divisions in Buddhism—Theravada, which is strongest in South and Southeast Asia, and Mahayana, which dominates East Asia. (Some would add a third: the Vajrayana, or esoteric, tradition, which is practiced in Tibet and to some extent in China; see page 295.) Various schools, such as Nichiren, Pure Land, and Zen, have arisen within the tradition of Mahayana Buddhism. Among the different schools, discussions have centered upon several aspects of Buddhist teaching: whether enlightenment is gradual (over the course of many lifetimes) or can be instantaneous, for example. There are also differences in meditation practice. Zen masters teach a form of *zazen* (seated) meditation, while Theravadans from Southeast Asia are more likely to emphasize the *vipassana* technique of "insight meditation" (see page 168). Finally, the traditions diverge concerning the role of a teacher or master in attaining enlightenment, and the importance of monasticism. (Interestingly, as Buddhist traditions are transplanted to the United States, many adherents are infusing them with American individualism, by de-emphasizing the importance of a master and focusing on the laity rather than the ordained monastic order.)

All of these Buddhist traditions are thriving on American soil. Zen masters, Theravadan *bhikkhus*, and Tibetan lamas all teach eager followers, some of whom are immigrants from predominately Buddhist countries, but many of whom are Euro-American converts who have discovered in Buddhism a peace that eluded them in Western religions. The presence of so many Buddhist traditions in one nation is unprecedented in human history. A Theravada Buddhist from Sri Lanka can meditate next to a Zen Buddhist from Japan and a Caucasian "bookstore Buddhist" from Vermont. Moreover, many American Buddhists are mixing Buddhism with other religions. Although some scholars estimate that there are nearly four million people who practice Buddhism in this country, many of them do not do so exclusively, but are members of other faith traditions.

New England is truly a Buddhist melting pot, with every option available. Most Buddhist centers in this country focus on a particular tradition—the Insight Meditation Center in Barre, Massachusetts, is Theravadan and stresses *vipassana* meditation techniques (see page 167), while the Cambridge Zen Center not fifty miles away emphasizes the Zen traditions of koans and *zazen* meditation (see page 122). But both centers welcome Buddhists and non-Buddhists of all persuasions and sometimes even offer courses or speakers from other Buddhist traditions.

As Asian immigration increases, some Buddhist temples cater specifically to certain nationalities and use their native languages alongside English. In Quincy, Massachusetts, the Thousand Buddha Chinese Temple (see page 151) practices Pure Land Buddhism, while a Theravadan Cambodian temple ministers to the immigrant community of Lynn, north of Boston (see page 145). In Vermont, the Buddhist retreat center Karmê-Chöling (see page 295) teaches in the Tibetan tradition, emphasizing the lineage of a master and the esoteric, or secret, nature of the most advanced teachings. Not far away is the Green Mountain Dharma Center and Maple Forest Monastery, founded by Vietnamese Buddhist teacher Thich Nhat Hanh to further Buddhist teachings and build interfaith understanding (see page 311).

CHRISTIANITY

Christianity remains the dominant religion in the United States, with more than 150 million adherents. Its three main branches are Roman Catholicism, Orthodoxy, and Protestantism; there are numerous Protestant denominations, some of which are treated in more detail below. In particular, the history of New England is intertwined with the Congregational Church, the spiritual descendant of the Puritan faith of sixteenth-century England. Other Protestant denominations that have been especially fruitful in New England include the Episcopal (Anglican) Church and the Unitarian Church; the latter got its start in Boston. Apart from theology, immigration patterns played an important role in determining which Christian traditions took hold in New England. There were, historically, very few Lutherans here, and relatively small numbers of Presbyterian and Dutch Reformed Christians (the group which dominated New Amsterdam, later renamed New York). Most early European settlers were of English descent, though a handful of French Huguenots settled in the multifaith haven of Rhode Island.

The well-established "mainline" churches, which typically include the Presbyterian, Methodist, Episcopal, Lutheran, and United Church of Christ denominations, experienced marvelous growth in the years immediately following World War II, but have since suffered from a drop in membership. In New England, this has resulted in some creative partnerships among many local churches, such as the sharing of a pastor for two congregations, or even the merger of churches that were once at odds with one another. Evangelical denominations, on the other hand, are on the rise. The term "evangelical" is often broadly used to refer to Christians who afford great importance to the Bible, sometimes to the point of literal interpretation, and who experience a personal "conversion" to Jesus Christ as Lord and Savior. There are evangelicals in nearly every Christian denomination, but they are most heavily concentrated among the Baptist, Pentecostal, Church of Christ, and Holiness denominations.

Anglicanism/Episcopalianism

The European, or "Continental" Reformation got its famous start in 1517, when Martin Luther (1485–1546) hammered his 95 Theses on to the door of a church in Wittenberg, Germany. The English Reformation occurred more than a decade later when King Henry VIII (r. 1509–47) wanted a divorce from his first wife, Catherine of Aragon. Because the pope would not grant one, Henry separated from the Roman Catholic

Church to form the Church of England, or Anglican Church. As "supreme head" of that church, Henry set about dissolving English monasteries and cutting all ties with Rome. Although his eldest daughter Mary (r. 1553–58), a devout Catholic, tried valiantly to restore the kingdom to Catholicism during her brief reign, the "Middle Way" of Queen Elizabeth (r. 1558–1603) consolidated the Church of England as a separate ecclesiastical body. Although Protestant in its theology, the new denomination followed Roman liturgies to some degree.

Anglicans, who were firmly established in the English colonies of Virginia and the Carolinas by the early eighteenth century, were not very welcome in Puritan New England. Since the Puritans had endured great persecution at the hands of Anglican magistrates back in England, they made life difficult for Anglicans in New England, particularly in Massachusetts. Because it was a royal colony, however, the Puritans did have to bow to the king's wishes when the Crown dictated in 1688 that an Anglican church would be established in the heart of Boston. That was King's Chapel, the first Anglican church in New England (see page 77).

Most Anglicans remained loyal to the English king during the American Revolution (1776–83), and New England churches are rife with wonderful stories from this period. Christ Church in Boston never omitted prayers for the king during the war, but Christ Church across the Charles River in Cambridge had to abandon services entirely because the town's anti-English sentiment resulted in a mob attack that looted the sanctuary and destroyed the pulpit and the organ (see page 119).

After the Revolution, the new nation's Anglicans went through something of an identity crisis. How could they redefine their religion and be loyal to their new American republic? During this postwar period, many of the Anglican churches and institutions in America were renamed. King's College in New York, for example, was rechristened Columbia University—in one stroke the college moved from honoring the king of England to commemorating Christopher Columbus. In Boston, King's Chapel began calling itself simply "Stone Chapel." During this period, the "Episcopal" church was born. The word *episcopal* comes from the Greek *episkopos*, or bishop, and pointed to the church's mode of governance. Uneasy Americans could rest assured that this was a church ruled by bishops, and not by a king across the Atlantic.

The Baptist Church

The Baptist Church in America, like several other religious groups, got its official start in New England. (Although similar groups arose in seventeenth-century England and the American South, Providence, Rhode Island, is considered the institutional birthplace of the Baptist Church.) When Roger Williams (1603–83) was banished from Massachusetts in 1635 for religious dissidence (according to the Puritan magistrates in Salem, he had "broached & divulged new & dangerous opinions" about Indian rights and the separation of church and state), he fled to the wilderness south of Boston. There, he found refuge in a place he called, aptly enough, Providence (see page 256). Aided by the Narragansett Indians from whom he had purchased the land, he was able to build a small shelter and eventually send for his family. It wasn't long before Providence, which opened itself to all faiths, began attracting colonists of many different backgrounds: Quaker and ex-Puritan, Anglican and Jew. It was here that Roger Williams began to formulate his religious ideas into creating a new church. The First Baptist meeting in Providence was gathered in 1638.

The name "Baptist" specifically refers to Williams's emphasis on "believer's baptism" rather than infant baptism. Infants, he said, should not be baptized since it is not their choice to embrace a life of faith. Rather, adults who had undergone a Christian conversion experience could join the church through baptism and a profession of faith. The Baptist movement spread slowly at first, but then enjoyed explosive growth in the decades immediately following the American Revolution. Baptist preachers (who did not need to meet the stringent educational requirements of Puritan ministers) traveled throughout the nation, urging sinners to repent and be baptized. A small sect, the Freewill Baptists, was founded in northern New England and proved particularly popular in Maine and New Hampshire (see page 331). With their emphasis on an individual's right to choose salvation (in contrast to the Calvinist/Puritan doctrine of foreordained "election"; see page 3), the Freewill Baptists captured the optimism of the residents of the new "United States," for whom all things seemed possible. Other Baptists preached the new doctrine of believer's baptism but maintained a Calvinist emphasis on God's sovereignty by rejecting the concept of free will.

The Baptist movement suffered an intense and severe national schism in the mid–nineteenth century, when many northern Baptists condemned the practice of slavery and many (but not all) southern Baptists condoned it. The denomination split in 1845, and in contrast to the now reunited Methodists (see page 18), the Baptists have never reaffiliated. The pre–Civil War divide still holds true geographically; the vast majority of *American Baptists* live above the Mason-Dixon line, and the majority of *Southern Baptists* live below it (and in California). With sixteen million members in the United States, the Southern Baptist Convention is the nation's second-largest Christian denomination after Roman Catholicism. The next-largest Baptist denomination is the mostly African American National Baptist Church, with 3.5 million members. All together, several African American Baptist denominations claim nearly sixteen million members, roughly equaling the size of the Southern Baptist Convention. The American Baptist Association has 1.4 million members.

There are several important Baptist sites throughout New England. Spiritual travelers can see the striking 1775 First Baptist Church in Providence, the spiritual home of the congregation founded by Roger Williams in 1638 (see page 258). Brown University is another Baptist-related spiritual site in Providence, famous not for its ties to the Baptist Church as for its determined independence from it: Although its founders were primarily Baptist, they wanted the university to remain free of denominational ties. Brown, founded in the 1760s, was the first educational institution in America that did not require students to adhere to any standard of religious orthodoxy (see page 260). Farther north in Boston, Tremont Temple reflects some of the Baptist denomination's discordant racial history. Founded in 1839 because another local Baptist church would not permit blacks to worship equally with whites, Tremont Temple was the nation's first racially integrated congregation of any denomination (see page 75). Moving still farther northward, New Durham, New Hampshire, is the birthplace of the Freewill Baptist denomination (which merged with the American Baptists in 1911). There, a small clapboard church bears witness to the importance of the Freewill Baptist movement in northern New England in the late eighteenth and nineteenth centuries (see page 331).

Christian Science

One of the first things you will hear if you take the tour of the Christian Science Mother Church (see page 99) in Boston is, "We are not the Church of Scientology." Indeed, there has been much confusion over this point in the press. So, for the record: Christian Science was founded in the late nineteenth century by Mary Baker Eddy (1821–1910) and is based in Boston. The Church of Scientology was founded by L. Ron Hubbard (1911–86), a science-fiction writer, in the 1950s, and is now based in Clearwater, Florida. Christian Scientists are anxious to distinguish themselves from Scientology and point to the fact that they follow the teachings of Jesus as recorded in the New Testament as evidence of this difference.

The First Church of Christ, Scientist, which is the official name of the organization, is based on the Bible and the teachings of Mrs. Eddy as recorded in her book, *Science and Health with Key to the Scriptures*, first published in 1875. Mrs. Eddy taught that individuals possessed the mental and spiritual power to overcome illness through prayer. The religion flourished in the late nineteenth and early twentieth centuries and was especially popular among women. Its membership has declined from a peak of more than 2,500 congregations in the early 1970s to approximately 2,000 at the beginning of the twenty-first century.

The spiritual traveler will find many Christian Science sites in New England that are of interest. In addition to the Mother Church, Administration Building, and Mapparium in Boston, Mrs. Eddy's home in the leafy suburb of Chestnut Hill is open for tours (see page 135). An earlier home of Mrs. Eddy in Lynn, Massachusetts, is also open to the public (see page 146).

Congregationalism (United Church of Christ)

Congregationalism was once so much a part of New England life that it spawned an expression, "the Congregational Way," to describe the colonies of Massachusetts and Connecticut. In a nutshell, Congregationalism is the direct ecclesiastical descendent of Puritanism and first arrived in Massachusetts with the Pilgrims in 1620. The early Puritans sought to create a "visible church" that would fuse the civic and the theological into one godly society. Puritans knew no easy distinction between church and state. Even their early meetinghouses served multiple functions as houses of worship, town halls, and strongholds to withstand attack (see page 40).

Although the Puritans had experienced grave persecutions when they attempted to practice their faith in England, that experience did not make them tolerant of dissenting faiths when they formed their own colonies. Quakers, Baptists, Roman Catholics, Jews, and other non-Puritans were personae non gratae in Massachusetts and Connecticut, the two colonies where Puritanism was most firmly entrenched. In the northern colonies of Vermont, New Hampshire, and Maine, which were established later, Puritanism had less of a presence.

Congregationalism literally means that the congregation, not a minister or a bishop or a board of trustees, makes all of the parish's decisions. For the descendants of the Puritans, this commitment to local church government had an unfortunate, unintended consequence: schism. In the 1730s and 1740s, Congregationalism experienced its first major schism in the form of the Great Awakening, an intercolonial—even transatlantic—

revival of colossal proportions (see page 185). Some ministers (called "New Lights"), such as Northampton theologian Jonathan Edwards (1703–58), supported the mass revival and welcomed itinerant preachers into their communities and churches. Others ("Old Lights") rejected the Awakening, clinging fast to Puritan traditions. In New Haven, Connecticut, we can still see a rather dramatic legacy of the Congregational divide: standing right next door to one another on the green are two churches, both descended from the original Puritan meetinghouse of the town. In 1742 one broke off from the other, allowing local Congregationalists the choice between "New Light" and "Old Light" congregations (see page 282).

At the end of the eighteenth and beginning of the nineteenth century, another schism threatened Congregational unity. This was the growth of Unitarianism (see page 26), a more liberal understanding of Protestant Christianity. The split was most pronounced in Boston and Cambridge, where the flagship institution, Harvard College, broke loose from its Puritan moorings and became Unitarian in 1804 (see page 117). In Boston, virtually every Congregational church had turned toward Unitarianism by 1809, when some concerned old-line Congregationalists founded Park Street Church to preserve the legacy of Christian Trinitarianism in Massachusetts (see page 73).

In the nineteenth century, Congregationalists failed to keep pace with the growth of other Christian denominations because they had no strong infrastructure or missionary presence outside of New England. In 1830, for example, more than 90 percent of the nation's Congregational churches were located in New England. Moreover, the Congregationalists did not capitalize on new immigration, but remained largely English in ethnic composition. The positive side of this regional dominance was that when the Civil War came, Congregationalism did not split along North–South lines as did the Methodists, Baptists, and Presbyterians. There were hardly any southern members with whom to feud.

Despite their relatively small size outside of New England when compared to the Baptists, Methodists, and certainly the Roman Catholics, Congregationalists exerted an influence far beyond their numbers. Harvard, Yale, Dartmouth, Williams, Bowdoin, Middlebury, and Mount Holyoke colleges were all founded by Congregationalists, who placed a high premium on education. They were also strongly represented in nineteenth-century reform movements such as abolition.

In the twentieth century, the Congregationalists merged with several small Protestant denominations to form the United Church of Christ, which in 1999 claimed just over 1.4 million members, after a 1960 peak of 2.2 million. The UCC is one of the most liberal Christian denominations; ironically enough, it shares this distinction with the old nemesis of Congregationalism, Unitarianism.

Methodism

Methodism was certainly a child of the new nation. Organized in 1784 just after the close of the American Revolution, it successfully capitalized on the westward growth of the country after the war. In 1784, there were 15,000 members of the fledgling Methodist Episcopal Church; by 1850 there were more than a million, stretching all the way from the Atlantic to the Pacific. Methodist circuit riders (traveling preachers) carried the gospel on horseback throughout the young nation, sleeping on the ground, preaching in the open air, and leading thousands to conversion.

Founder John Wesley (1703–91) had not originally intended to start another Christian denomination; he was an Anglican who sought to renew the Church of England from within through a message of warm-hearted piety and genuine religious conversion. But Anglicans were not delighted with this competing faith, and in 1784 Wesley broke with Anglican tradition by ordaining ministers himself, without the authority of a bishop. Somehow, this act set a precedent for the Methodist character: Methodists sought not to bow to tradition, but to what they perceived as the immediate prompting of the Holy Spirit. Early Methodists aspired to spiritual perfection, which they called "holiness."

The message of holiness was especially well-suited for the American frontier. Methodist camp meetings, or outdoor revivals, proved to be a phenomenally popular way to nurture the newfound faith. Over time, some of these camp meetings evolved into permanent summer revivals, such as the Martha's Vineyard Camp Meeting Association. Here, in what is now a tony resort haven, early Methodists cried over their sins and pledged their lives to God's service (see page 204).

Although the Methodists endured a particularly rancorous split over slavery just before the Civil War, the southern and northern branches reunited in 1939, and added a German evangelical denomination to their ranks in 1968. At that time, the "United Methodist Church" had eleven million members in the United States; it currently has just over eight million.

The mostly white United Methodist Church is by no means the only Methodist denomination. In the nineteenth century, African American Methodists formed their own churches and denominations, including the

African Methodist Episcopal Church and the smaller African Methodist Episcopal Zion Church. Early AME leader Richard Allen (1760–1831) explained that "The Methodists were the first people that brought glad tidings to the colored people," and that African Americans could benefit from the "plain and simple gospel" that the Methodists preached. In 1999, there were approximately 2.5 million members of the African Methodist Episcopal Church and just over one million members of the AME Zion Church in the United States. Although New England is not a regional stronghold for these denominations, there are some AME and AME Zion churches in the Boston area and in southwestern Connecticut, near New York City.

Mormonism (The Church of Jesus Christ of Latter-day Saints)

While many associate the Church of Jesus Christ of Latter-day Saints with Utah, the location of its international headquarters, its historical roots actually lie in New England and New York. The church's founder, Joseph Smith, Jr. (1805–44), was born in central Vermont. Smith inaugurated the church (then called the Church of Christ) with six members in 1830, and it has grown to over eleven million today. Approximately 5.2 million of those members, popularly called "Mormons," live in the United States, where they are known for the principle of tithing (donating a tenth of their income to the church), and for adhering to a health code that prohibits the consumption of alcohol, tobacco, coffee, tea, and harmful drugs.

The LDS Church does not consider itself a Protestant denomination, but it is Christian, expressing "faith in the Lord Jesus Christ." Mormons follow the teachings of the Bible, the Book of Mormon (believed to be an ancient text translated by Joseph Smith), the Doctrine and Covenants, and the Pearl of Great Price (other divine revelations and teachings). They believe that Joseph Smith was a prophet of God, and that the subsequent presidents of the church have all been prophets. Latter-day Saints place a high premium on the sanctity of the family, and believe that faithful Saints can be sealed to their family members for time and all eternity in a holy temple. One of the Church's temples is located outside of Boston, in the suburb of Belmont (see page 130). Only Mormons in good standing are permitted inside, but visitors are welcome to walk the grounds.

As a rule, Mormons are often very interested in American history, which is intricately tied with Mormon theology. The Mormon migration westward is one of the great epic tales of this nation. After they encountered persecution in states such as New York, Ohio, Illinois, and

Missouri—including the assassination of their leader, Joseph Smith, in 1844—many Mormons set about on a mass exodus to the West. Approximately 10 percent of that first company of 4,000 migrants did not survive the grueling winter journey. But under the pragmatic, visionary direction of their new leader, Brigham Young (also, incidentally, a native of Vermont), the Mormons' settlement in the Salt Lake Valley became one of the most successful permanent communities in the American West. It was a controversial religious group; the Mormon practice of polygamy (abandoned in 1890) earned the disapproval of many. One Presbyterian minister, for example, called Mormonism "the grossest of all the delusions that Satanic malignity or human ambition ever sought to propagate."

Despite such criticism, the persecuted minority faith of Mormonism gave rise, in the late twentieth century, to a global Christian movement. One prominent non-Mormon sociologist of religion, Rodney Stark, predicted in the mid-1980s that if Mormon growth could be sustained at the rate of the previous fifty years, there would be 265 million Mormons at the end of the twenty-first century. Many scoffed. But since he made that prediction, the rate of Mormon growth has even exceeded his initial expectations. Visitors to New England have the unique chance to see its humble beginnings; the site of the birthplace of Joseph Smith is open as a museum (see page 306).

Orthodoxy

Eastern Orthodoxy has been called America's "invisible religion" because although its membership numbers are on par with the larger faith groups in this country, it does not enjoy instant name recognition. Despite the presence of more than five million Orthodox Christians in the United States in the year 2000, a majority of Americans are unaware of the tradition's long history or its distinctive practices.

To be accurate, Orthodox Christianity is not just "Eastern Orthodoxy" anymore. Although most Orthodox churches in America were founded by immigrants of one particular ethnic group—Russian, Greek, Armenian, or Romanian, for example—those ethnic ties have become less important with each passing decade. Today, most Orthodox churches in the United States conduct their services in English and serve a mostly English-speaking constituency. Bishops and priests are more likely to be American-born than not. There is also increasing crossover between churches—a person who grew up in a Greek Orthodox church may attend one that is affiliated with the Russian-heritage Orthodox Church in America, for example. Even more commonly, converts to Orthodoxy whose ethnic background is not eastern European are attaching themselves to one or another of these ancient denominations. Orthodox Christians may be Hispanic, African American, or of any possible nationality. It is a tremendously diverse religious movement.

The Orthodox and Roman Catholic churches both lay claim to the longest history of any Christian group. In the first millennium after the death of Jesus of Nazareth, the united Christian church stretched across Europe and western Asia as a single entity, despite some nagging disagreements over doctrines and practices between its Eastern and Western (Roman) halves. Orthodox Christianity did not emerge as a distinct religious movement until 1054, when the church in Rome modified an important creedal statement without so much as discussing it with the Eastern Christians. In 1204 the division reached schismatic proportions when Western soldiers of the Fourth Crusade actually ransacked the city of Constantinople (Istanbul), the seat of the Byzantine Empire and the Eastern church, in the same way that they had looted and destroyed non-Christian cities. The Western and Eastern traditions of Christianity formally parted ways. They remain separate to this day, although there are signs of rapprochement. In 2001, during the first visit by a Roman Catholic pope to Greece in more than a millennium, Pope John Paul II formally apologized for the sacking of Constantinople.

Theologically, there are few differences among the major Orthodox denominations in the United States. All Orthodox Christians regard the ecumenical patriarch of Constantinople as a spiritual leader, although he has no power to interfere with the governance of the many "autocephalous" (self-ruling) Orthodox denominations. Orthodox Christians believe that icons are spiritually necessary to bear witness to the presence of Christ, emphasize the importance of liturgy and the Eucharist, and hold fast to the ancient traditions of the church. Orthodox services can be several hours long; traditionally, worshipers stand for the entire service, though some Orthodox churches in America now have pews for seated worship. Because many Orthodox Christians follow the Julian calendar and not the Gregorian one, the Christian liturgical year is somewhat different from the one celebrated by Roman Catholic or Protestant Christians. (The Julian calendar is slightly less accurate than the 1582 Gregorian calendar, and runs nearly two weeks behind. Therefore, many Orthodox Christians celebrate holidays such as Christmas and Easter at a later date than Western-tradition Christians.)

Orthodoxy first came to the United States in 1743—via Alaska, which was then a Russian territory. In 1794, formal missionary work began there, with eight Russian Orthodox priests seeking converts among the native Alaskan peoples. During the nineteenth century the Russian Orthodox presence spread southward down the western coast of the United States; in 1905, the denomination moved its American headquarters from San Francisco to New York City to minister to the many thousands of immigrants who were arriving there. Despite the serious problems that plagued the church in the wake of the Russian Revolution of 1917 (financial support virtually dried up, and American churches were left adrift without institutional aid from Russia), Russian Orthodoxy continued to thrive in America. So too did Greek Orthodoxy, which gained prominence with the arrival of Greek immigrants in the late nineteenth century.

The various Orthodox denominations range widely in size; the Albanian Orthodox Diocese of America reported just over two thousand U.S. members in the year 2000, while the Greek Orthodox Archdiocese of America had over two million. The Greek Orthodox Church is well represented throughout southern New England; Brookline, Massachusetts is a major hub of Greek Orthodoxy, with a seminary, college, and small monastery (see page 132). The Orthodox Church in America (Russian) enjoys its strongest regional presence in southwestern Connecticut, near New York City; however, its churches can be found in unexpected places throughout New England, such as the Holy Resurrection Orthodox Church in the northernmost section of New Hampshire (see page 317).

Quakerism (Society of Friends)

"Be patterns, be examples in all countries, places, islands, nations, wherever you come; that your carriage and life may preach among all sorts of people and to them; then you will come to walk cheerfully over the world, answering that of God in everyone. . . ."
—George Fox, 1658

It is perhaps difficult for modern Americans to realize that the Quakers—who are today most known for their tolerance, silent mode of worship, and belief that God resides in the heart of every person—were considered some of the most dangerous renegades of seventeenth-century society. Quakerism arose in 1650s England, when George Fox (1624–91) proclaimed that the spirit of Jesus Christ could speak directly to the soul of any human being. This radical egalitarianism in spiritual matters extended to temporal things as well. Because Fox's followers believed that God spoke to everyone equally, early Quakers challenged hierarchical authority; they refused to tip their hats to magistrates and nobility, used the familiar terms "thee" and "thou" with everyone, and affirmed the right of women to be leaders in the movement. They also rejected violence and all of its accouterments (including war taxes), a stance that angered many people in England. English authorities were concerned by the group's enthusiastic worship; the society's habits of groaning, sobbing, and quaking convulsively during meetings earned it the nickname "Quaker."

If the Quakers in England were indecorous and antiauthoritarian, the Quakers who risked their lives to bring their message across the Atlantic Ocean were the most fervent of all. Many of the missionaries and their early converts were, to be blunt, religious extremists. Some renounced family ties altogether; one English convert, Mary Clarke, left her husband and six children to preach God's message in New England. But the most famous Quaker in the Puritan colonies was Mary Dyer, who was hanged for her beliefs in Massachusetts in 1660 (see page 255).

In the seventeenth century, Massachusetts and Connecticut passed stringent laws prohibiting citizens from harboring Quakers or reading their literature. Quakers were welcomed in only one New England colony— Rhode Island. But that was not because the colony's founder, Roger Williams, had any great fondness for the followers of George Fox. Rather, Williams had a love of liberty that enabled him to grit his teeth and allow the Quakers to enjoy full religious freedom there, despite his personal misgivings about them. But the Quakers were not content to reside in Rhode Island and quietly pursue their faith; they were evangelizers who believed that God wished them to bring their message to those who labored most determinedly to reject it.

The tenacity of early New England Quakers is a trait to be admired. By the nineteenth century, after Puritanism/Congregationalism had forsaken its privileged status as the official religion of New England's colonies, Quakers were no longer persecuted, imprisoned, and publicly flogged in the region. In the absence of the overt public opprobrium that had long fueled the movement, the Quakers settled into being a more orderly, restrained religious group that largely ceased from proselytizing, although they continued to voice their strong social concerns against slavery and in favor of women's education and other reforms.

Today, there are approximately 100,000 U.S. members of the seven distinct Quaker denominations that are affiliated as the Society of Friends.

They are well known for their social activism, agitating on issues such as peacemaking, human rights, and poverty. In New England, most Quaker meetings follow the traditional pattern of being "unprogrammed" (silent) and having no ordained clergy. (In the Midwest and West, some Quaker meetings have clergy and "programmed" meetings for worship.) Many historic Quaker meetinghouses still exist in New England, including the Dover, New Hampshire, Friends Meeting (see page 323) and several on Cape Cod (see page 232). The Quakers had an especially strong presence on the Massachusetts island of Nantucket (see page 213).

Roman Catholicism

Roman Catholicism was the first Christian denomination to enter the United States, due to sixteenth-century Spanish settlement in the West and in Florida, and it is also the largest by a substantial margin. There are more than sixty-two million Roman Catholics in the U.S., and their number is growing at a healthy rate, due in no small part to immigration from heavily Catholic areas in Latin America and Asia. Roman Catholicism is especially strong in New England; Catholics make up two-thirds of the population of Rhode Island and enjoy a commanding presence in the five other New England states.

Catholics were not always gladly received in New England, however. In Massachusetts, for example, Puritans passed a law in the late seventeenth century that "no Jesuit or ecclesiasticall person ordained by the authoritie of the pope" could come within the colony's jurisdiction. Such colonial statutes did not survive long past the Revolution, but anti-Catholic prejudice persisted into the nineteenth century. In 1832, an outlandish novel by a woman who claimed to have "escaped" from a convent school in Charlestown, Massachusetts, became a best-seller in the Boston area. The work was fiction and not autobiography, but its charges of Jesuit conspiracies and illicit relations between nuns and priests were widely believed and held up as examples of the dangers of Catholicism. In 1834, an angry mob, stirred up by Congregationalist minister Lyman Beecher's sermon "The Devil and the Pope of Rome," torched the convent and burned it to the ground. Remains from that convent were incorporated into the architecture of the Cathedral of the Holy Cross, the magnificent 1875 cathedral that serves the Diocese of Boston (see page 103).

In New England, nineteenth-century immigration patterns meant that regional Catholicism was largely Irish, Italian, and Portuguese in character. The first major wave of immigration came as a direct result of the Irish potato famines of the late 1840s and early 1850s, which propelled 1.8 million Irish immigrants to seek a new life in America. Although Congregationalism was no longer the state religion of Massachusetts, its residents were deeply suspicious of the Irish Catholics who arrived daily in Boston Harbor. Most were poor, and critics accused them of being a burden on the government. During the Civil War, the tremendous efforts of Irish American Union soldiers won the Irish some respect in New England, and Irish Catholic growth continued unabated into the twentieth century. In 1960, New England's Irish Catholics realized a dream when John F. Kennedy, one of their own, was elected president of the United States.

Boston remains a hub of Irish-heritage Catholicism, though it also hosts a substantial Italian American Catholic community. Between 1880 and 1900, almost a million Italians immigrated to the United States, and by 1920 the Italian American population had grown to more than four million. In Boston, Italians settled in the North End, an area that is still home to a large community of Italian descent. Each summer, their national heritage and popular piety are both on display in the *feste*, devotional celebrations of various patron saints. These celebrations take to the streets, with parades, music, and glorious food (see page 86).

Boston and the shore towns of Massachusetts have also been bastions of Portuguese Catholicism. Portuguese-speaking fishermen and whalers from the Azores and Cape Verde began coming to New England in the eighteenth century, and developed a strong presence in such Massachusetts towns as Gloucester, New Bedford, and Provincetown. Many of those communities still have Portuguese Holy Ghost festivals each summer, often in conjunction with a Blessing of the Fleet ceremony (see page 143).

These three nationalities constitute the largest ethnic groups within New England Catholicism, but they are by no means the only ones present. In northern Vermont, the French Canadian influence is felt at such Catholic sites as Saint Anne's Shrine on Isle La Motte (see page 301). New England is also home to Polish, Mexican, and German Catholics, as well as thousands of African American Catholics (of whom there are more than two million nationwide).

New England boasts a large number of Roman Catholic shrines, churches, retreat centers, grottoes, and monasteries. Most of these monasteries, such as the Weston Priory in Vermont and Spencer Abbey in central Massachusetts, receive guests (see pages 312 and 191). The region's Marian shrines also attract thousands of visitors, from a replica of Lourdes in Litchfield, Connecticut (see page 271), to the Shrine of Our Lady of

Grace in northern New Hampshire (see page 318). Pilgrims come from far and near to commemorate the Virgin Mary's appearances and honor her with their devotions and prayers.

Shakerism

At the height of Shakerism in the mid–nineteenth century, there were nine Shaker villages scattered throughout New England: Massachusetts had Shaker communities at Hancock, Harvard, Tyringham, and Shirley; Connecticut had one village in Enfield; New Hampshire had villages in Canterbury and Enfield; and Maine Shakers built communities in Alfred and Sabbathday Lake.

Shakerism came to America in 1774 when one of its leaders, Ann Lee (1736–84, see page 189), arrived in New York with a band of nine followers. The movement had begun in England two decades earlier as an enthusiastic offshoot of Quakerism. The "Shaking Quakers" (later consolidated to "Shakers") thrived in late-eighteenth-century America, despite the trials of having their leaders imprisoned and being attacked by the occasional mob. The Shakers, whose official name is the United Society of Believers in Christ's Second Appearing, are most famous today for their furniture and crafts, but their theology often goes undiscussed. After Ann Lee's death, many Shakers believed that she had been a female incarnation of Christ; just as God was both male and female, Christ had appeared once in the form of a man, Jesus of Nazareth, and again in the form of a woman, Ann Lee. In the twentieth century, some Shakers downplayed the theological significance of Ann Lee, claiming that she was not a messiah figure so much as a beloved spiritual teacher.

Today, the only active Shaker community in the world is the one at Sabbathday Lake in Maine, which in 2001 was home to eight Shakers (see page 364). All of the other communities have closed, most of them in the early twentieth century. Many villages are open as museums, offering guided tours to visitors. Several of these Shaker communities are featured in this guidebook.

Unitarian Universalism

A popular New England saying holds that Unitarianism embraces "the fatherhood of God, the brotherhood of man, and the neighborhood of Boston." It is certainly true that Unitarianism is deeply connected to the soil of New England, particularly Massachusetts. This is where the movement began in 1786, when Boston's flagship Anglican church, King's Chapel, changed its affiliation to become the first Unitarian congregation in America (see page 77). And this is where it is still concentrated; the denomination's headquarters are located in Boston, and Massachusetts has historically had more Unitarian congregations per square mile than any other state.

Unitarianism was based in a theological rejection of the Trinity. Its early ministers and thinkers discarded the traditional Christian idea of God as three-in-one as unbiblical and, almost more importantly, irrational. A product of the Age of Enlightenment, Unitarianism placed a high premium on the importance of human reason and emphasized the ethical components of Christianity more than the religion's creeds or doctrines. In the early nineteenth century, what old-line Congregationalists called "the Unitarian heresy" began splitting the Congregational church right down the middle. Many became Unitarian in orientation, while others remained staunchly Congregational. Some churches, such as Park Street Church in Boston (see page 73), were founded specifically to combat the dangers of Unitarianism by reaffirming the Trinity and the central role of the Bible. Conservatives also founded Andover Seminary in 1808 to train Congregational ministers in traditional theology, because Harvard—once a training ground of Puritan leaders—had begun to lean toward Unitarianism (see page 117).

In 1961, the Unitarian denomination merged with the Universalists, another liberal Christian movement that had been particularly strong in New England. Universalism was predicated on a belief in universal salvation. If God were entirely benevolent, argued the Universalists, then he would certainly not damn human beings to eternal torment, but would "finally restore the whole family of mankind to holiness and happiness." Whereas Unitarianism was a rather sophisticated (even elitist) philosophical movement that flourished in urban areas like Boston, Universalism was more of a rural phenomenon and proved especially popular in the northern states of Vermont, New Hampshire, and Maine.

Theologically and socially, the two groups had come together sufficiently by the mid–twentieth century to consider a merger. Today, the Unitarian Universalist Association is a noncreedal denomination that teaches that "personal experience, conscience and reason should be the final authorities in religion." There are more than a thousand UU congregations in North America, and great diversity exists among them. Some, for example, are "green" congregations that emphasize earth-centered religious practices; the Covenant of Unitarian Universalist Pagans, founded in 1986, has many chapters throughout New England. Other UU churches, like First Unitarian Congregational Church in Wilton Center, New

Hampshire (see page 342), are "Christian Unitarian" and retain Christian practices such as scripture reading, hymn singing, and communion.

HINDUISM, JAINISM, AND SIKHISM

As New England has become increasingly ethnically diverse through immigration, *Hinduism* has gained a strong foothold in the region. The word *Hinduism*, however, is something of a Western construct, used by perplexed nineteenth-century Western tourists to describe the incredibly diverse religious traditions they observed while traveling in India. Approximately 85 percent of India's population is Hindu, though exactly what "Hindu" means varies greatly from region to region. In general, Hindus worship a pantheon of gods and goddesses that includes Vishnu, Krishna, Shiva, Kali, and many others. A popular saying is that there are 330 million gods, though this is not so much an exact number as a suggestion that Hindus regard the Divine as infinite. There are certainly many gods in Hinduism, but they are all considered different aspects of one life-source, a single soul that ties the entire universe together. This one spirit (*brahman*) inhabits all beings, including the natural world. Much of Hindu devotion emphasizes the unity of all life.

The religion—which has no date of origin, no founder per se, and no centralized organization—emerged nearly 4,000 years ago in northern India. Its central sacred text is the ancient Rig Veda, with later devotional texts, such as the Mahabarata and the Upanishads, occupying important roles in the faith as well. One especially popular devotional text is the Bhagavad Gita, which New England philosopher Ralph Waldo Emerson (1803–82) once called "the first of books." (Of course, Emerson also thought it was a Buddhist book, but even transcendental philosophers sometimes make mistakes.) He told his younger friend Henry David Thoreau about the Gita, and Thoreau brought it with him to Walden Pond when he lived in a tiny cottage there in 1845 (see page 137).

As a religion, Hinduism mixes ancient folk beliefs with its sophisticated hierarchy of deities. The cow is considered a sacred animal (though it is not worshiped, only honored), and dairy products are believed to purify the body and the spirit. Hindus do not eat beef or wear leather clothing; many are complete vegetarians. Many Hindus also believe in reincarnation—that beings may progressively improve their state and gain knowledge from one lifetime to another. Ultimately, all creatures hope to reunite with *brahman*, the life-source.

After the Immigration and Naturalization Act of 1965 (see page 7), Indian immigration shot up dramatically—2,800 percent in the seven years up to 1972. Although there had been some pockets of Hinduism (and its offshoots, including the Vedanta Society and Self-Realization Fellowship) in the United States before 1965, it only became a major faith group here in the late twentieth century. It is difficult to estimate how many Hindus there are in the United States, since the census no longer asks specific questions about religious affiliation and Hinduism by its nature is quite decentralized. It is obvious, however, that the number of American Hindus is growing at a very healthy rate.

Hindus in New England achieved a dream when they dedicated the Sri Lakshmi Temple in Ashland, Massachusetts, in 1990 (see page 127). Since 1978, Hindu families had planned, saved, and worked to have a temple for the gods in New England. In the week before the temple was dedicated, three thousand Hindus attended various dedicatory rituals, including the consecration of hundreds of pots full of river water—from the sacred Ganges River in India, but also from the Mississippi, Colorado, and Missouri Rivers in the United States. At the end of the week, this water was hoisted to the towering pinnacles of the temple and poured upon them, demonstrating the temple's significance as a sacred place for Hindus who were now also Americans.

Jainism is an ancient faith that, like Buddhism, had its origins more than 2,500 years ago in the teachings of a nobleman who renounced everything to embrace asceticism. Vardhamana, a king, abandoned worldly life and became a wandering monk, teaching others the path to faith. Jains hold that all life is sacred; the teaching of *ahimsa*, or nonharming, is a central tenet of the religion. They are strict vegetarians. Jain monks, for example, will sweep the path before them with a broom so that they will not accidentally step on and kill an insect. Jainism has flourished in pockets of India, particularly its northwestern regions, though it is numerically tiny compared to Hinduism. In America, too, it remains small (approximately 25,000 in the early 1990s) but is growing. There were thirty-four Jain temples in the United States in 1987, but more than sixty by the middle of the 1990s. The Jain center in Norwood, Massachusetts, occupies the building of a former Swedish Lutheran church (see page 158).

Sikhism is another Indian religion that has gained significant ground in the United States. Sikhism was begun in northern India by Guru Nanak

(1468–1539 C.E.), who combined elements of both Hinduism and Islam and stressed the oneness of God. Although U.S. Sikhism is most heavily concentrated in California, New Jersey, and New York, Boston has a Sikh Study Center, founded in 1968. In 1991, local Sikhs purchased a vacant church building in the Boston suburb of Milford (formerly a Kingdom Hall for the Jehovah's Witnesses) and created New England's first gurdwara, or Sikh temple (see page 130).

ISLAM

Many religions claim to be the fastest growing in the United States, but that distinction most likely belongs to Islam, which has nearly seven million American adherents. Organizationally, Islam is still in its early stages in this country; 32 percent of all existing mosques were established in the 1980s, and another 30 percent were founded in the 1990s. Approximately 80 percent of American mosques are located in metropolitan areas, and those mosques have a tremendously diverse ethnic makeup. Leading ethnic groups are the South Asians (including Pakistanis and Indians) at 33 percent, African Americans at 30 percent, and 25 percent from the Arabic-speaking world. American Muslims might be of Lebanese, Vietnamese, Egyptian, Hispanic, or European descent; Islam is truly a global faith whose many branches are amply represented under the single umbrella of "Islam in America." Approximately one-third of American Muslims are converts, primarily from Christianity.

The word *Islam* means "submission" in Arabic, and a Muslim is "one who submits." The central holy text is the Qur'an, which Muslims believe was given by God to the prophet Muhammad (570–632 C.E.) in the year 611. Like Judaism and Christianity, Islam is a Western religion that is deeply monotheistic. The Five Pillars of Islam consist of the belief that "there is no God but God, and Muhammad is his messenger"; daily prayer (men are obligated to cease all activities and pray five times a day while facing toward Mecca); almsgiving; the observance of a fast during the holy month of Ramadan; and a pilgrimage (*hajj*) to Mecca at least once during a lifetime. Muslims pray each day alone or in their families, except at midday on Friday, when they gather in mosques for *jum'ah* prayers. Islam prohibits eating pork, drinking alcohol, or engaging in nonmarital sexual relations, as well as participating in the practice of usury (borrowing or lending money at interest).

Despite its recent explosive growth in the United States, Islam has been subtly present here for centuries. It was actually one of the first nonnative religions to enter America, nearly a century before the Puritans arrived. Spanish explorers brought African slaves, some of whom were Muslim, with them to the New World. Some scholars have estimated that as many as a tenth of the African slaves who were brought to North America from the sixteenth to nineteenth centuries were Muslims. However, the oppressive regime of chattel slavery demanded that these Muslims abandon their religious convictions and practices. Islam, like traditional African religions, did not typically survive through generations of slavery.

Around the turn of the twentieth century, Islam began to reenter the United States through immigration, with the first American mosque being built in 1936 in the rather unlikely place of Cedar Rapids, Iowa, which was home to a small Lebanese American Muslim community. By World War II there were a handful of mosques and Islamic associations scattered around the country, but it was not until the immigration law changed in 1965 (see page 7) that Muslims became a real force on the American religious landscape. Since the mid-1960s approximately 25,000 to 35,000 Muslims have immigrated each year. With continued immigration and a strong rate of African American conversion, Islam has now surpassed Judaism as America's second-largest religion, after Christianity.

The first mosque in New England was constructed in Quincy, Massachusetts, in 1962, its membership consisting primarily of Lebanese

MOSQUE ETIQUETTE

Friday, which is the holiest day of the week in Islam, features a special noontime prayer service at the mosque. Called the *jum'ah*, the service lasts between a half hour and an hour and requires men and women to form separate prayer lines, facing toward Mecca, on either side of the mosque's main sanctuary. Non-Muslim visitors are asked not to participate in the prayer line, but to sit separately. (There are no pews or chairs for sitting in the mosque. Muslims pray on the floor, kneeling on tarps or more elaborate Oriental rugs.) Prayers are offered in Arabic, and the Qur'an is recited in Arabic. The imam, or spiritual leader, may offer a sermon.

Women should consider wearing a dress or skirt that covers the knees; modesty is an important value in Islam. Women may also be asked to wear a scarf to cover their heads while in the mosque. All visitors should leave their shoes neatly stacked by the entrance, since shoes are never worn inside a mosque.

Muslims who had immigrated to the United States in the early twentieth century (see page 7). They had been meeting in temporary quarters for nearly half a century before they were able to build a small mosque. Today, the mosque's members come from more than two dozen different nations.

There are approximately thirty mosques in New England, some of which are small storefront-style community centers; one of the first of these was located in a U-Haul dealership in Pawtucket, Rhode Island. As Islam gains a more visible foothold in America, its mosques are becoming more evident also. At the Islamic Society of Boston (which is actually in Cambridge; see page 124) Muslims conduct daily prayers, send their children to on-site Islamic schools, and attend lectures and workshops on their faith. A large mosque is in the planning stages for the Boston neighborhood of Roxbury; once completed, it will accommodate 1,600 worshipers.

"Do you not know, O people, that I have made you into tribes and nations that you may know one another?"

—The Qur'an

Sufism

In predominantly Muslim countries, Sufism is regarded as a mystical path to the divine, but one that is contained entirely within the rubric of Islam. Arabic-world Sufis follow Muslim practices, such as praying five times daily, and regard the Qur'an as their central text, a work of God. In the United States, the situation is a little different. The great popularizer of Sufism in the States, Hazrat Inayat Khan (1882–1927), was a Muslim himself, but he taught his American followers that it was not necessary for them to become Muslims to embrace the Sufi path. The leader of Khan's Sufi Order International today is his son, Pir Vilayat Inayat Khan. He has continued his father's emphasis on Sufism as an interfaith movement, offering insights to individuals of many religious traditions. Its mostly Euro-American followers often remain members of their own religious traditions while incorporating Sufi practices into their spiritual lives.

Traditional Sufi practices include deep meditation and ecstatic dancing. Sufism has been called "the religion of the heart," since it places a paramount emphasis on the devotee's relationship with the divine. Sufis often describe that relationship in sensual terms, referring to God as "the beloved" and seeking a mystical union with that beloved. Union can be reached when the Sufi succeeds in subduing the individual will, thereby allowing the divine presence to occupy the human heart.

The United States is home to many small groups of Sufi practitioners, the largest of which is Sufi Order International. It has more than a hundred centers throughout the nation, including one in the Jamaica Plain neighborhood of Boston (see page 112). Boston-area Sufis often participate in interfaith dialogues and events, seeking to create harmony among various paths to God. Other Sufi groups in the United States include the Naqshbandi order (which follows the spiritual leadership of Shaykh Muhammad Nazim al-Haqqani) and the International Association of Sufism.

JUDAISM

Rhode Island, the colony that granted unparalleled religious freedom in the seventeenth century, welcomed a small community of Jews in 1658, which became the second-oldest Jewish congregation in the United States. (The oldest had been founded in the Dutch colony of New Amsterdam—later renamed New York—four years earlier). It was a good thing that at least one New England colony welcomed Jews; Puritan-governed Massachusetts, for example, was not so friendly. In 1649 a Sephardic Jewish merchant named Solomon Franco had been "warned out" of Boston (i.e., told in no uncertain terms to leave) because of his religion.

Judaism did not experience explosive growth in New England until the nineteenth century. Around 1800, there were only 2,000 Jews and five synagogues in all of the United States. (These were located in Newport, New York, Philadelphia, Charleston, and Savannah.) An influx of immigrants from eastern Europe in the late nineteenth and early twentieth centuries brought the total number of American Jews to nearly 4.5 million on the eve of World War II. Today, there are more than six million Jews in the United States, making Judaism the nation's third-largest religion after Christianity and Islam. In New England, Jews are located primarily in western Connecticut (especially the suburbs of New York City) and the greater Boston area.

Judaism, like Christianity and Islam, is a monotheistic Western religion that traces its heritage to Abraham of the Hebrew Bible (which Christians call the Old Testament). Judaism's foundational text is the Torah ("law"), the first five books of the Bible. Throughout its history, the Torah has been explained, interpreted, and reflected upon; many of these expositions of Torah are contained in the Talmud, a compilation of rabbinic teachings on the law. Jews observe numerous religious holidays, the most important of which are Yom Kippur (the "day of atonement"), Rosh

Hashanah (the new year), and Passover. Jews also observe the Sabbath each week, from sundown on Friday to sundown on Saturday.

Although Judaism has remained generally unified outside the United States, something about the American religious propensity toward schism affected Judaism in the nineteenth century. Then, too, Jews in America came from many different ethnic backgrounds, contributing to the diverse traditions of Judaism in the United States. American Jews are typically affiliated with Reform, Conservative, Orthodox, or Reconstructionist synagogues. The Reform movement, founded by Isaac Mayer Wise (1819–1900), emphasizes the applicability of Judaism to modern life. Early Reform Jews challenged some Jewish traditions, favoring family seating over segregated-sex seating in the synagogue (which they called a temple), and an English-language service. Some Reform Jews abandoned dietary restrictions altogether. At the other extreme, the Orthodox movement stressed the importance of age-old ritual observance, Torah study, kosher laws, Sabbath keeping, and holy days. In the middle is Conservative Judaism, the denomination of choice for the largest number of American Jews. Conservative Judaism holds to many of the traditional values of Judaism, though it acknowledges that the religion has been shaped by historic change. Reconstructionism emerged in the 1930s as a left-leaning expression of Conservative Judaism; it is a more humanistic approach that emphasizes the religion's ethical values. Historian Jacob Neusner has reported that in 1990, 43 percent of American Jews were Conservative, 35 percent Reform, 9 percent Orthodox (including the ultra-Orthodox Hasidic Jews), and 2 percent Reconstructionist. (Some were not affiliated with a denomination.)

New England is home to a number of historic synagogues and Jewish sites. The Touro Synagogue in Newport, Rhode Island, dates to 1763 (though the congregation was formed a century earlier) and has intersected with American history in some important ways (see page 245). In 1781, George Washington visited the synagogue and proclaimed that if he were ever elected president of the new nation, he would ensure that Jews—and all others—could practice their religion freely. A younger but no less significant synagogue is the Vilna Shul in Boston, a 1919 Lithuanian synagogue that is the last intact early-twentieth-century synagogue in the city. The building is currently under restoration, with plans to open it as a Jewish cultural center and museum (see page 80). In the suburb of Chelsea, Congregation Agudath Sholom (Walnut Street Synagogue), built in 1909, is one of the oldest continuously used Orthodox shuls in New England. (See page 154. *Shul*, the Yiddish word for synagogue, is the term used by most Orthodox Jews.) And in Amherst, Massachusetts, the National Yiddish Book Center has, since 1980, dedicated itself to the preservation of Yiddish-language books, theater, and culture (see page 164).

NATIVE AMERICAN RELIGIONS

The usual phrase "Native American religion" should in fact be "Native American religions," as indigenous beliefs and practices actually spanned hundreds of ancient cultures over the course of millennia. The spiritual beliefs represented among American Indians are simply too diverse to be accurately generalized, even in broad and seemingly innocuous statements such as "Native Americans always respected the land," or "Native Americans lived according to the earth's rhythms." Moreover, historical accounts of Native American religious beliefs are often filtered through European perspectives and recorded by nonnative authors, complicating the situation still further. Having said that, Native American religions did (and do) typically arise from a special, symbiotic relationship with the earth. Many indigenous cultures have creation stories in which the first human beings issued from the core of the earth, as a baby emerges from its mother's womb. Some Native American cultures tracked the movements of the sun and the moon, and infused the planting and harvest seasons with special rituals to bless the crops that would sustain life. Some also professed a special kinship with animals and believed that animals possessed powerful spirits.

In New England, numerous indigenous nations were loosely connected to one another and shared a common Algonquin language, though they spoke very different dialects. The most prominent native groups were the Wampanoag, who settled mostly in southern Massachusetts, Cape Cod, and Rhode Island; the Pequot, who were primarily located in what is now Connecticut; and the Narragansett, who lived in Rhode Island. Other large tribes included the Mahican, whose lands extended from New York into western Massachusetts, and the Penobscot tribe of coastal Maine.

In their *New Historical Atlas of Religion in America*, Edwin Gaustad and Philip Barlow have cautioned that "any effort to divorce Native American religion from Native American culture and daily life is doomed." To that end, this book directs the spiritual traveler to a number of sites that seek to explain the history of indigenous cultures in New England. From the tiny Wampanoag Indian Museum on Cape Cod (see page 212) to the enormous, multimillion-dollar Pequot Museum in Connecticut (see page 275), spiritual travelers can glean an invaluable education about the language, history, and culture of some of New England's tribes. Native American religions are also inherently tied to a sense of *place*; for example, the Wampanoag, who have inhabited Martha's Vineyard for 10,000 years, have a special creation myth about the origins of the island itself (see page 209).

Despite the devastations of almost four centuries of European contact, Native Americans are still present in New England, and many nations have fought extensive legal battles to reclaim their tribal lands. In Mashpee, Massachusetts, the Wampanoag lobbied unsuccessfully for federal recognition as an official tribe, but on Martha's Vineyard the Wampanoag enjoy official tribal status. Federal recognition offers certain benefits, including the right to take advantage of casino gaming, a strategy employed with tremendous success by the Pequot of Connecticut.

One final note about indigenous beliefs. In the late twentieth century, a number of Euro-Americans began adapting elements of what they called "Native American spirituality" for their own spiritual growth. They beat drums, held "sacred circles" and emulated traditional native dances. While this appropriation was certainly well intentioned, Native American author Vine Deloria, Jr., has cautioned that it is a worrisome trend. In a 1992 essay in *For This Land: Writings on Religion in America*, he explained that "the non-Indian appropriator conveys the message that Indians are indeed a conquered people and that there is nothing that Indians possess . . . that non-Indians cannot take whenever and wherever they wish." In this vein, many Native American groups today hold rituals that are not open to the public. This guidebook points to some events, such as the Mashpee Wampanoag Powwow on Cape Cod and the Moshup Pageant on Martha's Vineyard, which are open to the public, and asks that readers not attempt to intrude on other, more private, rituals.

> "Our land, our religion, our life are one."
> —A Hopi man, 1951

WICCA

Wicca is a convenient term for a whole host of religious traditions that include neopaganism, druidism, witchcraft, and earth-centered religions. The name *Wicca* is adapted from *wicce*, an Anglo-Saxon word for sorceress or "wise one." Also called "the Craft," Wicca is eclectic by nature, and practitioners are sometimes involved in several religious groups. (In other words, since Wicca is a nonexclusive religion, practitioners may also consider themselves to be Buddhist or Christian or Jewish.) This fact, coupled with the reluctance of many Wiccans to "come out of the broom closet" for fear of persecution, makes it very difficult to gauge how many Wiccans there are in the United States. Some scholars believe that it is one of the nation's fastest-growing religious movements, but reliable numbers do not exist.

There are few rules and doctrines that apply universally to all Wiccans, but some general statements hold true. Most Wiccans seek to be in tune with the earth and its natural rhythms; worship some variation of a Mother Goddess; "bind the Rede" (adhere to a code of ethics called the Rede); and respect all living things. Contrary to popular belief, Wiccans do not worship Satan, who is a Judeo-Christian figure; since their religion is pre-Christian, Satan does not play a role in it. The central rule of Wicca is nonharming; magic is never to be used for personal gain at the expense of the health and well-being of other people and creatures. Wiccans believe in the Threefold Law—that any good or harm that is worked by a spell will come back threefold upon the person who cast it.

Apart from those central themes, there is tremendous diversity within Wicca. Some Wiccans are solo practitioners ("solitaries"); others join covens and practice in groups. Wiccans have many different traditions (called "trads"), including Dianic, Gardnerian, and Alexandrian. These traditions are named after famous practitioners. Wiccans may follow Celtic, ancient Egyptian, or other historic paths. Some Wiccans are "hereditary" Wiccans, meaning that they come from neopagan families. As neopaganism continues to take hold in the United States, it is becoming more common for some witches and warlocks to be second- or third-generation practitioners.

New England has several important gathering places for Wiccans, one of which is Salem, Massachusetts, home of the witchcraft hysteria of 1692 (see page 151). While Salem is famous for the horrors it perpetrated upon those suspected of witchcraft, modern-day witches convene here openly because they feel it is a place of sacred power. Similarly, "America's Stonehenge" in southern New Hampshire is considered an ancient and accurate astronomical calendar, its stones lining up on events such as solstices and equinoxes (see page 333). On the Summer Solstice, for example, many Wiccans and other practitioners of earth religions hold a sunrise celebration here, complete with flowers, dancing, and song.

.... ⌒ ....

CHAPTER TWO

*W*hat to Look For in New England's Houses of Worship

Houses of worship have historically been among New England's largest and tallest buildings, and their steeples long dominated the Boston skyline. The 219-foot steeple of Park Street Church was the highest point in early nineteenth-century Boston, clearly visible from the ships sailing into the harbor (see page 73). Before Park Street Church was built in 1809, the tallest steeple in the city belonged to Old North Church. This is why Old North was chosen to relay a message to American troops on April 18, 1775, the crucial night of Paul Revere's famous ride. By a prearranged signal, the sexton of Old North hung two lanterns in the 191-foot steeple, alerting American forces that the British troops were advancing by water, not by land (see page 86).

Size, however, was but one signal of architectural importance. Another was location. In the colonial period (before the American Revolution), many New England towns were settled in a very familiar pattern. The village would be centered around a small field, which was called a green in Connecticut and a common in Massachusetts and elsewhere. On or beside the common, the town would erect its first meetinghouse or church, usually in the Congregational tradition. Fine examples of New England's town layout can be seen in the Connecticut towns of Litchfield, where the church sits beside the town green (the original meetinghouse was located directly on the green; see page 270) and New Haven. New Haven's Center

Church Crypt also offers the opportunity to see a burying ground that was typical of the seventeenth century (see page 285). In the colonial period, graveyards were adjacent to churches, often on or near the common or green. New England towns, including Boston, eventually forbade new burials in the town centers, and most of the early burial grounds have been built over. A few quiet churchyards, such as King's Chapel Burying Ground (1630) and the Old Granary Burying Ground (1660), still exist in the heart of Boston, and they are the more precious for their rarity and calm (see pages 78 and 72).

This chapter suggests principal features to look for in houses of worship of different denominations and faiths. The entries for the individual buildings throughout the rest of the book, however, will not conform to a "checklist" of criteria, but treat each place according to its unique points of interest, whether they be its members' beliefs, the congregation itself, a building's architecture, its history, or the artwork it contains.

Architectural Elements

THE PLACEMENT AND SHAPES OF BUILDINGS

Churches traditionally face east. Worshipers in synagogues traditionally face toward Jerusalem; in New England that is east. Mosques are designed so that the congregation faces Mecca, and classical Hindu temples are oriented toward the east to face the rising sun. In the more crowded and urban areas of New England, however, not all churches, synagogues, mosques and temples have been able to observe an eastward orientation on their exterior plan, even if they can design the interior to achieve it.

The shape of a house of worship can itself reveal something about the congregation's beliefs. For example, the Church of the Transfiguration on Cape Cod is designed in the style of a fourth-century **basilica** because that architectural style predates the divisions of the Christian churches. That is, the basilica form was in use centuries before the 1054 split between the Eastern Ortho-dox and Roman Catholic Churches, not to

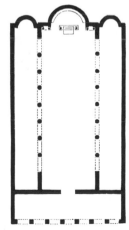

Floor plan of a church in the basilica style with a narthex and three aisles

THE PURITAN MEETINGHOUSE

While the phrase "New England meetinghouse" evokes romantic pictures of white-spired churches holding court on the village green, that image is of a later era. The earliest New England meeting-houses (1630–1700) were quite shockingly plain. Unfortunately, few examples survive. Possibly the most arresting example is the recon-structed Puritan meetinghouse at Plimoth Plantation, created to appear as it would have in 1627 (see page 221). The other example is the Old Ship Meetinghouse in Hingham, Massachusetts, whose wall frame dates to 1681, making it the oldest surviving Puritan meeting-house in the nation. With original dimensions of 55 feet by 45 feet, it appeared almost square when it was first built, which was typical for a meetinghouse of the seventeenth century. Later additions enlarged Old Ship, and a cupola and belfry were added to the roof. It now measures 73 feet long and 55 feet wide, giving it more of a rectangular appearance than it originally had, but its plainness still suggests the restraint of the early meetinghouses (see page 146).

In New England towns, the meetinghouse's physical location spoke of its centrality in the life of the town: the center of faith, of commerce, and of government. The style of seventeenth-century New England meetinghouses was influenced by English town halls, called market halls. Like the market halls, many meetinghouses were placed in the town square, rather than beside a road, as was common for Eng-lish parish churches.

Most New England meetinghouses were constructed to serve mul-tiple purposes. They were places of worship on Sundays, and commu-nity centers during the rest of the week. Many were the sites of town meetings and social gatherings, and some even served as temporary garrisons in times of attack. School was often taught there. This mul-tifunctionality served the Puritan ethos well, since for them, religion and daily life were always interwoven. The Puritans did not distin-guish between church and state. They also rejected the notion that a building could be sacred in and of itself; they believed that the "invis-ible church" of true believers was the home where God's spirit dwelt. Therefore they did not invest time, money, or energy into many of the architectural and artistic accoutrements that typically embellished European churches.

The building material favored in early New England was usually local wood, in direct contrast to late-seventeenth- and early-eighteenth-century buildings in the southern English colonies such as Virginia, where brick was favored. The Puritans' rationale for using wood was probably twofold. Wood made a modest impression, and modesty was a quality greatly sought by the Puritans. More importantly, timberland was plentiful in early New England, while building with brick and stone was prohibitively expensive.

Inside the meetinghouse, simplicity reigned. The congregants usually faced each other on plain benches, in contrast to the boxed and forward-facing pews that would characterize later New England churches. Of paramount importance was the position of the preacher: In keeping with the reformers' ideals of the priesthood of all believers, the minister remained in full view at all times. No screens or veils were allowed to separate him from the people. Likewise, the space had to accommodate the Puritans' reformed ideas about communion, which they renamed "The Lord's Supper" and divested of much religious symbolism. The Lord's Supper was blessed not at an altar, but at a simple "table," which was not considered holy in itself. No longer was the "bread" a wafer dispensed by a priest to individuals lined up at the altar to receive it. Puritans passed great loaves of bread to one another as they sat, then followed that with "large draughts" of wine drunk from a substantial, common cup.

Spiritual travelers who are interested in the architectural evolution of the New England meetinghouse should consider a visit to Old First Church in Northampton, Massachusetts (see page 187). Exhibited in the basement of the church are drawings of all five of the congregation's buildings from the mid–seventeenth century to the present, showing the evolution from a squat, square meetinghouse to a Gothic Revival brownstone church (1878). Old First Church's buildings reflect, in microcosm, the changes that were afoot elsewhere in New England.

mention the many schisms that occurred after the Protestant Reformation. The church's form therefore testifies to the ecumenical spirit of the Community of Jesus, the nondenominational Christian community that built it. (The church was dedicated in the year 2000; see page 216.) In the nineteenth century, that same ecumenical spirit was visible in the structure chosen for an interdenominational church in Richmond, Vermont. Richmond's Old Round Church is actually hexkaidecagonal, or sixteen-sided, but it gives the appearance of roundness. Its founders wanted to construct a place where Christians of all denominations would feel welcome (1813; see page 302).

The traditional New England meetinghouse was square (see sidebar below), though by the end of the colonial period the rectangle had become more common. The earliest rectangular, or longitudinal, churches in New England preserved part of the square **meetinghouse style** by having the pews facing one another, all looking toward a central **pulpit**. Gradually, the rectangular form evolved into the interior style we are more familiar with today, with the pews facing forward and the pulpit in the front. Called basilica design, it requires the congregation to come forward to approach the **altar** or pulpit. It has always been considered hierarchical, so the first Puritans explicitly rejected it. In the nineteenth century, however, many Congregationalists adopted this form.

A church in the form of a Latin cross, called **cruciform**, is considered even more hierarchical than a basilica design. The arms of the cross are called **transepts**, and the area where the transepts intersect the **nave** is the **crossing**. The altar may be placed in the center of the crossing, or it may

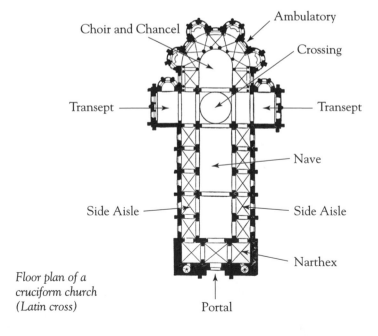

Choir and Chancel

Ambulatory

Crossing

Transept

Transept

Nave

Side Aisle

Side Aisle

Narthex

Floor plan of a
cruciform church
(Latin cross)

Portal

be pushed back away from the congregation into the **chancel**. The further the altar is removed from the congregation, the more hierarchical, or ceremonial, the plan is considered. A place to walk around behind the altar is called an **ambulatory**, and chapels may radiate from that. On a **Greek cross plan**, all arms radiating from the crossing are of equal length.

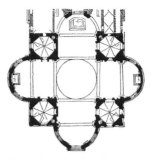

Floor plan of a church in the form of a Greek cross

Many places of worship, churches in particular, are divided into three parts: the **narthex**, an enclosed porch or vestibule at the entrance; the nave, at times divided by columns, piers, and side aisles; and the chancel, which may have an **apse**. A well-designed narthex in an urban house of worship serves as a "decompression chamber" from the hustle and bustle of street activity into the sanctuary of quiet contemplation. It may also accommodate fellowship and social assembly after a service.

Any church may have a tower with a belfry and steeple over the entrance, over the crossing, or placed asymmetrically, picturesquely, somewhere along the side of the sanctuary. Domes may be found in buildings of classically inspired styles: Romanesque, Renaissance, Baroque, or Classical Revival.

Many Christian buildings have clerestories. A **clerestory** (clear story) is often found in a basilica-plan building where the side aisles are lower than the central nave, and it has windows allowing light into the interior. Simply put, it is that part of the nave that rises above the side aisles and contains windows. Clerestories are important sources of light (gas lighting was introduced in the 1820s, but electric lighting not until the 1880s), and they also inspire people to look up and, perhaps, elevate their thoughts.

Architectural Styles

Congregations and their architects have always been concerned with the philosophical or historical associations of architectural styles. Well-known architectural images have great power. The common association of the Gothic style with Christian churches, for example, is a powerful metaphor.

Many of New England's houses of worship were built in the nineteenth century, when new building materials were introduced, such as iron and steel, but many of them echoed historic styles and even revived them. Their architects, however, were not simply archaeological reconstructors.

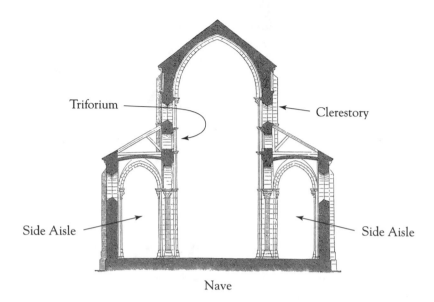

Triforium

Clerestory

Side Aisle

Side Aisle

Nave

A cut-away view of a Gothic church

They treated styles of the past as architectural vocabularies with which they could "say things" that were altogether their own.

No attempt to classify New England buildings in historical styles can be completely successful. Many builders were ignorant of stylistic purity, and frequently they inadvertently mixed styles in one or another of their buildings. Furthermore, many New England houses of worship have been built through the course of several years, and during those years the congregations' preferences changed. Different parts of these buildings may be in different styles. This is common among the old churches of Europe, and some American architects deliberately mixed styles in order to imitate and suggest such age.

Even the dating of houses of worship may be difficult. Some congregations commemorate the groundbreaking for their building, others the laying of the cornerstone, others the building's completion, first service, year of dedication, or year of consecration (usually when it's paid for). This book provides each building's date of dedication; if the congregation's founding predates the building, the date of the congregation's formation is also given. For general reference, the characteristics and connotations of the most popular sacred styles will be discussed in the following pages, in which we trace a history of architectural fashions from the eighteenth to the early twentieth century.

THE TRANSFORMATION FROM PURITAN MEETINGHOUSE TO CONGREGATIONAL CHURCH

In the eighteenth century, the New England meetinghouse evolved from the square to the longitudinal style we typically see today; with the exception of the Old Ship Meetinghouse, the oldest examples of New England meetinghouses date from the eighteenth century. And—in a development that is as important for its theological transformation as for its architectural evolution—New Englanders began to call their meetinghouses "churches" around the middle of that century. Most of these buildings still functioned as multipurpose town centers, cradling the forces of local government as well as faith, but some Puritans began to refer to them by their age-old name.

This relaxation of nomenclature suggests a larger transformation occurring in the Puritan mind. Meetinghouses became churches; and what was the harm, anyway, of making those church buildings a bit more attractive and special in their design? They were still clearly oriented around the preaching of the Word; a pulpit, not an altar, demanded all visual attention. But more expressive design elements began to insinuate themselves in the carving of the wood and the symmetry of the windows. Pitched and gabled roofs lent more elegance to the buildings. These new houses of worship still reflected the Puritan penchant for usefulness, however. The most common decorations were a clock and a bell tower, both essential devices for small-town life; some also had a weather vane, another pragmatic form of ornamentation.

The classic New England church has plain-glass windows throughout. The preference for plain glass was both theological and practical: early Puritans rejected the ornamentation of stained-glass windows, which they felt distracted from the spoken Word of God and might lead followers into idol worship. Plain glass also permitted the maximum amount of natural light—an important consideration in the days before electricity and central heating. Box pews were another innovation that proved practical as well as artistically elegant. Box pews helped to keep parishioners cozy; the pew door would keep drafts out, and in the cold months many people brought blankets and hot bricks to warm their feet. Church services were long and serious affairs, so a minimum degree of comfort was important.

In the mid–eighteenth century, Puritan/Congregational church buildings aspired to even greater elegance. Many were influenced by the church designs of British architect Christopher Wren (see below). New England Congregational churches inspired by Wren include Old South Meetinghouse in Boston (1729; see page 70), First Church in Wethersfield, Connecticut (1764), and Park Street Church in Boston (1809; see page 73). A New England architect, Charles Bulfinch (1763–1844), expanded upon many of Wren's ideas but substituted a dome for Wren's towering spire. Unfortunately, only one of Bulfinch's Congregational churches survives: First Church in Lancaster, Massachusetts (1817; see page 179).

The Wren-Gibbs, Georgian, and Colonial Revival Styles

A number of New England churches emulate a style developed by Sir Christopher Wren, who designed fifty-one new churches after the Great Fire of London in 1666. James Gibbs, whose most famous church is London's St.-Martin-in-the-Fields (1726), successfully copied Wren's classical style. The distinguishing exterior features of this **Wren-Gibbs style** include the combination of a classical **portico** (porch) with a tower and steeple. Wren transformed the Gothic spire into a classical square tower surmounted by a pyramidal or telescoping spire. He often centered the tower on the façade with the principal entrance at its base. At St. Martin's, Gibbs perched the tower and steeple farther back onto the roof ridge, concealing its structural support, and put a monumental portico with free-standing columns across the entire façade. This kind of tower can be seen in churches throughout New England, including Boston's 1729 Old South Meetinghouse (not to be confused with the 1877 Old South Church, which is Gothic Revival; see pages 70 and 95), Trinity Church in Newport, Rhode Island (1728; see page 249), and First Congregational Church in Farmington, Connecticut (1771).

Wren-Gibbs church interiors were among the first specifically designed to meet the requirements of Protestant worship, which focuses on preaching. Clear sightlines and audibility were essential; Wren actually called his churches "auditories." Balconies allow more of the congregation to be close to the minister by doubling up. Sounding boards often hover over wineglass-shaped pulpits. The windows in such churches were originally clear, and the interiors were bright, allowing the congregation to see the minister and to read in their own prayer and hymnbooks. The walls usually have a lower row of short windows and an upper row of higher rounded windows, as can be seen in the United Church on the Green in New Haven, Connecticut (1815; see page 282), or First Congregational Church in Bennington, Vermont (1805; see page 297).

Many American builders owned a copy of Gibbs's *Book of Architecture*, and the Wren-Gibbs type of church was further popularized by America's first how-to architectural handbook, Asher Benjamin's *The Country Builder's Assistant* (1797). This book inspired many of the Congregational churches in New England, although economical New Englanders frequently omitted the enormously expensive porticos.

The term **Georgian** often refers to the architecture of the reigns of England's first three Georges (1714–1820). The Georgian style was classical, imitating northern Italian late–Renaissance architecture, particularly that of Andrea Palladio. Characteristics include a formal dignity and symmetry, solid proportions, ornate frames for doorways, stone **quoins** (blocks used to reinforce or decorate the corners), and **Palladian windows**.

Wren-Gibbs and Georgian classical architecture enjoyed new popularity in the United States in the 1920s and 1930s, when it was called **Colonial Revival**. In New England, several Colonial-style churches that had been decorated in High Victorian styles in the late nineteenth century returned to their classic roots during the Colonial Revival movement. In 1929, for example, the First Congregational Church in Litchfield, Connecticut, began extensive restorations to its 1829 Wren-Gibbs style building (see page 270).

Greek Revival

Late-eighteenth-century archaeology spurred an interest in antique architecture and decoration, and both Greek and pre–Imperial Roman styles found favor in the United States. Greek architecture was thought to represent democratic government, and Roman to represent republican government. Thomas Jefferson's Virginia state capitol (1785–92), modeled after the Roman Maison Carrée in Nîmes, France, was the modern world's first example of a public building in the temple form.

The most easily identifiable features of **Greek Revival**–style buildings are a portico across the front and a roof with a ridge running from front to back. All doors and windows are **trabeated** (rectangular, since they are built with posts and beams), because ancient Greeks did not use arches. The windows are clear glass.

By the 1820s, the Greek Revival style flourished for churches, although New England did not adopt this style as readily as it did the popular Wren-Gibbs style. In 1819, Boston's Episcopalians deliberately broke with Anglican architectural traditions by choosing the Greek Revival style for the Cathedral Church of Saint Paul (see page 79). Other Greek Revival–style churches are scattered throughout New England, including the relatively late example of Mary Keane Chapel in Enfield, New Hampshire (1934; see page 327).

A Gothic pointed arch

Gothic Revival

The romantic movement of the nineteenth century idealized the Christian medieval past and spurred a **Gothic Revival** style of architecture. **Pointed arches** are the most typical feature, but other characteristics include **buttresses** (structures built against walls for support), stained-glass windows, **tracery** (curvilinear openwork shapes creating a pattern within openings), large **rose windows** (circular windows with tracery), and sculpture with medieval inspiration. Early Gothic Revival buildings are usually monochromatic, but later buildings, called **High Victorian Gothic**, often used stone in contrasting colors.

Gothic Decoration Is Not Gothic Construction

Some nineteenth- and twentieth-century churches were built according to medieval Gothic methods of construction, but others only display Gothic decoration. True Gothic construction, the Gothic of the Middle Ages, is the grandparent of the modern skyscraper. In those buildings a skeleton of strong piers—stone in the Middle Ages, steel in the present—supports the building. The walls are not holding up the building but are themselves being held up by the skeleton. They are mere curtains to keep out the rain. The Gothic churches of Europe and modern skyscrapers everywhere demonstrate that curtain walls can even be made of glass. The construction of Europe's great Gothic **cathedrals**, however, absorbed the efforts and finances of whole communities for decades, or even centuries, and nineteenth-century American congregations demanded fine new houses of worship in a hurry. Therefore, most nineteenth-century Gothic Revival churches in America are Gothic in their design and decoration, but they were not built according to medieval Gothic construction methods.

A rose window

America's first Gothic Revival buildings were made of wood, and Gothic-style details and decoration were added. Even structural elements that have no function in wooden buildings were copied from the medieval stone buildings. For example, most large Gothic churches need buttresses along the outside to support the high walls against the outward thrust of the heavy stone roof **vaults**. Sometimes even freestanding piers, called **flying buttresses**, extend supporting arms against the wall. In wooden churches, however, the vaults are made of plaster. From inside, these are indistinguishable from stone vaults, but they are hung from wooden roof supports, more or less as in any plaster ceiling. With plaster vaults, weight-supporting buttresses are unnecessary, but many wooden Gothic Revival churches have them anyway. These buildings are often called **Carpenter's Gothic**, to differentiate them from true **Stonemason's Gothic**.

A Gothic finial

New England's Gothic-Style Churches

Richard Upjohn (1802–78) cinched the popularity of the Gothic with his design for Trinity Church in New York City (1846), which was immediately hailed as a masterpiece. Upjohn wrote a handbook for the construction of wooden churches for rural parishes, *Rural Architecture* (1852). It provided patterns for churches that still stand throughout New England and elsewhere. St. Matthew's Episcopal Church in Hallowell, Maine, for example, was directly modeled after one of the rural church designs in Upjohn's book. Upjohn himself designed another Gothic Revival church in Maine: First Parish Church in Brunswick (1846; see page 355). Richard Upjohn's son, Richard M. Upjohn, joined him in the architect's profession and designed the Gothic Revival Church of the Covenant in the Back Bay neighborhood of Boston (1867; see page 102).

The Gothic Revival style came to be associated with the Episcopal denomination, but other faith groups adopted its architectural language as well. Roman Catholics were particularly attracted to Gothic Revival, which testified to the medieval grandeur of the Roman Catholic faith. Saint Bridget's Roman Catholic Church (1861) in West Rutland, Vermont, is in the Gothic Revival style, as is the Cathedral of the Holy Cross in Boston (1875; see page 103). Both were designed by Patrick Keely, an Irish-born architect who specialized in Gothic Revival buildings.

Other denominations, too, including Congregationalists, Methodists, and Baptists, were attracted to the beauty of the Gothic Revival style. They incorporated Gothic features into their buildings, but retained the liturgical arrangement of their interior spaces (for example, the floor plans were seldom cruciform). Several New England synagogues also adopted the Gothic Revival style, including the Ahavath Gerim in Burlington, Vermont (1902; see page 301).

Romanesque Revival

Romanesque was the architectural style that had *preceded* the Gothic in European history, but in America it enjoyed a revival of interest more than a half-century *after* the Gothic Revival began, around 1814. Reverend Leighton Parks, rector of St. Bartholomew's Church in New York City, identified five characteristics of Romanesque architecture that he believed carry spiritual significance: First, the **round arch** to him signified thankful acceptance of life on earth, rather than the striving toward heaven

A Romanesque round arch

represented by the Gothic pointed arch. Second, Parks argued that the chancel should be in the form of an apse. The chancel is the area in which the clergy performing a service move or sit; an apse is a semi-circular area terminating a space. An apsidal chancel, in Parks's view, recalled the early democratic church organization, when there were no bishops' thrones, but the whole clergy sat on benches around the wall of the apse. Third, a

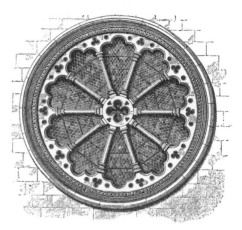

A wheel window

dome would symbolize the tents first used for worship among the Jews. Fourth, the purity of clear glass, rather than stained glass, would represent redemption, and, fifth, a bell tower (or **campanile**), which was a Romanesque architectural innovation, would reflect the idea that the church was open to new ideas. **Romanesque Revival** churches also often have **wheel windows**—large round windows having distinctly radiating spokes. If the churches' façades have two towers, one is usually taller than the other.

America's master of the Romanesque Revival style was undoubtedly Henry Hobson Richardson (1838–86), although his individual stamp differentiates his work from European precedents. **Richardsonian Romanesque** is characterized by stone construction, round arches framing deeply recessed windows and doors, rough textures, and a horizontal heaviness to the buildings. The church generally considered Richardson's masterpiece is Trinity Church in Boston's Back Bay neighborhood (see page 93). Completed in 1897, more than a decade after his death, Trinity's style was widely copied throughout the country.

A particularly ornate form of medieval Romanesque architecture, called **Byzantine**, is characterized by complex vaulting, large open spaces, and lavish decoration with precious marbles, mosaics, and gilding. It was especially popular in New England at the turn of the twentieth century. In Boston in 1905, the Mother Church Extension of the First Church of Christ, Scientist adopted a Byzantine style with Italian influences (see page 100). The following year, Holy Trinity Orthodox Church in Lowell, Massachusetts, commissioned a church in the Byzantine style, its multiple domes recalling such Byzantine gems as the Hagia Sophia in Constantinople (today's Istanbul).

Synagogues

In order to be a synagogue, a structure only needs to be a place where at least ten adult male Jews (a **minyan**, the minimum necessary for an Orthodox service) assemble regularly for prayer. Synagogue is from the Greek *synagein*, "to bring together." Some traditions prescribe architectural details, but these have been open to interpretation or change through the years. For example, the synagogue should be the tallest building in a city, but this cannot always be achieved.

Any synagogue must have an **ark**, which is a receptacle containing the **Torah** scrolls, and the ark should be placed against the wall facing Jerusalem. Torahs (scrolls containing the first five books of the Hebrew scriptures: Genesis, Exodus, Leviticus, Numbers, and Deuteronomy) are handwritten in Hebrew on leaves of parchment sewn together to create scrolls. Portions of the Torah are read regularly in the synagogue, the minimum being on the Sabbath and during festivals. The Torah scrolls may have small caps (*rimmonim*) of silver or brass. Torahs are considered

The Ark in Vilna/Vilner Shul, Boston

sacred, second only to human life, and they are, in fact, buried when they are no longer usable. In front of every ark hangs a continuously burning lamp (today often electric), the *ner tamid*. This symbolizes the eternal light that burned in the Temple in Jerusalem.

The wall facing Jerusalem may also display a painted curtain. It is said that when the Messiah comes to Jerusalem, the curtain will part to reveal a view of the city. Traditional Jewish congregations interpret the Second Commandment's prohibition against "graven images" (Exodus 20:4) to forbid the representations of humans or animals in décor. (All Muslims and the most traditional Protestant denominations also observe that prohibition, but other Christians, including Roman Catholics, believe that God's appearance on earth as Jesus Christ moderated that commandment.) Stenciling, usually of ornate geometric or foliate patterns, is popular on the walls of synagogues (although seldom of words, as can be found in some Christian churches and in mosques).

Each synagogue has a platform (*bimah* to the Ashkenazim; *tebah* to the Sephardim) with a lectern from which the Torah is read. One tradition holds that this must be located in the center of the synagogue so that everyone can hear, but many Reform synagogues place the *bimah* in front of the ark along the eastern wall. The **cantor** may stand on the *bimah* or at a separate lectern.

Another common decorative object is a **menorah**, or candelabrum. Seven-branched menorahs were found in Solomon's temple in Jerusalem. We can see them on the Arch of Titus in Rome, which was erected in 81 C.E. to commemorate the capture of Jerusalem and the looting of the Temple eleven years before. Orthodox synagogues generally avoid having seven-branched menorahs because they want to avoid imitating the Temple, but Reform synagogues might have seven-branched menorahs. A special nine-branched menorah is used during the festival of Hanukkah.

Orthodox synagogues have no instrumental music (an organ immediately reveals that the synagogue you are in is not Orthodox); the congregation worships with covered heads, and men and women sit separately. In Reform, Conservative, and Reconstructionist synagogues, there is no segregation by sex.

Synagogues have always reflected the community and time in which they were built. The first synagogue in New England, built in 1763 in Newport, Rhode Island, was modeled after sketches of great Sephardic synagogues of Europe (see page 245). When nineteenth-century migrations brought more Ashkenazim to New England, many new congregations at first simply purchased existing Protestant church buildings and adapted them for use as synagogues. These buildings were given rabbinical approval because they did not contain any statuary or other graven images, and the ark could often comfortably fit into what had been an apse. Other synagogues were patterned after Christian churches. The Gothic Revival structure built for Ahaveth Gerim Synagogue in 1902 still stands in Burlington, Vermont (see page 301), but this style was soon associated with Christianity so exclusively that few other Gothic-style synagogues are to be found. Romanesque Revival became a popular style for New England synagogues around the turn of the twentieth century; both Temple Beth Israel in Hartford, Connecticut (1876; see page 269) and Congregation Agudath Sholom in Chelsea, Massachusetts (1909; see page 154) feature this style.

Newer buildings reflect a mixture of contemporary tastes and the architectural styles of the people's countries of origin, as well as pan-Jewish history. Temple Israel in Swampscott, Massachusetts, for example, is hexagonal in shape, recalling the six-pointed symbol of Judaism, the Star of David (1946; see page 155). The National Yiddish Book Center in Amherst, Massachusetts (1997; see page 164), was designed to resemble a traditional eastern European *shtetl* (village).

Mosques (Masjids)

Islam means "submission [to God's will]," and "one who submits" is a Muslim. When Muslims gather for Friday midday prayers and a sermon, it must be in a space whose purity reflects that of the believers. A mosque is

fundamentally an enclosure for community prayer, not ritual. Muslims traditionally show little concern for the architectural "style" of the building in which they pray. The first houses of worship for New England Muslims were created inside buildings used for other purposes (the first mosque in Rhode Island, for example, was actually housed in a U-Haul dealership). Over time, Muslims in New England have been able to raise sufficient funds to erect permanent

Geometric design

mosques. They accomplish this without incurring any debt, since Islam prohibits the practice of borrowing or lending money at interest.

Mosques can properly be built in any architectural style, but they often reflect those of Islam's Middle Eastern cradle. Characteristic features suggest shelter—originally from the hostile desert environment—including courtyards with covered arcades, and pools and channels of water. Tall slender towers called minarets are used to call the people to prayer. Unlike Christian steeples, **minarets** often stand apart from the body of the mosque.

Masonry domes, vaults, and arches span the large interior spaces, and although mosques may have few windows, intricate grilles allow light to filter in. Muslim architects created the horseshoe arches that were later copied on synagogues. Interior walls are often elaborately carved plaster or stone, or surfaced with brilliantly colored, glazed tiles. Islam prohibits figural art, so it has developed a rich decorative art based upon abstract geometric patterns and natural flower and plant forms. Quotations from the Qur'an, the sacred text of Islam, in the flowing forms of Arabic calligraphy, are also used to splendid effect.

Horseshoe arch

The main feature of a mosque's interior is the **mihrab**, a shallow apse in the wall that identifies the direction of Mecca. That wall is called the **qibla**. The *mihrab* is sometimes interpreted as a symbolic door or gateway to heaven, and it may boast decorative arches or pilasters. The members of the congregation, arranged in parallel rows, pray facing the *qibla*. Near to the *mihrab* are usually two pulpits. A small one, called a **kursi**, may be used by the imam to lecture or preach on ordinary occasions. The other is the **minbar**, a high pulpit, often canopied, reached by a straight staircase. The *minbar* is used only during Friday services and on holidays. There are no pews; the congregation stands and kneels, and women pray separately from the men. Music does not play a part in Muslim prayer, so mosques have no choir loft or organ.

All mosques will have facilities for ritual purification, usually at or near the entrance. Muslims must wash their arms, hands, faces, and feet before praying. Also near the entrance are shoe racks, since all who enter the prayer room must first remove their shoes.

Hindu Temples

Although Hindu temples in India are often devoted to just one god or goddess, Hindu temples in the United States are usually designed flexibly to accommodate a great variety of divine images or languages, or even to serve as cultural or community centers. New England's largest Hindu temple does, however, reflect traditional considerations; Sri Lakshmi Temple in Ashland, Massachusetts (1990; see page 127), follows the exact proportions laid out in the *vastu shastras*, ancient Hindu sacred texts on temple building. For example, temples must face the rising sun; they should be built near a river or pond; the architect must undergo special rites of purification. Every stage of the construction process is carefully monitored to ensure that building occurs at astrologically auspicious times.

The principal structural symbols in Hindu sacred architecture are mountains and cavelike spaces within them. A temple represents an earthly model of the entire cosmos, so it should resemble a mountain, which is the center of that cosmos. Few Hindu communities in America can afford the lavish sculptures and bas-reliefs of deities found on the exteriors of temples in India, although Sri Lakshmi Temple is ornately decorated with dozens of stone images of the gods. Other Hindu temples in New England may not be immediately identifiable from their exteriors; for example, the Sri Akshar Purushottam Swaminarayan Temple in Stow, Massachusetts, occupies a former Protestant church and is still crowned by a cross (see page 179).

Inside Hindu temples, cavelike spaces represent the womb's generative and regenerative powers. There are many variations in Hindu temple architecture, but most temples have a large room (**natmandir**) where worshipers sit or stand. This room will usually have an east-west alignment. The image of the principal deity resides in the womb-chamber (**garbha-griha**) of the temple at the western end, gazing toward the rising sun and the approaching devotee. Around the perimeter of an American temple are shrines to many different Hindu gods, depending on the devotional leanings of the temple community. Traditional details and figures are often imported from India. Temples traditionally have no pews or chairs; the only seat is reserved for the god.

Sikh Temples

A Sikh temple is called a **gurdwara**, which means "Gate to the Guru." It may be a home, rented space, or specially built temple, but the focus will always be on the scriptures, which are usually covered with a cloth at the front of the room, under a canopy. Sikhs avoid turning their backs to them. Worshipers and visitors must leave their shoes in an entry area, and everyone sits on the floor as an act of humiliation, equality, and respect. During services, hymns are sung and the scriptures are read. There are virtually no "decorative" requirements for a *gurdwara*, nor is there any additional architectural symbolism. Boston-area Sikhs have a *gurdwara* in the suburb of Milford; the building was once a Kingdom Hall for Jehovah's Witnesses (see page 130).

Buddhist Temples

The primary Buddhist monument is the dome-shaped **stupa** (the upper part of which evolved into the **pagoda** of East Asia). The form derives from ancient royal funeral mounds, but it was adopted by Buddhists as a **reli-**

A *pagoda*

quary. According to legend, Buddha's remains were divided into ten portions, and a consecrated mound was built over each relic. Later stupas were constructed for the remains of other holy figures such as saints and monks. As in Hinduism, the dome represents a symbolic mountain, and its interior represents the womb. Some buildings in New England are clearly and intentionally Buddhist in orientation; others are less obviously Buddhist. Temple Vietnam in the Boston neighborhood of Roslindale, for example, occupies a cinderblock structure that is a former day care center; its Buddhist orientation is signaled more by the seven-foot-tall exterior statue of the bodhisattva Kuan Yin than by the temple's architecture.

Inside, Buddhist temples vary widely. Most, but not all, feature at least one main altar. It may hold a statue of the main Buddha for that temple, and it is usually located at the front of the sanctuary. The altar itself is a symbolic mountain, and that symbol can be enhanced by the addition of a terrace or tiers of altars. Side altars often contain statues or pictures of the founder of the temple's lineage, which is a line of teachers and student followers through history. The principal feature of most Buddhist temples is the large open space that is reserved for meditation. A few temples have pews (particularly in the Jodo Shinshu tradition), but most others have just pillows or meditation cushions on the floor.

Church Interiors

The interior design of any Christian house of worship will reveal something about the beliefs of the people who worship there.

High or Low

A distinction commonly used to differentiate churches is between **High Churches** and **Low Churches** (usually capitalized in this special meaning). This expresses the degree to which any congregation believes that pomp and ceremony are appropriate for religious celebration. High Churches favor ceremony, formality, and elements of mystery; ornate vestments, candles, and incense; and artistic and symbolic decorations, including crosses (especially **crucifixes**, which are crosses with an image of the crucified Christ on them). Low Churches, by contrast, forego decoration and ceremony. They express their piety in plain and simple furnishings and ceremonies.

The distinction between High and Low can sometimes be drawn not only between denominations, but even among individual churches within one denomination. Many of the Episcopal churches discussed in this book were refurbished Higher in the late nineteenth or early twentieth century. Chancels were deepened or decorated more elaborately; transepts were added; altars replaced communion tables; **reredoses** (altar screens) were added, and crosses or even crucifixes were displayed.

Ritual or Nonritual

A second differentiation can be drawn between ritual and nonritual churches. **Ritual** (or **liturgical**) faiths, which include the Catholic and the High Episcopal churches, focus their worship on the altar. The altar is given great visual prominence as the site of the ritual sacrifice of the Eucharist, and the entire congregation must have an unobstructed view. Houses of ritual worship also usually need space for processions and for the numerous clergy. These requirements will usually result in a large narthex, at least one wide aisle, and a broad and deep chancel. Ritual churches may also need a **sacristy**, which is a room near the chancel where the robes and altar vessels are stored and where the clergy vest themselves for services.

Changes in Roman Catholic liturgy defined at the Second Vatican Council in 1965 necessitated architectural changes in Roman Catholic churches. Before Vatican II, the priest celebrated the mass in Latin with his back to the congregation. He faced an altar attached to the back wall of the sanctuary, and this area was set off by a communion rail. Today, however, the mass is celebrated in the language of the people, and the priest faces the congregation across a freestanding altar. This liturgical change raised the problem of what to do with the existing, frequently ornate altars and the communion (or altar) rails that created a barrier between the priest and the congregation. Generally, rails have been removed, and new low altars have been built forward from the back wall, often at the crossing.

Several other details to look for in Roman Catholic churches derive from their belief in the doctrine of **transubstantiation**. This is the belief that the ceremony of mass reenacts Christ's last supper. Christ's words to his disciples, "This is my body, which is given for you," are interpreted literally. Transubstantiation means that in the act of consecration of the host, an ordained priest is the instrument for transforming bread and wine into the actual human flesh and blood of Christ. Any leftover portions of this transubstantiated bread are, therefore, still the body of Christ. These portions will be kept in a small repository, called a **tabernacle**, on or near the altar. Most Roman Catholic churches have some consecrated hosts in the tabernacle all the time, and their presence is noted by the burning of the **vigil light**, or **sanctuary lamp**, which usually hangs beside the tabernacle and is usually red in color.

Most Protestant faiths do not believe in transubstantiation, but believe that the communion is a symbolic sharing of bread and wine. Episcopalians leave undefined the nature of the communion bread and wine. Some Episcopal and Lutheran churches speak of the "Real Presence" in the Eucharist when received.

Roman Catholic churches may display relics of saints in reliquaries on altars or in dedicated chapels. In Catholic teaching, relics are devotional objects, like holy water and the rosary. It is not necessary to believe in them; that is, they are not *de fide* (essentials of the faith). A **shrine** is a special chapel dedicated to the worship of a particular saint, and shrines often contain relics of that saint.

Orthodox churches are also ritual churches. In them, the sacrament of the Eucharist is performed by the priest out of sight, and the bread and wine are brought forth from that holy place. An **iconostasis**, or screen covered with icons (sacred images), conceals that space. The priests' doorway through the iconostasis is called a Royal Door because Christ, the King of Heaven, passes through it in the form of the Eucharist.

Nonritual (or **nonliturgical**) denominations include most Protestant groups—Methodist, Baptist, and so forth, as well as some Low Church Episcopalians. For these groups the most important part of the service does not consist of performing rituals at an altar, but of listening to the Word, so their liturgy and church design focus on the pulpit. The entire congregation must be able to see the pulpit and to hear the sermon. The ideal form for nonritual churches is the auditorium, a preaching space in which the largest possible congregation can be brought within the range of the human voice, as in Wren's "auditories."

Nonritual churches do not require either a large chancel or pathways for processions, but a wide center aisle may facilitate communion. A table may be set up all the way from the head to the foot of the aisle, and members sit at the table in relays to be served the bread and wine by elders. Altars in these churches are not elaborate. Reformed Protestants (members of the Calvinist-heritage Congregational, Presbyterian, or Dutch Reformed denominations) do not even call them altars, but communion tables. For the Puritans in seventeenth-century New England, a simple wooden table, the Lord's Board, sufficed.

Furnishings

Most Christian churches have three basic items: a **pulpit**, from which the minister delivers the sermon; an altar or communion table, from which the sacrament of the Eucharist, or the Lord's Supper, is shared; and a **font**, for the sacrament of baptism. Some churches also have a **lectern**, or Bible stand. Lecterns often display an eagle, the symbol of St. John's Gospel, which begins "In the beginning was the Word." Christian Science churches have two lecterns for the two readers.

Many Roman Catholic and some Episcopal churches have confessionals, although these booths are being replaced in most churches by reconciliation rooms. Roman Catholic and Orthodox churches also have containers for holy water at church entrances, so that entrants can cross themselves, in remembrance of their baptism.

Pews

Today, most churches allow people to sit wherever they choose, but this was not true in the past. Pews were pieces of real estate held by regular members of the congregation, and few were available for visitors. "Free" churches did exist, but these were usually chapels in poor neighborhoods supported by wealthy churches elsewhere.

Many New England churches began to abolish pew rents in the nineteenth century; Park Street Church in Boston was among the last to relinquish the practice, in the mid-twentieth century. As annual pledges and weekly collections came to replace pew rent as most churches' main source of income, slip pews replaced box pews. The box pews that still exist in a few New England churches are generally open to all on a first-come-first-served basis.

Other Interior Furnishings

Most decorations in ecclesiastical buildings carry symbolic meaning, and the study of these is called **iconography**. One of the most common symbols is the paired first and last letters of the Greek alphabet, alpha and omega (A and W). This signifies that all things begin and end in the Lord (Revelation 22:13).

Churches dedicated to specific saints feature their portraits. The patron of a church is often represented on the **trumeau** (the column in the center of the main door holding up the **tympanum** above), and saints can be identified by distinctive objects they carry or have around them, called **attributes** or **emblems**. These usually symbolize the personality of the

THE ORGANS OF NEW ENGLAND

Each organ is a completely unique mix of sets of pipes in an acoustically unique environment. Each is suitable for producing a distinctive type of music, depending upon the specific liturgy, the traditions of that denomination or individual congregation, and the tastes of the music director or organist. This is to say nothing of the tastes and prejudices of the listeners. Still further, each organ is in a different state or condition. Some of what, by general agreement, would be the finest organs in the region are wheezing along at only a fraction of their capacity, because the cost of maintaining and restoring these mighty instruments is prohibitive.

New England has a wonderful history of organ music, beginning with King's Chapel in 1713. King's Chapel was the first church in the American colonies to have an organ. Although the Fisk organ that now stands at the rear of King's Chapel is not the original 1713 instrument, it is highly regarded for its excellent sound, and undergirds the church's outstanding program in sacred music (see page 77). Also in Boston, the organ of the Christian Science Mother Church Extension is among the world's ten largest, with 13,290 pipes. The 1952 organ was entirely refurbished in 1995, and is played for religious services as well as concerts (see page 100). In the Boston suburbs, the Wellesley College Chapel has a rare twentieth-century reconstruction of a temperament that dates to the time before Johann Sebastian Bach. (This is not a well-tempered instrument, in the style of post-seventeenth-century instruments, but has separate keys for G sharp and A flat, for example.) The organ is entirely mechanical and has no electronic components. This rare organ makes it possible for music students and professionals to hear music from before the time of Bach (e.g., by Buxtehude and other sacred composers) the way it would have originally sounded (see page 157).

The 19th-century organ at the Church of the Immaculate Conception, Boston

saint, the saint's occupation or acts, or how the saint suffered martyrdom. The four evangelists, Matthew, Mark, Luke, and John, for example, are traditionally accompanied by an angel, a lion, an ox, and an eagle, respectively. All four symbols are often winged. Roman Catholic churches may display the **stations of the cross**, which are fourteen specific scenes from Jesus' trial and crucifixion.

Visiting a House of Worship

Houses of worship generally welcome visitors of all faiths. Different congregations do hold services on different days at different hours. For example, the principal services of the week in mosques are on Friday at noon, and in Christian churches on Sunday morning. Synagogues hold services on Friday evening and Saturday morning; call individual congregations for times and details.

Houses of worship do not vary much in the behavior expected. In all, respectful quiet is always appreciated. Eating or drinking is prohibited. Some houses of worship will have dress codes posted, and these usually require at least long trousers for men; women's clothing should cover the arms, and hems should reach below the knee (to the ankles in mosques). Women's heads should be covered in mosques and Orthodox synagogues. Men are requested to wear a small skullcap (*yarmulke*) in Orthodox and Conservative synagogues, but to remove headgear in most other houses of worship. All worshipers and visitors to mosques, Sikh temples, Hindu temples, and some Buddhist temples must remove their shoes. If you have any questions, simply telephone ahead of your visit.

Don't be confused by moments of sitting, standing, or kneeling during services. You may wish to follow the lead of those around you, but if that makes you uncomfortable, few regular worshipers will take offense if a visitor remains quietly seated.

It is rude to photograph individuals at their private devotions, but some sacred places will allow you to photograph portions of the interior. If you are in doubt, ask an official for permission.

Chapter Two by Edward F. Bergman and Jana Riess

CHAPTER THREE

·············· ❧ ··············

Boston and Cambridge

BOSTON IS THE OFFICIAL capital of Massachusetts and the unofficial capital of the entire region of New England, with more than half a million residents in Boston itself and nearly five million inhabitants in the greater Boston area. It is a city rich in history and tradition. Its first inhabitants were Native Americans, particularly of the Massachusett and Pawtucket nations. They spoke languages that were related to Algonquin and enjoyed an agrarian culture that followed centuries of tradition. The area's history took an entirely different course in 1630, when a party of more than 1,000 English Puritans passed over Salem and Charlestown to settle in what was then called Shawmut Peninsula. (There had been some English migration prior to this; in fact, the Puritans purchased a good deal of their Boston land from the Reverend William Blackstone, an Anglican priest who had already settled there.) The Puritans, who placed a high premium on the ownership of land, quickly scattered the native peoples. The Massachusett tribe had already been decimated by a terrible plague in 1617, and by 1630 only numbered about 500 people. They could do little to stop the English tide.

The Puritans' influence indelibly marked New England, especially Boston. Their emphasis on education resulted in the founding of Harvard College in Cambridge in 1636, still regarded as one of the finest universities in the United States (or, as MIT students like to say, "the most prestigious university in Harvard Square"). The Puritan character encouraged thrift and industry, as God-fearing men and women used their work to demonstrate the salvation they believed God had granted to the elect. This meant that within a generation, the once-hardscrabble frontier that

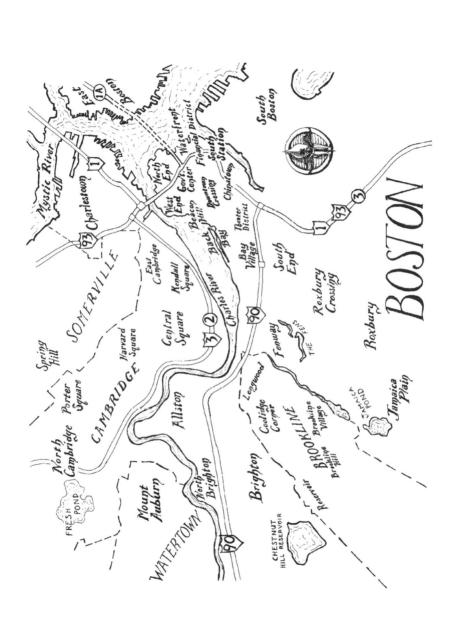

was eastern Massachusetts had been transformed into a series of well-planned communities, with a Puritan meetinghouse at the center and a series of prospering businesses clustered around it.

Today, Boston is a cosmopolitan city, its ethnic composition becoming richer with each passing decade. Its Puritan heritage is still visible in the church-dotted landscape and in some slow-to-die traditions, such as prohibitions about selling alcohol on Sundays. But today's city is a spiritually eclectic version of its early self. In the mid–nineteenth century, its primarily English character gave way to successive waves of Irish immigration, and in the late nineteenth century, thousands of Eastern Europeans and

NAVIGATING IN BOSTON

Boston is—to put it politely—a driver's nightmare, the downtown area streets having been laid out from the original cow paths of the city. Streets are narrow and often only one-way, making navigation difficult in a car. (One famous local saying is "You cahn't get theah from heah"—i.e., "You can't get there from here.") The generally bad driving conditions are even worse just now, with "The Big Dig" construction project on Interstate 93 expected to be finished by 2004 at the earliest. Also, Boston drivers are notoriously assertive, which may intimidate a tourist who does not know the lay of the land. Then, there is the additional problem of where to "pahk youh cah," since parking is extremely limited on the street and often prohibitively expensive in the charge-by-the-hour garages.

Do yourself a favor and explore Boston on foot. Boston is a remarkably compact and walkable city; all of the downtown sites are within easy distance of each other. Walking affords opportunities to leave the well-trod tourist path and make delightful discoveries of your own—a tiny Italian café or a neighborhood grotto in the North End, for example.

Alternatively, take the "T," the city's subway system. To help you learn the T's routes, each entry in this chapter includes information about the closest T stop to every site. The T is fast, convenient, and astoundingly inexpensive. (History buffs will also want to know that it is the nation's oldest subway system, constructed in 1897.) Tourists may purchase passes that are good for unlimited rides for a specified number of days, which is a real bargain if you take several rides each day.

Italians poured into the area. These transformations resulted in an increasing religious diversity. Whereas Massachusetts had an established Congregational (formerly Puritan) Church until 1833, with the minister's salary and the church's upkeep paid for by local and state taxes, by the late nineteenth century the city was home to many immigrant communities of Catholics and Jews. Moreover, the New England region gave rise to some new religions of its own, including The Church of Christ, Scientist, which is headquartered in Boston. In addition to these religious groups are Muslims, Hindus, Buddhists, and Latter-day Saints (Mormons), who all have a strong presence in the Boston area.

The entries in this chapter are organized by neighborhood. Given the city's rich diversity and importance in American history, not every sacred site or noteworthy house of worship can be included here. It is hoped that readers—spiritual pilgrims themselves—will use these entries as starting places in their own voyage of discovery.

Boston Common and Downtown

Downtown Boston, the area surrounding the Common and beyond, was the heart of the city in the colonial era, and that remains true today. The Massachusetts State House and the various skyscrapers of the Financial District mark the neighborhood as an important center of both government and commerce, while various historic churches and sacred sites attest to its spiritual significance. Here we find some of the city's oldest cemeteries, churches and parks, juxtaposed with modern life.

America's Oldest Public Park
BOSTON COMMON
Year created: 1630.

Boston Common is bordered by Tremont, Park, Boylston, and Beacon Streets. T Stop: Park Street on the Green and Red Lines. The Information Booth is on the Common at Tremont Street, a five-minute walk from the Park Street subway station.

Boston Common, more affectionately called "the Common," takes its stately place as the oldest public park in America. In 1630, just months after the Puritans had landed in Massachusetts Bay, they donated

Boston Common and Park Street Church

their pounds and shillings to preserve approximately fifty acres for public use. Three hundred and fifty years ago, we might have seen Puritan families enjoying recreation and grazing their cows and goats on this land. Puritan mothers breast-fed their infants publicly in the Common's open spaces. (It is perhaps a bit ironic that contemporary American culture is offended by practices that the supposedly straight-laced Puritans regarded as a matter of course.) At times, colonial militias held training exercises here. Above all, this land was set aside for the needs of the community.

Centuries ago, the community's needs demanded a place for public executions. Numerous dissidents and criminals met rather ghastly ends here; Quaker martyr Mary Dyer (see page 255) was hanged in the Common in 1660 alongside three of her spiritual compatriots, accused of religious heresy for their Quaker beliefs. (Incidentally, because the Puritans considered the Quakers to be personae non gratae in the eyes of God, they were not permitted a Christian burial. Their ashes were scattered in the Common itself, perhaps nurturing the very trees we see today.) In 1643, a young woman executed for adultery publicly exhorted young female witnesses to remain chaste, and in 1656, a Native American named Matoonas was tied to a tree here and shot. In the colonial period, executions such as these were considered opportunities for a grand holiday. Hundreds, and even thousands, of spectators attended public executions, some bringing their small children and a picnic lunch, prepared to make a day of it.

The Common has played an important role in our nation's history. During the Revolution, it was used for the hundreds of tents and campfires of the colonies' ragtag militia—and alternately for the more nattily attired Redcoats. It was here that Ralph Waldo Emerson persuaded the young

Walt Whitman to revise some of the more salacious passages from Whitman's poetic manifesto, *Leaves of Grass*, and during the Civil War the country's first regiment of black soldiers met in the Common to enlist. In the Common, Presidents have been saluted—and criticized, as Vietnam War protesters made their voices heard.

After the Revolution, the city of Boston painstakingly removed some

PILGRIM OR PURITAN?

Although they are often used interchangeably in travel guides and local histories, the terms "Pilgrim" and "Puritan" connote two distinct groups. The Pilgrims were the first English settlers in New England, who created Plymouth Colony in 1620 (see page 221). The Puritans, on the other hand, first arrived in Massachusetts Bay in 1630, led by John Winthrop. Over time, both groups melded into the single label, "Puritan," despite their early distinctions; the Pilgrims had been a more radical group than the Puritans in the early seventeenth century, and felt that the Anglican Church was far too theologically corrupt for them to remain within it. The Puritans, on the other hand, hoped to "purify" the Anglican Church from within—or rather, they did until they were well settled in America and realized that the differences between Anglicanism and nonconformist Protestantism were simply too great.

When they despaired of ever bringing about a reunion, Puritans began to view themselves as "separatists," like the Pilgrims had before them, belonging to a new and separate church. And although it was the Puritans who were persuaded to the Pilgrim point of view, the name "Puritan" stuck for the ages to describe the blended group. (The name "Pilgrim" did not disappear altogether in local history though—it was the original name of Boston's baseball team, now called the Red Sox.)

Puritan churches had a congregational polity (form of church government), meaning that individual congregations could decide who to call as minister or how to maintain their buildings. In the eighteenth century, "Congregational" with a capital C replaced "Puritan" as the moniker for the Puritan churches. In this book, congregations that began earlier than 1700 are designated "Puritan/Congregational," while those that were formed after 1700 are called simply "Congregational."

of the public buildings (such as an almshouse and the granary) in favor of more green space. Until World War II, a lovely wrought-iron fence encircled the entire park, but it was torn down during the war for use as scrap metal. Today, visitors can enjoy the park's winding paths, wade in its Frog Pond, and throw coins into the Brewer Fountain, modeled after a fountain from the Paris Exposition of 1855. Spiritual travelers may be particularly interested in the tremendous religious diversity that can be witnessed in the park. Hare Krishnas distribute literature, saffron-robed Buddhists meditate, and the controversial Boston Church of Christ holds regular mass baptisms in the Common. (What would the Puritans have thought?)

Prelude to the Boston Tea Party
OLD SOUTH MEETINGHOUSE
Puritan/Congregational. 310 Washington Street at Milk Street. Year consecrated: 1729 (congregation dates to 1669). Architect: Joshua Blanchard.
☎ 617-482-6439 🖳 www.oldsouthmeetinghouse.org

T Stop: Downtown Crossing on the Red and Orange Lines. Open daily from April through October from 9:30 A.M. to 5 P.M., and from November through March from 10 A.M. to 4 P.M. Admission fee.

This site, which was purchased by the Old South congregation in 1669, is the oldest continuously owned piece of property in Boston. It has not been in use as a church since the late nineteenth century, but has been wonderfully preserved and is now open as a museum. The first small church on this site burned to the ground in 1711 and was replaced in 1729 by the current brick building. Its attached freestanding tower, which narrows into an octagonal spire at its top, resembles the London churches of Christopher Wren. It's the second-oldest church building in Boston (after Old North, whose present structure dates to 1723; see page 86). Old South retains many of its original fixtures, including its tower clock, which has told time perfectly since it was installed in 1770.

The Old South Meetinghouse is a stop on Boston's famous Freedom Trail (see sidebar), which connects the major sites in the city related to the Revolution. It enjoys this distinction for good reason. Its large, uncluttered interior offered the perfect spot for the colonies' dissenters to hold their meetings and protest loudly for change. It was here, on December 16, 1773, that Samuel Adams proffered up a rousing speech on boycotting

British goods. (In 1773, Britain's "Tea Act" had repealed all taxes on tea within England but continued such taxes in the colonies, infuriating Boston's citizens.) The crowd of 7,000 people could not all cram into the church, so many spilled out into the street and strained to hear. After Josiah Quincy stirred up the masses even further, they thronged out of the meetinghouse and into the streets. The famous result? The Boston Tea Party, when colonists disguised as Indians dumped 342 chests of tea— worth roughly $700,000 today—into the harbor. This outrageous act of destruction further damaged the already strained relations between England and the colonies, fanning the flames of war.

Perhaps because Old South Meetinghouse was such a hotbed of patri- otism, British soldiers made a special point of desecrating the building while they occupied it from 1774 to 1776. The pulpit was destroyed and the pews hacked apart for kindling, leaving a vast open space in what is to this day New England's longest meetinghouse, 96 feet long and 67 feet wide. The British army turned the building into a riding ring, spreading sand on its wood floors to accommodate their many horses. British officers drank hard liquor in the galleries and looked on as their horses were exer- cised on the floor below. After the colonists had succeeded in expelling the

THE FREEDOM TRAIL

Visitors to Boston can take a walking tour of seventeen of the city's (and the nation's) most important historical sites by following the Freedom Trail, which begins in Boston Common and includes churches, monuments, burying grounds, historic houses, and gov- ernment buildings. You are welcome to walk the trail on your own or partake of a guided tour. National Park Service Rangers give free ninety-minute tours of the Freedom Trail daily, starting at the National Park Service Center (15 State Street). Tours depart at 10 A.M., 11 A.M., 2 P.M., and 3 P.M. on Saturday and Sunday; 10 A.M. and 2 P.M. on Monday; and 2:00 P.M. only on Tuesday through Friday. Rangers also give short historical talks in Faneuil Hall each day, every half hour from 9 A.M. to 5 P.M.

From late May to early September, ninety-minute guided tours are also offered by the Freedom Trail Players, costumed actors who discuss the historical significance of each site and portray everyday life in the eighteenth century. There is a fee for these tours.

For information on all tours, 🖳 www.thefreedomtrail.org

British from Boston, they began the difficult work of restoring the meetinghouse to its pristine prewar state. The high pulpit was finally replaced in 1808.

When this neighborhood became more urban and populous during the nineteenth century, Old South's members began looking for new digs. In 1875, most of them left for the new Gothic Revival structure in Back Bay (see page 95), with a small but committed contingent remaining behind, determined to save this building. It had mercifully escaped the horrible Boston Fire of 1872, which destroyed so many other downtown Boston landmarks, and these congregants could not bear the thought that the historic building would be torn down by their own hands after it seemed to have been so providentially spared during the fire. They formed the Old South Association and raised the substantial $400,000 purchase price (in 1870s dollars) to rescue the building. This is widely regarded as the first large-scale example of historic preservation in America.

Puritan Headstones and Epitaphs
THE OLD GRANARY BURYING GROUND
Park and Tremont Streets. Year created: 1660.

T Stop: Park Street on the Green and Red Lines. Open daily from 9 A.M. to 5 P.M. No admission fee.

Tucked behind the busy modern thoroughfare of Tremont Street is this oasis of tranquility, one of the most historic cemeteries in New England. It was opened in 1660 as the city's third cemetery (after King's Chapel and Copp's Hill Burying Grounds), and is named for that part of the old Common that was used to store grain. Many patriots have found rest here, including John Hancock, Paul Revere, Samuel Adams, and the five victims of the Boston "Massacre." Some of the Puritan graves are nearly three centuries old, the stones featuring skeleton heads and hourglasses (symbolizing the transience of the body) and depictions of the paradise to come (symbolizing the eternal nature of the soul).

One tombstone you shouldn't miss is for Ann Pollard, considered the first English female to set foot on the peninsula that is now Boston. She was just ten years old. Despite her famous pipe-smoking tendencies, she lived to be 105, and much of Boston turned out to pay their respects at her funeral in 1725. Her portrait still hangs at the Old South Meetinghouse nearby—she had it painted when she was a youthful 103.

A Trinitarian Standard-Bearer
PARK STREET CHURCH
Congregational/Conservative Congregational Christian Conference. Park
and Tremont Streets. Year consecrated: 1809. Architect: Peter Banner.
☎ 617-523-3383 💻 www.parkstreet.org

T Stop: Park Street on the Green and Red Lines. Open July through
August, 9:30 A.M. to 3:30 P.M. Open in winter by appointment.

Park Street Church is the most imposing edifice on "Brimstone Corner"—so named not because of the hellfire sermons preached there, but for
the gunpowder that was stored in the church's basement during the War of
1812. But the church has also had no shortage of fire-and-brimstone
preaching in its two-century history. It was founded, in fact, to combat the
liberalizing tendencies in the Congregational Church in the early nineteenth century—most specifically, the "heresy" of Unitarianism (see page
27). Park Street would stand as a bastion of Christian orthodoxy (read:
Trinitarian theology) when other churches transformed themselves into
Unitarian almost overnight.

Park Street Church was founded in 1809, with its charter members
constructing this remarkable building in record time. The architect, Englishman Peter Banner, incorporated some designs by Christopher Wren.
For many years, its 217-foot steeple was the tallest landmark in the downtown area. There are some unusual decorative elements for a Puritan-
descended church, including a stained-glass window, dedicated in 1904.
(In keeping with the modest and functional theme of Puritan architecture,
however, a plain-glass window has been placed in front of the stained-
glass one, so that the stained glass is invisible from the street.) The pulpit
is prestigiously located in the center of the sanctuary, unlike the Anglican-
legacy churches, where the pulpit is to the side and the altar is in the
center. The pulpit-centered arrangement emphasizes the importance of
preaching in the church.

The church's interior has changed somewhat since the nineteenth
century; in 1880, the original box pews were replaced by the row pews we
see today. (Incidentally, the rental of pews here, as in other New England
churches, continued well into the twentieth century.) In the church's early
years, it employed two "tithing men" to walk outside the church property
on Sundays and chastise any children who were playing or climbing trees
in Boston Common. Sermons in those days were two to three hours long,

so the church also utilized sticks during worship services to rap the heads of dozing adults or misbehaving children.

Although it is not the oldest Congregational church in Boston (Old South bears that distinction), Park Street is likely the most famous, and is one of the stops on the historic Freedom Trail. Many historical firsts have taken place here: William Lloyd Garrison preached his first radical abolitionist sermon from this pulpit in 1829 (it was so controversial that some audience members thought he should be lynched). The patriotic standard "My Country 'Tis of Thee" (also known as "America") was sung here for the first time on July 4, 1831, and the church has sponsored the longest-running radio broadcast program in the country, bringing its services to the listening public every Sunday morning and evening. It also pioneered the first prison ministry program in America. (Many guidebooks credit Park Street Church with establishing the first Sunday school in the country, but this last "first" is incorrect. Methodist Sunday schools had been active in the United States since 1790.)

When the first subway in the United States was constructed across the street in 1895, an enormous geyser of water erupted from a broken main, spewing water with such force that it broke the windows in the pastor's study. Fuming, he preached in his evening sermon that the subway was "an infernal hole and an unchristian outrage, sponsored by the devil himself." Today, however, that subway is the means of transportation that most of the congregation's youngish membership use to get to church (particularly for the two youth-oriented services on Sunday evenings). Park Street Church is well known for its vibrant college and international outreach programs, its "Seekers" fellowship of young adults meeting on Sunday afternoons, and its support of missionaries worldwide. Unlike many Congregational churches that have become part of the liberal-leaning United Church of Christ (UCC) denomination, Park Street has hoed the straight and narrow by upholding evangelical theology.

Self-guided tours are available, with church volunteers on hand to answer questions. A five-minute film about Park Street runs continuously, describing some highlights of the congregation's history. In the hallway, photographs commemorate some of these events, including the church interior being draped in black after President Lincoln's assassination.

A Drop-in Center for Spiritual Seekers in the Heart of Boston
PAULIST CENTER
Roman Catholic/Paulist Fathers. 5 Park Street. Year consecrated: 1970.
☎ 617-742-4460 💻 www.paulist.org/boston

> *T Stop: Park Street on the Green and Red Lines. Masses are held Monday*
> *through Friday at 7:55 A.M. and 12:05 P.M.; Saturday at 6 P.M.; and*
> *Sunday at 10 A.M., noon, and 6 P.M.*

Across from Boston Common, and just steps away from Park Street Church and the Massachusetts State House, this subdued storefront gives little hint of the vitality of the ministries housed within. The Paulist Center is operated by the Paulist Fathers, a Roman Catholic missionary organization founded in the United States in 1858. Following World War II, the Paulist Fathers had the visionary idea of creating drop-in centers in America's metropolitan areas. These would be informal places where Catholics, lapsed Catholics, and non-Catholics could stop by for a heart-to-heart conversation with a priest or to receive helpful reading materials.

This spiritual center in the heart of downtown Boston is evidence of the success of their vision. The chapel is open daily for public mass and private prayer, with many outreach ministries meeting the needs of the Catholic community. There is a group called "Landings" to facilitate returning Catholics' readjustment to the fold, and an RCIA (Rite of Christian Initiation of Adults) program to prepare new Catholics for the responsibilities of church membership. Other outreach programs include a "Divorced Catholics Group"—the first group of its kind in the nation— and a food pantry, open on Tuesday and Thursday afternoons.

America's First Interracial Congregation
TREMONT TEMPLE
American Baptist. 88 Tremont Street. Year consecrated: 1895 (congregation dates to 1839). Architect: Clarence Blackall. ☎ 617-523-7320

> *T Stop: Park Street on the Green and Red Lines. Sunday worship is at*
> *11 A.M. Each Wednesday evening at 6:30, there is a Bible study and*
> *prayer meeting.*

Tremont Temple was founded in 1839, when Charles Street Baptist Church member Timothy Gilbert challenged his congregation's segrega-

Tremont Temple

tionist seating policies by welcoming some black friends into his pew one
Sunday morning. The church did not look kindly on this transgression of
boundaries, and Gilbert was asked to leave. He and some other abolitionist
Baptists founded First Baptist Free Church, later renamed Tremont
Temple, which is considered to be the first integrated congregation in
America.

In the nineteenth century, this church played host to all manner of
lectures, symposia, and rallies. Evangelists such as Dwight Moody, Evange-
line Booth, and Billy Sunday preached here, and temperance activist
Frances Willard convened the first triennial conference of the Woman's
Christian Temperance Union. Before the Civil War, Tremont Temple was
an important forum for the antislavery movement, with many abolitionist
meetings held in its vast sanctuary. That auditorium-style sanctuary also
hosted numerous theatricals and evenings of secular entertainment. When
Charles Dickens came to Boston in 1867, he read selections from *A Christmas Carol* and *David Copperfield* to standing-room-only crowds.

In 1895, the congregation erected the present Venetian-style stone
edifice, with a large auditorium seating 1,850 people. Today, Tremont

Temple is a thriving American Baptist congregation, with numerous foreign-language services and international ministries. Special services are offered each Sunday for Korean, Ethiopian, Cambodian, and Hispanic congregations.

New England's First Anglican—and Unitarian!—Congregation
KING'S CHAPEL
Unitarian Universalist (formerly Anglican). Tremont and School Streets. Year consecrated: 1749 (congregation dates to 1686). Architect: Peter Harrison. ☎ 617-523-1749 🖳 www.kings-chapel.org

T Stop: Park Street on the Green and Red Lines. Open daily in summer, with more limited hours during the rest of the year. Sunday worship is at 11 A.M.

Numerous historic American churches have made some odd theological transformations through the years, but King's Chapel must be the granddaddy of them all. It began as a staunch Anglican establishment—the first Anglican congregation in Puritan New England, in fact. Those early Anglicans had a rough time of it. The Puritans—whom the Anglicans had persecuted in England—clearly considered the Anglican arrival in New England as opportunity for payback. They simply refused to sell the Anglicans any land on which to build their first church.

Finally, in 1686, they pawned off some subprime real estate—a corner of their burying ground. (Other stories claim that the Anglicans simply took the plot of land without a purchase.) And here King's Chapel got its inauspicious start. The first building on the site was a small wooden chapel, built in 1688 and expanded in 1710. The present quarried-stone building (minus its 120-foot steeple, abandoned for lack of funds) was designed by Peter Harrison and erected in 1749. The Anglican presence was still a thorn in the side of Puritan Boston, and the building's cornerstone ceremony was marked by angry residents throwing garbage and animal carcasses at Anglican congregants.

King's Chapel remained loyalist during the Revolution, a touchy time for Tories in the colonies.

While the war still raged, the congregation did a doctrinal about-face and embraced the newfangled teachings of Unitarianism, which was just taking hold in Boston. In 1783, Reverend James Freeman was ordained as the first Unitarian minister in America (or anywhere, for that matter), and in 1786 the congregation became the nation's first Unitarian church. The congregation has remained Unitarian ever since—although, as the church's brochure proudly states, it espouses "a Unitarian Christian theology, an Anglican form of liturgy and a congregational form of governance." So, King's Chapel is an ecclesiastical American melting pot.

The church's fine Georgian design is atypical of New England architecture, its hand-cut Quincy granite exterior differing markedly from the clapboard churches more typical of the region in the mid–eighteenth century. This was an intentional decision, with the architecture striving to evoke the great cathedrals of England rather than the simple, pragmatic meetinghouses of New England. But the stonemasons did not have the techniques or the tools to create a polished exterior, resulting in rather roughly textured granite blocks.

The forbidding façade, which architectural historian Robert Mutrux calls "quite clumsy," is balanced by a magnificent and well-conceived interior. The box pews, which are original, offered warmth during Boston's wintry mornings, making the long church services bearable in the days before central heating. One very special box pew sits on the right side of the nave, facing the altar. Crowned with a royal red canopy, this was the royal governor's pew, still called by that name although Massachusetts has not had a royal governor in over 200 years.

Plain-glass Palladian windows fill the chapel with natural light. The communion table was a gift from joint monarchs William and Mary in 1696. The pulpit was built in 1717 for the earlier, wooden King's Chapel. It is the oldest pulpit in the United States that has been in continuous use on the same site. At the rear of the chapel stands the late twentieth-century Fisk organ that is the pride of the congregation. King's Chapel was actually the first church in America to have an organ, its original instrument having been bequeathed by a local merchant in 1713. Today, the church offers an expansive program of sacred music, including brief instrumental concerts on many Tuesdays at lunchtime.

Boston's Oldest Cemetery
KING'S CHAPEL BURYING GROUND
Tremont and School Streets. Year created: 1630.

T Stop: Park Street on the Green and Red Lines. Open during daylight hours.

CEMETERY ETIQUETTE

In order to preserve cemeteries as historic sites, visitors are usually asked to keep to the path and not wander between the tombstones. You will still be able to see the most important gravestones, which have been moved to the path for this reason. In all New England cemeteries, be sure to follow simple etiquette: don't lean on the stones or make rubbings from them. Leave Rover and Fido at home. And most importantly, respect the privacy of other visitors, who may be mourning their loved ones.

King's Chapel Burying Ground is Boston's oldest cemetery, offering some of the best examples of Puritan headstones anywhere in New England. (Look for the grave of Rebecca Gerrish, which depicts a skeleton and an angel holding an hourglass, reminding visitors of the brief transience of human life.) Unfortunately, as with many old cemeteries, some of the stones have been moved from their original locations, as grave keepers attempted to maintain an orderly arrangement of stones along the walking paths. Some of the stones are also partially buried in the ground, obscuring their unique carvings.

This cemetery is the final resting place of some prominent New Englanders; the colony's first governor, John Winthrop, is buried here alongside two of his sons, both Connecticut governors. Behind the Winthrops lies the Reverend John Cotton, an early Puritan minister of some renown. Their presence here, in the shadow of Boston's first Anglican church, is somewhat ironic. But the church was erected after they and other first-generation Puritans were already several feet under, and incapable of protesting too much. Other famous folks have connections to the cemetery. Nathaniel Hawthorne used to enjoy walking here, and legend has it that the character of Hester Prynne, the much-maligned adulteress of *The Scarlet Letter*, was based on Elizabeth Paine (alternately spelled Pain), who is buried near the rear of the cemetery. Her grave is easy to spot.

NEARBY

➥ **St. Paul's Episcopal Cathedral**, consecrated in 1820, was the first Greek Revival structure in the city. Its design was intentional; the founders wanted a building that would create a very different aesthetic than the typical New England meetinghouse. The church was elevated to the status of cathedral in 1908 and serves the largest Episcopal diocese in the United States. It has been renovated numerous times, most recently in 1986. *138 Tremont Street, across from Park Street Church. Open Monday through Friday, 9* A.M. *to 5* P.M. *Sunday services are at 8* A.M., *10* A.M., *12:30* P.M. *and 6:30* P.M. ☎ 617-482-8431 💻 www.stpaulboston.org

Beacon Hill and the West End

Its stately red brick townhouses and narrow, winding streets have long made Beacon Hill one of Boston's most enviable addresses. It became known in the nineteenth century as a tony neighborhood, home of Boston Brahmins such as Senator Charles Sumner and President John Quincy Adams. Today, it retains much of its old-world charm, with gaslamp street-lights and window boxes spilling over with colorful flowers.

If Beacon Hill was the "upstairs" of nineteenth-century Boston, then the neighboring West End was its "downstairs" counterpart, home to successive waves of immigrants who served the Beacon Hill families as domestics and tried to make ends meet in the new land. The West End was also home to a substantial population of free African Americans in the early nineteenth century, who forged their own institutions in a city that gave no official sanction to slavery but still practiced severe racial discrimination.

The Last Remaining Synagogue in the West End
VILNA/VILNER SHUL
Jewish (Orthodox). 16 Phillips Street. Year consecrated: 1919 (congregation dates to 1893). ☎ 617-523-2324
💻 www.jewishboston.com/synagog/vilna/

> *T Stop: Park Street on the Green and Red Lines, or Charles on the Red Line. Tours of Vilna Shul are offered most Sunday afternoons from 1* P.M. *to 3* P.M. *Call beforehand if you are with a large group.*

One of the spiritual crowns of Boston's West End is the Vilna (alternately spelled Vilner) Shul, a Lithuanian Orthodox synagogue that held services from 1919 until 1985. The congregation was founded in 1893, when Lithuanian immigrants formed a *landsmanshaft*, or communal organization. As the group developed into a congregation and its membership grew, it required a more permanent house of worship, and moved to this location in 1919. The synagogue was constructed mostly by volunteer labor, and its distinctive L-shape is modeled after the synagogues of medieval Europe. Yet its simplicity—it is a two-story brick edifice lit primarily by three large skylights in the sanctuary—stands in harmony with the style of the New England meetinghouse. Inside, the synagogue's glory is its two-story wooden ark, featuring carvings of the Ten Commandments and the Lions of Judah, among other things. The ark is capped by that most American of symbols, an eagle. In these emblems the Jews of Vilna Shul celebrated both their religious heritage and their newfound political freedom.

At the turn of the twentieth century, the heyday of the Jewish presence in the West End, there were fifteen shuls (which are traditional, or orthodox, synagogues) and approximately 25,000 Jews in the neighborhood. Today this is the only intact synagogue remaining in the West End, and the oldest that survives in Boston. Given its tremendous historical importance, the building is undergoing restoration, with plans to reopen it as the Vilna Center for Jewish Heritage, "Boston's only historic Jewish cultural center and museum." In October of 1994, Partners for Sacred Places,

JEWS IN BOSTON

Although Solomon Frankel (also spelled "Franco"), the first Jew in Boston, arrived in 1649, he was soon banished from the Massachusetts Bay Colony because of a "trade dispute." This accusation was likely just a pretext. Puritan-governed Boston was loathe to accept Jewish immigrants during the colonial period; in fact, Jews were not granted full citizenship rights in Massachusetts until 1821, nearly half a century after it had become a state of the new American nation. "Full citizenship rights" apparently did not extend to the dead: it wasn't until 1844 that Jews could be legally buried in Massachusetts.

There was a trickle of German Jewish immigration in the mid–nineteenth century, but full-scale Jewish immigration only began in the 1880s, when eastern European Jews settled in America by the tens of thousands. In Boston, they initially favored the North and South Ends, with the West End becoming well-populated with Jews at the turn of the century. In 1900, fifty-three synagogues served the Boston Jewish community, most of them located in the North, South, and West Ends. By the late 1960s, however, most Boston Jews had relocated to tree-lined suburbs such as Brookline and Newton.

a national organization dedicated to the preservation of historic religious properties, recognized the Vilna Center with its "Award for Sacred Place Reclaimed."

The Oldest Surviving Black Church Building in the United States
AFRICAN MEETINGHOUSE/
ABIEL SMITH SCHOOL
Baptist. 8 Smith Court. Year Consecrated: 1806. Architect: uncertain; adapted from a townhouse design by Asher Benjamin. ☎ 617-742-5415 🖥 www.afroammuseum.org

> *T Stop: Park Street on the Green and Red Lines. Open daily from 10 A.M. to 4 P.M. (closed Sundays from Labor Day to Memorial Day). No admission charge. Donations welcome.*

The neighborhood around Joy and Pinckney Streets had a high concentration of African American residents in the early nineteenth century, living alongside whites (mostly immigrant Irish). In that era, this was a working-class community, in stark contrast to its image today as one of the toniest sections of Boston. These blocks offer fascinating glimpses of African American history and spirituality, encapsulated in the Museum of Afro-American History. The museum contains both the African Meetinghouse and the Abiel Smith School next door. Since 1980, National Park Service Rangers have helped to guide visitors through these two sites (as well as a third that is owned by the museum, located on Nantucket; see page 215).

Cited as "the oldest black church edifice still standing in the United States," the **African Meetinghouse** served dual purposes in the nineteenth century as a house of worship and a community meeting place for African Americans. Before 1805, blacks in Boston had no church to call their own and faced much prejudice in the predominantly white churches. This building was constructed in 1806 by black workers, many of whom volunteered their time. The money was raised within the community. A plaque at the door commemorates the $1,500 donation of one Cato Gardner, a former slave who single-handedly provided a fifth of the building's total construction costs. Gardner also provided much of the organizational impetus for the church's erection.

The church has simply been called "the African Meetinghouse" throughout most of its two-century history. It was initially Baptist in persuasion, but denomination mattered far less than racial unity in nineteenth-century Boston, when African Americans dealt with racism and persecution in a highly segregated society. Many blacks worshiped here who did not consider themselves to be Baptists, but simply Christians.

The meetinghouse was more than a religious center; it was a political platform as well. Many Bostonians referred to it as the "black Faneuil Hall," comparing it to the famous building on State Street that housed important meetings during the American Revolution. Like Faneuil Hall, this too was a "cradle of liberty." Throughout its history, the meetinghouse hosted such speakers as Frederick Douglass and the early-nineteenth-century feminist Maria Stuart, the first black woman to address a mixed-gender audience in the United States. In 1832, the radical white abolitionist William Lloyd Garrison organized the New England Anti-Slavery Society here, beginning a wave of organized abolitionism among the region's white and black residents. The church also had a hand in education: the Abiel Smith School met in the church's basement until it acquired its own building next door (see below).

One interesting fact about the meetinghouse is that when the African American community began moving further out of downtown Boston toward Roxbury and the South End, Jewish immigrants bought this structure and used it as a synagogue for more than seventy-five years, until 1972. Few traces remain of this period in the building's history, though it offers one of many examples throughout New England of a sacred site that has been home to several diverse religious communities.

Next door to the African Meetinghouse is the **Abiel Smith School**, considered the first public school for black children in Boston. Dedicated in 1835, its story begins nearly half a century earlier in 1787, when a black Bostonian named Prince Hall petitioned the Massachusetts legislature to allow his children access to a public education. His petition was denied, just as a similar appeal by many black parents was turned down eleven years later. In protest, blacks started their own school in Hall's home, moving it to the basement of the African Meetinghouse when they outgrew this space. In 1835, the present edifice was constructed, thanks to the generosity of a white donor named Abiel Smith. It was in use until 1855, when the Massachusetts legislature struck down its segregation law, permitting black children to attend the public schools closest to their homes. In 1887, this building became a headquarters for black Civil War veterans.

THE BLACK HERITAGE TRAIL

The first African Americans were brought to Boston as slaves in the seventeenth century; by 1705, Boston had about 400 slaves and some free blacks. When America became a nation, slavery was phased out of Massachusetts. By 1790, Massachusetts was the only state to record no slaves in its first federal census, and by the early nineteenth century, Boston had a sizeable community of free blacks living in the West End. Most were concentrated in the neighborhood bordered by Joy, Charles, Pinckney, and Cambridge Streets, in the blocks now known as the North Slope of Beacon Hill.

A short walk up the hill from the Common are fourteen important sites on the Black Heritage Trail, a 1.6-mile guided walking tour of the neighborhood. The Museum of Afro-American History calls the Black Heritage Trail "the largest collection of historic sites in the country relating to the life of a free African American community prior to the Civil War." The only buildings that are open to the public are the Abiel Smith School and the African Meetinghouse, though the others are explained thoroughly while visitors stand outside. The tour includes the Robert Gould Shaw and 54th Regiment Memorial (see below) and various homes and meeting places. To catch the entire free guided tour of the Black Heritage Trail, meet at the Shaw Memorial at the corner of Beacon and Park at 10 A.M., 12 P.M. and 2 P.M. each day. Tours are conducted by National Park Service Rangers.

NEARBY
➥ Opposite the State House on the corner of Beacon and Park Streets is Augustus Saint-Gaudens's **Robert Gould Shaw and Massachusetts 54th Regiment Memorial**, which commemorates the Civil War service of the Massachusetts 54th Regiment of African American Volunteers. The regiment was commanded by a white Bostonian named Robert Gould Shaw (1837–63). The 1,000 soldiers of the 54th were recruited from all over the North, and included two sons of Frederick Douglass and a grandson of Sojourner Truth. One of the 54th's soldiers, William H. Carney, was the first African American to be awarded the Congressional Medal of Honor. It took Saint-Gaudens (see page 322) fourteen years to complete this monument, a bronze bas-relief that was unveiled on Memorial Day in 1897.
💻 www.nps.gov/boaf/site1.htm

➥ **The Charles Street Meetinghouse**, a forum for antebellum abolitionists such as Frederick Douglass and William Lloyd Garrison, was erected in 1807. Although it is now a commercial building, it is a frequently photographed site in Boston, as much for its history as for its architectural design by Asher Benjamin. *At Charles and Mount Vernon Streets. T Stop: Charles Street on the Red Line.*

➥ Veteran PBS watchers may recognize the Hatch Shell at **The Esplanade** from the televised Fourth of July celebrations that occur here every year. This nine-mile strip of verdure along the banks of the Charles River

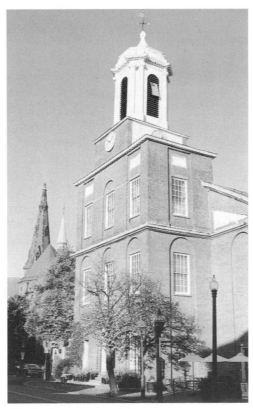

Charles Street Meetinghouse

is a favorite destination for nature and sports enthusiasts, and thousands throng here each Independence Day for the Boston Pops concert and subsequent fireworks. Many other free (and far less crowded) concerts and cultural events take place on the Esplanade on summer evenings.

The North End

The North End is the city's oldest neighborhood, having been continuously populated since the first Puritans arrived in Boston in 1630. Its proximity to the harbor made it the logical residence of seafarers and fishermen alike. In the mid–nineteenth century, Irish immigrants came to dominate the neighborhood, but it became predominately Italian in the

FEAST DAYS OF THE VIRGIN

If you are looking for a special time to visit Boston, consider coming for one of the many feast day celebrations that take place throughout the year. Some particularly vibrant celebrations take place here in the North End near the end of August, when parishioners carry colorful statues of the Virgin Mary through the streets, blending the sacred traditions of Roman Catholicism with a carnival atmosphere of joy. Be sure to generously sample the pasta!

late nineteenth century as immigration patterns changed. (When Bostonians today are asked to characterize the North End, their usual response is that the neighborhood is home to some of the finest Italian restaurants in Boston—or the country, for that matter.) The area is replete with sacred history, from the early Congregationalists to the present-day Italian Catholic presence. Often, this history overlaps in the very same church buildings and sites; Sacred Heart Italian Church, for example, sits on the same spot as one of the first Congregational meetinghouses in the city, which burned to the ground during the Revolution.

The Midnight Ride of Paul Revere
CHRIST CHURCH/OLD NORTH CHURCH

Anglican/Episcopal. 193 Salem Street. Year consecrated: 1723. Architect: uncertain; inspired by the designs of Christopher Wren. ☎ 617-523-6676 🖳 www.oldnorth.com

T stop: Haymarket on the Orange and Green Lines. Open June through October daily from 9 A.M. to 6 P.M. (until 5 P.M. the rest of the year).

"One, if by land, and two, if by sea. . . ." While this historic cry is perhaps a bit romantic, it is indeed true that a famous warning was issued from the spire of this very building, the oldest standing church in Boston. The church stepped into the annals of history on the night of April 18, 1775, when Robert Newman, the sexton (caretaker) of Old North climbed out of the rear window of his house to meet a young silversmith named Paul Revere. Revere gave him the news: The British Regulars were coming by water. The two then split up; Revere set out on his famous ride to warn fellow patriots John Hancock and Samuel Adams of the attack, and Newman furtively scaled the 154 steps to the top of Old North's steeple (the church had been chosen because it had the tallest steeple in the city, at 191 feet). There, he placed *two* lanterns—the signal that had been prearranged if the British were discovered to be advancing by water—to alert the Whigs of Charlestown. They purportedly got the message and prepared for attack.

Old North Church thereby takes its place among the most historic houses of worship in the United States—without which, perhaps, there might *be* no United States. A collection box in the church carries the sign, "If it weren't for Old North Church, you might be making donations in pound notes now." That about sums it up.

Paul Revere Mall and Christ Church/ Old North Church

Old North's official name is Christ Church, and it was the second Anglican (later called "Episcopal") church in Boston, built in 1723. (The first was King's Chapel, consecrated in 1686.) It was an ironic place to have played such a pivotal role in the Revolution, since it was something of a Loyalist stronghold and had a Tory minister. (During this period, the Anglican liturgy included prayers for the king as a matter of course, and whether to include them or not became something of a watershed issue for New England Anglicans during the Revolution. Christ Church never omitted the prayers for the king, demonstrating its loyalty to England.) Paul Revere was not a church member here, as some guidebooks claim; his family was Congregationalist. But it may be true that one of Revere's many sons worshiped here in the nineteenth century. And it is certainly true that Paul Revere himself was a bell-ringer here in his adolescence; the church still owns a 1750 contract that Revere and five other boys signed, detailing their musical services. The bells here, which date to 1744, are the oldest in any church in the United States. The bell tower was restored in 1894 and again in 1975.

Unfortunately, the famous steeple that Newman once climbed was destroyed in the Great Gale of 1804. Local architect Charles Bulfinch was hired to replace the steeple, which he did with all respect to its earlier manifestation. But Bulfinch's steeple was also lost to history in 1954, the victim of a hurricane. The present-day steeple dates to 1954, and is a faithful replica of the original.

Tombs of Forefathers and Mathers
COPP'S HILL BURYING GROUND
Hull Street. Year created: 1659. ☎ 617-635-4505

T Stop: Haymarket on the Orange and Green Lines. Open daily year-round from 9 A.M. to 5 P.M.

Boston's second-oldest cemetery dates to 1659, but it actually contains a grave from 1625—five years before the first Puritans settled in the area. This strange circumstance is explained by the fact that one of Plymouth Colony's first female settlers had died in 1625, and when her husband moved to Boston some years later he moved the grave with him.

The cemetery contains the graves of three generations of the Mather family, all Puritan ministers of great renown. The Puritan tendency toward simplicity in death and mourning is somewhat belied by their grand family brick tomb. Old North sexton Robert Newman (see above) is also interred here, in somewhat simpler style. Unfortunately, many of the tombstones show evidence of having been used for target practice by British troops during the Revolutionary War. (One gravestone, for a Captain Daniel Malcolm who died during the war, bears the marks of three musket balls. Was this British revenge for his epitaph, which boasted that he was "a true son of liberty"?)

The northwest corner of the cemetery is an eighteenth-century African American burial ground, containing the graves of approximately one thousand black Bostonians. Many lived nearby in a black residential neighborhood that was called New Guinea during the colonial era. As was the custom of the time, they were segregated even in death from their white American counterparts.

From Congregational to Unitarian to Roman Catholic
ST. STEPHEN'S CHURCH
Roman Catholic. Hanover and Clark Streets. Year consecrated: 1804. Architect: Charles Bulfinch. ☎ 617-523-1230

T Stop: Haymarket on the Green and Orange Lines. Mass is offered on Saturday at 5:15 P.M. and Sunday at 8:30 A.M. and 11 A.M.

One of the last stops on the Freedom Trail is St. Stephen's Church, which, in true American fashion, has changed names and denominations a good many times. It was once New North Congregational (to distinguish it from nearby "Old North"), developed into Second Unitarian in 1814, changed to St. Stephen's (Irish Catholic) in 1862, and finally became Italian Catholic by the turn of the twentieth century. The present red brick edifice (1804) was designed by the prominent architect Charles Bulfinch (1763–1844) and is the only church of his still standing in Boston. Bulfinch, whose architecture merged the Federal and classical styles, also created the Massachusetts State House just north of the Boston Common. His trademark blind-arch windows are in full evidence at St. Stephen's, and his predilection for simplicity can be seen in his adoption of a basic dome instead of the traditional Congregational spire.

In 1870, Hanover Street was widened to its present size, and a faction of the St. Stephen's congregation wanted to tear the church down to make way for the road. Instead, the Archdiocese of Boston raised funds to move the entire building sixteen feet backward to accommodate the wider street. This costly action not only saved an architectural landmark, but also preserved a house of worship that had been home to several different religious traditions and ethnic groups. In recent times, the church has been most famous for its association with the illustrious Kennedy clan: matriarch Rose Kennedy was baptized here in 1890, and her funeral was held here as well in 1995.

NEARBY
➡ **St. Leonard's Church**, built by Italian immigrants and consecrated in 1873, was the first Italian Catholic parish in New England. Services are still offered in both English and Italian. In the basement of the church

St. Leonard's Church Peace Garden

there is a shrine to St. Anthony; the church also sponsors a festival of St. Anthony each June. A small garden, dedicated to peace, is adjacent to the church. *At the corner of Hanover and Prince Streets.*
☎ 617-523-2110
➥ A famous bronze statue of Paul Revere top his horse sits at the entrance to the **Paul Revere Mall**, a small brick plaza in the center of the neighborhood. In keeping with the North End's Italian character, many locals refer to this simply as "the Prado." It was created in 1933. *Hanover Street, across from St. Stephen's Church.*

Back Bay

Back Bay may have the distinction of being the only area in Boston where the streets are laid out in an orderly, understandable grid. (In fact, the cross-streets are even in alphabetical order, making navigation a relative breeze.) All of this well-managed harmony stems from the fact that Back Bay was a planned community, a late-nineteenth-century attempt to expand the city by claiming some of the swampy marshland of the Charles River. Boston's population had increased dramatically over the course of the nineteenth century—from 54,000 people in 1825 to nearly ten times that figure by the end of the century. To accommodate the bursting population, the Back Bay landfill project (which took place over a span of forty years) added 450 acres to Boston and permitted rail lines to extend into the downtown area for the first time.

Back Bay's settlement was hastened by the Great Fire of 1872, which leveled 776 buildings in the downtown area. Thousands of residents settled in Back Bay's well-planned streets after the devastation of the downtown fire, and many reestablished their churches in their new neighborhood. Today, Back Bay is a fashionable district, home to some of the Victorian era's most philanthropic institutions (the Boston Public Library, the Public Garden) and some opulent churches, including Trinity Church and the Mother Church Extension of the First Church of Christ, Scientist.

Swan Boats and Ducklings
PUBLIC GARDEN
Bordered by Beacon Street, Charles Street, Boylston Street, and Arlington Street. Year created: 1859.

T Stop: Arlington on the Green Line.

The twenty-four acres of Boston's Public Garden were some of the first to be created in the Back Bay; this land was filled in around 1837 and dedicated for public use in 1859. It retains more of a family-oriented reputation than nearby Boston Common; it is here that you can take the famous fifteen-minute ride on a Swan Boat, first created in 1877. The six Swan Boats, which were inspired by a scene in Wagner's opera *Lohengrin*, carry passengers across a man-made pond in the center of the rectangular park. Another child-friendly attraction is a group of duckling sculptures, placed in the northeast section in 1987 in honor of the popular children's story *Make Way for Ducklings*, which is set here in the garden.

John Singer Sargent's "Triumph of Religion"
BOSTON PUBLIC LIBRARY
700 Boylston Street. Year created: 1895 (institution dates to 1848). Architect: Charles Follen McKim. ☎ 617-536-5400 💻www.bpl.org

T Stop: Copley on the Green Line. Open from 9 A.M. to 9 P.M. Monday through Thursday; 9 A.M. to 5 P.M. on Friday and Saturday; and 1 P.M. to 5 P.M. on Sunday (Sunday hours from October through May only).

The Boston Public Library, founded in 1848 and located in this grand Renaissance Revival edifice since 1895, is considered a granddaddy of public institutions. It was the first free metropolitan library of significant size in America, and its architecture (loosely inspired by the Bibliotheque Nationale in Paris) influenced many other public buildings across the country. When architect Charles Follen McKim completed the building, he called it "a palace for the people," and it remains that to this day. It

contains over six million books and 1.2 million rare books and manu-
scripts, and hosts numerous special exhibitions throughout the year that
are free to the public.

A special treat for the spiritual traveler is the Sargent Gallery, a series
of fifteen magnificent murals on the third floor that are the work of American artist John Singer Sargent (1856–1925). The work is considered
unusually symbolic for Sargent, who specialized in portraiture (be sure not
to miss his famous depiction of Isabella Stewart Gardner in the museum
that bears her name; see page 107). Sargent chose the theme of the development of religion, particularly the Jewish and Christian traditions. Using
various media, including paint, metal, paper, and jewels, Sargent's religious
history begins with Egypt's oppression of the Israelites and continues
through the prophets of the Hebrew Bible/Old Testament to culminate in
the crucifixion of Christ.

While the artistic techniques drew upon the work of Michelangelo and
Raphael, the subject matter—depicting how religion has progressed to its
"modern" position as an ethical force—had parallels in the writings of Sargent's contemporaries, most notably William James and Ernest Renan.
The driving idea behind the *Triumph of Religion* was to depict noninstitu-
tionalized, ethically focused religion as the pinnacle of history. The project
took Sargent a total of twenty-four years, with the final panels being
installed in 1919. The large rectangular area over the stairs remains empty;
Sargent intended to create a mural of Jesus' Sermon on the Mount (the
quintessential Christian statement on religion as ethics), but it was never
completed.

On the second floor, be sure to peek in on the magnificent barrel-
ceilinged reading room, which was restored in 1997. The second floor also
contains a series of wall paintings called *The Quest and Achievement of the
Holy Grail* by Edwin Austin Abbey. The fifteen paintings depict the legend
of the pursuit of the Holy Grail, which many medieval Christians believed
to be the very cup that Christ had drunk from at the Last Supper.

The **Boston Public Library Courtyard** is a secluded but fully utilized public space that was inspired by the enclosure of the Palazzo
della Chancelleria in Rome. The roofed courtyard, with its airy skylights,
is a favorite destination for bibliophiles of all descriptions, many of whom
you may encounter whiling away their lunch hours with a good book. In
2000, the courtyard was restored to its original design, including the rein-
stallment of an Epicurean statue called *Bacchante and Infant Faun*. The
library's architect donated the sculpture a century ago, but Boston prig-
gishness at the time prohibited a display of nudity on the courtyard green.

Richardsonian Romanesque
TRINITY CHURCH
Episcopal. 206 Clarendon Street, Copley Square. Year consecrated: 1877
(congregation dates to 1733). Architect: Henry Hobson Richardson.
☎ 617-536-0944 🖳 www.trinitychurchboston.org

> *T Stop: Copley on the Green Line. There is a free guided tour each
> Sunday after the 11 A.M. service. Self-guided tours are available on other
> days for a small fee.*

Ask most parishioners who was responsible for their house of worship
and they will give you a blank stare. Not so at historic Trinity Church,
which features no less than seven representations of its most famous rector,
Reverend Phillips Brooks (1835–93). Brooks came to Boston from
Philadelphia when he was just a young man, but he had already earned
some renown as a preacher and as the author of the hymn text for
"O Little Town of Bethlehem." After the Great Fire of 1872, he undertook
the monumental task of moving Trinity from its downtown location to
this newly created neighborhood called Back Bay. Although many people
questioned the wisdom of relocating one of Boston's oldest congregations
to the dusty wasteland that was then Copley Square, Brooks was a great
man with great ideas, and he carried the day.

Architecturally, this church is one of the premiere achievements of

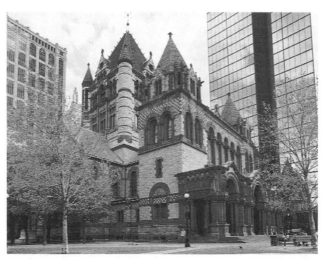

Trinity Church

Henry Hobson Richardson (1838–86), who had been a Harvard acquaintance of Brooks. Richardson was influenced by the French Romanesque designs of the great medieval churches in Auvergne, and favored brightly colored stonework, low arches, and massive towers. Although he originally designed a large, octagonal tower for the church, the project's engineers questioned its stability, and in the end it was replaced by a 167-foot-tall tower, modeled after the cathedral in Salamanca, Spain. The church took five years (1872–77) to plan and build, with the exterior West Porch added in 1897.

The man who seems to have been responsible for alerting Richardson to the design of the Salamanca tower was the very artist who went on to create the striking interior of Trinity Church: John La Farge (1835–1910). It is because of La Farge's contribution, and not just Richardson's talent, that this is considered one of the great churches of New England. (For the record, La Farge was paid $8,000 for his contributions to the interior, while Richardson earned slightly less than that designing the entire building.)

Stepping into the building in the middle of the day requires an adjustment, both of the eyes and of the spirit; the church's very dark interior shows each modulation of light as the day progresses, and calls attention immediately upward to heaven. La Farge believed that the entire interior was a canvas for decoration, in sharp contrast to the plain New England meetinghouse style. The paintings in the pendatives above the windows—mostly Old Testament prophets and other Biblical scenes—have regrettably become quite dark through the years. The church has recently undertaken an ambitious cleaning and restoration project of La Farge's expansive murals, but it is a time-consuming process; La Farge used many different media (oils, tempera, etc.) in the same paintings, making them difficult to restore. In the nave, one painting tucked between two stained-glass windows has been cleaned. It took four months just to do the first tiny corner of the painting, but the results are magnificent.

La Farge is best known for his stained glass, and visitors will not be disappointed by the windows he designed for Trinity Church. In particular, note the portrayal of Christ in the main window above the main entrance; La Farge used up to seven layers of glass to create that window's sense of depth and reality. His Christ is so vivid, so purposeful, that it appears as though he is striding right into the church building. The flanking windows use bright purple, turquoise, and teal circles in a special glass technique that molts whole clumps of glass together. The pieces are actually the size of baseballs, though they of course appear much smaller from the floor of the church.

Until the early twentieth century there was no altar in the chancel, an extremely unusual situation for an Anglican or Episcopal church. Traditionally, the Anglican liturgy has privileged the sacrament ("communion" or "Eucharist") over the preaching of a sermon. But at Trinity, the pulpit, with its high, central position and ornate design, was the clear focus of attention. This pulpit was erected in 1916 and features carvings of great preachers such as Martin Luther, St. Paul, and—but of course!—Phillips Brooks.

Today, Trinity Church evokes a tranquil sense of timelessness in the busy financial district that is now Copley Square. It might seem less impressive when its reflection is photographed against the sleek, rising panes of glass that distinguish its neighbor, the John Hancock Tower. But Trinity holds its own against the mistrals of change, an attitude that is carved into the very structure of the church. As you exit the building, note the intricate frieze running along its exterior. Against a backdrop of rough-hewn stone, these delicately carved decorations around the porch tell the story of the Bible, from Genesis to Paul. The frieze ends abruptly—to symbolize the sacred history that has yet to be written.

Don't miss the church's tiny **Cloister Garden**, tucked into a quiet courtyard that faces the Clarendon Street entrance by the bookstore. A lovely fountain and a sculpture of St. Francis holding a dove provide a focal point of tranquility in the center of the garden.

A Gothic Congregational Church
OLD SOUTH CHURCH
United Church of Christ (formerly Puritan/Congregational). 645 Boylston Street. Year consecrated: 1877 (congregation dates to 1669). Architects: Willard Sears and Charles Cummings. ☎ 617-536-1970
💻 www.oldsouth.org

T stop: Copley on the Green Line. Sunday worship is at 11 A.M.

Yet another "Old South" congregation in Boston? This church is often confused with the Old South Meetinghouse in Downtown Crossing—and with good reason. They were once the same congregation. When the Back Bay became a fashionable neighborhood after its marshy area was filled with land, the overcrowded Old South Meetinghouse abandoned its noisy locale downtown and sent many of its parishioners here to start a daughter

Old South Church

church. A small delegation persevered at the old meetinghouse, dedicated to preserving the structure when many in the congregation wanted to sell it or tear it down (see page 72).

The new church on Boylston, which was completely renovated in 1985, is as grand and opulent as the old meetinghouse was simple and functional. It was designed by the architectural team of Willard Sears and Charles Cummings, who adopted a "Ruskinian Italian Gothic" style (modeled after the neo-Gothic designs of nineteenth-century Englishman John Ruskin). Its stained-glass windows, designed by the English firm of Clayton and Bell, emulated English stained glass of the fifteenth century. Just as medieval European churches sought to teach the gospel through art to the illiterate masses, Old South's windows are didactic (despite the fact that the church's upper-crust Victorian membership did not exactly have a literacy problem). The left wall of the nave depicts the prophets of the Old Testament and the evangelists of the New. Opposite these are imaged some of the parables of Jesus: the workers in the vineyard, the wise and foolish virgins, the good Samaritan, the prodigal son and the sower. In an accompanying side chapel (1933), a series of windows represents the passion and crucifixion of Christ. One very special stained-glass window in the chapel emulates a thirteenth-century Gothic geometric design, with four lancets and a tracery.

The church's grand architecture—and the simple fact that it was regarded as a church and not just a meetinghouse—reflects the tremendous changes that came upon New England's Congregationalists in the nineteenth century. It was a radical departure from the congregation's first barnlike 1669 structure on Washington Street to this glorious, no-expenses-spared testimony of God's providence and New England's material success.

In 1957, this church became part of the newly formed United Church of Christ denomination, which is regarded as one of the most liberal of the Protestant traditions. A famous 1966 photograph in *Life* magazine rocked the nation by showing young hippies dancing in the aisles of the church. In January of 1968, its pastor offended some congregants by preaching a Sunday sermon against the war in Vietnam, and in April of that year he mourned with the nation after Martin Luther King, Jr., was assassinated. He reminded his congregation that the Civil Rights leader had sometimes worshiped with them when he was a student at nearby Boston University. "You see, we never know who our neighbor is, do we?" he asked. "We never suspect what our neighbor may become!" Today, Old South Church is a leader in many Boston initiatives on behalf of the homeless and the poor. It is highly regarded for its musical excellence, its outreach ministries, and its fellowship for gays and lesbians, established in 1988.

A Cradle of Unitarianism
ARLINGTON STREET CHURCH
Unitarian-Universalist (originally Presbyterian, then Congregational, then Unitarian). 351 Boylston Street. Year consecrated: 1861 (congregation dates to 1729). Architect: Arthur Gilman. ☎ 617-536-7050
🖳 www.world.std.com/~ascuua/index.html

T Stop: Arlington on the Green Line. Open Monday through Friday from 10 A.M. to 5 P.M., as well as for Sunday worship at 11 A.M.

This pillar of the Back Bay was William Ellery Channing's church, the flagship Unitarian church of the nineteenth century. Channing (1780–1842) was one of the most vocal Unitarian ministers in early nineteenth-century Boston, whose "Baltimore Sermon" of 1819 helped to clarify and codify Unitarian belief. Channing was also a prominent abolitionist, and his published thoughts on social issues became topics for discussion among all levels of Boston society.

Today, Channing's church retains his early focus on social justice. In the early 1960s, one of Arlington's ministers was killed while campaigning for civil rights in Selma, Alabama, and the church also hosted a draft card–burning service during the Vietnam War. Arlington Street Church made an early start in citywide efforts to feed the hungry and still sponsors a Friday Night Supper program every week that feeds approximately 250 Bostonians. Sunday services draw from "the great thinkers of all ages and the sacred books of all religions," an ecumenism that is reflected in the outreach programs of the church. Alongside more traditional offerings like the "Minister's Tea" are weekly tai chi classes and a yoga group. The church even has its own small Zen center.

Arlington is renowned for its architecture and well-conceived interior, a high point of Victorian design. Built from 1859 to 1861, this was the first great public building in the newly created neighborhood of Back Bay. (The congregation dates back a century before that, its Presbyterian-turned-Congregational-turned-Unitarian meetinghouse located in a barn at the corner of Federal and Franklin Streets downtown. That site now hosts the Bank of Boston building.) The architect for Back Bay's Arlington Street Church was Arthur Gilman, who modeled the structure after St. Martin-in-the-Fields, in London. The most notable features of the church's interior are its Tiffany stained-glass windows. Installed between 1898 and 1933, the windows represent the full flowering of Tiffany techniques in draping, folding, and the use of multiple layers of opalescent glass. These windows are believed to constitute the largest grouping of Tiffany windows in a single church.

> "God deliver us from all prejudice and unkindness, and fill us with the love of truth and virtue."   —William Ellery Channing, 1819

The Mother Church of Christian Science
CHRISTIAN SCIENCE CENTER
Church of Christ, Scientist. 175 Huntington Avenue. Year consecrated: 1894 (denomination dates to 1875). Architects: I. M. Pei designed the Colonnade Building and the Administration Building; Chester Lindsay Churchill designed the Publishing Society building. ☎ 617-450-2000
🖳 www.tfccs.com

T Stop: Symphony or Prudential on the Green Line. In summer, tours of the original Mother Church and the Extension are offered every hour on the hour on weekdays between 10 A.M. and 4 P.M., and Sundays at 11:30 A.M.

There are so many interesting things to see in the Christian Science complex of buildings that travelers may want to budget an entire half day to visit them all and enjoy some leisurely, contemplative time by the Plaza's famous fountain. This fourteen-acre complex in Back Bay is at the heart of many Christian Science activities and outreach programs (including the famed and well-respected newspaper, the *Christian Science Monitor*). The buildings are centered around a lovely urban plaza, designed in the 1960s by the architectural firms of I. M. Pei and Araldo A. Cossutta. The plaza's reflecting pool, at 670 feet long, offers a tranquil area for contemplation. The church's community has worked to make this plaza a center of Boston's public life, with free concerts and events for all ages taking place throughout the year. Pei designed the Colonnade Building and the skyscraping Administration Building (1973), whose twenty-fifth-floor ledge is home to a family of peregrine falcons.

The Original Mother Church. Tours begin with this lovely building, erected in 1894 to accommodate the growing movement that was Christian Science. Its Romanesque Revival design paid homage to some of the great architectural traditions of the past. Upon entering the sanctuary, many visitors will be struck by the church's glorious stained-glass windows. Even more interesting than the windows' artistic sensibilities is their subject matter: Unlike other New England stained glass, which depicts the activities of the apostles, these focus on themes of healing, resurrection, and women's religious leadership. The prevalence of women in the windows is exceptional. Artistically, some of the windows are noteworthy because of their use of the "draped glass" technique, in which the twisting of the hot molten glass enables details such as the folds of a robe to actually be three-dimensional. Be sure not to miss the Rose Window, a gift to the church from the board of directors. If you look in the center of that window, you will see the artist's rendering of Mrs. Eddy's textbook *Science and Health*, its pages open for the eager reader.

The Romanesque-style interior features an expansive fresco treatment that weaves around the ceiling of the church like a ribbon. It was all hand-done by craftspeople painting on wet plaster through a stencil. The floor is hand-laid marble. The interior fixtures are all original; the church was already wired for electricity when it was dedicated in 1894.

Mother Church Extension. The turn of the century was a period of tremendous growth for Christian Science, and the opulence of the Byzantine-style Mother Church Extension, located next door to the original Mother Church, reflects the growing importance of Christian Science in that era. Completed in 1906, it can seat 3,000 people.

MARY BAKER EDDY, "FOUNDER AND DISCOVERER" OF CHRISTIAN SCIENCE

In an era when most women could not vote, hold property, or become ordained ministers, Mary Baker Eddy dared to challenge society's expectations and create her own religious movement. She was born in Bow, New Hampshire, in 1821, and battled illness through much of her childhood and young womanhood. For her, the traditional path of marriage and motherhood was not a very happy one; her husband died two months before their first child was born, and for years she had to depend on the charity of relatives and friends for a place to live. In 1866, Mrs. Eddy fell on the ice in Lynn, Massachusetts, and believed that she would die from the serious injuries she sustained. Instead, a verse she read in her Bible (possibly about the paralytic man healed by Jesus) caused "a healing Truth" to dawn upon her, and she got up and dressed, feeling in excellent health.

Ever after, Mrs. Eddy sought to teach others about the healing that was available to them through the power of God. Healing "miracles," she felt, were not really miracles so much as the result of carefully applied scientific techniques for wellness. Healings were "natural demonstrations of divine power." She taught that illness was neither a natural nor an inevitable state, but the direct result of a limited, mistaken sense of God. She wrote of her findings in a landmark 1875 book, *Science and Health with Key to the Scriptures*, which has gone through many editions and is now in print in seventeen languages and Braille. Christian Scientists regard *Science and Health* as a text to be used in conjunction with the Bible.

Mrs. Eddy became very famous—some might say infamous—in her day, as revered by her followers as she was denounced by her critics. She was once taken to court by a disgruntled ex-Scientist; the ensuing courtroom drama provided front-page news for a public eager to discredit the controversial woman-healer, who was fully exonerated. (It was in part because of this negative publicity, much of it untrue, that Mrs. Eddy decided to found the *Christian Science Monitor*, a newspaper whose object would be "to injure no man, but to bless all mankind.") Mrs. Eddy died in 1910. Today, her reputation has enjoyed something of a well-deserved renaissance, as feminists recover her message about God being Mother as well as Father, and those interested in the mind-body-spirit connection discover her teachings on healing.

Mrs. Eddy, concerned by the importance some followers were attaching to herself and other charismatic healers, created a worship service that is unique in its impersonality. Instead of a human pastor, each of the more than 2,000 Christian Science churches around the world has an "impersonal pastor": the Bible and *Science and Health*. Today, there is no ordained clergy per se, but each branch church elects two "Readers" to convey the assigned lessons to the congregation. There is no sermon, but the service includes hymns, the Lord's Prayer, silent prayers, a collection, and organ music.

The organ at the Mother Church Extension is quite exceptional. It is one of the ten largest working organs in the world, with eight divisions of pipe work totaling 13,290 pipes. This organ was built by the Aeolian-Skinner Company in 1952 and was reconditioned and refurbished in the 1990s. The church must be kept at a constant temperature to maintain the organ's tuning. Organ concerts are held occasionally in the Extension, featuring some of the best instrumentalists in the country as well as the full-time organist employed by the church. On New Year's Eve, the Extension is often open for very popular First Night concerts, and a recent Women's History Month featured an organ concert called "Praise Her."

In addition to Sunday morning services, the Extension also hosts the Wednesday evening testimony meetings that speak to the heart of the Christian Science experience. These meetings, which are open to the public, include a lesson (such as a spiritual perspective on an issue that has been in the news) and readings from the Bible and from *Science and Health*. After the lesson, the congregation is invited to offer informal testimonies of their healing experiences, which range from cancer and broken bones to financial and emotional problems. The meetings usually last about an hour and provide a fascinating glimpse into the beliefs and practices of Christian Scientists.

Mapparium. This one-of-a-kind exhibit, located on the first floor of the Christian Science Publishing Society building, reopened in June 2002 after renovations to the building. The "Mapparium" is a large (thirty feet in diameter) stained-glass globe depicting the world as it was in 1932, when the globe was created. Its 608 stained-glass panels were kiln-fired to attain their brilliant colors. The tour guide can demonstrate the room's amazing acoustics; the glass surface of the globe does not absorb sound, so what is whispered in one end of the room can be heard at the other.

Mary Baker Eddy Library for the Betterment of Humanity. Opened to the public in September of 2002, this $50 million library is the largest ever devoted to a woman in the United States. It houses a 500,000-document collection of letters, periodicals, journals, and other materials, including most of Mrs. Eddy's unpublished work. The library will be a repository for materials related not just to Mrs. Eddy but to women, medicine, and religion in nineteenth-century America. It will also host conferences and seminars on spiritual healing. A satellite library in Seneca Falls, New York (the birthplace of the American women's movement), is scheduled to open in March of 2003.

NEARBY

➥ Architect Richard M. Upjohn (son of Richard Upjohn; see page 49) designed the Gothic Revival **Church of the Covenant**, which was completed in 1867. New England poet Oliver Wendell Holmes called its 242-foot spire "absolutely perfect," a sentiment echoed by many Bostonians. The church features a panorama of Tiffany stained-glass windows. *67 Newbury Street (at Berkeley Street). T Stop: Arlington on the Green Line.*
☎ 617-266-7480   💻 www.churchofthecovenant.org

The South End

Just south and slightly east of Back Bay is the South End (not to be confused with South Boston, which is even further east). This neighborhood became a desirable address in the mid–nineteenth century, as the recently created land that became Back Bay brought new traffic and residences to this part of Boston, also a former marshland. After 1870, the neighborhood fell into a century-long period of decline, with slumlords taking advantage of the immigrants who typically resided here. But because of the neighborhood's exciting ethnic diversity, the South End became a home to Catholics of many nationalities, including Italian,

Polish, and Irish. Today, it is an urban neighborhood that is undergoing intense renewal (some would say "gentrification"); its Victorian mansions are being restored to their original grandeur, with rents to match.

A Roman Catholic Presence in Boston
CATHEDRAL OF THE HOLY CROSS
Roman Catholic. 1400 Washington Street. Year consecrated: 1875. Architect: Patrick Keely. ☎ 617-542-5682
💻 www.rcab.org/tourofcathedral/default.html

T Stop: Back Bay on the Orange Line, or Copley on the Green Line. Walk south on Dartmouth Street, which turns into Dedham Street, to Washington Street. Mass is offered in English on Monday through Saturday at 9 A.M., and on Sunday at 8 A.M. and 11 A.M.

The Cathedral of the Holy Cross is a grand edifice that bears testimony to the growing presence of Roman Catholics in Boston. In the early nineteenth century, there were few Catholics in Massachusetts, which was still so steeped in Puritan belief that "papists," as the Congregationalists called Catholics, were not wanted. In 1833, Massachusetts at last disestablished the Congregational Church as the official state religion, ending the practice of utilizing public tax money to fund Congregational churches and their ministers. This change paved the way for greater religious diversity throughout the state, and Boston became the choice

The Cathedral of the Holy Cross

destination of many Irish immigrants who fled the midcentury Potato Famine.

The presence of Catholics was still challenged by many old Bostonians. Although it seems ridiculous today, Catholics in the nineteenth century were accused of all manner of heinous acts. Many Americans believed that because Roman Catholics swore allegiance to the pope (a foreigner!), they could never be considered true Americans. Samuel Morse, famous for the invention of the telegraph, warned in 1835 that "foreign political conspiracy is identified with that creed." Anti-Catholic tracts and exposés claimed that nuns and priests engaged in illicit sexual relations and that Irish immigration was part of a papal plot to infiltrate a democratic American society and bring the United States to its knees. In the 1830s, anti-Catholic hysteria reached a fever pitch and resulted in some truly horrific acts of violence against Roman Catholics. In fact, this very cathedral bears witness to that prejudice. In 1834, anti-Catholic rioters burned down an Ursuline convent in Charlestown across the river. Some of the brick remains of that convent were relocated here and form the archway that separates the front vestibule from the nave. From the ashes of anti-Catholic prejudice arose a pillar of faith, a cathedral that announced to all naysayers that Roman Catholicism was in Boston to stay.

The cathedral, which was constructed from 1866 to 1875, was designed by Patrick Keely, an Irish-born Brooklyn architect who also created the cathedrals of Chicago, Hartford, Providence, Buffalo, Newark, and Cleveland. He settled on a Gothic Revival cruciform style, and used pudding-

CHURCH OR CATHEDRAL?

What is the difference between a church and a cathedral? A cathedral is not merely a particularly large or grand church. It is the seat of the bishop—in Latin, the word *cathedra* means throne or seat. As such, there can only be one cathedral in each diocese. In Boston, the Cathedral of the Holy Cross is the Roman Catholic bishop's official base, serving the needs of more than two million area Catholics, 373 parishes and seven missions. The Cathedral is also a thriving parish church.

Cathedrals are not just a Roman Catholic phenomenon; Episcopalians (Anglicans) have their own system of cathedrals and bishops. Although Methodists are also governed by bishops, they do not have cathedrals.

stone quarried from neighboring Roxbury for the exterior of the building, which is nearly as large as Paris's famed Notre Dame Cathedral. The interior, which can seat 2,000 people, seems all the more vast because its nave is "clear space," or space that is almost entirely unfettered by obstructive columns or pillars. Downstairs, a crypt contains the tomb of John B. Fitzpatrick, the third bishop of Boston, as well as the altar from the cathedral's first building on downtown Franklin Street. Fitzpatrick was instrumental in moving the cathedral here from its Franklin Street location and in making it such an impressive European-style house of worship. Today, the cathedral continues to fulfill Fitzpatrick's stated desire to "set before the world the splendor and majesty of Catholic worship."

A Hard-Won Historic Landmark
THE JESUIT URBAN CENTER AND THE CHURCH OF THE IMMACULATE CONCEPTION
Concord and Harrison Avenues. Year dedicated: 1861. Architect: Patrick Keely. ☎ 617-536-8440 🖥 www.jucboston.org

> *T-stop: Orange Line to the Back Bay or Massachusetts Avenue stations. From there it is about a ten-minute walk. Open Monday through Friday from 7:30 A.M. to 5:30 P.M., and weekends for services and special activities. Mass is offered weekdays at 8 A.M. and noon, and Sundays at 8 and 10 A.M.*

The New England Province of the Society of Jesus (the Jesuits) appears to have engaged Irish-born architect Patrick Keely (see page 50) to design the Church of the Immaculate Conception. Completed in 1861, it served for more than fifty years as the chapel for Boston College and then for Boston College High School. (Boston College moved to Chestnut Hill, a Boston suburb, in the early twentieth century, and the high school moved to South Boston in 1953.)

Built of New Hampshire granite, the church is a significant example of Renaissance Revival architecture with Baroque detailing. Arthur Gilman, who was responsible for designing the master plan for Boston's Back Bay, is thought to have designed the interior of this church.

As the demographics of Boston's South End changed, this church became a little-used jewel. In 1986, its owners began interior demolition in order to convert it to housing. Boston's preservation community, neighbors, and musicians united in opposition, petitioning to designate the

Church of the
Immaculate
Conception

interior as a historic landmark. The Organ Historical Society submitted, to the pope and the head of the Jesuits in Rome, a petition with over five thousand signatures protesting the destruction of an outstanding nineteenth-century organ in a room with perfect acoustics. The Landmarks Commission designated the interior and permitted certain changes, to which the Jesuits conformed. However, the Massachusetts Supreme Judicial Court eventually declared that this designation violated the Massachusetts Constitution.

With new leadership and now known as the Jesuit Urban Center, this splendid church now gathers several hundred people each week, and has a special ministry to the area's gay and lesbian communities. In addition, it hosts a varied menu of outstanding musical programs using the superb acoustics and world-renowned E. & G. G. Hook organ. Its leadership is committed to the preservation, enhancement, and intensified use of this space.

NEARBY

➥ The Baha'i Faith has actually been present in Boston for more than a century; the first group was founded in 1899 and bolstered by a visit from Abdu'l-Baha, the son of the Baha'u'llah. Today the **Boston Baha'i Center**, established in the 1980s, continues to be a place of worship for a small, multiethnic group of area Baha'is as well as the Tahirih Peace Institute, an outreach and service center for the neighborhood. The Institute offers ESL classes, instruction on job skills, and a youth workshop. On Friday evenings at 7:30, the Baha'i Center hosts informal gatherings that feature discussion of Baha'i teachings and the music of the One Human Family Gospel Choir. *595 Albany Street. T Stop: Massachusetts Avenue on the Orange Line.* ☎ 617-695-3500 💻 www.bostonbahai.org

Kenmore Square/The Fenway

The district around Kenmore Square and the Fenway is a study in contrasts: it is home to venerable cultural institutions such as the Isabella Stewart Gardner Museum and the Museum of Fine Arts, yet the area feels youthful and rather avant-garde. Indeed, this neighborhood at the western edge of Back Bay has it all: culture, sports, elite educational institutions (including Boston University and Harvard Medical School), and casual restaurants and cafes. It houses Symphony Hall and also Fenway Park, home to Boston's on-again, off-again Red Sox. Babe Ruth got his professional start here, as did a divinity student named Martin Luther King, Jr.

A Venetian-Style Courtyard
ISABELLA STEWART GARDNER MUSEUM
280 The Fenway. Year opened: 1903. Architect: Willard T. Sears.
☎ 617-566-1401 💻 www.boston.com/gardner

T Stop: Museum Stop on the Green Line "E" train. Open Tuesday through Sunday from 11 A.M. to 5 P.M. Admission fee.

Boston's indomitable Isabella Stewart Gardner (1840–1924) once remarked that what America needed most was art, and art of the best kind. This museum is a testament to that vision, with over 2500 objets d'art from thirty centuries. It is particularly strong in Italian Renaissance painting, but the collection also includes fine sculptures, tapestries, furniture, ceramics, and paintings of many other periods. The museum's eclecticism only adds to its charm; this was the personal collection of one remarkable lady, a collection that she housed in a palace that she designed for the enjoyment of the world. It was also Gardner's home from 1901 until her death in 1924; she lived in a suite on the fourth floor.

Gardner ("Mrs. Jack," as she was popularly known) was an eccentric society woman who routinely traveled across Europe with her husband, shipping magnate John Lowell Gardner, searching for artistic treasures to ship home. She had wide-ranging tastes. Some of the museum's highlights include works by Rembrandt, Titian, Botticelli, Vermeer, Degas, Manet, Matisse, and Boston's own John Singer Sargent, who seems to have perfectly captured Gardner's spirit in a daring portrait that was the talk of fin-de-siècle Boston. (Her husband asked that the painting not be displayed again until after his death; she honored his wish and kept the portrait under wraps until after her own death, a quarter of a century later.) Tragically, the museum lost some priceless pieces in 1990, when thieves stole two Rembrandts and a Vermeer, along with seven other paintings. The art has not yet been recovered. Apart from the loss of those paintings, the collection, according to Gardner's will, has remained unchanged since her death. Also according to her wishes, the museum offers only sparse descriptions of each work of art. Gardner desired each visitor to experience the art on a personal level, and to deeply interact with it, rather than simply read a placard and then move on.

Gardner had a deep appreciation for shrines and altars, and the museum contains many examples of both. The third-floor chapel is a treasure of Christian art, with sixteenth-century Italian choir stalls and stained-glass windows from the Milan cathedral. Spiritual travelers should also spend some time in the Spanish Cloister on the first floor. Gardner cobbled this cloister together with seventeenth-century Mexican tile and a Spanish-themed painting by Sargent, and the result is quite inspiring.

The glass-roofed interior courtyard of the museum is, in and of itself, worth a trip. Gardner, an avid horticulturist, designed it, four stories high, in the style of a fifteenth-century Venetian palace, with many flowering plants and fountains. During her lifetime, she supplied the flowers from her greenhouses in nearby Brookline. Today the gardeners tend the courtyard as beautifully as ever; its Venetian balconies explode with colorful fresh flowers, comforting the winter-weary souls of Bostonians each snowy season. The floral displays change monthly, with the Eastertide season offering a particularly stunning pageant of nasturtiums, lilies, and orchids. (A note to visitors: because of its valuable mosaics and sculptures, the courtyard is for viewing only, not for entering.)

Sacred Art from Around the World
MUSEUM OF FINE ARTS
465 Huntington Avenue. Year opened: 1906 (museum dates to 1870). Architect: Guy Lowell. ☎ 617-267-9300 🖳 www.mfa.org

*T Stop: Museum Stop on the Green Line "E" train. Open Monday and
Tuesday from 10 A.M. to 4:45 P.M.; Wednesday through Friday from
10 A.M. to 9:45 P.M.; Saturday and Sunday from 10 A.M. to 5:45 P.M.
Admission fee.*

New England's premier art museum is daunting in its sheer size:
350,000 objects of art clamor for the viewer's attention, and the museum's
540,000 square feet of space threaten to overwhelm. If you only have a day
and are interested primarily in sacred art from the world's major religious
traditions, there are quite a few items in the museum that you ought to see
(in addition to the Monets, Renoirs, and Cassatts, of course).

Buddhist art. Although the museum is most famous for its European
and American paintings, its collections in Buddhist art are scarcely
equaled in the West, and its body of Japanese Buddhist art is considered to
be the most extensive collection anywhere outside of Japan.

Hindu art. The collection offers several examples of sculptures of the
Hindu gods, including a tenth-century C.E. statue of Shiva, god of destruction (and, ironically, of life as well).

Christian art. Of course, a substantial portion of the paintings—and
all of the icons—in the museum's extensive European collection were in
some way inspired by the Christian faith, if not used liturgically in historic
churches. Be sure not to miss Duccio di Buoninsegna's fourteenth-century
triptych called *The Crucifixion, the Redeemer with Angels, Saint Nicholas and
Saint Gregory*. Also, a Catalonian chapel has been reassembled here in its
entirety, and features a twelfth-century C.E. fresco in the apse.

Egyptian art. The MFA has a stunning collection of ancient Egyptian
artifacts, fueled by a forty-year research expedition with Harvard University in the early twentieth century. The pieces here come from tombs and
temples throughout Egypt, and are believed to comprise the finest collection of Egyptian artifacts outside of Cairo's Egyptian Museum.

The museum's 100-square-foot **Japanese garden** strives to evoke Zen
Buddhist mindfulness through its utilization of large stones and
raked gravel. The pebbles represent the sea, with boulders symbolizing
islands in that sea. The garden was designed from 1986 to 1988 by Kinsaku
Nakane, who also created the Japanese garden at Atlanta's Carter Library
and a tea garden in Washington, D.C.'s National Gallery. The MFA's
Japanese garden is inspired by the traditional gardens of Zen monasteries,
where raking the gravel each day is considered an act of meditation. A
stone path leads to a terrace with benches for seated contemplation.

Holy Trinity Russian Orthodox Cathedral

NEARBY

➥ Built in 1910, the **Holy Trinity Russian Orthodox Cathedral** belongs to the Orthodox Church in America denomination. Although the cathedral's heritage is Russian, more than half of the current membership is comprised of adult converts of many different nationalities. *The Fenway at 165 Park Drive. T Stop: Museum of Fine Arts on the Green "E" Line. Vigil for the Resurrection is held each Saturday evening at 5 P.M., and Vespers is Tuesday and Thursday at 6:30 P.M. Divine Liturgy is offered on Sunday morning at 9:30 A.M.* ☎ 617-262-9490 🖥 www.holytrinityorthodox.org

Jamaica Plain

A "Rural Cemetery" in the Heart of the City
FOREST HILLS CEMETERY
95 Forest Hills Avenue. Year created: 1848. Landscape designer: Henry Dearborn. ☎ 617-524-0128 🖥 www.foresthillstrust.org

> *T Stop: Forest Hills at the end of the Orange Line. Exit through the Hyde Park exit and cross Washington Street to Tower Street. Walk up Tower Street to the cemetery entrance. Open daily from 7:30 A.M. to dusk.*

Colleen McDannell's book *Material Christianity* recounts a story that illustrates why Forest Hills and other Victorian cemeteries of its era were created. In 1835, a five-year-old Philadelphia girl lost her life to scarlet fever and was buried in one of the city's Quaker graveyards. Her father, John Jay Smith, tried to visit her there, but was exceedingly distressed when he could not be perfectly certain that he had found his little girl's grave. Graves were often very simply marked in Puritan and Quaker cemeteries, in an attempt to discourage elaborate mourning practices that focused too heavily on this earthly life. Sometimes, as in the case of King's Chapel Burying Ground (see page 78), graves were moved altogether when things became too crowded. The bereaved father became enraged when the Quakers who owned the graveyard placed their new Arch Street Meeting House right on top of it. His solution? He created the Laurel Hill Cemetery in Philadelphia, the mid–Atlantic region's first parklike cemetery, in 1835, and thus helped launch what is called "the rural cemetery movement."

Forest Hills, established in 1848, is Boston's answer to Laurel Hill (see also Mount Auburn Cemetery, page 121). As New England shifted from the sternness of its Puritan heritage to a more sentimental nineteenth-century view of God as a loving and benign Father, its citizens changed their methods of mourning and burying their loved ones. Death became less a dreaded time of judgment than a long-awaited opportunity to begin the life eternal. The cemetery itself became a sacred landscape to celebrate immortality, not merely a repository for the corpses of the dead.

"Rural cemeteries" such as Forest Hills, which were not directly tied to a church or denomination, became immensely popular in the mid-to-late nineteenth century. Despite their newfound autonomy from a sponsoring church, these new cemeteries were hardly secular places; in fact, they were laid out to create a sense that the very grounds were sacred and hallowed by death. Instead of having graves jumbled together or following the common practice of having multiple bodies in one grave, the rural cemeteries highlighted the individual. Each grave was permanent and had its own stone, often an elaborate one. (Plots in the rural cemeteries came with a hefty price tag; the rural cemeteries reflected the material divide between haves and have-nots, with the wealthy opting for temples and mausoleums over the traditional stone markers.) While the cemetery called attention to the individual, single graves were often grouped together with their kin in the "family plot," an innovation that reflected the emerging Victorian ideal of the home as a sort of training ground for celestial life.

At Forest Hills, there is a good deal of carefully measured, orderly space between one grave and the next. Here, no father need fear that his daughter's grave might be overrun or simply lost to history. He would be comforted by the idea that while her soul was in heaven, her body rested in an earthly setting almost as tranquil, in land set aside as a reminder of the wonders of God's creation. In their rustic—but still well-controlled—loveliness, rural cemeteries offered visitors an affirmation of abundant life amidst the harsh reality of death.

They also offered urban dwellers a rural paradise—in the case of Forest Hills, one slightly on the outskirts of the city. In the late nineteenth century, many Boston families would undertake the long journey here and spend the entire day, visiting the graves of deceased loved ones and marveling in the cemetery's 275 well-manicured acres. Landscape artists and many groundskeepers were employed to create a parklike Elysium of rolling hills and floral borders. Mourners were encouraged to decorate the graves with cascades of flowers and plants, creating natural shrines to their deceased. The drive to produce a paradise on earth even resulted in Hibiscus Lake, a graceful man-made lake in the cemetery.

Today, Forest Hills is a marvelous place to find tranquility in the midst of the city (which has now, of course, swallowed up the once-rural environs of Jamaica Plain). Nearly 100,000 people are buried in its vast acreage, including the poet e. e. cummings, abolitionist William Lloyd Garrison, playwright Eugene O'Neill and suffragist Lucy Blackwell Stone. A special time to visit is in mid-July, when the Annual Lantern Festival is held on Hibiscus Lake. At nightfall, families launch lanterns on to the water, following an ancient Buddhist tradition in which the lanterns represent the souls of the dead, and are freed by being floated out to sea.

"Stones have been known to move and trees to speak."
—William Shakespeare, *Macbeth*

American Sufis
BOSTON SUFI ORDER
Sufi Order International. 83 Elm Street. ☎ 617-522-0800
🖳 www.meditation/hnt.com

T stop: Green Street Station on the Orange Line. From the subway, walk one block west on Green Street (toward Centre Street), and take a left onto Elm Street. Walk three blocks to 83 Elm, on the southwest corner of Elm and Greenough. Classes are held each Thursday evening.

The Boston Sufi Order is housed in a large, stately house on a tree-lined street in Jamaica Plain. Its community, founded in the 1970s, meets here for Thursday evening classes, readings, and meditation practice. Many of the classes focus on the teachings of the founder of the Sufi Order International, Hazrat Inayat Khan, who helped to establish Sufism in America in the early part of the twentieth century. Khan's introductory text, *The Sufi Message of Spiritual Liberty*, became a best-seller when it was published in England in 1914. Because of the book, many Westerners became attracted to Sufism's mystical emphasis on love and ecstatic devotion as the path to God. Although Sufism originated as a mystical movement within Islam, the more than 100 Sufi Order centers in the United States consider themselves to be interfaith. Khan and his son, Pir Valayat Inayat Khan, who now leads the movement, opened Sufi practice to people of all backgrounds, making even the most esoteric traditions of Sufism accessible to a broad audience. Many of the practitioners who attend classes here are members of other religious traditions. On the third Sunday of each month, a Universal Worship Service is held here, where candles are lit for all major religious traditions and readings are taken from many different sacred texts. Even the regular classes and meetings here emphasize interfaith dialogue: In a recent Thursday evening meditation class, practitioners focused on a musical CD of Tibetan Buddhist chant; Islamic-style prayer rugs and cushions adorned the floor; and a sign above the fireplace wished everyone a Happy Hanukkah. A Jewish menorah sat in the front window, and a Victorian angel adorned the piano in the corner of the room. Readings were taken from the teachings of founder Hazrat Inayat Khan.

Many special events take place at the Sufi Order throughout the year. On the first and third Fridays of each month, Sufis and others gather at the Cambridge Friends Meeting (5 Longfellow Park, Harvard Square) for Dances of Universal Peace, honoring the sacred traditions of the world. The movements include basic folk dances done to the chants and songs of traditions such as Judaism, Islam, Christianity, Buddhism, Hinduism, and others. There is no charge for classes or services, though donations are welcome; there is a sliding-scale fee for retreats. Occasionally, Pir Valayat Khan visits the Boston Sufi Order, and his teaching sessions are attended by upwards of 2,000 people.

The Crown Jewel of the Emerald Necklace
ARNOLD ARBORETUM
125 Arborway. Year created: 1872. Landscape architect: Frederick Law Olmsted. ☎ 617-524-1718 🖳 www.arboretum.harvard.edu

T Stop: Forest Hills on the Orange Line. From there, walk northwest one block on the Arborway to the Arboretum's Forest Hills gate. Open year-round every day from dawn to dusk. Visitors Center open Monday through Friday, 9 A.M. to 4 P.M.; Saturday and Sunday from 12 P.M. to 4 P.M. A small donation is requested. Guided tours begin on the front steps of the Hunnewell Building at 10:30 A.M. on selected Saturdays, weather permitting.

On a Sunday in mid-May, garden enthusiasts from all over New England gather at the Arnold Arboretum to celebrate a floral treasure: the lilac. At that time, the Arboretum is bursting with the colors of 500 lilac bushes in more than 230 varieties. As visitors stroll the wide Arboretum paths, they marvel at the flowers' astounding colors—not just pink, purple, and white, but yellow, blue, and burgundy!—and drink in the lilacs' heavy scent. While they pass, they learn something about botany from the carefully worded signs that accompany each specimen.

This annual tradition is the sort of thing the arboretum's benefactor, James Arnold, dreamed of when, in 1872, he set aside a substantial parcel of land in Jamaica Plain for the cultivation of trees and shrubs for scientific research and public enjoyment. These 265 acres, which formed the first public arboretum in the nation, are the crown jewel of the "Emerald Necklace" designed by Frederick Law Olmsted. Olmsted believed that public spaces should be resplendent with beauty, inspiring citizens to heightened morality and spiritual purpose. Today, the space is used as he once hoped; although the arboretum is owned by Harvard University, it has a thousand-year lease agreement with the city of Boston for public use of the land. The arboretum offers a carefully planned landscape of woods, meadows, hills, and valleys, merging seamlessly into one another. It is open to the public from dawn to dusk every day of the year, and functions very much like a municipal park (except for its prohibition of picnics).

The paths are laid out according to the types of plants they showcase; the arboretum intends to provide a microcosm of all of the species of trees and shrubs that can grow in this climate, so the layout seems rather vast. Its living collections include more than 7,000 plants, with special emphasis on the woody species of North America and Eastern Asia. Teams of researchers have scoured Japan and other Asian countries for new specimens; one turn-of-the-century researcher survived malaria and the Chinese Boxer Rebellion in his fifteen-year pursuit of exotic plants. The collection is particularly strong in beech, crabapple, honeysuckle, oak, bonsai, and lilac, and its Chinese Path offers a breathtaking variety of flowering trees and shrubs from throughout Asia. In all, the Arnold Arboretum is considered one of the largest collections of woody plants anywhere in the world. As a research institution, it is also responsible for the preservation of endangered plants—the dawn redwood, now a staple of many public gardens in this country, would have become extinct without the arboretum's timely intervention.

> "One impulse from a vernal wood,
> Will teach you more of man,
> Of moral evil and of good,
> Than all the sages can."
> —William Wordsworth

NEARBY

➥ Calling itself "Lourdes in the land of the Puritans," **The Basilica of Our Lady of Perpetual Help** was founded in 1871 by the Redemptorist Fathers. Their mission was to reach out to others with the message of the love of the Blessed Virgin Mary, giving rise to the nickname "The Mission Church." This basilica houses a shrine to Mary, where the faithful light candles, say prayers and gaze at the serene portrait of Mary above the altar. *1545 Tremont Street. T Stop: Brigham Circle on the Green Line "E" train. The basilica is three blocks up on the left side (at Tremont Street).* ☎ 617-445-2600 🖥 www.themissionchurch.com

➥ In the Boston neighborhood of Roxbury, **Twelfth Baptist Church** is a direct descendent of the African Meetinghouse in Beacon Hill (see page 82). This daughter congregation was founded in 1840 and has a long history of activism in causes such as abolitionism and civil rights. It moved to this location in 1957. It was at one time the church home of the Reverend Martin Luther King, Jr. *160 Warren Street.* ☎ 617-442-7855 🖥 www.tbcboston.org

Cambridge

First, a point of clarification: Cambridge is not a neighborhood of Boston. It is a full-fledged town in its own right, established in 1638, with its own character and its own tourist attractions. Cambridge has traditionally enjoyed a reputation as a well-educated community, partly due to the presence of Harvard University and the Massachusetts Institute of

Technology. Cambridge has more bookstores per capita than any other city in America and was home to the first printing press in the American colonies. Its streets also have a rich spiritual history, from the Puritan founders of yesteryear to the Zen Buddhists who now sit in *zazen* meditation in Harvard Square. Folk singer Joan Baez got her singing start as a street and café musician in Harvard Square, and the famous philosopher William James first tried out his newfangled ideas about religion on his students at Harvard University. The area around Harvard is simply buzzing with cutting-edge ideas, international music, and interesting conversations in multiple languages.

But Cambridge is more than Harvard Square, and the town's sacred history encompasses far more than its Puritan origins. Its spiritual diversity now includes Buddhists, Muslims, Jews, and Christians of all denominations, extending from Central Square to distant Porter Square. Its more industrialized eastern area has been a haven for many immigrant groups, bringing with them new spiritual traditions.

Sacred Spaces for the Living, and Memorials to the Dead
HARVARD UNIVERSITY'S MEMORIAL HALL AND MEMORIAL CHURCH

Nondenominational (originally Puritan/Congregational). Harvard Yard. Memorial Hall consecrated: 1870. Memorial Hall architects: William Ware and Henry Van Brunt. Memorial Church consecrated: 1932. Memorial Church architects: Coolidge, Shepley, Bulfinch, and Abbott. Memorial Church ☎ 617-495-5508 🖳 www.memorialchurch.harvard.edu

T Stop: Harvard Square on the Red Line. During the academic year, Memorial Church holds Sunday services at 11 A.M. in the sanctuary, and daily prayer from 8:45 to 9 A.M. from Monday through Saturday in Appleton Chapel. All are welcome.

Harvard University (pronounced Hah-vahd if you wish to sound like a native, or simply "the university" if you want to really hammer the point that you belong) is by most accounts the premier university in America. It is certainly the oldest. Founded in 1636 as a college for training Puritan ministers, Harvard is one of only a handful of seventeenth-century educational institutions in the nation. Much has changed at Harvard; a babbling stream no longer cuts through the center of Harvard Yard, as it did in the seventeenth and eighteenth centuries, and residents have ceased grazing their sheep in the Common. Moreover, Harvard is of course no longer the bastion of Puritan orthodoxy that it was founded to be. It started slipping from its Puritan moorings at the beginning of the nineteenth century, when its faculty and president turned Unitarian, and has never looked back.

Two important buildings commemorate the many young Harvard graduates who died in the nation's wars. **Memorial Hall**, which is used primarily as a theater and concert hall, was erected in 1870 to honor the 154 Harvard men who lost their lives in the Civil War. Memorial Hall is easily the most ascendant structure on campus, its sheer size commanding all attention. The Victorian Gothic structure has been criticized as "a cathedral mated with a railroad terminal," a vast edifice that is somehow out of character with the Colonial architecture that pervades throughout the campus. Although its original tower was destroyed by fire in 1956, leaving a 35-foot square base in its stead, the tower has been recently restored to its original 190-foot height and splendor.

Where Memorial Hall is a testimony to Victorian grandeur, **Memorial Church** (1932) harkens back to colonial simplicity. Its tall spire, white painted pews, and wooden trim draw upon New England's classic meetinghouse structure and decor. Like Memorial Hall, the church was erected to honor Harvard's war dead—in this case, those who fell during World War I. WW I names, hundreds of them, are listed by class in a special vestibule to the right side of the sanctuary. The frieze at the top reads, "While a bright future beckoned they freely gave their lives and fondest hopes for us and our allies that we might learn from them courage in peace to spend our lives making a better world for others." A banner proclaiming Harvard's motto, *Veritas* ("truth"), notes that 11,398 Harvard men entered the service from 1914 to 1918. Not all, it should be noted, fought on the same side.

Although Memorial Church was designed to honor Harvard's World War I heroes, the twentieth century's ruthless pursuit of warfare meant that the Harvard graduates who made sacrifices in other conflicts required honoring, too. On the right as you walk down the nave of the church, nearly an entire wall is devoted to the Harvard students, listed by class or graduate school, who gave their lives in World War II. Among these was a chaplain in the German armed forces. Memorial Church has also expanded its focus to include the university's dead of later wars; other plaques list Harvard students who were killed in Vietnam and Korea.

Memorial Church regularly hosts some of the nation's most famous preachers at its 11:00 A.M. service on Sundays. Although daily prayer has not been compulsory for Harvard students since 1886, voluntary daily prayer services continue to be held in Appleton Chapel (the chancel area behind the pulpit), a tradition that has not been interrupted since Harvard's founding in 1636. The fifteen-minute service features a brief address by a member of the university community and music from a small group of singers drawn from the university choir.

> *If you would like a full tour of the Harvard campus, free guided tours are available each day at Holyoke Center, 1350 Massachusetts Avenue. In the summers, tours are offered on Monday through Saturday at 10 A.M., 11:15 A.M., 2 P.M., and 3:15 P.M., and on Sundays at 1:30 P.M. and 3 P.M. During the academic year, tours are scheduled at 10 A.M. and 2 P.M. on weekdays, and at 2 P.M. on Saturdays.*

NEARBY

➼ Also on campus, be sure to see the **Fogg Art Museum**, the university's oldest museum (1895). The museum is especially strong in Italian early Renaissance, British pre-Raphaelite, and nineteenth-century French art. *32 Quincy Street (at Broadway). T Stop: Harvard Square on the Red Line. Open Monday through Saturday from 10 A.M. to 5 P.M., and Sunday from 1 P.M. to 5 P.M. Admission fee.* ☎ 617-496-8576
🖳 www.artmuseums.harvard.edu
➼ Across the street from the Fogg is the **Arthur M. Sackler Museum**, which houses the university's collections of Islamic, Asian, and ancient art. The museum is renowned for its holdings in Chinese jade, Korean ceramics, and Japanese woodblock prints. *485 Broadway. T Stop: Harvard Square on the Red Line. Open Monday through Saturday from 10 A.M. to 5 P.M., and Sunday from 1 P.M. to 5 P.M. Admission fee.* ☎ 617-496-8576
🖳 www.artmuseums.harvard.edu
➼ **The Peabody Museum of Archaeology and Ethnology**, which opened in 1877, is one of the world's oldest anthropology museums. It is particularly strong in the Mesoamerican cultures of the Aztec and Mayan peoples. *11 Divinity Avenue. T Stop: Harvard Square on the Red Line. Open daily from 9 A.M. to 5 P.M. Admission fee.* ☎ 617-496-1027
🖳 www.peabody.harvard.edu
➼ **Harvard Divinity School**, established in 1816, now fulfills Harvard College's original purpose of training ministers, though in traditions far more wide-ranging than the Puritan divines would have thought possible.

BOSTON AND CAMBRIDGE ～ 119

(Today's students come from more than fifty-five denominations and religious traditions.) Andover-Harvard Theological Library is also one of the best theological libraries in the world, but you need to be a member of the Harvard University community or the Boston Theological Institute (a consortium of area divinity schools) to use it. There is also a bookstore (14 Divinity Avenue) stocking more than 6,000 books in religion and the humanities. *Divinity Avenue. T Stop: Harvard Square on the Red Line.* 🖳 www.hds.harvard.edu

➡ **The Monastery of Saint John the Evangelist** near Harvard Square, operated by the Anglican order of the Cowley Fathers, welcomes retreatants for individual, group, and directed retreats. Guests are housed in private rooms and are invited to use the chapel, gardens, and meeting rooms for prayer and meditation. Meals are taken in silence. Parking is limited, so retreatants are urged to use public transportation. *980 Memorial Drive. T Stop: Harvard Square on the Red Line. Take the "Harvard Yard" exit from the subway. Walk four blocks along John F. Kennedy Street toward the Charles River. The monastery is on the right side, past Harvard University's JFK School of Government and JFK Park.* ☎ 617-876-3037 🖳 www.ssje.org

George Washington Prayed Here
CHRIST CHURCH
Anglican/Episcopal. Zero Garden Street. Year consecrated: 1759. Architect: Peter Harrison. ☎ 617-876-0200 🖳 www.cccambridge.org

> *T Stop: Harvard Square on the Red Line. Open daily from early morning until 6 P.M.*

Christ Church, founded in 1759, is the oldest house of worship in Cambridge. It has not, however, operated continuously—and therein lies a story. Its most famous interruption of services occurred in 1778, when the Tory-leaning church was occupied by British soldiers. A British officer was fatally shot in Cambridge, and Christ Church hosted a special memorial service for the man. But when the patriotic citizens of Cambridge learned of the service, they became enraged and stormed the sanctuary. They smashed the pulpit, destroyed the organ, and overturned the communion table. Gunshots were fired; it is believed that the bullet hole in the church entry dates from this looting. You can still see the hole, about seven feet up on the right side. The overall damage was so severe that the church was abandoned for twelve years, its windows left open to the rain and snow. Although services were resumed in 1790, the struggling Anglican (turned Episcopal) parish could not afford to repair the damaged building until 1825.

Pew 93 marks the spot where George Washington once worshiped. On New Year's Eve in 1775, while the Washingtons were visiting Boston, Martha Washington requested that they attend services here. General Washington was accompanied by a military escort, replete with fife and drums. Although pew 93 is situated in the same place where the Washingtons sat, it is not the original pew. The church's eighteenth-century high-backed pews, purchased and furnished by individual families, were replaced in the 1850s with slip pews. The same wood was used to build the new pews.

Many other famous people have worshiped here; Harvard student Teddy Roosevelt used to ring bells here, but was asked to resign as a Sunday school teacher because he would not become an Episcopalian. In 1968, the Reverend Martin Luther King, Jr., held a press conference here with child-care expert Dr. Benjamin Spock, stating their opposition to the Vietnam War. It was one of the few churches in town that would allow antiwar protestors to speak.

Resting Place of Harvard Presidents and Revolutionary War Heroes
GOD'S ACRE/THE OLD BURYING GROUND
Zero Garden Street. Year created: uncertain; first graves date to the 1650s.

> *T Stop: Harvard Square on the Red Line. If the gate next to Christ Church is not open during daylight hours, ask the sexton to please open it for you.*

As you exit Christ Church, turn to your right and go through the small wrought-iron gate that leads to the Old Burying Ground. Though not large, this is one of the most fascinating cemeteries in the Boston area, home to some of Cambridge's most famous sons and daughters. To your left, a modest pillar pays homage to some of the Cambridge men who fought in the Revolutionary War and are buried in this cemetery. We know of at least fifteen soldiers, including the African American patriots Neptune Frost and Cato Stedman, who came to rest here. Some stones are tiny and, sadly, illegible; others have weathered the decades more gracefully. Several of the headstones are in Latin. Some of the oldest are located in the far left corner, adjacent to a Unitarian-Universalist church. The earliest graves date from the mid–seventeenth century, not long after Cambridge (then called "New Towne") had been settled. Those who chose to have their epitaphs engraved in stone rather than in an attached metal plaque have fared better in the annals of history. During the Revolution, the Americans were so desperate for ammunition that they melted down the metal plaques of many tombstones to make musket balls.

* At least eight of Harvard's presidents are buried here in a grove adjacent to the U.U. Church. The inscriptions are long and have weathered so much as to be difficult to decipher, even if your Latin isn't rusty.

America's First Garden Cemetery
MOUNT AUBURN CEMETERY
580 Mount Auburn Street. Year created: 1831. Founded by: Dr. Jacob Bigelow and Joseph Story. ☎ 617-547-7105

> *T Stop: Harvard Square on the Red Line. Change to the Watertown bus #71 or walk along Mount Auburn Street (approximately fifteen minutes). The cemetery is open daily from 8 A.M. to 5 P.M. Maps that locate famous graves and special trees are available for no charge in the office.*

Founded in 1831, this cemetery was the nation's pioneer in the rural cemetery movement (see also page 110). It boasts ten miles of winding walkways, its curving paths encouraging visitors to take their time and enjoy the scenery. In traditional churchyard cemeteries, the headstones were very close together, almost piled one on top of another; sometimes graves were partially exposed, with decomposing bodies on view. Multiple graves were fairly common. Mount Auburn was the first cemetery in New England to challenge this paradigm—to create what its founders called a "garden cemetery," or rural cemetery.

Try to visit Mount Auburn Cemetery and God's Acre, the small burying ground near Harvard Square, on the same day (see above). Then you will see most clearly how radical the rural cemetery idea actually was. A cemetery as a park? As a landscape garden? It had never been done, and some Boston Brahmins viewed the notion as vaguely distasteful. But others—many, many, others—felt it was an idea whose time had long since come. Mount Auburn's 170 acres enjoyed instant popularity as a final resting site, particularly for New England's most prominent citizens. Here, there were no foul odors of human decay, only the pleasant scent of flowers in bloom. From the cemetery's gently sloping paths, visitors could gaze out at the Charles River or enjoy the occasional flowered hilltop or pond. Many of the path names, christened after trees and flowers, emphasize the wonders of the natural world.

Many famous people found rest in Mount Auburn Cemetery, which has been called "a bucolic Westminster Abbey." Its list of permanent residents reads like a "Who's Who" of the nineteenth century: art collector Isabella Stewart Gardner, Christian Science founder Mary Baker Eddy, poet Henry Wadsworth Longfellow, painter Winslow Homer, actor Edwin Booth, and even cookbook guru Fannie Farmer. The plots were quite large—fifteen feet by twenty feet—and more expansive meant more expensive. Many prominent New Englanders bypassed the usual tombstone in favor of granite monuments, detailing their many achievements, and grand family crypts. There is even a Gothic Revival chapel on the grounds.

This cemetery is famous for the arboreally and ornithologically inclined—in other words, aficionados of trees and birds. There are more than 580 kinds of trees here, and over 30,000 trees in all. The cemetery even contains a special garden and fountain that are dedicated to the memory of botanist Asa Gray. And the birds! In springtime, this cemetery is one of New England's migration hotspots, as birds return from their winter vacations to their northeastern home base.

A terrific way to see Mount Auburn—and on a fine day, much of Cambridge and Boston—is to climb the tower that is located on Mount Auburn Hill, a 125-foot hill in the cemetery's center. It's a sixty-foot additional climb to reach the pinnacle of the tower, but the view is well worth the exertion.

The Boston Area's Oldest Residential Zen Center
CAMBRIDGE ZEN CENTER
199 Auburn Street (Central Square). Year founded: 1973. ☎ 617-576-3229
🖥 www.cambridgezen.com

T Stop: Central Square on the Red Line. Walk south on Magazine Street for three blocks. Turn right onto Auburn Street and walk one block.

Cambridge Zen Center is part of the Kwan Um School, a Zen Buddhist tradition from Korea that has sixty centers worldwide. The Kwan Um

School crystallized around the teachings of Zen Master Seung Sahn, who was the first Korean Zen master to bring his teachings to the West. This center was founded in 1973, making it the oldest residential Zen center in the Boston area. It was also the first Kwan Um center to have a woman named as Dharma heir. Presently, one of the center's two resident Zen masters is a woman.

There are currently about thirty-five practitioners (mostly lay) in residence here. Training in Zen techniques is open to anyone, regardless of background or meditation experience, and visitors are always welcome. Tuesdays at 5:30 P.M. the Cambridge Zen Center hosts a simple vegetarian meal. A small donation is requested. Most Thursdays at 7:30 P.M. there is a free talk on some aspect of Zen practice, and free drop-in meditation instruction is available each Monday at 7 P.M. The center's regular daily practice is also free and open to the public, beginning with the 108 bows at 5:15 A.M. each day.

Retreats are available, and are usually held either the second or third weekend of the month. Retreat days follow a tight schedule of sixteen hours of meditation practice, work periods, formal vegetarian meals, private interviews with the retreat leader, and rest time. A longer retreat called a *kyol che* ("coming together") is also available twice a year at the Providence Zen Center (see page 242). These retreats, modeled after the winter and summer retreats held in Korean temples, are conducted in silence and last for several weeks, though shorter stays can be arranged.

> "If you wish to find the Buddha, first you must look into your own mind. Outside of the mind, there is no Buddha."
>
> —Hakuin (1686–1769 C.E.)

NEARBY

⇒ The **Cambridge Insight Meditation Center**, a satellite of the Insight Meditation Center in Barre, Massachusetts (see page 167), was established in 1985 to offer instruction in *vipassana* meditation. In addition to classes, retreats, and workshops on meditation, CIMC also hosts a Wednesday Evening Program that consists of "mindful housework," public sitting meditation, and a dharma talk. A small donation is suggested. *331 Broadway (near Central Square). T Stop: Central Square on the Red Line. Walk north on Prospect Street three blocks. Turn left on Broadway. After one block, CIMC will be on the right.* ☎ 617-441-9038 🖳 www.dharma.org

➥ Located in Central Square is **St. Mary's Antiochian Orthodox Church**, a pan-Orthodox congregation serving Christians of Middle Eastern, Ethiopian, Slavic, Greek, and other backgrounds. Services are conducted entirely in English. *8 Inman Street. T Stop: Central Square on the Red Line. The church is opposite the Inman Street side of City Hall. Saturday Vespers are at 5* P.M.*; Sunday Liturgy is at 10* A.M. ☎ 617-547-1234

➥ Cambridge is home to a large and active community of Sunni Muslims. The **Islamic Society of Boston**, a small mosque in Central Square, can no longer house the throngs of Muslims who live in the area, so other mosques are rapidly springing up around Boston, and major events are sometimes held at larger secular halls in the city. This building is open for five daily prayers, Friday prayer, daily *Iftar* during the holy month of Ramadan, and *Eid* prayers. Throughout the week, there are often special speakers who address Islamic law and other topics. There is a bookstore on-site. A Weekend Islamic School offers lessons in the Qur'an and in the Arabic language; a full-time weekday Islamic School opened its doors in 1996. *204 Prospect Street. T Stop: Central Square on the Red Line.* ☎ 617-876-3546

A Modernist Achievement
MIT CHAPEL
Nondenominational. Massachusetts Avenue and Vassar Street (near Kendall Square). Year consecrated: 1955. Architect: Eero Saarinen.
☎ 617-253-7973 🖳 www.mit.edu

> *T Stop: Kendall Square on the Red Line. From there it is a ten-minute walk through MIT's campus and the "infinite corridor." Open daily from 7* A.M. *to 11* P.M.

Even MIT students, famous for their all-night "tool-and-die" sessions, must occasionally take time to nurture the spirit. To encourage this, the university has one of New England's most unusual houses of worship, the MIT chapel, built in 1955. The brick chapel is shaped like a cylinder and capped by a modernist sculpture spire by Theodore Roszak (b. 1933). Most unusual is the tiny moat that surrounds the chapel, which is reached by a small bridge. An oculus window in the ceiling functions as a sort of skylight, permitting light to filter down into the windowless chapel. Light is then refracted off an altar-to-ceiling mobile sculpture of small bronze fragments, the work of Harry Bertoia (1915–78).

The chapel was designed by Finnish-born architect Eero Saarinen (1910–61), who also created the "Gateway to the West" arch in St. Louis, various corporate centers, and the distinctive egglike structure of Kresge Auditorium, also at MIT. (Campus legend insists that just after its construction, an MIT graduate student wrote a thesis predicting that Kresge was structurally unsound and that its ceiling would crack. According to tradition, angry professors refused to grant him his degree until the ceiling did, in fact, crack, and the student's reputation was redeemed. There is no truth to the story, though it's an outstanding example of the disdain with which many Techies regard the unorthodox campus buildings of Saarinen.) Although the chapel is hailed in architecture books as a unique modernist achievement, many MIT students have rejected its aesthetic of bricks, concrete, and stone, preferring to hold informal religious meetings in the nearby Student Center. The chapel's excellent acoustics, however, make it a perfect setting for small concerts and chamber music.

CHAPTER FOUR

Greater Boston

SPIRITUAL TRAVELERS who begin—but then end—their New England sojourns in Boston will miss the marvelous treasures that lie to the north, west, and south of the city. If Boston is the heartbeat of New England, then the suburbs and outlying areas comprise the region's veins and arteries, bringing life to the city and revitalizing themselves in its proximity. Greater Boston is alive with sacred history and a strong legacy of religious diversity.

Greater Boston encompasses three distinct regions: the North Shore, the western suburbs, and the South Shore. Both of the shore areas are distinguished, of course, by their rich history of seafaring and fishing. This maritime world often intersects with the sacred, as evidenced by the Blessing of the Fleet (in Gloucester) or the Old Ship Meetinghouse (in Hingham)—a church that physically resembles the keel of a boat. Then, too, the North and South Shores provide an abundance of natural beauty for the spiritual traveler: sandy beaches, lapping waves, and unforgettable sunrises over the Atlantic Ocean. The abundance of monasteries and retreat centers located near the sea is testimony to the importance of natural beauty for spiritual renewal.

The western suburbs, from Brookline and Chestnut Hill out to Wellesley and Natick, have long been known for their relative affluence. Here we find the stately home of Christian Science founder Mary Baker Eddy and the tree-lined campuses of Wellesley College and Brandeis University, two institutions which have been noted innovators in their dedication to religious pluralism. Here, too, we discover evidence of America's increasing religious diversity, in the first Hindu, Jain, and Mormon temples to be

erected in New England. And in the western suburb of Concord we learn much about America's literary heritage in Ralph Waldo Emerson's teachings on spiritual Transcendentalism, Henry David Thoreau's experiment in simplicity, or Louisa May Alcott and her unusual family.

Ashland

New England's First Hindu Temple
SRI LAKSHMI TEMPLE/NEW ENGLAND
HINDU TEMPLE, INC.

117 Waverly Street. Year consecrated: 1986. Architect: Sri Ganapathy Sthapathy. ☎ 508-881-5775 🖳 www.srilakshmitemple.org

From Route 90, get off at Exit 13. After the toll booth, bear right toward Framingham on Route 30 West. At the fifth traffic light, bear left onto 126 South. Go two miles to downtown Framingham. After the railroad

*crossing, take Route 135 West into the town of Ashland. The temple
entrance is on your left, one-tenth of a mile after you pass the entrance sign
for Ashland.*

The first authentic Hindu temple in New England is a glory to behold.
It was conceived in 1978, when the growing community of Boston-area
Hindus decided that the time had come for a temple of their own. Every
member pledged a seed donation of $101 to help to build the temple,
which was a labor of great love and energy for many families. Since many
of the temple's founders were immigrants who believed that they had
found a new abundance of blessings in America, it was dedicated to the
goddess Sri Lakshmi, who bestows prosperity. In Lakshmi's honor, her holy
day of Diwali was the first festival celebrated by the congregation in
1978—although since the temple was not yet completed, the Diwali celebrations were held nearby at a Knights of Columbus hall.

An architect from Tamil, India, was hired in the early 1980s, with the
long-awaited groundbreaking occurring in June of 1984. Worship began in
the fall of 1986, but the temple's intricate decorations and sculptures were
not completed until 1990. Traditionally, Hindu temples are distinguished
by their vivid sculptural detail, often covering every inch of the exterior
walls. These sculptures are richly symbolic, some depicting scenes from the
lives of the gods, while others are inspired by the Vedas or other classic
scriptures of Indian spirituality. Hindu temple-building is a precise science,
with several sacred texts delineating the exact geometric proportions a
temple must be if it is to be a meeting place for human beings and the
gods. Nothing is left to chance; there are ancient prescribed rituals for
consecrating the land, and construction must occur at a time that is
deemed astrologically propitious. Even the building materials used are
recommended in the ancient Vastu Shastras, the holy texts on temple
making. A brick temple is a hundred times more meritorious than a
wooden one, and a stone temple ten thousand times better than wood.

Sri Lakshmi temple is a stone structure; its interior is a large, open
space with several individual shrines rimming its perimeter. The temple's
architecture reflects its status as a divine abode: The central sanctuary
(*vimana*) contains a smaller chamber called a *garba griha* (literally, "womb
house") for the reception of the divine being. Thus, worshipers shed the
trappings of the outside world in the vestibule and then proceed through
areas of the temple that become increasingly holy.

Each of the shrines contains a sculpted, dressed image of a deity—Lakshmi, Vishnu, or Ganesha, for example—who stands or sits behind a gate. Here, worshipers may recite prayers and perform a *pooja*, or ritual of devotion. Devotees may leave *prasadam*, or offerings, at the base of the gate. Offerings may include fruit, coconuts, flowers, or camphor; on a given day you may see bananas, oranges, apples, pears, and rosebuds at each shrine. The worshiper is to treat the deity's image as if he or she were a royal guest, making every effort to accommodate the deity with luxuries.

Many of the sculptures were handcrafted in India and shipped here. Special ceremonies were held to consecrate and breathe life into these granite images of the divine. Hindus do not believe that these are "graven images" or that the images themselves are holy; they become holy because they offer devotees a temporary window through which the deity may descend, to dwell among humankind for a brief time.

Sri Lakshmi Temple is staffed by a full-time priest, who provides regular services and also performs weddings and other rituals. Every Saturday, for example, Lord Vishnu is honored with a royal shower; The Thousand Names of Vishnu are recited in Sanskrit while the priest makes offerings of water, milk, honey juice, and turmeric to an eight-foot statue of the god. Since the temple also functions as a community center for Hindus in greater Boston, it hosts cultural events and concerts as well. Visitors must remove their shoes upon entering.

NEARBY

➥ **Garden in the Woods** in **Framingham** offers more than 1,600 varieties of wildflowers and native plants, the largest collection anywhere in New England. Its forty-five acres have several miles of walking trails, a lily pond, a pine barren, and cultivated deciduous woodlands and meadows. In 1997, the owners created a new garden of rare and endangered plants, featuring over 100 species. *180 Hemenway Road, Framingham. Take Route 128 to Route 20 West. Go eight miles on Route 20 to Raymond Road (the second light after the traffic lights in South Sudbury). Go 1.3 miles to Hemenway Road and follow the signs for Garden in the Woods. The garden is open from April through October, Tuesdays through Sundays, from 9 A.M. to 5 P.M. (until 7 P.M. in May). Admission fee.* ☎ 508-877-7630
💻 www.newfs.org/garden.htm

➥ Spiritual travelers who are interested in what the world's religions have to say about peace would enjoy a visit to **Peace Abbey**, a retreat center in **Sherborn** that is committed to social change through nonviolence. The

Abbey's many programs include the "Veganpeace Animal Sanctuary," which provides shelter to animals who have been rescued from slaughterhouses, and the Pacifist Memorial, an on-site monument commemorating Mahatma Gandhi and thirty other men and women who struggled for peace. *2 North Main Street, Sherborn. From Route 95 South, take Route 16 West to Sherborn. At the T intersection, turn left onto Route 27 South (still 16 West). Peace Abbey is a quarter of a mile ahead on the left, before the fork in the road. Open daily from 10:30* A.M. *to 7* P.M. ☎ 508-650-3659
🖳 www.peaceabbey.org

➡ In **Milford**, the **New England Sikh Study Circle** meets in a former Kingdom Hall, which the Sikhs purchased from the Jehovah's Witnesses in 1990. The congregation is primarily Punjabi. Sunday *Kirtan* lasts from 7 A.M. to 2 P.M., but visitors can attend an abbreviated program from 10 A.M. to noon. *204 East Main Street, Millford.* ☎ 508-478-2469

Belmont

A Temple for Mormons in New England
THE BOSTON TEMPLE
The Church of Jesus Christ of Latter-day Saints (Mormon). 86 Frontage Road. Year consecrated: 2000. ☎ 617-993-9993
🖳 www.bostontemple.org

From I-95, take Route 2 east to Exit 57 (Dow Avenue/Arlmont). From the exit, follow Frontage Road (which runs alongside Route 2) past Ledgewood Place until the temple entrance appears on the right. The grounds are open daily from dawn to dusk. The public is not admitted into the temple.

Dedicated in October 2000, this was the hundredth Latter-day Saint (LDS) operating temple in the world. Being the hundredth was a great honor, for in 1998, the president of the LDS Church, Gordon B. Hinckley, had announced the church's intent to have 100 temples in operation by the end of the year 2000. The rapid growth of Mormonism around the world is demonstrated by the intense wave of temple construction during the last decade of the twentieth century, doubling the fifty temples that existed in 1990.

The Boston temple, built on a hill in Belmont, has already seen a bit of controversy. Even before ground was broken for its construction, neighbors in the mostly residential area began to protest the idea of having an LDS temple here. Most of them objected to the traffic the temple would generate, while others rejected the proposed design of the $30 million building. The LDS Church compromised by scaling back the design; the originally planned spires and 139-foot steeple were not built at the time of the build-

WHY CAN'T I GO INSIDE?

Once they have been formally dedicated, LDS temples are considered holy buildings, consecrated for sacred use. As such, they are not tourist destinations, though visitors are welcome to stroll the grounds, which are lovingly maintained by church volunteers. Entrance to the temple is reserved for "active" Mormons in good standing: that is, those who have a strong spiritual life and who adhere to certain behavioral expectations. These include keeping the "Word of Wisdom," a dietary law that prohibits the use of alcohol, tobacco, nonprescription drugs, coffee, and tea; tithing 10 percent of one's income to the church; abstaining from all premarital or extramarital sexual activity; supporting church leaders and LDS doctrines; and being "honest in all dealings" with other people. Members who meet these criteria and who desire to enter the temple must meet with their local bishop and stake president for interviews to ascertain their worthiness. Those who are worthy to enter receive a card called a "temple recommend," to be shown at the temple's entrance for admission.

What, however, are temples for? They're not for Sunday-morning church—Mormons have thousands of ordinary meetinghouses, called "ward chapels," for that purpose. Temples are, in fact, often open every day *except* Sunday, when church members are having their three-hour services in those local ward chapels. Temples are special, holy places, where adult Latter-day Saints participate in rituals that only take place here. Members may "receive their endowments," making covenants of faithfulness and learning more about their roles in eternity. They learn about their premortal existence, their purpose on earth, and about the life to come. Marriages are also sealed "for time and all eternity." Latter-day Saints believe that with the proper priesthood authority to perform a marriage, the family bond is sealed to last beyond death for eternity and that all children who are "born in the covenant" to such parents will be united with them forever.

ing's dedication in 2000, resulting in a more modest structure. However, in May of 2001 the Supreme Judicial Court of Massachusetts ruled that the steeple addition could go forward, rejecting the opponents' argument that it did not constitute a "necessary" part of LDS worship. (Chief Justice Margaret Marshall noted that since the court did not have the authority to decide whether a rose window at Notre Dame Cathedral or a balcony at St. Peter's Basilica were "necessary" to the faith served by those buildings, it also did not have the power to dictate what architectural features were appropriate for the Latter-day Saints.) On September 21, 2001, the new steeple was completed, with a statue of the Angel Moroni standing at the top.

Despite the local protests, many Boston-area residents welcomed the temple. More than 82,000 visitors (mostly non-Mormons) attended the "open house" in the weeks before the temple's dedication. Now that it has been dedicated, entry is reserved for active Latter-day Saints.

NEARBY

➡ In 1955, sociologist Will Herberg penned a foundational text called *Protestant-Catholic-Jew: An Essay in American Religious Sociology*, in which he argued that America's Protestant heritage must be expanded to include Catholicism and Judaism as major religious forces. As if on cue, that same year Brandeis University (the first Jewish-sponsored nonsectarian university in the United States) in **Waltham** constructed the **Brandeis University Interfaith Center**—three chapels, one each for Protestantism, Catholicism, and Judaism. All three chapels, designed by Max Abramowitz, are equal in stature and of the same gray brick, joined together by a walking path and a reflecting pool. *415 South Street, Waltham. From Boston, take I-90 West to Exit 15 (Route 30). Turn right at the end of the ramp, then right again at the first traffic light to access Route 30. Turn left at the next traffic light (South Street). Brandeis University is two miles ahead on the left side.* ☎ 781-736-2000 🖥 www.brandeis.edu

Brookline

An American Acropolis
HOLY CROSS GREEK ORTHODOX SCHOOL OF THEOLOGY
50 Goddard Ave. Year founded: 1937. ☎ 617-731-3500
🖥 www.hchc.edu

> From Route 128 South, take Exit 20A (Route 9) heading east. Go
> through eight sets of lights. At the ninth light, bear right on to Lee Street.
> Get into the left lane and drive on this road until it ends at a traffic light.
> Turn left. At the fork in the road, stay left on Goddard Avenue. The
> campus will be on the right after eight-tenths of a mile.

The "Acropolis" of Greek Orthodoxy in America, this Brookline
campus houses Hellenic College, an undergraduate school; a publishing
company; the offices of *The Greek Orthodox Theological Review*; offices for
the archdiocese; a bookstore specializing in Eastern Christian theology,
patristics, and Byzantine history; and Holy Cross Greek Orthodox School
of Theology, the main seminary for training Greek Orthodox priests in the
United States. Holy Cross, founded in 1937, is one of the most important
Greek Orthodox educational institutions outside of Greece. Its presence in
Boston is fitting; many Greek Americans have labeled Boston the "Athens
of America" because of the preponderance of educational institutions in
both cities. Students come from all over North America, with a smattering
of international students, who attend classes and perhaps sing in the
Byzantine Choir.

As part of its commitment to Orthodox unity, Holy Cross welcomes
students from other Orthodox churches, as well as those from other faiths
who wish to study Orthodoxy. The seminary's chapel hosts a number of
services each week, including evening vespers and "Great Vespers," which
are open to the public. Morning devotions called *Orthros* are also offered
daily in the chapel.

Self-Empowerment through Yoga
THE BOSTON BK RAJA YOGA CENTER
Brahma Kumaris World Spiritual Organization. 1821 Beacon Street.
☎ 617-734-1464 🖳 www.bkwsuboston.com

> *T Stop: Green Line trolley toward Cleveland Circle, and get off at the
> Englewood Stop. The center is right in front of you.*

Although it is a relative newcomer to the United States, the Brahma
Kumaris World Spiritual Organization has already made quite a name for
itself here. From the movement's founding in 1936 until 1971, when it

established its first overseas centers in the United Kingdom, it was exclusively located in India and Pakistan. The movement now has over 3,200 centers in seventy countries. Its headquarters and university are still based in Rajasthan, in northern India. It is considered an NGO (Non-Governmental Organization) and has received the United Nations Peace Messenger Award seven times.

Even though it is not a women's organization, BKWSO is unusual in that it is mostly administered by female leaders. The founder, an Indian man named Prajaptita Brahma (1876–1969), surrendered all of his property to a team of eight young women leaders in 1938, believing that they would manage the trust responsibly to the benefit of the movement he created. Today, the world leader of the BKWSO is a woman named Dadi Prakashmani, who was just fourteen years old when she was chosen as part of that original eight-woman leadership team.

The BKWSO seeks to promote self-empowerment and self-realization through the practice of yoga meditation. Its members are vegetarians, who emphasize traditional Indian beliefs such as karma and reincarnation. The BKWSO teaches that meditation offers improved self-awareness, and that it holds the key to world peace. This is part of the reason why every class at every BKWSO center is offered free of charge as a community service.

NEARBY

➥ Also in Brookline is the **Boston Dharmadhatu/Shambhala Meditation Center**, in the Tibetan Buddhist tradition. The mostly Euro-American community was founded in the 1970s, and moved to this location in the mid-1990s. The center offers classes on all levels, from one-day introductory courses in mindfulness meditation on the first Saturday of each month to ongoing Shambhala training programs over the course of five weekends. Meditation takes place in the large and airy Main Shrine Room, where bright red and yellow mats and cushions are spread invitingly on the floor. *646 Brookline Avenue. T Stop: Green Line D/Riverside Train to the Brookline Village stop. Walk away from Washington Street (eastward) one and a half blocks down Pearl Street until it runs into Brookline Avenue. Shambhala Center is across the street.* ☎ 617-734-1498
🖥 www.shambhala.org/centers/boston/index.html
➥ Referred to as the "mother church" of Greek Orthodoxy in America, **Annunciation Greek Orthodox Cathedral of New England** is one of the oldest Greek Orthodox churches in the country. With its five Byzantine-style domes and ornate iconography, it is also one of the most architecturally impressive. *162 Goddard Avenue.* ☎ 617-731-6633

Chestnut Hill

Mrs. Eddy's Gracious Estate

MARY BAKER EDDY HISTORIC HOME

400 Beacon Street. ☎ 617-566-3092 💻 www.marybakereddy.org

Driving from Boston, take Route 9 (Huntington Avenue) west from the city. After about six miles, turn right on to Hammond Street. At the next traffic light, turn left on to Beacon Street. The home is .1 mile on the left. By subway: take the "D" outbound train to the Chestnut Hill stop. Turn right onto Hammond Street and walk a half mile to North Beacon Street. Turn left at the Beacon Street traffic light. The home is .1 mile on the left. Free guided tours are offered Wednesday through Friday from 10 A.M. to 4 P.M. and Saturday from 1 P.M. to 4 P.M. Daily carriage rides are also offered on those days.

This grand home in a tree-lined suburb of Boston was where Mary Baker Eddy, the founder of Christian Science, lived from January 1908 until her death in 1910. She purchased it sight unseen, and was quite unhappy when she first encountered it. The eighty-six-year-old woman believed that the stone edifice was too large and immediately set about modifying many of the rooms to make them smaller and cozier.

The house has stayed much the same as it was in Mrs. Eddy's last years; it is elegantly furnished in the manner favored by post-Victorians, with heavy drapes in rich colors and three pianos throughout. The house was quite technologically innovative for its day, with a comprehensive inter-com system and even an elevator (installed by Mrs. Eddy so she could enter and exit privately through a side door). The tour begins in the formal living room just off the foyer; a tour guide offers basic information about Mrs. Eddy, the church she founded, and her role in spiritual healing and women's history. This living room, with its twelve-foot ceilings, was too large and formal for Mrs. Eddy's liking and was used by the various staff members living here (up to twenty-five at one time) but not often by her. So many people lived here and visited the home that dinner in the courtly Victorian dining room was sometimes served in two shifts. Mrs. Eddy, how-ever, preferred to take her meals more simply in her rooms upstairs.

On the second floor are the reception room and library, where she gov-erned many of the affairs of the church and met her visitors. The tour also

Mary Baker Eddy's Chestnut Hill home

includes her bedroom (small, at her insistence), which still has her own linens, monogrammed with her initials. Mrs. Eddy died in this room in 1910, in her sleep. Next-door to the bedroom is her private study, where she did her work (commenting on many articles for *The Christian Science Monitor*, for example) and kept up with her voluminous correspondence. Each morning, she spent at least an hour in prayer and Bible study in this room, before beginning her daily work.

Mrs. Eddy's private parlor—also pink, a color she loved—was used by the entire staff as a place to gather. Here they would read aloud bits from the *Monitor*, discuss the affairs of the church, play the piano or listen to the Victrola. An adjacent small front sitting room features a wicker chair decorated with the Christian Science insignia of cross and crown. This handwoven rocker was a gift from the prisoners of the New Hampshire state prison, in gratitude for the church services being held there at Mrs. Eddy's request. That prison ministry continues to this day.

The final stop on the tour is the Carriage House. Mrs. Eddy was famous for her love of carriage-riding and tried to go out daily. Eight carriages are housed here, including Mrs. Eddy's two favorites. Although there was an automobile kept here for staff use, she rode in it just once, feeling more warmly toward her horses than the newfangled motorcar.

 The eight acres of grounds are open to the public and feature rolling hills and magnificent trees. When Mrs. Eddy lived here, there were no other houses in view; although Boston's growth has encroached a bit, it is still possible to forget that these grounds are on the edge of a major city.

There is a formal flower garden, with roses, peonies, and irises in full bloom in late spring and early summer. Mrs. Eddy's original birdhouse still stands, and its pole is at least two stories high.

Concord

Ralph Waldo Emerson (1803–82), a native of Concord, popularized Transcendentalism (see pages 139 and 177), a movement catalyzed by the philosophical ideas in his 1836 book *Nature*. Other writers and thinkers who were attracted to Transcendentalism came to Concord to associate with Emerson, transforming this small Massachusetts town into a literary giant in the mid–nineteenth century.

Thoreau's "Life in the Woods"
WALDEN POND
Walden Street. 🖥️ www.nanosft.com/walden

From Route 2, take Route 126 approximately 1.5 miles south of Concord. The pond is open daily from 5 A.M. until half an hour after sunset. There is a fee for parking. No dogs are permitted.

Today, Walden Pond is primarily a recreation site (and a place of hazing by Boston-area fraternities who throw unsuspecting freshmen into the cold New England waters). But a century and a half ago, before the automobile traffic buzzed ignominiously by on Route 2, this was the scene of a tremendous spiritual experiment. Henry David Thoreau (1817–68), who was a *beatnik* a century before "beatnik" was even a word, opted to drop out of society for a time and determine just how simply a human being could live. He constructed a tiny cabin on land owned by his friend, Ralph Waldo Emerson, and lived in it from July 1845 to September 1847.

During these two years and two months, Thoreau made his own furniture and spent, by his own reckoning, only about twenty-seven cents each

"To be a philosopher is not merely to have subtle thoughts, nor even to found a school, but so to love wisdom as to live according to its dictates, a life of simplicity, independence, magnanimity, and trust."
—Henry David Thoreau, *Walden*

Walden Pond

week on food. His goal was to support himself entirely by the work of his own hands. He did not, as many have imagined, withdraw completely from society—he often walked into town by way of the Fitchburg Railroad causeway. He would take in a meal, converse with friends, and sometimes play a good game of cards. Then he would return to this rustic cabin to Think Great Thoughts, Alone.

Thoreau recounts all sorts of adventures in *Walden, or Life in the Woods*, a book he published in 1854 about his bucolic stint. His nitpicky explanation of every food expenditure even includes a rather comical account of eating a woodchuck. Thoreau "went so far as to slaughter a woodchuck which ravaged my beanfield . . . and devour him, partly for experiment's sake." He decided not to continue the woodchuck diet "though it afforded . . . a momentary enjoyment, notwithstanding a musky flavor." Even the nature-loving Thoreau had his limits.

Thoreau entertained himself mostly by reading, a subject to which he devotes an entire chapter in *Walden*. "My residence was more favorable, not only to thought, but to serious reading, than a university," he claimed, and the list of works read during his lakeside tenure is impressive to be sure. Visitors to the site today may well entertain a vision of the stalwart Thoreau, sitting in a simple chair he made himself, swatting mosquitoes and reading the classics. As Thoreau remarked, people should "stand on tiptoe" for the privilege of reading, a task to which we must "devote our most alert and wakeful hours."

Walden Pond has undergone numerous metamorphoses in the century and a half since Thoreau lived here. In the late nineteenth century, a public park was built adjacent to the pond, complete with concession stands, bathhouses, and dance halls. Around 1890, a baseball diamond was added, a nod to America's new favorite pastime, and a cinder track catered to cyclists and runners. This all burned to the ground in 1902 and was never replaced, though the area around the lake continued to see an enormous onslaught of leisure travelers. With the advent of the automobile, crowds became even more numerous—up to 25,000 visitors on a fine Sunday. When Massachusetts environmental authorities assumed responsibility for Walden Pond in the 1970s, they set a limit of 1,000 visitors per day, and also began to restore the lake's eroded banks.

The site of Thoreau's cabin is still accessible by a walking trail and is marked by a cairn of stones. The site was excavated in 1945, the hundredth anniversary of the Walden experiment, by a fan of Thoreau's writ-

THE TRANSCENDENT INDIVIDUAL

As is so often the case, the movement that became Transcendentalism was ignited by a book. In 1836, Ralph Waldo Emerson anonymously published *Nature*, a small treatise based on his ten years of reflections about the natural world. A group of literati that included Margaret Fuller, Bronson Alcott, and Henry David Thoreau began discussing the book's ideas. And thus a religion—or at least a diffuse philosophical movement—was born on New England soil. Transcendentalism was a prominent movement in New England from the late 1830s through the 1850s and marked a definitive rejection of both enlightened rationalism and industrialization.

The Transcendentalist movement emphasized the primacy of the individual over any institution. Those who imagine society to be "wiser than their own soul," Emerson told a bewildered Harvard Divinity School graduating class in 1838, would be amazed to realize that their souls are "wiser than the whole world." Intuition, not doctrine or convention, was to become the Transcendental creed. The movement also heavily emphasized the presence of the divine in nature. Since the divine (or "the Oversoul") had imbued nature with divinity, human beings—who were also infused with the divine presence—could find the sacred through the natural world. In essence, Transcendentalism eloquently furthered the age-old mystical assertion that the individual spirit, rather than canon or creed, reigned supreme.

ings. After some effort, he discovered the cabin's old chimney and dedicated a fieldstone plaque on the old hearthstone. In addition to the stones marking the actual site of the cabin, there is also a replica of the tiny home near the parking lot, giving visitors a vivid sense of Thoreau's life on Walden Pond.

Little Women
ORCHARD HOUSE
399 Lexington Road. Year built: Precise date unknown, but sometime in the early eighteenth century. ☎ 978-369-4118
🖳 www.louisamayalcott.org

> *From I-95, take Exit 30B (Route 2A West). Follow 2A past the entrance to Hanscom AFB toward Concord Center. At the fork in the road, 2A bears left, but you will bear right, following the signs to Concord Center. Proceed 2.5 miles. Orchard House is on the right, just before Concord Center. Park in the Wayside lot. The house is open for guided tours from April through October from 10 A.M. to 4:30 P.M. on Monday through Saturday and from 1 P.M. to 4:30 P.M. on Sunday. From November through March, weekday hours are from 11 A.M. to 3 P.M., and weekend hours same as above. Admission fee.*

In this house, in 1868, Louisa May Alcott (1832–88) wrote her most famous novel, *Little Women*. The Alcotts lived here from 1858 to 1877, which were penurious times for the family. Bronson Alcott, Louisa's philosopher-father, was never much good at supporting the household (see page 176 for an explanation of the ill-fated Fruitlands commune he founded in 1843), although during this period he served as superintendent of the Concord schools. Louisa eventually took pen in hand and brought in some money through her writing. "I will make a battering-ram of my head and make my way through this rough and tumble world," she vowed in her journal.

Louisa May Alcott died on March 6, 1888, outliving her beloved father by just two days. Today, Orchard House is open for regular guided tours, offering an introduction to the family's unusual lifestyle and literary work. Approximately three-quarters of the furnishings in this house were owned by the Alcotts; standing in the dining room today, one can easily imagine the conversations the family must have had about philosophy and abolitionism while enjoying their vegetarian repasts.

NEARBY

➥ **Concord Museum**, founded in 1886, is the cream of the crop of local history museums. It has most of Ralph Waldo Emerson's library, the furniture from Henry David Thoreau's cabin on Walden Pond, a lantern hung at Boston's Old North Church on the night of Paul Revere's legendary ride, and many artifacts relating to the Emersons, Thoreaus, Alcotts, and Hawthornes. *200 Lexington Road. Open April through December from 9 A.M. to 5 P.M. Monday to Saturday and noon to 5 P.M. on Sunday. From January to March, open Monday to Saturday from 11 A.M. to 4 P.M. and 1 P.M. to 4 P.M. on Sunday. Admission fee.* ☎ 978-369-9609 🖳 www.concordmuseum.org

➥ **Ralph Waldo Emerson House** offers guided half-hour tours of the home where the philosopher lived for nearly half a century (1835–82). Most of the furniture here belonged to Emerson, and the dollhouse in the nursery may have been made by Emerson's friend and neighbor, Henry David Thoreau. *28 Cambridge Turnpike at Route 2A. Guided tours offered April through October, Thursday through Saturday from 10 A.M. to 4:30 P.M., and 2 P.M. to 4:30 P.M. on Sundays. Admission fee.* ☎ 978-369-2236

➥ Another interesting Emerson family site is **The Old Manse**, where Ralph Waldo's grandfather Reverend William Emerson is said to have stood at the window on April 19, 1775, to watch the battle on nearby North Bridge. (The literary grandson later memorialized that "rude bridge" in his poem, "Concord Hymn.") This house also hosted Nathaniel Hawthorne and his new bride Sophia from 1842 to 1844. *269 Monument Street, next to the North Bridge Visitors Center. Guided tours are offered from April to October from 10 A.M. to 5 P.M. Monday through Saturday and noon to 5 P.M. on Sunday. Admission fee.* ☎ 978-369-3909 🖳 www.thetrustees.org

➥ The elevated section called "Authors' Ridge" at **Sleepy Hollow Cemetery** contains the graves of Thoreau, Emerson, Hawthorne, and the literary Alcotts, among others. Emerson's grave is an unshaped natural stone with a plaque noting the date that the philosopher "lent his hand to the great soul," in April 1882. *On Bedford Street. From Concord Center, turn right onto Route 62. The cemetery is the second gate on the left. Open daily from 9 A.M. to sunset.* ☎ 978-318-3233

➥ **Minute Man National Historic Park** is the site of one of the most famous battles of the American Revolution. Each Patriot's Day (April 19), the battle is reenacted by authentically kitted-out redcoats and colonists. (The recreated battle on the Lexington Green begins with a British officer yelling, "Lay down your arms, you damned rebels, and disperse!") The historic park encompasses 900 acres and offers walking tours with informative plaques describing the events of April 19, 1775. *The Battle Road Visitor Center is off Route 2A in Lexington. Open daily from 9 A.M. to 5 P.M. from May until October; 9 A.M. to 4 P.M. in other months.* ☎ 978-369-6993 🖳 www.nps.gov/mima

Gloucester

Portuguese American Heritage
OUR LADY OF GOOD VOYAGE CHURCH
Roman Catholic. 142 Prospect Street. Year consecrated: 1893.
☎ 978-283-1490

From 128, cross the A. Piatt Andrew Bridge and go to a rotary. Bear right onto Washington Street. Cross the railroad tracks. Take a left on Railroad Avenue. Go left on Prospect Street. The church will be on the left-hand side. The church is open on weekdays from 10 A.M. to 4 P.M.

Our Lady of Good Voyage Church, Gloucester

Inspired by Portuguese architecture, this 1893 church is ornately decorated, its interior walls anchored with models of various fishing boats. Atop the church, a statue of Our Lady of Good Voyage is perched between two blue-capped cupolas. The Madonna's purpose is to guide seafarers safely into the harbor. And sailors might indeed feel a bit safer when they see what she cradles in her arms: not the baby Jesus, but a fishing schooner. Fans of the novel and the blockbuster film *The Perfect Storm* will recognize the church's famous Madonna, testimony to the way the faith of Gloucester's residents has, for most of its history, been inextricably tied with the capricious, unfathomable sea.

Our Lady of Good Voyage is a

famous reminder of Gloucester's maritime history and of the community's tremendous Portuguese heritage. A group of immigrants from the Azores came to settle in Gloucester, the nation's oldest seaport, around 1845. Many native Portuguese moved to the North Shore in the mid–nineteenth century to participate in various aspects of the whaling industry. They completed this church in 1893 and constructed the nation's first carillon (a series of chromatic bells) in the tower.

With the decline of the whaling industry in the late nineteenth century, many Portuguese Americans left the area for California and other destinations. Others remained, their numbers bolstered by a new wave of immigration after the Portuguese monarchy fell in 1910. Many began working in the textile mills that emerged in Fall River, Lowell, and other communities. By 1912, the greater Boston area boasted the second-largest expatriate Portuguese population of any nation in the world, after Brazil.

HOLY GHOST FESTIVALS AND THE BLESSING OF THE FLEET

Holy Ghost festivals are common in Portuguese-heritage churches throughout Massachusetts and Rhode Island, and are often accompanied by a **Blessing of the Fleet**, a custom that merges the faith and the working lives of many Portuguese New Englanders. No two festivals are alike, but most last a full weekend and feature parades, fireworks, and music. In addition to the famous Gloucester celebration each June, there is also a Fourth of July Blessing of the Fleet in Provincetown, Massachusetts, a tradition established in 1947. In New Bedford, Massachusetts, the entire ceremony takes place at the port, where clergy of many different faiths offer blessings on the fishing fleet.

Traditionally, the blessing begins in the church, with local fishermen carrying banners with the names of their boats printed upon them in bright colors. The bishop of the Roman Catholic Diocese of Fall River celebrates the mass, which is followed by the whole congregation marching in procession to the pier for the blessing of the boats. These have been meticulously cleaned and decorated for the occasion. Not all is joyous celebration, however; the ceremony also offers the opportunity to remember those men and women whose lives have been tragically taken by the sea, and to pray for a successful year of fishing.

To this day, the church's Portuguese heritage is reflected in its celebration of the *Festa do Espírito Santo* (Festival of the Holy Ghost), held each June. The *festa* has an interesting history; in the late nineteenth century, a Portuguese American captain found himself and his crew in a terrible storm. He promised God that he would sponsor a Holy Ghost Festival if the ship and its crew were spared. They survived, and the captain made good on his foxhole conversion.

An Oceanside Mansion for Spiritual Renewal

EASTERN POINT RETREAT HOUSE

Roman Catholic (Society of Jesus/Jesuit). 37 Niles Point Road.
☎ 978-283-0013

> *From Boston, take Route 128 North until it ends, going through two traffic circles and two sets of traffic lights. Go straight through the last light and up a hill, bearing left. Continue on East Main Street past Niles Beach on the right. Proceed between two pillars marked "Private: Eastern Point." Follow this narrow, winding road to the retreat center.*

Jesuit retreat centers do not often conjure up images of mansions by the sea, but that is what you can expect at this marvelous house an hour north of Boston. Built in 1921, it was acquired in 1957 by the Jesuits, who promptly added a wing to accommodate fifty visitors at a time. And they certainly do come, from all over the world and from many different

Eastern Point Retreat House, Cape Ann

LIGHTHOUSES OF THE NORTH SHORE

Boston's North Shore is justifiably famous for its lighthouses, some of which are open to the public. **Eastern Point Lighthouse**, located at the tip of Eastern Point on Cape Ann, is one of the most-photographed lighthouses in New England. It still flashes its light every night, sending a beacon into the darkness every five seconds. Some lighthouses, like Salem's **Derby Wharf Lighthouse**, are quite tiny—Derby Wharf is only twenty-five feet tall, but its position at the end of Salem's long wharf made it visible to seafarers from miles away. Tall, elegant twin lighthouses, erected in 1861, mark the entrance to **Thacher Island** and are thought to have saved the lives of President Wilson and his entourage when they returned from the Versailles Peace Conference in 1919. The night was so foggy that the passenger liner *America* would surely have collided with Thacher Island's rocky shores if it had not been for a loud foghorn blast coming from one of the lighthouses. Boats to Thacher Island leave regularly from Rockport and Gloucester. In Newburyport (a Coast Guard base and shipbuilding center near the New Hampshire border), you may also catch a boat to historic **Plum Island Lighthouse**, a popular tourist destination on the north end of Plum Island Point. For more information about Massachusetts lighthouses, call the Lighthouse Preservation Society ☎ 1-800-727-BEAM.
🖳 www.lighthousepreservation.org

religious backgrounds. Retreatants find peace in the lapping waves of the Atlantic, which can be seen and heard from many guest rooms and from the bay windows of the dining room, where meals are taken in silence.

Each year there are twenty-two directed retreats for individuals, which typically last for eight days; fifteen weekend retreats (four of which are for twelve-step participants); and guided retreats of various lengths for groups. Month-long silent retreats are quite popular. Each January and July, Eastern Point Retreat House offers the "Full Spiritual Exercises of Saint Ignatius" on a directed basis for individuals.

NEARBY
➥ A substantial Cambodian community has arisen in the northern suburb of **Lynn**, with over 4,000 Cambodian residents. Their **Sanghikaram Wat Khmer** temple is housed in a former Baptist church. A house across

the street serves as a monastery residence for the temple's monks. *109-110 Chestnut Street, Lynn.* ☎ 781-581-7266

➠ The **Mary Baker Eddy House**, also in **Lynn**, was home to the founder of Christian Science from 1875 until 1881. Its front parlor was the site of the first meeting of the group that would become The Church of Christ, Scientist. *12 Broad Street, Lynn.* ☎ 617-450-3793

Hingham

The Nation's Oldest Puritan Meetinghouse
OLD SHIP MEETINGHOUSE
90 Main Street. Year consecrated: 1681, with enlargements in 1729 and 1755 (congregation dates to 1635). ☎ 781-749-1679

Open daily from noon to 4 P.M. in July and August, and by appointment in other months. Donation requested.

While many church buildings in New England boast of being the "first" this or the "oldest" that, such claims are often unsubstantiated. But here, as they say, is the real McCoy: Constructed in 1681, this is the oldest Puritan meetinghouse still standing in America. Although "Old Ship" is the name by which it is now popularly known, this church should more aptly be called First Congregational Meetinghouse, Hingham. It got its name because of its unusual shape: The interior roofing is curved like the hull of a ship, with exposed roof beams. (This may have been no accident, since the church was allegedly constructed by local shipbuilders who simply followed a form that they knew well.)

It is rather remarkable that Old Ship Meetinghouse is still standing—three centuries plus is an exceptional tenure for a wooden church. Its frame and walls were constructed in 1681, while the interior furnishings—pulpit, pews, and gallery—were added in 1755. The building is square and spartan, devoid of decoration or ornate details. The pews and interior furnishings are not painted, permitting the warmth of the natural wood to shine forth in simple elegance. The meetinghouse's clear-glass windows show the only hint of decoration, with diamond-paned leaded glass. The building is topped by a simple spire with a bell and weathervane. This octagonal belfry was, however, added later, and it is a reasonable question whether the Puritans might have approved of it.

*Old Ship
Meetinghouse,
Hingham*

The meetinghouse was nearly torn down in 1791, when the congregation voted to build a flashier church; fortunately, they never got around to it. After the Civil War the members succumbed to the temptations of Victorian grandeur and redecorated the meetinghouse with great fanfare, employing every frill and furbelow. The Colonial Revival movement of the 1930s encouraged them to restore the building to its original simplicity, and so it remains today.

Benedictine Hospitality
GLASTONBURY ABBEY
Roman Catholic (Benedictine). 16 Hull Street. Year opened: 1954.
☎ 781-749-2155 🖳 www.glastonburyabbey.org

> *From Boston, take I-93 South to Route 3 South (Cape Cod). From Route 3, take Exit 14 (Route 228) and take a left at the light at the end of the exit ramp. Continue on Route 228 North through the town of Hingham. Continue through the intersection with Route 3A and then bear left at Hull Street. The abbey will be on the left.*

In this tranquil abbey, the "Black Benedictines" (so called because of the long black cowls they wear) attend to their daily prayers and the needs of their retreatants. The abbey can house approximately thirty people (both individuals and groups), who are warmly cared for in the tradition of Benedictine hospitality. The abbey purchased this property, which includes sixty wooded acres, in 1954. There are some marked trails for contemplative walking. Guests are invited to share in the abbey's spiritual life, including prayer five times each day, and daily mass. They are also asked to uphold the abbey's observation of silence in the chapel and the two retreat houses, Stonecrest and Whiting House.

NEARBY

➥ On 250 acres of secluded peninsula is **World's End**, a nature preserve fourteen miles south of Boston that was designed by Frederick Law Olmstead. Visitors may well feel that they have reached the end of the world, so secluded are the preserve's meadows and paths. A hiking trail leads to a spot on the peninsula with views of Boston. *Martin's Lane, near Route 3A, Hingham. Take Route 3A south past Hingham Harbor and enter the rotary. Go right onto Rockland Street. At the first traffic light, turn left onto Martin's Lane. The park is at the end of the lane. Open daily from dawn to dusk.* ☎ 781-821-2977

➥ The **Cohasset Common First Parish Meetinghouse** is a fine example of eighteenth-century New England meetinghouse architecture. Its simple wooden structure is capped by a square tower and octagonal belfry. Once Puritan/Congregational, the church became Unitarian in the late eighteenth century. *23 North Main Street, on the Cohasset Common.* ☎ 781-383-1100

➥ In 1894, the first Vedanta Society branch was founded in the United States by Swami Vivekananda (1862–1902), and the society has a formal membership of several thousand people nationwide. Many more, however, have sought yoga instruction and philosophical guidance from the society, which offers the **Cohasset Vedanta Centre**, the continuation of the Boston Vedanta Centre that was founded in 1909. Vedanta, one of the earliest threads of Hinduism to reach the United States, has incorporated some Christian elements from American culture, and celebrates Christian holy days as well as Hindu and Buddhist festivals. The Cohasset Centre's worship service is held on Sundays at 11 A.M. *130 Beechwood Street.* ☎ 781-383-0940

Peabody

Attention, Shoppers

ST. THERESE CARMELITE CHAPEL

Roman Catholic. North Shore Shopping Center. Year dedicated: 1960.
☎ 978-531-8340

> *The chapel is open during regular mall hours, usually from 10 A.M. to*
> *8:30 P.M. on weekdays.*

"Goin' to the chapel, and we're . . . gonna go shopping?" Visitors can
do just that at St. Therese Carmelite Chapel, one of several mall-based
houses of worship that have sprung up across the country. St. Therese's is
located on the ground floor of the North Shore Shopping Center, just
below jewelry stores, gift shops, and clothing boutiques. It's a bit jarring to
find a quiet Roman Catholic chapel in the midst of a suburban den of commercial exchange, but the chapel's founders felt the need to bring God's
message where the people are. And these days, many people spend their
Sundays at the mall.

By mall standards, St. Therese's is quite old: It has been in this location
for more than forty years. It was the brainchild of Cardinal Richard Cush-
ing, who said in 1960 that he wanted to "bring God into the marketplace."
Judging by the chapel's attendance numbers, it would seem that his vision
has been a success. In a time when many Roman Catholic churches are
forced to cut back on daily masses and consolidate their priestly leadership,
St. Therese's continues to celebrate mass three times daily and is led by an
entourage of six retired priests. Attendance at weekday mass ranges from
fifty to a hundred people, with several hundred people crowding into the
chapel for mass on weekends.

Many welcome the spiritual anonymity that comes with worshiping
here. The priests say that while some people feel embarrassed by going to
confession in a parish church, where all of the neighbors know them, they
have no qualms about slipping in to the confessional at St. Therese's. If
anyone were to ask, they could just say they were out shopping.

Quincy

New England's First Mosque

THE ISLAMIC CENTER OF NEW ENGLAND

470 South Street. Year built: 1964 (congregation dates to 1937).

☎ 617-479-8341 💻 www.ia-ne.org/icne/

> From I-93, take Exit 8 and follow the signs toward Furnace Brook
> Parkway and Quincy Center. At the first traffic light, turn right onto
> Copeland Street, which becomes Water Street. At the end of the street,
> turn right onto Quincy Avenue. At the third traffic light, turn left onto
> S. Artery/Route 53 North. At the first light, turn right onto South
> Street/Des Moines Road. Take the second left onto Chubbuck Street.
> The ICNE is located on the corner of Chubbuck and South Streets.
> Jum'ah prayer is held on Friday at 12:45 P.M. and Sunday at 1 P.M.
> The mosque is also open for regular daily prayer.

Not far from the birthplace of President John Quincy Adams is another historic site: the first mosque in New England. The congregation began in the early twentieth century, when Lebanese and Syrian immigrants who worked in the Quincy shipyards began coming together regularly for prayer. In 1934, they formed a congregation and met for the next thirty years in members' homes, using a volunteer imam (spiritual leader). In 1964, after years of saving and planning, they dedicated this mosque on South Street.

After the 1965 Immigration and Naturalization Act permitted

The Islamic Center of New England, Quincy

more Asians and Arab Americans to enter the United States, the ethnic character of the mosque changed dramatically. While in 1964 the members were still primarily Lebanese and Syrian Americans, by 1974 the overall membership had tripled, and members hailed from many parts of the world. Today, the mosque includes members from over two dozen countries and has a full-time imam, Talal Eid, who participates in interfaith educational initiatives as well as tending to his rapidly expanding community.

In 1990, the mosque was the target of an ugly anti-Muslim act. An arsonist set fire to the building, causing half a million dollars' worth of damage and laying waste to the dome, prayer hall, and education wing. Although the police confirmed that it was an act of arson, there was not enough evidence to make an arrest. Using the money from insurance proceeds and an outpouring of financial support from the Quincy community, the mosque was fully repaired. In 1995, the Islamic Center of New England opened a satellite mosque (also called the Islamic Center of New England) in the Boston suburb of Sharon to further accommodate the local Muslim community.

NEARBY

➥ **The Thousand Buddha Temple**, dedicated in 1996, has several hundred members, primarily ethnic Chinese. This temple is part of the Pure Land School of Buddhism, which stresses devotion to Amida (an enlightened buddha who inhabits the Pure Land of perfect enlightenment). In Pure Land Buddhism, liberation can be achieved through chanting, vows, and visualization. Special celebrations are held here for the birthdays of Buddha, Guan-Yin, and Amida. *53-55 Massachusetts Avenue.*
☎ 617-773-7745

Salem

A Bewitching Destination

Most of the tourist destinations in Salem are accessible on foot—park your car for the day and enjoy the walk. The Salem Witch Museum (978-744-1692—the last four digits of the phone number are no coincidence—or www.salemwitchmuseum.com) is located on Washington Square, just across from the Salem Common. Witch House (978-744-0180) is located at 310 1/2 Essex Street. The House of the Seven Gables (978-744-0991

or www.7Gables.org) is at 54 Turner Street. The Haunted Happenings
hotline is 978-744-0013; www.salemhauntedhappenings.com.

Salem is justifiably famous for two things. Its port once served as the
launching site for ships bound for India, China, Europe, and the Carib-
bean, giving the town its nineteenth-century nickname as the "Venice of
the New World." Fortunes were made and lost on the cargoes carried by
these ships: sugar, spices, coffee, china, and—regrettably—African slaves.
Another historical incident mars Salem's past: its role in the witchcraft
hysteria of 1692.

In the winter and spring of 1692, the sleepy village came alive with
witchcraft accusations, arrests, and executions. It began with a group of
young girls, ranging in age from twelve to nineteen, who suddenly experienced "fits" and "distempers" and made "foolish, ridiculous speeches."
They began pointing fingers to explain their odd behavior, claiming that
other people, mostly women, had bewitched them. Throughout the spring,
Salem remained a flurry of uncertainty and accusation, as neighbors
indicted neighbors and the accused individuals were put into jail without
trial. (To be fair, the reason that these "witches" did not get a speedy trial
was that there was no legitimate government in Massachusetts at the time.
The colony's charter had been revoked several years earlier and had not
yet been replaced, so all of Salem had to wait with bated breath until a
new governor, with charter in hand, arrived on May 14, 1692.) One
"witch" was incarcerated in chains for nine months, together with her
four-year-old daughter, Dorcas, who had implicated her mother.

The trials proceeded through the summer of 1692, with the verdict of
"guilty" being rendered in nearly every case. The punishment for witchcraft activity was death, according to the Bible and to English law.
Although popular imagination sees these twenty unfortunates as having
been burned at the stake (as had occurred in Europe throughout the
Middle Ages), all but one were in fact hanged. One accused wizard, Giles
Cory, was pressed to death by heavy stones piled upon his body. It took a
full two days for him to die.

One of the women, as she awaited her hanging, was offered one last
opportunity to confess her sins before God and the gathered crowd. "I am
no more a witch than you are a wizard," she declared to the church's assistant minister. "And if you take away my life, God will give you blood to
drink." No record of this minister's remorse exists, although a gratifying
scene in Nathaniel Hawthorne's novel The House of the Seven Gables has a

fictitious witch-trials judge later choke to death on his own blood. But many of the real-life accusers in Salem found occasion, later in life, to deeply regret their involvement in sending twenty presumably innocent persons to their deaths. In 1697, Samuel Sewall, one of the judges who convicted the accused witches, stood before his congregation and begged for God's forgiveness.

Today, the witchcraft connection has become Salem's stock in trade, making the town one of the most popular tourist destinations in the Boston area. The **Salem Witch Museum** uses a light-and-sound show with thirteen different stage sets to tell the tragic story, while **Witch House**, the 1642 building that was home to trial judge Jonathan Corwin, is the only building remaining that has a direct connection to the witch hysteria. Pretrial hearings and grand jury sessions may have been held here. There is also **The House of the Seven Gables**, immortalized by Nathaniel Hawthorne in his 1851 novel of the same name. Hawthorne had a bit of a connection to the witch trials himself: born Hathorne, he allegedly added

WHY DID THIS HAPPEN IN SALEM?

Although witchcraft accusations—and also executions—were never exactly rare in New England, they were generally isolated incidents. Salem stands alone as the single mass-execution site of accused witches in U.S. history. Its scope was terrifying, and also puzzling. What was different about Salem? Theories range from the geographic (all of the accused lived in Salem Village, while all of the accusers resided in Salem Town) to the socioeconomic. One scholar has discovered that many of the accused female witches in New England owned or stood to inherit property, thereby interfering with the customary pattern of passing property from father to son. Other historians have focused on the fact that young girls—a group without much social power in Puritan America—were the primary accusers, perhaps reflecting intergenerational and gender-based tensions. And while traditional accounts have centered on the idea that Tituba, the Carib Indian slave who belonged to the town's Puritan minister, first taught Salem's young girls about Vodou and "black magic," Elaine Breslaw's book *Tituba, Reluctant Witch of Salem* argues that Tituba probably taught them nothing of the kind. Whatever the case, Salem's history will continue to disturb and fascinate students of human nature, if not the supernatural.

the "w" to his surname to distance himself from his ancestor John Hathorne, a Salem witch trials judge.

Charter Street Cemetery is the burial site for two of the witchcraft trial judges, and a memorial to the twenty victims of 1692 is imbedded in the sidewalk just to the east of the burial ground. Because witches were believed to be in league with Satan, they were not permitted a Christian burial, and their bodies were tossed into a shallow pit near the gallows.

Salem as a tourist destination is not all gloom and doom, however. There are interesting shops vending all manner of witch kitsch, capitalizing on Salem's reputation today as a haven for self-described witches who are attracted to the spot because of its spiritual history. Things really heat up in October, when the town readies its tourist act for Halloween. Salem's Haunted Happenings, which typically run for the last three weeks in October, include special tours, costume balls, psychic fairs, haunted houses, and the like.

NEARBY

➥ Founded in 1799, the **Peabody Essex Museum** in Salem is the nation's oldest continuously operating museum. It specializes in maritime artifacts and the decorative arts of China, Korea, Japan, India, and other parts of the world. In 2003, the museum's 100,000-square-foot, $100 million expansion will open its doors to visitors. It features six new art galleries, public gardens, a public memorial park, and a three-story glass atrium. *East India Square, Salem. From Boston, take I-93 North to Exit 37A (which is I-95 North) to Route 128 North. Take Exit 25A. Follow route 114 East into Salem. In Salem, follow the signs to the Salem Visitor Center, Museum, and Historic Sites. Admission fee. From April through October, the museum is open Monday through Saturday from 10 A.M. to 5 P.M. and Sunday from noon to 5 P.M. From November to March, it is closed on Mondays.* ☎ 978-745-9500 🖳 www.pem.org

➥ The 114 acres of **Sedgwick Gardens at Long Hill** in **Beverly**, feature two miles of woodland walking paths, several ponds, an apple orchard, and an estate garden. *572 Essex Street, Beverly. From Route 128, take Exit 18 (Route 22) and go north for 1.3 miles. Bear left at the fork in the road, and continue for two-tenths of a mile to the brick gate entrance on the left. The grounds are open daily from 8 A.M. to sunset. Donation requested.* ☎ 978-921-1944 🖳 www.thetrustees.org

➥ Constructed in 1909, the Romanesque Revival **Congregation Agudath Sholom (Walnut Street Synagogue)** is the work of architect Harry

Dustin Joll. When this synagogue was built, nearly a third of the population of **Chelsea** was Jewish. Today the congregation is far smaller, but the synagogue is still in use, making it one of the longest continuously operating Orthodox shuls in New England. Be sure to see the wall frescoes, painted by local turn-of-the-century Jewish artists. *145 Walnut Street, Chelsea.* ☎ 617-884-8668

➧ The rambling gardens of **Glen Magna Farms** in **Danvers** have a rather romantic history: The land was originally purchased by a sea captain to conceal the considerable treasures the Americans stole from the British during the War of 1812. In the 1880s, the property was bought by a British landscape architect named Joseph Chamberlain (father of Neville, the prime minister). One of his dear friends, the famous landscape architect Frederick Law Olmsted, helped Chamberlain design the estate's many gardens, including an Italianate perennial garden and the formal Peabody Garden to the rear of the house. *Ingersoll Street, Danvers. The gardens are open weekdays from 9 A.M. to dusk, and weekends from 9 A.M. to noon (the site is quite in demand for weekend afternoon weddings).* ☎ 978-774-9165

➧ In **Ipswich**, home to six generations of the Whipple family, the **John Whipple House and Garden** is a trove of information on seventeenth- and eighteenth-century American life. Of special interest is the recreated Puritan garden, thought to be one of the most authentic examples of a seventeenth-century kitchen garden in America. *1 South Village Green, Ipswich. Open from May through September, Wednesday through Saturday from 10 A.M. to 4 P.M. and Sunday from 1 P.M. to 4 P.M. Admission fee.* ☎ 978-356-2811 🖳 www.ipswichma.com

➧ The modern Conservative Jewish synagogue **Temple Israel**, founded in 1946, is tucked away in a serene residential neighborhood of **Swampscott**. Its hexagonal shape evokes the six-pointed Star of David. This active synagogue attracts many well-known speakers (e.g., Ralph Nader, Desmond Tutu and Lech Walesa) and operates numerous outreach programs. *837 Humphrey Street, Swampscott. From Boston, take Route 1-A North through Revere and Lynn. Follow the signs for Swampscott through the rotary. Follow Route 129 East into Swampscott. Go through the town, and bear left at the Getty gas station. Follow Humphrey Street for one mile. Bear left at the fork, and Temple Israel will be on the right side.* ☎ 781-595-6635 🖳 www.templeisraelswampscott.org

➧ **Rocky Hill Meetinghouse** in **Amesbury**, built in 1785, is considered the most perfectly preserved eighteenth-century meetinghouse in Massachusetts. It has remained essentially unchanged since its construction, with the original high pulpit, three-quarters gallery, and box pews all intact. These pews are the original unfinished wood, mellowed with age. *4 Elm Street, Amesbury. Located on the corner of Elm Street and Rocky Hill Road. Open by appointment. No admission fee.* ☎ 617-227-3956

Somerville

The Nation's First Havurah
HAVURAT SHALOM
Jewish Renewal. 113 College Avenue. Year founded: 1968.
☎ 617-623-3376 🖳 www.TheHav.org

> *T stop: Davis Square on the Red Line. Walk up College Avenue to 113, a five-minute walk. Wheelchair accessible. Shabbat services are held on Friday evenings at 6:30 P.M. (7 P.M. during Daylight Savings Time) and Saturday mornings at 10 A.M.*

Tucked in the quiet residential streets of Somerville is the nation's oldest *havurah*, or lay-led alternative to a synagogue. It was founded in 1968 and had its beginnings in this three-story house as a seminary for young Jewish American men who wished to avoid the draft. (According to draft law at the time, men could be exempt if they demonstrated full-time enrollment in higher education.) From there, it was transformed into an egalitarian community that stressed Jewish renewal and spirituality, offering Shabbat services on Fridays and Saturdays, community holiday observances to mark the major and minor Jewish holidays, and many community events. It is not affiliated with any of the major Jewish movements, although it does have ties to other *havurat* around the country.

Havurat Shalom does not have an ordained rabbi, but relies on its small but very active membership to run the congregation's many programs. Members take turns in planning and leading services and holiday celebrations. They are dedicated to creating gender-inclusive worship services and have even drafted their own English and Hebrew *siddur* (prayer book) for congregational life. Services are mainly in Hebrew and include a fair amount of singing alongside traditional prayer.

Although the membership is small, with approximately thirty full members, Havurat Shalom's classes and outreach programs draw many more participants from Jewish and non-Jewish backgrounds. Classes have dealt with Judaica topics such as Jewish mysticism, feminism, and social justice.

Wellesley

From a Protestant to an Interfaith College Community

HOUGHTON MEMORIAL CHAPEL, WELLESLEY COLLEGE

110 Central Street. Year college founded: 1875. ☎ 781-283-1000
🖳 www.wellesley.edu

From the Massachusetts Turnpike (I-90), take Exit 16 (West Newton).
Follow Route 16 West for 4.7 miles to the town of Wellesley. At the
five-way intersection, go straight on Route 135 West. At the third traffic
light, make a left into the college entrance.

When Wellesley College was founded in 1875, Protestant Christian principles formed the bedrock of its existence. Founder Henry Fowle Durant had been just fifteen years old when he dedicated his life to God's service. In creating Wellesley College nearly four decades later, he offered his land and part of his vast fortune as well. He believed that Bible study should be part of college life and encouraged the young women who attended Wellesley to devote themselves to the pursuit of Christian ideals. The college's motto (*Non ministrari, sed ministrare*) attested to this as well: Young women were not "to be ministered unto, but to minister."

More than a century later, Wellesley's principle of service to humanity remains fully intact, but the religions that serve as vehicles for that service have diversified tremendously. The college was one of the first educational institutions in America to realize that having a single college chaplain—who always happened to be a Protestant—was a bit out of date. In the early 1990s, Wellesley created the position of Dean of Religious Life, one person who would oversee the chaplains for Christian, Muslim, Buddhist, Wiccan, Jewish, Sikh, and Baha'i traditions, among other groups. Wellesley has offered a new model of religious diversity for other campuses, and while its transition from Protestant to multifaith college has not always been easy, it has proven very successful. In 1998, Wellesley sponsored a national conference on religious diversity that examined the challenges and insights to be gained from interfaith awareness, educating people from other campuses and businesses on the importance of religious understanding.

Perhaps no other tradition reflects Wellesley's recent transformation as well as Flower Sunday, the oldest continuous tradition on this campus of old and continuous traditions. Quite early in the college's history, a minister came to campus one Sunday to deliver a message of hellfire and damnation. Founder Durant didn't like that sermon much and decreed that one Sunday a year should be entirely dedicated to the message that "God is love." As the tradition evolved, the chapel was always filled with flowers on that day, with older students (big sisters) offering flowers to younger students (little sisters) to welcome them into the college community. Flower Sunday has kept pace with the campus's changing religious landscape. It is still a colorful, flower-filled celebration, but it now includes African drumming, Hindu dancing, and readings from the Qur'an and the Torah as well as the New Testament.

The Jain Center of Greater Boston in Norwood

NEARBY

➥ Tucked on a quiet side street of **Norwood**, about twelve miles southwest of Boston, is the **Jain Center of Greater Boston**, obscurely housed in a former Swedish Lutheran Church. Please call ahead to make an appointment. Although the Jain community in the United States is small (see page 29), it is growing; this center now has a membership of 275 families. In the spirit of the Jain tradition of *ahimsa* (nonharming), the center sometimes hosts public lectures or seminars on topics of spiritual and ethical interest, and is a regular sponsor of the Boston Vegetarian Food Festival. *15 Cedar Street, Norwood. From Route 128 South (I-95), take the exit for Route 1 South. At the first traffic light, turn right onto Everette Street. Follow Route 1A South, passing through the center of Norwood. At the fork, bear right to continue following 1A South. At the third traffic light after the fork, turn left onto Chapel Street. Then turn right onto Cedar Street. The center is half a block down on the right side. Call for hours and availability.*
☎ 508-762-9490 🖳 www.jainworld.com/society/gboston.htm

Weston

Ignatian Spiritual Retreats
CAMPION RENEWAL CENTER
Roman Catholic (Society of Jesus/Jesuit). 319 Concord Road. Year opened:
1975. ☎ 781-894-3199
🖳 www2.bc.edu/~conlanwa/campion.htm

> *From Route 128, take the Route 20 Exit heading west. After about a mile,*
> *bear right at the fork onto Boston Post Road. Go through Weston Center*
> *and turn right on Concord Road. Go over a railroad pass. Fork left from*
> *Merriam Street. Wind up the hill; Campion is on the left.*

In a quiet suburb twenty miles west of Boston, retreatants at Campion
Renewal Center immerse themselves in Ignatian spirituality. Administered by the Society of Jesus (Jesuits), the center is dedicated to enhancing
people's lives for spiritual renewal. That includes Catholics, but also
people from all faiths and those who have been alienated by organized religion. Here, time is marked by the rhythms of the daily liturgy, and individuals lose themselves in quiet prayer and meditation.

Campion opened as a retreat center in 1975 and provides a variety of
programs to meet guests' needs. Day-long programs discuss how to pray the
psalms, or teach about the cadences and rhythms of the liturgical calendar.
Weekend retreats, which take place in an atmosphere of silence, seek to
encourage retreatants' individual prayer lives, and include instruction in
Ignatian prayer and poetry, beginning prayer, prayer in the Celtic tradition, and the "Stations of Joy" (an Easter equivalent to the stations of the
cross). Longer silent retreats are also available.

NEARBY
➥ The **Center of Traditional Taoist Studies** (formerly the New England
Center of Tao) was founded in 1979. It was the first Taoist temple in the
United States to be recognized by the Quan Zhen Taoists of Shanghai,
China. Dedicated to the practical application of Taoism, the center offers
instruction in Taoist meditation and philosophy, as well as Tai Chi, Kung
Fu, Chi Quong, and holistic healing. Lectures are held on Saturdays. *Apple
Crest Road.* ☎ 781-899-7120 🖳 www.tao.org

West Newbury

A Quiet Anglican Retreat Center
EMERY HOUSE
Episcopalian (Society of St. John the Evangelist). Emery Lane. Retreat house dates to 1745. ☎ 978-462-7940 💻 www.ssje.org

> *From I-95, take Exit 57 (Newburyport/West Newbury). After the ramp, turn right onto Highway 113 and drive 1.1 miles west to Emery Lane, which will be on the right. The lane is marked by a small white sign with the society's name.*

The Society of St. John the Evangelist (SSJE), established in 1866, was the first Anglican order of religious men to be organized after the sixteenth-century Reformation. This British order arrived in Boston in 1870 and today operates the St. Mary and St. John monastery and retreat center near Harvard Square in Cambridge (see page 119). The brothers also have this rural retreat center approximately an hour's drive north of Boston. Here, brothers who have undertaken a life of poverty, celibacy, and obedience pray the Daily Office four times each day, and also celebrate the Eucharist daily. Visitors are always welcome in the monastery chapel, which is open throughout the day and evening for prayer and meditation.

Retreats are offered here for individuals and groups (no larger than fourteen people), and retreatants of all faiths will be warmed by the brothers' tradition of extending hospitality. Most retreat topics relate to issues of prayer and spirituality. Guests can have as much or as little interaction with monastery life as they wish. Emery House is located on 120 acres of woods and fields, bordered by the Merrimack and Artichoke Rivers. A 450-acre state park is adjacent to the property, perfect for contemplative walks.

Retreatants may stay in the main house, which dates to 1745, or in the Coburn hermitages, a group of six cottages that are designed for solitary and group use. Although the word *hermitage* brings to mind a sense of self-mortification, these cottages were designed to be quite comfortable, with rocking chairs, private baths, central heating, wood-burning stoves, and kitchenettes. Meals are simple but scrumptious, featuring primarily vegetarian fare.

CHAPTER FIVE

Central and Western Massachusetts

WHILE MENTION OF BOSTON is likely to conjure images of the nation's most historic city, replete with outstanding restaurants and cultural attractions, the oblique phrase "central and western Massachusetts" is just as likely to elicit blank stares. Many visitors to Massachusetts, who begin their sojourn in Boston and end with a few days on the Cape, are unaware of the delightful charms of the Bay State's interior. In this chapter, we will venture into the land beyond Interstate 495, visiting towns that are as irresistible as they are abundant with spiritual history.

The central and western areas of Massachusetts reflect the state's firm historic ties with Puritanism, as seen in Northampton, the longtime pulpit of New England's most famous eighteenth-century divine, Jonathan Edwards. But these regions are also home to a famous Roman Catholic shrine, the nation's first Buddhist meditation center in the *vipassana* tradition, an interfaith center founded by musician Arlo Guthrie, and the nation's largest research facility for Yiddish-language books. Cultural attractions rival those of Boston, including world-famous music, theater, and dance festivals. The poet Emily Dickinson spent her entire life here, and painter Norman Rockwell adopted western Massachusetts as his adult home. Natural beauty abounds, highlighted by the majesty of the Berkshires and the state's numerous cultivated and wild gardens. So take a few days to enjoy the spirited back roads of central and western Massachusetts.

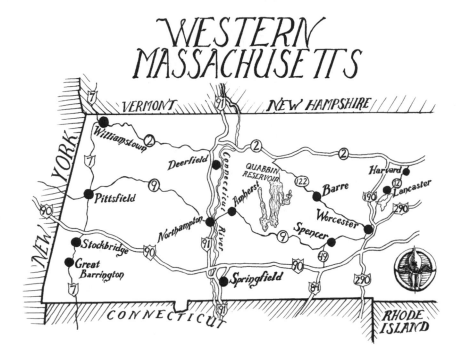

Amherst

The Belle of Amherst
EMILY DICKINSON HOMESTEAD
280 Main Street. Year built: ca. 1813. ☎ 413-542-8161
💻 www.dickinsonhomestead.org

Take I-91 to Exit 19 (Route 9 East). Drive on Route 9 five miles to the Amherst town limits. Once in Amherst, continue straight up a long hill (about 1 mile) to a traffic light. Turn left onto South Pleasant Street toward Amherst Center. At the next light, turn right onto Main Street. The Homestead is three-tenths of a mile ahead. Tours of the Dickinson Homestead are offered on select afternoons from March through mid-December; call for a schedule. If you want to take the combined tour of the Homestead and the Evergreens house next door, you will need to make a reservation ahead of time. Combined tours are offered only a few mornings each week, and are limited to a maximum of twelve people.

One of Amherst's most famous tourist attractions is the home where Emily Dickinson (1830–86) lived most of her life and wrote nearly all of her 1,800 poems. The Dickinson family was very prominent in the Amherst community; Emily's father and grandfather, both lawyers, served in the state legislature, and her father also served one term in the United States House of Representatives. Her grandfather, a staunch Trinitarian (see page 27), helped to found Amherst College as a theologically sound alternative to Harvard after the Cambridge college began to bend toward Unitarianism, which he considered heretical.

Emily experienced surprisingly little pressure to marry, and devoted her life to her writing and her beloved home. A recluse, she was essentially unknown in her lifetime, having published just a few of her poems. In fact, it was not until the publication of her complete works in 1955 that she began to earn the reputation she now holds—as one of America's premier poets.

When Dickinson lived here, the house's red brick exterior was painted a soft yellow, and the land surrounding it was just the fourteen acres of rolling fields owned by her father. The small shrubs that graced the landscape out front in Dickinson's day have grown to majestic trees. Inside

A ROAD LESS TRAVELED

"Stopping by woods on a snowy evening"? Then there is a lovely hiking trail that you must not miss. A path has been created in honor of Amherst's other famous literary resident (apart from the reclusive Dickinson)—twentieth-century poet laureate Robert Frost (1874–1963), who taught at Amherst College for more than two decades. Frost's stunning poetic images of apple orchards and bucolic retreats have become, for many Americans, the quintessence of New England. In 1982, a group of conservationists sought to preserve a portion of the land that Frost loved so deeply. The **Robert Frost Trail** connects nine towns in the Central Connecticut River Valley, encompassing both public and private lands. Forty miles long, this pedestrian path is one of the five longest hiking trails in the state and is marked by bright orange blazes. *Begin the hiking trail at Holyoke Range State Park in South Hadley. Brochures are available from The Kestrel Trust, P.O. Box 1016, Amherst, Mass. 01004, or at the Notch Visitors Center at Holyoke Range State Park.* ☎ 413-253-2883
🖳 www.amherstcommon.com/recreation/rftrail.html

the house, great efforts have been made to restore the rooms to their nineteenth-century state. Emily and her sister lived here until their deaths (Emily died in 1886, Lavinia in 1899).

The highlight of the tour is Emily Dickinson's bedroom on the second floor, which features her writing table and a bed that was almost certainly hers. In this room, she wrote poetry and copious letters (of which more than a thousand survive), contemplated ethereal things, watched the town's comings and goings, and read voraciously. Although she rarely left the confines of her home and garden after age thirty, she remained vitally interested in the world until her death.

The Nation's Largest Center for Yiddish Books
NATIONAL YIDDISH BOOK CENTER
1021 West Street. Year opened: 1997. Architect: Allen Moore.
☎ 413-256-4900 or 800-535-3595 🖥 www.yiddishbooks.com

From Amherst Center, take Route 116 South and go three miles to the main entrance of Hampshire College. Turn right on to the campus, then left at the first intersection. The National Yiddish Book Center is a quarter mile past the intersection, on the left. The center is open Sunday through Friday from 10 A.M. to 3:30 P.M., and is closed on Saturdays, Jewish holidays, and national holidays. No admission fee.

Tucked away in a lovely apple orchard on the campus of Hampshire College in Amherst is one of the most exciting Jewish sites in New England: the National Yiddish Book Center. In 1980, Aaron Lansky, a twenty-three-year-old graduate student in Yiddish literature, realized that tens of thousands of Yiddish books were being rapidly lost, possibly forever, as English-speaking Jews of the second and third generations threw away inherited Yiddish books that they could no longer understand. Lansky set about on an ambitious crusade to rescue these books, organizing a national campaign of *zamlers* (volunteers) to collect and catalog them.

When he began his campaign, scholars guessed that there were just 70,000 Yiddish books in existence, but in fact the center has collected 1.5 *million* Yiddish books since 1980, and they keep pouring in at the rate of 1,000 books a week. The National Yiddish Book Center is not a lending library, but a research facility and a clearinghouse for the purchase of Yiddish books. While in 1980, only a few libraries maintained Yiddish col-

National Yiddish Book Center, Amherst

lections, the center now sells books to over 450 libraries around the world, including one in mainland China.

Amherst may seem an unlikely spot for the world's foremost center for the preservation of Yiddish books, but that is intentional. Hampshire College was chosen, in part, because Lansky is an alumnus, but more importantly because he felt that bucolic western Massachusetts is a "Jewishly neutral location." The center is not affiliated with any of the Jewish divisions (Reform, Conservative, Orthodox, Reconstructionist) in America.

The center is housed in a beautiful 1997 wooden building, a 37,000-square-foot space designed by architect Allen Moore to be comfortable and full of light. Lansky and his supporters wanted a structure that would resemble, but not caricature, an Eastern European *shtetl*—yet that would also fit seamlessly into the New England landscape. The eight-million-dollar structure was built with the support of large-scale philanthropists (such as Steven Spielberg's Righteous Persons Foundation) and the smaller donations of more than 9,300 of the center's members.

Visitors to the center are treated to a brief but valuable tour and then invited to wander the building, the exhibits, and the excellent bookstore, which features mostly English-language books and gifts. They are also welcome to roam the stacks, which contain about 100,000 of the center's current collection of 1.5 million Yiddish books. (The others are in a warehouse facility in Holyoke, eight miles away.)

One of the highlights is the Yiddish theater, an interactive exhibit that teaches visitors about the importance of Yiddish drama, comedy, and music. It contains a "listening corner" with an old wind-up Victrola and headphones, where guests can listen to Yiddish radio broadcasts dating from 1925 to 1955. As part of its ongoing commitment to help visitors understand the importance of Yiddish culture, the center offers many lectures, concerts, and screenings of the 300 Yiddish films that have now been restored (with English subtitles). On many Sunday afternoons, the center hosts special speakers and performers. Some of the events are especially for children, such as a Yiddish reading of *Vini-der-Pu* (a.k.a. Winnie the Pooh). Donations are welcome, to help preserve the precious *yerushah* (legacy) of Yiddish culture.

NEARBY

➡ **Second Congregational Church/Jewish Community of Amherst.** During the Revolutionary War, a number of Amherst's patriots were dissatisfied with First Congregational Church pastor David Parsons's Tory sympathies. They founded this church in protest. The original building was razed in 1839 to make way for this roomier structure in the Greek Revival style. In 1976, the dwindling Congregational membership sold the building and merged once again with First Church—history coming full circle. The building is now home to a faith that the Puritans had, once upon a time, banished to Rhode Island (see page 81): Judaism. The Jewish Community of Amherst has a membership that includes Reconstructionist, Reform, Conservative, and cultural Jews, and its program offers weekly Shabbat services, holiday celebrations, a Hebrew school, and an adult education program. Services are held in the sanctuary, with its *bimah*, white pews, organ, and stained-glass windows. *742 Main Street.*
☎ 413-256-0160 🖳 www.j-c-a.org/
➡ Marked only by a plaque, it's easy to miss the important **Amherst Academy Site** on Amity Street. From 1814 to 1861, this lot housed the three-story brick school that educated several of New England's most important religious figures, including poet Emily Dickinson, Mary Lyon (the founder of nearby Mount Holyoke College), and Sylvester Graham, the Presbyterian minister who invented a unique dietary system in the nineteenth century (see sidebar). In the 1860s, local African Americans used the crumbling structure as a meetinghouse, serving both religious and political needs. Frederick Douglass once lectured here, as did other prominent activists in the post–Civil War cause of uplifting African Americans. The original building was demolished in 1868. *Amity Street.*

THE ORIGINS OF
THE GRAHAM CRACKER

One of the Amherst Academy's most famous students was Sylvester Graham (1795–1851), who was once mocked in the press as the "Philosopher of Sawdust Pudding." This was because Graham, a Presbyterian minister and reformer, believed that refined white flour was dangerous for the human body and soul. In his 1837 "Treatise on Bread, and Bread Making," he advocated a strict diet of "Graham flour," a coarsely ground whole-grain flour that should be baked into homemade bread. He encouraged followers to grind their own wheat and decried the "artificial process" of removing the natural bran from the whole grain. He was also a vegetarian who believed that the consumption of meat defiled human beings and caused them to adopt base, animal behavior. While many ridiculed Graham's teachings, others jumped onto his dietary bandwagon; many boarding-houses and restaurants throughout the 1840s advertised themselves as serving "Graham bread."

Some of Graham's ideas, such as the importance of whole grains and vegetables to a healthy diet, are now embraced by the medical establishment. And of course, there is the cracker that bears his name—but it is unlikely that Graham himself would have been pleased at this particular turn of events, since much of his message involved the rejection of all processed foods.

Barre

Vipassana *Meditation in a Bucolic Setting*
INSIGHT MEDITATION SOCIETY
Theravada Buddhist. 1230 Pleasant Street. Year founded: 1975.
☎ 978-355-4378 🖳 www.dharma.org

Insight Meditation Society is located approximately two miles north of Barre. From the Massachusetts Turnpike, take Exit 8 (Palmer), then Route 32 approximately twenty-five miles north to Barre. In Barre, take Route 122/32 one block past the library and post office. Do not follow 122/32 as it wends left after the post office, but bear right onto Pleasant Street, and drive for 2.2 miles. The IMS will be on your right.

In 1975, a group of Theravada Buddhists (see sidebar below) founded a *vipassana* retreat center here on eighty acres in Central Massachusetts. The goal of *vipassana*, or "insight meditation," is "the moment-to-moment observation of the mind/body process through calm and focused awareness." This is accomplished in near-total silence, as serious meditators learn to understand the constantly changing nature of existence. Meditation can take place individually or in groups, while sitting, walking, or working, but always with the goal of increased insight into the mind-body process.

IMS welcomes beginning *vipassana* students for group retreats throughout the year. A typical day begins at 5 A.M., with most of the retreat time spent in some form of meditation. Daily instruction is offered, as well as evening discourses on various aspects of meditation. It should be noted that some of the most significant movers and shakers in the world of Buddhism are featured speakers at IMS each year; Jack Kornfield, Sharon Salzberg, and other luminaries maintain close ties. Some of the evening discourses are open to the public; please call in advance for a schedule and to inquire about attendance restrictions. More experienced meditators— that is, anyone who has practiced meditation in a similar *vipassana* style— may schedule individual retreats.

All retreatants should be aware that a strict code of silence is observed at IMS, and that other distractions—even reading—are not seen as helpful to meditation. Meals are vegetarian and served buffet-style.

BUDDHIST TRADITIONS
IN THE UNITED STATES

Buddhism has changed significantly since its beginnings in India in the sixth century B.C.E.. As it passed through nations as diverse as China, Thailand, Japan, and Tibet, Buddhism became layered over indigenous cultural and religious practices. This resulted in many different national Buddhist traditions, most of which have emigrated to the United States, all under the umbrella of "Buddhism." They do share basic doctrines: a worldview that sees suffering as endemic to the human condition, and desire as the basic cause of suffering; an emphasis on the personal story of the Buddha as a man who renounced worldly things and discovered enlightenment; a pacifist perspective; a reliance on the practice of meditation to help others come to enlightenment; and the goal of nonattachment. All Buddhists take refuge in the "Three Jewels": the Buddha, the Dharma (teaching), and the Sangha (the enlightened community).

But there are also many differences. Buddhism is a tolerant and syncretic philosophical system, and as it spread to diverse cultures it adapted to its local environs. There are two basic divisions within Buddhism. Theravada ("Tradition of the Elders") Buddhism is more widespread in southeast Asian cultures such as Thailand, Sri Lanka, Burma, and Cambodia. It emphasizes meditation techniques, two of which are called *vipassana* and *shamatha*, and the importance of mindful breathing. The other major strand of Buddhism is called Mahayana ("Great Vehicle"), and is most prevalent in China, Japan, Korea, Vietnam and Tibet. The teachings of love and compassion take center stage in Mahayana Buddhism, though the various schools within Mahayana (Pure Land, Zen/Ch'an, and Vajrayana, for example) have adopted a variety of practices.

In the United States, Mahayana Buddhism has been more popular than Theravada, but immigration patterns and increasing interest may change this somewhat. Zen Buddhism (from Japan) has had a significant impact in the United States, as has the Dalai Lama, the exiled spiritual leader of Tibetan Buddhism. Buddhism in the United States—what scholar James Coleman has called the "New Buddhism"—blends ancient Eastern traditions with Western emphases on egalitarianism and individualization. Many American Buddhists mix different elements of the various schools of Buddhism together, or even merge Buddhist practice with belief in Western religions such as Judaism and Christianity.

Dedicated to the Study of All Buddhist Traditions
BARRE CENTER FOR BUDDHIST STUDIES
149 Lockwood Road. ☎ 978-355-2347 🖳 www.dharma.org/bcbs

Follow the same directions as for IMS. Lockwood Road intersects Pleasant Street one-half mile before IMS. Turn right onto Lockwood Road. The Barre Center for Buddhist Studies is set back from the road, so watch carefully.

Although the Barre Center for Buddhist Studies does not grant academic degrees, many individuals who come here earn professional and academic credits for their time from their own educational institutions. That's because the center is a serious institution in its own right, with a library of several thousand volumes and programs for students of all levels. The center, which maintains close ties to the Insight Meditation Society nearby, sits on ninety acres of wooded land, and its primary facilities exist in a renovated eighteenth-century farmhouse.

The Barre Center is at the vanguard of a movement emphasizing dialogue among different Buddhist traditions. In the United States today, practitioners can find centers offering every form of Buddhism under the sun; this diversity is found nowhere else in the world. The Barre Center believes that this unprecedented situation offers a unique opportunity for intra-Buddhist discussion and learning. Its library contains volumes on Theravadan, Tibetan, and Zen Buddhism, including original-language works as well as English translations. A second focus of study is the inter-action of Buddhism with other world religions.

The center can accommodate up to forty-five students for a weekend, and has twenty spots for longer-term residential courses. One-day courses are also available. In addition to dormitory facilities, there are now two cottages on the grounds to accommodate the scholars and advanced students who comprise the independent study program. Recently, the Barre Center also opened a branch campus in Cambridge, Massachusetts.

Deerfield and the Mohawk Trail

A Restored Colonial Community
HISTORIC DEERFIELD
☎ 413-774-5581 🖳 www.historic-deerfield.org

> *Historic Deerfield is located ninety miles west of Boston. Coming from Springfield on I-91 North, take Exit 24. Go six miles north on Routes 5/10 and turn left into the historic village. The museum houses and museum store are open 362 days a year from 9:30 A.M. to 4:30 P.M. Admission fee. Visitors can purchase a one-museum pass or a general admission ticket that is valid for one week.*

When the Works Progress Administration compiled its classic guide to Massachusetts in 1937, it lauded Deerfield as "not so much a town as the ghost of a town," saying that "to all intents, nothing has happened there for two hundred years. . . . The whole history of its greatness is crowded into the first three decades of its existence, the violent and dreadful years from 1672 to 1704, when it was the northwest frontier of New England,

The **Mahican-Mohawk Trail** is a 100-mile modern trail that aims to retrace the path that many Native American groups used when they traveled in the area. Roughly tracing the path of the Connecticut, Deerfield, Hoosic, and Hudson rivers, the route has been carved as closely as possible to the original footpath. Although the most prominent native group in western Massachusetts was once the Pocumtuck, by the colonial period, when this path was named, the Mohawk had annihilated the Pocumtuck, and the trail bears the Mohawk name.

The modern trail was created in 1914, the first scenic route in New England. It begins in historic Deerfield, winding its way northwest through Williamstown and into southern Vermont and northwestern New York. It is primarily a motor route, so it makes a convenient, educational, and beautiful thoroughfare for tourists traveling west from Deerfield. Part of the route can be traveled by foot through the beautiful country of the Mohawk Trail State Forest. *For more information, call the Mohawk Trail Association at* ☎ 413-743-8127 🖳 www.mohawktrail.com

On the Mohawk Trail

the spearhead of English civilization in an unknown and hostile country." Today, Deerfield residents are bound to protest the WPA's assertion that nothing interesting has occurred there since 1704, but it is certainly true that it offers a mecca for travelers interested in colonial, Native American, and religious history. Visitors will find these interests sated at Historic Deerfield, a painstakingly restored colonial town in the Connecticut River Valley. Many of the houses along the village's one-mile stretch are privately owned, but more than a dozen buildings are open to the public.

Deerfield was founded in 1669, and for the next century found itself the target of numerous attacks by both Native Americans, who felt that the English were encroaching ever farther into their land, and the French. Deerfield's most famous raid occurred on the night of February 28, 1704, when a party composed of Abenaki, Pennacook, Huron, and Mohawk (*Kanien'kehaka*) Indians successfully attacked the enclosed fortification around the center of the town.

The raid tore some families apart. Reverend John Williams (1664–1729), the Congregational minister of the town, saw his two youngest

EUNICE WILLIAMS,
"THE UNREDEEMED CAPTIVE"

The Mohawk (*Kanien'kehaka*) Indians who captured Reverend Williams's seven-year-old daughter Eunice were not interested in trading her for profit. She was adopted into an extended Mohawk family and raised as a member of the Mohawk nation. She received a new name, *A'ongote*, which meant something akin to "taken and made a member of the tribe." Within two years of her kidnapping, Eunice had forgotten how to speak English, and by 1713—even worse, in her father's eyes—she had been rebaptized and confirmed as a Catholic. Although the Williams family lobbied extensively for her return, Eunice chose to remain with the Mohawk. As a teenager, she married a tribe member and had at least three children. After her father's death, her brother wrote and persuaded her to make the journey to Deerfield for a visit, bringing her children with her. This opened the door for three more visits before her death. Today, many descendents of Eunice Williams still live in the region of Kahnawake, Quebec, and have gathered in Deerfield with other Williams descendents for family reunions.

children (including baby Jerusha, just six weeks old) hacked to death as the older children and adults were gathered up as captives for the long winter march to Quebec. Many New England captives were sold by Native Americans to the French, who in turn used them as leverage in negotiations with the English to release French prisoners held in Boston. Nearly every Deerfield household suffered losses; of the 109 people captured, twenty-one died en route, twenty-nine remained in Quebec for the rest of their lives, and fifty-nine were eventually "redeemed" (returned home). Williams's wife Eunice could not survive the journey and perished en route to Quebec. Within a few years, Reverend Williams and all but one of his children—also named Eunice—had been returned home.

Deerfield's Local History
MEMORIAL HALL MUSEUM
8 Memorial Street. Year founded: 1880. ☎ 413-774-3768
 www.old-deerfield.org/museum.htm

> *Open daily from May through October, 9:30 A.M. to 4:30 P.M. At the corner of Memorial Street and Routes 5 and 10. Follow directions for Historic Deerfield. Admission fee.*

Memorial Hall, the oldest building of the Deerfield Academy, opened as a local history museum in 1880, making it one of the first community museums in the country. It's a hodgepodge of artifacts. The centerpiece of the second floor is possibly the most interesting exhibit in the museum, called "Deerfield: The Many Stories of 1704." The display reflects recent historians' commitment to presenting a native perspective, recognizing that in the events leading up to the raid, the English settlers had butchered and displaced many Native Americans. The exhibit also depicts the pro-English traditional party line about the 1704 raid being a brutal Indian massacre. (An entire wall of nineteenth-century plaques memorializes those town members lost as "victims to starvation or the tomahawk.") The exhibit contains an enormous door with a hole in the center—the hole allegedly put there the night of the attack, when the raiding party tried to hack their way through the solid structure of the Sheldon House and could not do so.

HISTORIC DEERFIELD

The Ashley House, the last house on the left side as you walk from the Information Center, was the home of Reverend Jonathan Ashley for almost half a century, from about 1730 (when it was built) until his death on August 8, 1780. He was the town's second minister (following in the famed footsteps of Reverend John Williams), and an unabashed Tory during the Revolutionary War. One of the town's stories (possibly apocryphal) holds that one member of his congregation became so angry when Ashley had preached a pro-England message that the following Sunday, Ashley stood up to preach and found his pulpit locked.

The original stockade is designated with a box on all maps of historic Deerfield. It includes what is now the First Church of Deerfield. First Church, which has merged the community's first Congregational and Unitarian congregations, is not open to the public for tours but welcomes visitors for Sunday worship. Also included within the boundaries of the original stockade are Deerfield Academy, the quintessential New England preparatory school, and the Barnard Tavern, the town's watering hole at the end of the eighteenth century.

The Old Burying Ground, Historic Deerfield

Be sure to see **The Old Burying Ground**, a few blocks west of the Town Common. Here lie John Williams and both of his wives—Eunice, who perished on the harsh captivity trek north to Quebec, and his second wife, Abigail, with whom he spent a relatively peaceful old age. Their red sandstone graves lie in the center of the small cemetery, surrounded by two tall trees. Abigail's tombstone is unusual in that it contains a clock face depicting the continuing passage of time, rather than the more typical Puritan hourglass to indicate the finite nature of time. Eunice's tombstone notes that she "fell by the rage of ye Barbarous Enemy March 1, 1703/4." The scripture verse chosen for the epitaph is ironic, considering that her namesake daughter was raised a Catholic and a "barbarian" by her captors: "Prov. 31:28. Her children arise up & call her Blessed." Other tombstones in the burying ground also speak to the irrevocable tragedy wrought the night of the raid; one memorial stone refers to a man who was carried captive into Quebec and never returned.

NEARBY

➧ Eight miles west of Greenfield in **Shelburne Falls** is the **Vipassana Meditation Community**, one of the first *vipassana* centers in the United States (established in 1982). Its meditation programs, which typically last ten days or longer, now attract more than 1,500 students each year. From its original eight acres, the Community now owns 100 acres of rolling farmland; a special outdoor pagoda offers advanced students a serene spot for meditation. *386 Colrain-Shelburne Road, Shelburne Falls. From I-91, take Exit 26. Follow Route 2 West (Mohawk Trail) toward North Adams. After about 3.5 miles, turn right at Strawberryfield Antiques, heading toward Colrain. Follow this road for about two miles, passing Orchard Hill Antiques. The Center is on the left side of the road, a large white building with blue trim.* ☎ 413-625-2160 🖳 www.dhara.dhamma.org/

➧ South of Historic Deerfield, but not within walking distance, is an unusual used bookstore that is worth a detour. It's one of many examples of Congregational churches in New England that have been adapted to serve new uses (see sidebar below). Called **Meetinghouse Books**, it contains over 20,000 volumes and is especially strong in literature, history and the arts. *70 North Main Street. The shop is generally open Wednesday to Friday from 10 A.M. to 6 P.M., and weekends from 12 P.M. to 6 P.M., though the friendly owners note that they are also open "other times by chance or by appointment."* ☎ 413-665-0500 🖳 www.meetinghousebooks.com

NEW WINE IN OLD WINESKINS

From colonial times, New England churches were meant to be practical. The classic style of a New England meetinghouse called for simplicity of design, so that worshipers would not be distracted from their spiritual purpose by worldly trappings. The traditional decorations of New England churches included a bell, a weathervane, and a clock—all fundamentally pragmatic design elements (see page 40). Form followed function.

Due to the numerical decline of the established New England denominations (most of the former Puritan/Congregational churches are now called United Church of Christ, and the Anglicans became Episcopalians after the Revolution), many of these traditional meetinghouses have been sold off. Some, like the Second Congregational Church of Amherst, have remained religious communities; that church is now home to the Jewish Community of Amherst (see page 166). Others have become commercial enterprises, such as Meetinghouse Books in Deerfield, or have been converted to private homes. (The First and Second Congregational Churches in Newport, Rhode Island are now luxury condominiums.) Perhaps none has had a more fascinating history than Trinity Church in Housatonic, now home to the Guthrie Interfaith Spiritual Center (see page 180). Whatever their current use, the thrifty New England character has demanded that these functional buildings be recycled to meet the needs of new generations.

Harvard

A Transcendental Experiment
FRUITLANDS
102 Prospect Hill Road. Year founded: 1843. ☎ 978-456-3924
🖳 www.fruitlands.org

Fruitlands is located approximately six miles from the junction of Route 2 and Interstate 495 near the town of Harvard. Take Route 2 to Exit 38A. Bear right at the end of the ramp and take the first right onto Old Shirley Road. Fruitlands will be on your right after two miles. From mid-May to

the end of October, the museum is open daily from 10 A.M. to 5 P.M.
Admission fee.

Just as California proved a haven for experimental religious movements in the 1960s and 1970s, New England was home to a number of utopian communities in the 1840s and 1850s. This was an era of political unrest, intense debate over moral issues such as slavery, and a softening of many of the restrictive Calvinist doctrines of the past. Many embraced the teachings of Unitarianism (see page 26). Some believed that Unitarianism's creedless Christianity was simply not radical enough; literary leader Ralph Waldo Emerson, who had been one of New England's pioneering Unitarian ministers, traded in his clergy robes for something new altogether—a spiritual movement called Transcendentalism (see page 139). Emerson had for a long period been itching within the constraints of organized religion, even one so liberal as Unitarianism. In "The Lord's Supper," his final sermon to his congregation, he expressed some of his doubts to the flock. "Two of the evangelists, namely Matthew and John, were present" on the occasion of the last supper, he said. "Neither of them drops the slightest intimation of any intention on the part of Jesus to set up anything permanent." From rituals and sacred texts and institutions, Emerson turned to inner wisdom and nature and the individual. And while he may not have persuaded any of his parishioners with that farewell sermon, many others were attracted to what became known as Transcendentalism.

Several years into the movement, Bronson Alcott (1799–1888), a philosopher and Transcendentalist of great repute, conceived the idea of starting a utopian community in Harvard. Here, the Transcendentalists' lofty ideals of individualism would be carried out: There would be few rules, and the faithful could decide for themselves how to spend their days and cultivate their spiritual interests. They called their community Fruitlands, after the orchards they expected would keep the community self-sufficient. The members eschewed the ownership of personal property, transferring ownership of Fruitlands to a trustee and sharing all things in common. They began each day with an ice-cold bath and adhered to a strict Graham diet (see page 167) of whole grains, fruits, and vegetables. Most radically, they wore simple brown linen tunics designed by Alcott, who rejected wool because it was the coat of an animal, cotton because it was grown using slave labor, and silk because it required the lives of innocent silkworms.

The Fruitlands community commenced with high ideals in June of

1843. Bronson Alcott, his wife Abigail, and their four daughters were the core members. (One of these daughters was Louisa May, then just ten years old; see page 140.) The other participants reflected a hodgepodge of the reform movements of the day: One was a Transcendentalist who had previously lived at Brook Farm (another utopian community in West Roxbury, Massachusetts) and was rumored to have subsisted for an entire year on crackers, and another year just on apples. Another later embraced the teachings of Shakerism. With the exception of Mrs. Alcott and one other woman who lived at Fruitlands for a short time, all of the adult residents were men.

After Fruitlands had been up and running for a month, the Alcotts' good friend Emerson came to visit. "I will not prejudge them successful," he wrote in his diary. "They look well in July; we will see them in December." Emerson's words were prophetic. By winter, it became clear that the experiment's emphasis on individual cultivation meant that no one was cultivating the orchards. The crops were neglected, and the bulk of the chores had fallen squarely on Mrs. Alcott's shoulders. At harvest time, her husband had taken off on a proselytizing tour, seeking converts for his utopian experiment. In January, the community evaporated and the various individuals went their separate ways. Louisa May, who eventually came to support the family through her successful writing career, later wrote a hilarious parody of Fruitlands called *Transcendental Wild Oats*. In it, she speculated that one of the former utopians who had since joined the Shakers found the Shaker community to be precisely the opposite of the Fruitlands group, meaning that "the order of things was reversed, and it was all work and no play."

Today, the Fruitlands farmhouse has been restored and is part of a four-building museum called Fruitlands, which "offers an intimate look at 5,000 years of life on the land in New England." The other buildings include a Shaker Museum (housed in an original Harvard Shaker community building, moved to this site in 1920), an American Indian Museum, and a picture gallery with landscapes by the Hudson River School. Visitors can also see an authentic Native American wigwam and hear an introduction to ancient native land practices. There are three miles of walking trails at Fruitlands, including some of the most spectacular panoramic views in New England atop Prospect Hill.

> ". . . Nature is the symbol of the spirit."
> —Ralph Waldo Emerson, *Nature*

NEARBY

➡ **The Harvard Shaker Community**, which operated from 1791 to 1918, is not a working museum. The original Shaker Trustees' Office was moved to Fruitlands, just a few miles away, for historic preservation in 1920. Many of the sites here are now private homes, and visitors are therefore strongly encouraged to remain on the roads and designated conservation trails so as not to disturb the owners. Having said that, the Harvard community is listed on the National Register of Historic Places, and there is still a good deal that is of interest here, including a special Shaker cemetery. This one-acre burying ground is unique among Shaker communities in that it has preserved the tombstone markers of individual Shakers, including their death dates. These are called "lollipop" markers because of their unusual shape. *The Harvard Shaker Village Historic District is located on Shaker Road. A brochure is available for a self-guided walking or driving tour of the Harvard Shaker community, and can be picked up at the Fruitlands museum or by writing to Harvard Shaker 200 Committee, Harvard, Massachusetts, 01451.*

➡ Designed by famous architect Charles Bulfinch in 1816, the **First Church of Christ (Unitarian)** in **Lancaster** is often cited as an example of the full flowering of New England meetinghouse style. Located on the coveted property of the town common, First Church dominates the community's center, its federalist dome replacing the tall spire that is more typical of New England churches. The church was restored in 1987 and is in pristine condition. *Town Green, Lancaster. Follow Route 2 to Lancaster, then turn south on Main Street.* ☎ 978-365-2427

➡ In the village of **Stow**, the **Sri Akshar Purushottam Swaminarayan Hindu Temple** occupies a former Congregational Church. While the building's exterior appears to be a traditional nineteenth-century Protestant church (complete with a cross atop the building), its interior is alive with vibrant colors and shrines to the gods. This Hindu *mandir* (temple) opened in 1990 and is part of the Bochasanwasi Shree Akshar Purushottam Swaminarayan sect (BAPS). Bochasanwasi Hindus believe that the spirit of Lord Vishnu once inhabited the body of an Indian saint, Lord Swaminarayan (1781–1830 C.E.), and that each successor of Lord Swaminarayan is also an incarnation of the divine. BAPS is a "socio-spiritual organization" that emphasizes volunteerism, health, education, environmentalism, and other reforms. The five principal vows of the faith prohibit stealing, adultery, alcohol, meat, and impurity of body and mind. *4 Marlboro Road, Stow. From I-495, take Exit 26 for Route 62 (Hudson and Berlin). Take Route 62 East through Hudson into Stow. The mandir is 100 yards after the Stow city limit sign.* ☎ 978-562-0727 🖳 www.swaminarayan.org

Housatonic

....

Alice's Restaurant
THE GUTHRIE CENTER/THE INTERFAITH
SPIRITUAL CENTER
4 Van Deusenville Road. Year consecrated: 1991 as an interfaith center
(Episcopal congregation dated to 1829). ☎ 413-528-1955
🖳 www.guthriecenter.org

> *Old Trinity Church, which houses the Guthrie Center, is located in*
> *Housatonic, near Great Barrington. From Housatonic, take Front Street*
> *heading south out of town. It will turn into Van Deusenville Road (total*
> *distance, about two miles). The center is open from 11 A.M. to 4 P.M. on*
> *Tuesday through Friday.*

You can get any religion you want at Alice's restaurant. But how that
came to pass is something of a long story. The lovely church building that
now houses the Guthrie Interfaith Spiritual Center wasn't always a haven
for all faiths. It was originally Trinity Church, a by-the-book Episcopal
congregation that arose in 1829, when western Massachusetts experienced
a healthy financial boom from the iron industry. Trinity Church was all
about the Holy Trinity (to counterbalance that Unitarian "heresy" sweeping through Massachusetts—see page 27): There were three steps leading
to the altar, three sides to the stained-glass windows, three petals on the
lilies featured in those windows, and a triangular shape to the building.
The church was a monument to a Christian God as three-in-one.

After the Great Depression, which hit this industrial region particularly hard, the congregation of Trinity Church fell on difficult times. Its
mother church deconsecrated the building and put it up for sale in the
early 1960s, never guessing who the eventual owners might be. In later
years, the bishop of western Massachusetts was so upset by what happened
at Trinity that he issued a decree that all deconsecrated Episcopal churches
within his jurisdiction were to be torn down rather than used in ways "dis-
turbing to the faithful."

What disturbed the faithful was seeing "long-haired youths in strange
clothes driving their motorcycles up a ramp and right through the church
door," as Laura Lee recounts in her book *Arlo, Alice, & Anglicans: The*

The Guthrie
Center,
Housatonic

Lives of a New England Church. Ray and Alice Brock, a young couple with high ideals, had spent $2,000 to purchase the church and a bit more to convert it into their home. They opened it to youth from all walks of life, offering meals and a floor to sleep on, no questions asked. Dozens of youth found sanctuary in the old sanctuary.

Unexpected fame came when musician Arlo Guthrie (son of folk singer Woody Guthrie) spent Thanksgiving here in 1965 and offered to take the garbage out. Noticing that garbage already cluttered a nearby hill, he and his companion merely added their trash to the heap. They were arrested for littering, and spent a night in jail. He described the whole experience in his most famous song, "Alice's Restaurant Massacree," an eighteen-minute epic declaration for peace, youth, and American freedom. It is still a cult favorite—the most requested song on Thanksgiving Day at some radio stations, although its excessive length prevented it from ever topping the singles charts.

Even more memorably, the story became the inspiration for a full-length feature movie, filmed at the old Trinity Church. The film premiered in 1969—appropriately enough, just a week after Woodstock. The movie got surprisingly positive reviews as an artistic expression of the nation's emerging youth culture, and the director received an Academy Award nomination. It also spawned a sort of countercultural tourist industry in the Berkshires, as youth from across the country made pilgrimages to see the church where it had all begun. Many wanted to eat at "Alice's Restaurant." (There never was a restaurant here in the church, although Alice Brock did pen a best-selling cookbook.) Others simply wanted to absorb the openness of the place.

The church-turned-hippie-haven passed into private hands in the early 1970s, after the Brocks divorced and the mini-utopia they created

NATURAL BEAUTY
OF THE BERKSHIRES

Many visitors to southwestern Massachusetts can recall a time, as a James Taylor song recounts, when "the Berkshires seemed dreamlike" in their intense natural beauty. Several special places in the area beckon to the spiritual traveler, offering a respite from a busy itinerary of touring. About fifteen miles southwest of Great Barrington, there's **Bash Bish Falls**, an eighty-foot waterfall that descends into a series of deep gorges and then a cascading pool. Bash Bish Falls is located in **Mount Washington State Forest**, which has thirty miles of wilderness trails for hiking and camping. In Sheffield, fifteen miles south of Great Barrington on the Connecticut border, is **Bartholomew's Cobble**, a natural rock garden that sits beside the lovely Housatonic River. Visitors can see rare wildflowers and more than 200 species of birds along the Cobble's "Ledges Interpretive Trail," a hiking path that winds through the Housatonic River valley. Less than five miles north of Great Barrington on Route 7 is **Monument Mountain**, whose 1,735-foot summit is named Squaw Peak after a young Indian woman who allegedly took a fatal plunge here. Visitors who brave the trek up to the mountain's peak will be rewarded by a panoramic view of the Berkshires.

Bash Bish Falls: ☎ 413-528-0330
　💻 www.state.ma.us/dem/parks/bash.htm

Bartholomew's Cobble: ☎ 413-229-8600
　💻 www.berkshireweb.com/trustees/barth.html

Monument Mountain: ☎ 413-298-3239
　💻 www.berkshireweb.com/trustees/monument.html

had largely dissolved. When the building came up for sale again in the early 1990s, Arlo Guthrie organized a national campaign to purchase it. He had a notion to create a spirituality center guided by his personal guru Ma Jaya Sati Bhagavati, a Jewish woman from New York who had embraced Hinduism. Guthrie, who grew up as a nonobservant Jew and has explored both Catholicism and devotional Hinduism as an adult, believes that all paths lead, eventually, to God. "I am sure that all true lovers of the truth go to the truth, whatever they call it, whether they are Buddhist, Hindu, Jew[ish], Christian, or whatever," he wrote in 1999.

Today, the Trinitarian symbols in the sanctuary are as likely to be interpreted as representations of Shiva, Vishnu, and Brahma as they are of the Christian Father, Son, and Holy Spirit. The Guthrie Center (named after Woody, not Arlo) housed in the church hosts seminars on holistic healing, extends outreach to AIDS victims, invites abused and neglected children to play music with Arlo Guthrie, and regularly opens the building for community meetings.

Lenox

"Yoga and a Whole Lot More"
KRIPALU CENTER FOR YOGA AND HEALTH
West Street, Route 183. Year founded: 1983. ☎ 800-741-7353
🖳 www.kripalu.org

> From I-90, take Exit 2 (Lenox, Lee, Pittsfield) and bear right at the exit ramp onto Route 20 West. After four miles, Route 7 merges with Route 20. A hundred yards past the merger, turn left at the traffic light onto Route 183. After one mile, you will be at the monument in the center of Lenox. Follow signs to Tanglewood, staying on 183 for another 1.6 miles. At the Town of Stockbridge sign and junction with Richmond Mountain Road, bear left; the entrance to Kripalu Center is immediately on your right.

Tucked into the woodsy, mountainous region of northwestern Massachusetts is Kripalu Center for Yoga and Health, the nation's largest center for yoga and holistic health. This massive building, with space for nearly

300 guests, was built in 1957 as a dormitory for a Jesuit seminary. In 1983, individuals associated with the Kripalu Yoga Fellowship in Pennsylvania purchased the property and renovated it for use as an *ashram*, or traditional Indian yoga center. It now welcomes more than 15,000 guests each year for its yoga programs for students of all levels, from novice to lifetime practitioner.

In the late 1980s the Kripalu Center began conducting programs on holistic living, since its leaders felt that yoga practice is but one facet of a well-balanced spiritual life. Teachers here aim to help students blend yoga practice with vegetarian diet and mind-body techniques, for example. The goal is to help guests "experience the heart of yoga and learn how to take yoga off the yoga mat and into their daily lives."

In 1994, Yogi Amrit Desai resigned from leadership of the Kripalu Center (unfortunately, in response to allegations of misconduct). Although yoga has traditionally been taught under a paradigm of the guru-disciple relationship, with students learning from a wise yogi, Kripalu has taken the departure of its leader as an opportunity for the center to explore "a [new] paradigm of self-sourcing and empowering the learner." Guests are still taught by yogic masters who have spent a lifetime cultivating their practice, but they are also told that they are responsible for undertaking their own spiritual development and that paths may differ from one individual to the next.

Accommodations are simple, ranging from bunk-bed quarters to dormitory rooms with twin beds, most with shared bath. In keeping with the center's emphasis on *ahimsa* (nonharming), meals are vegetarian, with limited use of eggs. Meals are served buffet-style and in silence, and feature the cuisine of many different cultures. The main meal occurs at noon, with a lighter meal offered in the evening to encourage a restful night's sleep. (Yoga practice begins each day at 6 A.M., so a good night's sleep is especially important.)

NEARBY

➡ One of the Berkshire region's quintessential churches is the **Church on the Hill**, situated on Main Street in Lenox. Although the congregation was established in 1806, this building dates to 1895, and was designed by architect Benjamin Goodrich. Kennedy Park, a lovely 300-acre public park, is located just behind the church. *55 Main Street, Lenox.* ☎ 413-637-1001

Northampton

Northampton, now famous for Smith College, was home to one of America's foremost theologians in the eighteenth century. Although most schoolchildren today know Jonathan Edwards (1703–58) only for his brimstone sermon "Sinners in the Hands of an Angry God," he was at the vanguard of the Great Awakening, the first major religious revival the colonies ever witnessed. It all started here. Edwards came to Northampton in 1727 to help his elderly grandfather Solomon Stoddard tend to his duties as minister of the Congregational Church. Edwards was just twenty-three, but he was precocious: he had graduated from Yale College at the tender age of sixteen, and had been working as a tutor there.

Something began happening in Northampton a few years after Edwards's arrival. Young people swooned in worship. Others began shouting excit-

GEORGE WHITEFIELD AND THE GREAT AWAKENING

The revival in Northampton soon spread through the Connecticut River valley and throughout New England, aided greatly by the sophisticated promotion techniques of an Englishman named George Whitefield (1714–70). Whitefield remained an Anglican all his life, though he preached revival and maintained deep and cordial ties with Methodist founder John Wesley. On his second trip to the American colonies in 1739, the twenty-five-year-old Whitefield stirred thousands of hearts to religious fervor. He had a precocious sense of the importance of publicity and advance promotion, plugging his meetings months in advance and attracting crowds of up to 20,000 people. Every move he made was front-page news during his trip to the colonies. Whitefield, who had once studied acting, became such a polished orator that Philadelphia newspaperman Benjamin Franklin wrote that "without being interested in the subject, one could not help being pleased with the discourse." Franklin, who had not intended to give a single penny to Whitefield's cause of a home for orphan boys, was so overcome by the revivalist's preaching that he found himself emptying his pockets of every cent he had.

edly during services. Edwards's own wife exhibited signs of a unique spiritual awakening. Edwards wrote about this in his treatise "A Faithful Narrative of the Surprising Work of God," a brief 1737 account of the community's intense revival. As Edwards's "Faithful Narrative" gained an audience throughout New England, the revival also spread, with communities across the region reporting a renewed interest in matters of religion. It wasn't until 1739, however, that the revival truly became an intercolonial event, fueled by the arrival of a celebrity—George Whitefield.

Unfortunately, none of the buildings from Edwards's tenure in Northampton remain. Few in his congregation would probably have believed that he would become the town's most famous adopted son, since he left the church in some disgrace after being asked to resign in 1750. (Edwards had caught some young people reading a manual for midwives—with diagrams!—and tried to punish them for it. Their parents, however, were angry with Edwards for embarrassing the youths.) The forced resignation was a bitter disappointment for Edwards, who felt he had given his all to the Northampton congregation, which he had served for twenty-three years. He was banished to Stockbridge, where he served as a missionary to Native Americans. While in Stockbridge in the 1750s, free from the cares of shepherding a congregation, Edwards wrote some of the most thoughtful treatises of his career, catapulting himself to modest fame in New England and beyond.

Calvin Coolidge's Congregation
EDWARDS CHURCH
Puritan/Congregational. 297 Main Street. Year consecrated: 1959.
☎ 413-584-5500

> *Follow directions for First Church, but continue a quarter of a mile past First Church on Main Street.*

There is a church on Main Street called "Edwards Church," but this is not the site of Edwards's own congregation. This congregation was founded in 1833, when First Congregational could no longer accommodate all of its members and required a branch church for the overflow. The original nineteenth-century building was destroyed by fire in 1870, and the brick church that replaced it was razed in 1957. In the early twentieth century, the Calvin Coolidge family worshiped here, and President Coolidge's funeral was held here. The present-day building, a stone and glass edifice built in 1958 and consecrated in 1959, reflects a Scandinavian modernist style.

Jonathan Edwards's Church
OLD FIRST CHURCH
Puritan/Congregational and American Baptist. 129 Main Street (at Center Street). Year consecrated: 1878 (congregation dates to 1654). Architects: Peabody and Stearns. ☎ 413-584-9392
💻 www.firstnorthampton.com

> *129 Main Street in Northampton, next-door to the courthouse. Take I-90 West to Exit 4 (W. Springfield/Holyoke), bearing left after the ramp. Merge onto I-91 North. Travel ten miles to Exit 18 (U.S. 5), bearing left after the ramp. Turn left onto Pleasant Street, and stay on Pleasant for nearly a mile. Turn left onto Main Street. The church is at the corner of Main and Center Streets.*

Old First Church on Main Street is actually the fifth church to stand on this site. Built in 1878, it is an imposing Gothic Revival structure in brownstone. The second and third buildings were of the Edwards era. As you enter the front door, a plaque informs you that the semicircular stone in the sidewalk just below the front steps was the step to the third meetinghouse on this site (1737–1812), where Jonathan Edwards preached from 1727 to 1750. The third and fourth meetinghouses were quintessential colonial churches, two stories tall with a bell tower complete with clock and weathervane.

Today, the church retains some of the eighteenth-century silver cups used in communion services, but that is the only tangible link to Edwards's era. Ideologically, much has also changed; the church where Edwards once preached of wormlike sinners squirming in the hands of an angry God now posts on its marquee that it is an "open and affirming" congregation. The United Church of Christ, the ecclesiastical descendent of the Puritan churches, was one of the first denominations to begin openly ordaining gay and lesbian clergy in 1972. It is fascinating to imagine what Edwards might have thought of these transformations.

Pittsfield

Home of the Round Barn
HANCOCK SHAKER VILLAGE
At junction of Route 20 and Route 41. Year consecrated: 1783.
☎ 413-443-0188 💻 www.hancockshakervillage.org

> *Hancock Shaker village is located at the junction of Route 20 and*
> *Route 41, approximately five miles west of Pittsfield. From Memorial Day*
> *weekend through mid-October, it is open for daily tours from 9:30 A.M. to*
> *5 P.M., with more limited hours in early spring and late fall. The café and*
> *museum shop welcome all visitors, and a research library is open by*
> *appointment.*

With six "families" and 300 residents at its height in the nineteenth century, Hancock Village (which the Shakers called their "City of Peace") was one of the largest Shaker communities in America. Its proximity to the leading community in Mount Lebanon, New York (just a few minutes' drive over the state border), meant that it was at the vanguard of Shaker life. Its early founding in 1783 meant that Mother Ann Lee (1736–84) visited here at least once and is said to have preached in the Trustees' House on the topic of charity to the poor.

The Five-Story Brick Dwelling, Hancock Shaker Village

MOTHER ANN LEE

A nn Lee, born Ann Lees in Manchester, England, on February 29, 1736, was the second of eight children in a working-class family. She never learned to read or write, and little is known about her early life except that she married a man (a blacksmith, like her father) named Abraham Standerin in 1762 and bore him four children. All of them, tragically, died in infancy, which may be one reason why Ann Lee later decided to renounce marriage and embrace a celibate lifestyle.

Four years before her marriage, she had become involved with a small religious sect in England called the Shaking Quakers, or Shakers. Although Lee is usually credited with founding the movement, it had been going for eleven years before she joined; its original founders, John and Jane Wardley, had already begun teaching some of the tenets that would become hallmarks of full-fledged Shakerism (including celibacy, although they were a married couple).

The Shakers were so named because of their enthusiastic habits of shaking, dancing, singing, shouting, and even shoving one another during worship. The Shakers encouraged women to be religious leaders, and during the 1760s Ann Lee arose within the movement as a spiritual leader of great charisma. In 1770 she had a vision in which she saw herself as Ann the Word, the Woman Clothed with the Sun (Rev 12). As Christ had once come into the world as a man, Jesus of Nazareth, Ann Lee preached that Christ had come a second time as a woman—herself. This belief gave rise to the official name of the religious movement that had been (and still is) popularly known as the Shakers: the United Society of Believers in Christ's Second Appearing.

Around the year 1774, Ann Lee led the first small band of Shakers to the American colonies and welcomed new converts to the Shaker ranks. Under her leadership, the movement prospered in America but also weathered great controversy. Many New Englanders were distressed by the radical, woman-led religious sect that had settled in the colonies, and Ann Lee and her followers suffered mob attacks and prison sentences on many occasions. (Alongside the religious controversy was the thorny fact that Lee had arrived from Mother England precisely at a time when the colonists were very, very suspicious of the home country. All of her imprisonments occurred during the Revolutionary War, which begs the question whether she was truly incarcerated on religious grounds or because the Shakers, like the Quakers before them, were pacifists who refused to fight in the conflict.) Ann Lee died at the age of forty-eight in 1784, surrounded by her beloved followers.

As a historic site, Hancock is one of the best-preserved Shaker villages in the United States. This is because it was one of the last to close. As the Shaker movement dwindled in the twentieth century, Hancock became a site of consolidation, with Shakers from many other communities living out their last days here. The village was sold in 1959 to a friend of the community, who set about the task of historic preservation. Today, Hancock is one of the few Shaker villages to maintain not only its buildings but also its considerable land holdings in period style; animals and crops are raised using traditional Shaker methods, and the herb garden features authentic nineteenth-century varieties, many of which the Shakers used medicinally. In the summer tourist season, special classes and

HANDS TO WORK

Many visitors to Shaker villages are surprised by the forward-thinking technological gadgets that were invented there. Shakers in Canterbury, New Hampshire, created the first industrial-size washing machine, an invention they patented and from which they enjoyed a healthy profit when the hotel industry adopted the technology. Shaker brothers in nearby Harvard, Massachusetts, invented the circular saw. And the most memorable building in Hancock Shaker Village is the Round Stone Barn, which enabled one individual to feed dozens of cows at a time.

Shakers have never feared technology, but have embraced it when it could be used to save them precious time. In the early twentieth century, Shakers were sometimes the first people in their communities to own cars, and they used trucks and tractors to help them farm more effectively. At Hancock Village, visitors can see the Shakers' four-car brick garage, built in 1916—with heating. Mother Ann Lee is famous for her saying, "Hands to work, hearts to God." Her Shaker followers honored these sentiments by inventing labor-saving devices that would free their time for the all-important task of worship.

demonstrations are available on animal husbandry, gardening, and cooking techniques.

Because there were Shakers living in Hancock for nearly 300 years, visitors can glimpse many architectural styles, from the spartan functionality of the meetinghouse to the Victorian-influenced Trustees' Office and Store. Highlights of the tour include the 1826 Round Stone Barn—possibly the most photographed Shaker building of all time—and the 1793 meetinghouse. Another very famous building is the five-story brick dwelling, a dormitory that the Shakers erected in just ten short weeks in 1832. (That's impressive, considering that the structure contains 350,000 bricks, 100 doors and 95 windows!) The brick dwelling, with its exact symmetry and separate doors for men and women, reflects the Shakers' strict separation of the sexes.

Spencer

A Trappist Monastery in the Heart of Massachusetts
ST. JOSEPH'S ABBEY
Roman Catholic/Cistercian (Trappist). 167 North Spencer Road. Year consecrated: 1952 (community dates to 1825). ☎ 508-885-8700
🖳 www.spencerabbey.org

From the Massachusetts Turnpike, take Exit 10. Go west on Routes 12 and 20 for three miles to Route 56 North. From there, it is eight miles to Leicester. Turn left at Route 9 and drive six miles to Spencer. Turn right on Route 31 North, and proceed for five miles. The Abbey will be on your left. On Wednesdays and Saturdays at 2:30, there is a slide presentation about monastic life in the reception room. The visitors' chapels are open for prayer and meditation each day from 3 A.M. to 8 P.M. The gift shop/ bookstore is open from 9:30 A.M. to 5 P.M. Monday through Saturday, and from 1 P.M. to 4:30 P.M. on Sunday.

St. Joseph's Abbey is a Roman Catholic monastery in the Trappist tradition, located on almost 2,000 acres of lovely groves, pastures, and meadows. The more than seventy monks here lead a contemplative life marked by round-the-clock prayer and strict adherence to the Rule of St. Benedict. The community rises in the wee hours to fulfill its daily prayer obligations, observing vigil from 3:30 A.M. until 4:15 A.M. The service of

St. Joseph's Abbey, Spencer

Lauds begins at 6:45 A.M. At 8 A.M., the monks gather to pray, then scatter to their various occupations; they reconvene at noon to pray again and have a communal meal. During the afternoon, normal chores are interrupted by brief services at 2 P.M. (None), and 5:40 P.M. (Vespers). The monks close out their day with "the dear little office" of Compline at 7:40 P.M. The monks' daily lives would seem austere to the outside world. Breakfast consists of "bread and hot liquid," and lunch—the largest meal of the day—is eaten in silence as the monks listen to a spiritual reading. Supper, taken between Vespers and Compline, is a light repast. The monks are vegetarian, with meat reserved for visitors and the infirm.

The Spencer community originated in Nova Scotia in 1825, after Cistercian monks fled political unrest in their native France. From 1900 to 1950, they lived in Rhode Island, then moved here after a fire destroyed their monastery. Although the classic stone buildings at St. Joseph's suggest medieval architecture, with their thatched roofs and small paned windows, they are only half a century old.

According to the Rule of St. Benedict, each monk is required to contribute to the economic vitality of the community, which at St. Joseph's generally means helping to produce the dainty jams, jellies, and marmalades for which the monastery is famous. (Be sure to pick up some of these "Trappist Preserves" in the gift shop near the entrance.) The community also operates the Holy Rood Guild, which designs and manufactures liturgical vestments and other church supplies.

Only male retreatants are generally permitted to stay on the monastery grounds, with one week each month reserved for women retreatants. At other times, women and families may stay at Mary House, a retreat house a quarter of a mile away that is affiliated with the monastery. Retreats are centered around the monastery's schedule of mass and the Liturgy of the Hours. An atmosphere of shared silence is encouraged.

Springfield

Episcopal and Ecumenical
CHRIST CHURCH CATHEDRAL
35 Chestnut Street. Year consecrated: 1876 (congregation dates to 1817). Architects: Lord, Fuller & Wadlin. ☎ 413-736-2742
 www.christchurchcathedralspringfield.org

From I-91, Take Exit 7 (Columbus Avenue). Go straight at the first light, left at the second light onto State Street, and straight through two lights. After the Civic Center (on your left), turn right onto Dwight Street, then get into the left lane and reverse direction by driving around a 180°-left-hand curve. At the traffic light, cross State Street. Christ Church Cathedral is immediately on the right, at the top of a small hill.

On March 25, 2001, the pews of this historic Episcopal cathedral were packed—and not just with the church's own parishioners or the congregants of the sixty-six other diocesan parishes served by the cathedral. The church was also filled with area Lutherans and Roman Catholics, who had come to celebrate an agreement reached by the Episcopal Diocese of Western Massachusetts, the Roman Catholic Dioceses of Springfield and of Worcester, and the New England Synod of the Lutheran Church in America. The ceremony unified the dioceses in a unique covenant, promising cooperation in the areas of worship, study, and service. Since the three denominations regard baptism as a sacrament that unites the traditions, the four bishops signed the agreement by the cathedral's baptismal font.

Such ecumenical cooperation has been a hallmark of Christ Church's role in the Springfield community since the early nineteenth century. In the 1820s, many of its services were held at a Methodist church until the congregation constructed its own house of worship. The present building, which is in the Norman style and constructed of Longmeadow brownstone, was consecrated in 1876. In 1929, it became the cathedral for the Diocese of Western Massachusetts.

Today, Christ Church is known for its glorious vocal music, provided by a fifty-voice Cathedral Choir. In English fashion, the choir includes some children, who are paid a small stipend and given an intensive musical education.

NEARBY

➥ The 1968 synagogue of **Congregation Beth El** has been lauded as "one of the great contemporary synagogues in the United States," an imaginative blend of Percival Goodman's architecture and religious art by Ibram Lassaw, Adolph Gottlieb, and Robert Motherwell. The original 1953 building burned to the ground in 1965 and was replaced by a synagogue of the same design, slightly expanded. Services are held daily at Beth El at 7 A.M. each weekday morning, 9:30 A.M. each Shabbat and festival morning, and 8 A.M. on Sundays and secular holidays. *979 Dickinson Street. Take I-90 West to Exit 6 (I-291). Turn left off the exit. Follow signs to I-91 South (toward Connecticut). Continue on I-91 South to Exit 1 (Route 5 South, Longmeadow/Forest Park). Bear left off the exit. Continue on Route 5 (Longmeadow Street) .9 miles to the second traffic light. Turn left at the light onto Converse Street. Continue 1.2 miles on Converse Street through a traffic light. Turn left onto Dickinson Street. Continue .5 miles on Dickinson Street to Temple Beth El on the right.* ☎ 413-733-4149
🖳 www.uscj.org/ctvalley/springfield/

➥ **Stanley Park** in **Westfield** offers an unusual mix of natural and human-made sacred elements in its 275 acres. There is an arboretum, a rose garden, an English herb garden, a wildlife sanctuary, and a Japanese garden complete with a bamboo tea house. Fans of sacred music will thrill to the sounds of the bells at the Stanley Park Carillon Tower. Since 1950, the eighty-six bells in the tower have been rung regularly in honor of world peace. From May to October, full Carillon Concerts are offered on the first Sunday of the month at 3 P.M. *400 Western Avenue, Westfield. From Springfield, drive west on Route 20. Turn left on Elm Street, left on Court Street, and bear left on Granville Road. Open daily year-round, 8 A.M. to 6 P.M.* ☎ 413-568-9312 🖳 www.stanleypark.org

➥ The first Congregational parish to be founded in western Massachusetts was **Old First Church**, gathered in 1637. This 1819 meetinghouse, designed by Captain Isaac Damon, is the fourth to be build on this site. The building was named to the National Historic Register in 1971. It features a sixty-pound, four-foot-high rooster weathervane atop the steeple, a reminder of how Peter's denial of Jesus can help Christians to become faithful and loyal disciples. *Court Square, Springfield.* ☎ 413-737-1411 🖳 www.old-first-church.org

Stockbridge

Lourdes in the Berkshires
NATIONAL SHRINE OF THE DIVINE MERCY
Roman Catholic (Congregation of Marians of the Immaculate Conception). 2 Prospect Road. Year consecrated: 1960. ☎ 413-298-3931
🖳 http://www.marian.org

> *The National Shrine of the Divine Mercy is located on Eden Hill, just south of the Massachusetts Turnpike near Stockbridge. Take Exit 2 (Lee) from the turnpike and follow Route 102 to Stockbridge. From the Red Lion Inn, go north on Pine Street. At the first intersection after the stop sign, go left and follow the road up the hill to the shrine. The shrine is open daily from 7 A.M. to 6 P.M. Mass is held on weekdays at 7:15 A.M. and 2 P.M.; Saturdays at 8 A.M. and 2 P.M.; Sundays at 10:30 A.M. and 2 P.M. Each day, there is also an Hour of Great Mercy at 3 P.M., including the Divine Mercy Novena and Chaplet, benediction, and sacrament of penance.*

The Congregation of Marians of the Immaculate Conception have created "this little bit of Eden" tucked in the Berkshires of western Massachusetts. It is visited by approximately 35,000 pilgrims annually, many of whom have claimed miraculous healings at the site. The shrine was inspired by the spiritual life of Our Lady of Mercy Sister Maria Faustina Kowalska (1905–38), a Polish nun who received a vision asking her to disseminate the message of God's mercy to the world. The price for this honor was that she would have to endure terrible physical pain herself so she could better model Christ's own suffering and mercy. Although she did not speak of her physical agony to many people, she did record her experiences in a diary, which has become a widely popular devotional. Sister Maria Faustina died of tuberculosis at the tender age of thirty-three, but her legacy lives on in her writings and at this site, which commemorates

NOVENA

A novena consists of special prayers that are offered for nine consecutive days, or one day a week for nine weeks. (*Nov* is the root of the Latin word for "nine.") The practice has its origins in the tradition of nine days of prayer before Pentecost. These devotions can be public or private, corporate or individual.

her example. In 2000, she was canonized on Mercy Sunday (the Sunday after Easter), with that day henceforth declared "Divine Mercy Sunday."

The grounds include approximately 350 acres and feature a Lourdes Grotto, modeled after the shrine to Our Lady of Lourdes in France. The grotto contains a candle shrine, built in 1997, with more than 1,600 candles.

NEARBY

➥ **The Mission House** in Stockbridge reflects the town's history as a Christian mission center to Native Americans. Stockbridge was founded in 1734 for the purpose of preaching the gospel to the Mohican Indians, and its original Mission House (established for the minister who taught here) still stands. Although it has been moved from its original site, the frame house retains its original entranceway and many period furnishings. It is now a museum, offering guided tours in summer. *Main Street, Stockbridge. From the intersection of Routes 7 and 102 at the Red Lion Inn in Stockbridge, take Route 102 (Main Street) West two-tenths of a mile to*

The Mission House, Stockbridge

Mount Auburn Cemetery,
Cambridge, Massachusetts

Left: King's Chapel, Boston

The Public Garden, Boston

Vilna/Vilner Shul, Boston

Lourdes in Litchfield, Connecticut

The New England Hindu Temple, Ashland, Massachusetts

Left: Hancock Shaker Village, Pittsfield, Massachusetts

Eastern Point Lighthouse, Cape Ann, Massachusetts

Christian Science Center, Boston

Old Meeting House, Jaffrey Center, New Hampshire

First Congregational
Church, Litchfield,
Connecticut

Old Narragansett
Church, Wickford,
Rhode Island

Townshend,
Southern
Vermont

Sargeant Street on the right. Open Memorial Day weekend through Columbus Day, 10 A.M. to 5 P.M. daily. Admission fee. ☎ 413-298-3239 🖥 www.berkshireweb.com/trustees/mission.html

➦ **Berkshire Botanical Garden**, created in 1934, is a nonprofit educational institution that showcases some of the Berkshire region's most stunning native flora. It is well known for horticultural education programs and its public gardens, which are among the oldest in the United States. *At intersection of Routes 102 and 83, two miles from the Stockbridge Center. Open daily from 10 A.M. to 5 P.M., May through October. Admission fee.* ☎ 413-298-3926 🖥 www.berkshirebotanical.org

➦ In the late nineteenth century, Stockbridge became a summer residence for many wealthy Americans, and the twenty-six-room "cottage" called **Naumkeag** was the vacation home of Joseph Hodges Choate (1832–1917), a Gilded Age attorney who once served as ambassador to Britain. Today, the home is open for tours; it offers fine furniture and the family's extensive collection of Chinese porcelain. But it is the garden that is truly extraordinary. Choate's daughter and heir, Mabel Choate, hired the landscape designer Fletcher Steele to create an innovative garden complete with "outdoor rooms," a Blue Stairs waterfall and an elegant rose garden. *From the intersection of Route 7 and Route 102 in Stockbridge, take Pine Street north. Bear left on Prospect Hill Road and go a half mile. The garden entrance is on the left. Open daily from 10 A.M. to 5 P.M., Memorial Day through Columbus Day. Admission fee.* ☎ 413-298-3239 🖥 www.berkshireweb.com/trustees/naumkeah.html

Williamstown

The Birthplace of Foreign Missions
MISSION PARK
Williams College campus. Year monument erected: 1867.
☎ 413-597-2568 🖥 www.berkshireweb.com/mohawktrail/haystack.html

Mission Park and the Haystack Monument are located a brief walk north of the First Congregational Church and Chapin Hall on the Williams College campus. Open daily.

The nineteenth century has been called the Century of Missions, and this small monument on the Williams College campus commemorates a group of men who, in no small way, helped to earn that designation. In

August 1806, a group of five Williams College students gathered in a grove of maple trees to pray and discuss their hopes for furthering the kingdom of God. In their minds, that meant foreign missions—bringing their faith to people in distant lands who had never heard the Christian message. Rain began pelting down on the gathered students, but rather than end their meeting early, they simply relocated it to the shelter of an obliging haystack, overcome with zeal for their cause.

In 1808 they formed a student society called "the Brethren," and in 1810 their efforts paid off on a larger scale: they organized the American Board of Commissioners for Foreign Missions, and began dispatching missionaries around the globe. With their motto, "The Field is the World," these earnest men set out to evangelize all nations, and created an American missions movement that ballooned into a multimillion-dollar global enterprise by the end of the nineteenth century.

The Haystack Monument was erected in 1867 to honor the original young men who dreamed big dreams on this site. It is a twelve-foot statue of local marble, topped by a globe that is three feet in diameter. Although Williams College has never been affiliated with a particular denomination, it is proud of its historical legacy, and since 1956 (the sesquicentennial of the original Haystack meeting), the college has offered the "Haystack Fellowship" to support undergraduates from foreign countries who wish to study at Williams.

NEARBY

➥ The **Williams College Museum of Art**, considered one of the premier college art museums in the country, is particularly strong in modern and contemporary art. It is housed in the school's original library, a neoclassical 1846 structure that was significantly expanded in the 1980s to house the collection of more than 12,000 works of art. *15 Lawrence Hall Drive. Open Tuesday through Saturday, 10 A.M. to 5 P.M., and Sunday from 1 P.M. to 5 P.M. No admission fee.* ☎ 413-597-2429 🖥 www.williams.edu/WCMA

➥ **Mount Greylock State Reservation** features more than 11,000 acres on the state's highest mountain, Mount Greylock (3,491 feet). On a clear day, visitors can see for up to 100 miles, making this the most panoramic vista in western Massachusetts. If the spirit is willing but the flesh is weak, have no fear: You can drive your car up to the summit. *From Williamstown, follow Route 2 East until you see signs for Mount Greylock.*
☎ 413-499-4262
🖥 www.berkshireweb.com/mohawktrail/mtgreylock.html

ARTS IN THE BERKSHIRES

It must be true that natural beauty inspires great art, because the Berkshires are home to some of the most outstanding cultural attractions in New England—or even the nation. You can almost expect to bump into some of the finest stars of stage and screen that New York and Hollywood have to offer at the **Williamstown Theatre Festival** each summer. Williamstown, in fact, has become a trial run and workshop city for many plays before they attempt to mount a Broadway or off-Broadway production. On the art front, there's the **Williams College Museum of Art** (see entry above) and the **Sterling and Francine Clark Art Institute**, which is famous for its paintings by European impressionists and Old Masters. More than 185,000 fans of the *Saturday Evening Post* illustrator visit the **Norman Rockwell Museum** in Stockbridge every year, savoring the world's largest collection of Rockwell's work. His personal art studio has also been moved into the museum and remains just as he left it—with an unfinished canvas on the easel. For music lovers, concerts at the **Tanglewood Music Center** near Lenox run from late June to early September. Since 1936, Tanglewood has been where the Boston Symphony Orchestra lets its collective hair down each summer and becomes the Boston Pops. Dance afficionados are also in luck; the **Jacob's Pillow Dance Festival** in Becket has been staging some of the world's most famous and complex ballets and dance programs since 1933. Its Ted Shawn Theatre, which opened in 1942, is considered the first theater in the United States to have been designed especially for the dance.

Williamstown Theatre Festival: ☎ 413-597-3399
🖥 www.wtfestival.org

Sterling and Francine Clark Art Institute: ☎ 413-458-2303
🖥 www.clarkart.edu

Norman Rockwell Museum: ☎ 413-298-4100 🖥 www.nrm.org

Tanglewood Music Center: ☎ 617-266-1492 🖥 www.bso.org

Jacob's Pillow Dance Festival: ☎ 413-243-0749
🖥 www.jacobs-pillow.com

CHAPTER SIX

.... ❧ ....

Southern Massachusetts and Cape Cod

"There I had got the Cape under me, as much as if I were riding it bare-backed. It was not as on the map, or seen from the stagecoach; but there I found it all out of doors, huge and real, Cape Cod! as it cannot be represented on a map, color it as you will; the thing itself, than which there is nothing more like it, no truer picture or account; which you cannot go further and see."

—Henry David Thoreau, *Cape Cod* (1864)

IT'S BEEN A CENTURY and a half since Thoreau made his famous walks along the shore of Cape Cod, yet no writer since has succeeded so well in capturing the perfect joy that accompanies a thorough investigation of the wild shores of Massachusetts. Jutting out from the mainland like a "bare and bended arm," Cape Cod has always been inextricably tied with its ocean surroundings. When the Puritans landed here in 1620, they spent five weeks in what is now Provincetown at the tip of the Cape before deciding to try their luck further inland. The Cape was wild, barren country—more suited to the occupations of fishing and whaling, which became the Puritans' livelihood, than it was to farming, which they had intended to pursue.

The Cape developed spiritually as it cycled through generations of Native Americans, immigrants, whalers, and fishermen. Today, the Cape's population, once so staunchly Calvinist/Puritan, is predominantly Roman

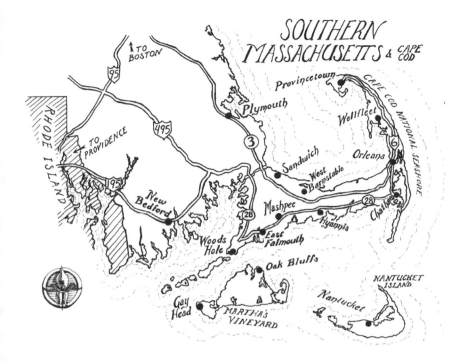

Catholic. More than thirty of the Cape's roughly 150 places of worship are Catholic, compared to sixteen United Church of Christ congregations. And since the membership of most Catholic parishes is significantly larger than the rosters of Protestant churches, Roman Catholicism is the dominant religion here by a margin of more than two to one. In the nineteenth century, Irish immigrants dotted the Cape's landscape with Irish Catholic parishes; this heritage is perhaps today best celebrated in the many local Catholic sites that boast an allegiance to the Kennedy clan. To a lesser extent, the Cape Verdeans and Azoreans who settled in Falmouth and its surrounding areas demonstrated the rising importance of Portuguese-heritage Catholic parishes. The Portuguese legacy is still felt in the fishing towns of Provincetown and New Bedford, which continue their annual Blessing of the Fleet celebrations to this day.

Other religious groups have been prominent on the Cape at one time or another. In the early nineteenth century, the Methodists founded a "camp meeting" on Martha's Vineyard that is now a permanent attraction, known for its lovely gingerbread cottages as much as for its ongoing Christian revival. The Quakers also found a home on the Cape. Although they were not officially welcome in this overridingly Puritan area until long after their seventeenth-century arrival, many Quakers established homes and businesses here. Their presence was especially felt on the tiny island of Nantucket.

But before European encroachment, Native Americans had lived on Cape Cod for approximately 10,000 years. While many history books rightly note that the Wampanoag were "the Indians who met the Pilgrims," there is far more to Wampanoag history than that. Some books also claim that the tribe is extinct. That is not true, although the ravages of war and disease did nearly wipe out the Wampanoag nation in the seventeenth century. Today, there are approximately 4,000 Wampanoag, many of whom still live in southeastern Massachusetts and Rhode Island. The Wampanoag ("People of the Dawn" or "People of the First Light") are concentrated in the town of Mashpee and on the island of Martha's Vineyard, with the Martha's Vineyard community being the only Wampanoag group recognized as an official tribe by the federal government. The Wampanoag have preserved their heritage and spiritual legacy in several museums in the area, and their annual summer powwow, which showcases the tribe's heritage, is open to the public.

A WORD ABOUT TRANSPORTATION

You will need a car to travel to most of the sites on Cape Cod; the Mid-Cape Highway conveniently stretches all the way to the tip of Provincetown, making most sites quite convenient. That is, of course, unless you're visiting during the high tourist season between Memorial Day and Labor Day—during those months, traffic can be backlogged for hours on the Cape. In particular, try to avoid the highly congested travel days of Friday and Sunday.

Although you'll need a car on the mainland, don't try to bring one to Martha's Vineyard or Nantucket. It is technically possible to do this (despite the exorbitant price to ferry a car), but the islands are so congested that drivers spend a good portion of their precious holiday hours fighting traffic and searching for elusive parking places. Island streets are confoundedly narrow, and road rage is not conducive to spiritual travel—so try taking the ferry (a wonderful experience in itself) and walking the islands.

Hyannis (Cape Cod)

Hyannis, on the southern shore of Cape Cod, seems to be best known for two things among the tourist set: You can catch the ferry for Nantucket and Martha's Vineyard here, and it is the site of the famous Kennedy compound. Unfortunately, many people do not venture beyond the dock or depart from the ruthless parade past all things John and Jackie. This is a shame, for Hyannis boasts an interesting religious history—much of it intersecting with America's most famous family. It is the Cape's largest town, approaching city size. (But travelers beware—it also suffers from some of the Cape's worst traffic jams.)

"The Kennedy Church"
SAINT FRANCIS XAVIER CHURCH
Roman Catholic. 347 South Street. Year consecrated: 1874.
☎ 508-775-0818 🖥 www.sfxp.org

> *From Route 6 (Mid-Cape Highway), take Route 132 (Iyannough Road)*
> *for 2.8 miles. At the roundabout, take the second exit onto Barnstable*
> *Road. After .2 miles, bear right onto Winter Street. After .7 miles,*
> *turn right onto Main Street. After .2 miles, turn left onto Pine Street.*
> *After .1 miles, turn left onto South Street. Mass is offered daily at 7 A.M.*
> *and 12:10 P.M. Monday through Saturday. Sunday masses are held at*
> *7:30 A.M., 8:30 A.M., 10 A.M., 11:30 A.M., 3 P.M. (Spanish), 5 P.M.,*
> *and 7:30 P.M. (Portuguese).*

As with many other sites in Hyannis, Saint Francis Xavier Church has a long association with the Kennedy family, particularly with matriarch Rose Kennedy, who attended mass here daily while on the Cape. The second pew from the front on the east side is dedicated to President John F. Kennedy, who worshiped here occasionally during his vacations. The altar has a memorial to JFK's older brother, Joseph, a lieutenant who was killed in action in World War II when his fighter plane crashed into the English Channel. Joseph and Rose Kennedy donated the altar in 1946. On either side of the altar's crucifix are images of St. George (representing England) and Joan of Arc (representing France); hanging above these are the U.S. Navy Wings.

The church continues to be an important stomping ground for the Kennedys; on April 26, 1986, Maria Shriver (daughter of Eunice Kennedy Shriver) made Arnold Schwarzenegger's day in this building, by promising to be his wife. And on a tragic note, the pews were crammed in July 1999 with thousands of worshipers who prayed here for the Kennedys after John F. Kennedy, Jr.'s plane went missing.

NEARBY

➥ Hyannis has one of America's last beech trees, located in a courtyard behind Main Street. Over 200 years old, this **Weeping Beech Tree** has weathered thousands of storms and witnessed enormous changes in Hyannis.

Martha's Vineyard

The tourist mecca called Martha's Vineyard was not always home to vacationing celebrities such as Spike Lee and the Clinton family. In fact, this island five miles off the coast of Cape Cod has only become a vacation destination within the last century and a half. But its status as a premier tourist attraction is confirmed each morning in the high season (July and August) when ferry boats unload their passengers at the dock in Oak Bluffs. The northern and eastern sections of the island, which contain the towns of Oak Bluffs and Edgartown, are the most heavily trafficked, while the western point of Gay Head enjoys day-tripping tourists but quiets down at night, since there are so few inns on that side of the island. Gay Head, called Aquinnah by the Wampanoag who have inhabited the area for generations, is the site of the spectacular Gay Head Cliffs.

Revival Meets Recreation
MARTHA'S VINEYARD CAMP MEETING ASSOCIATION
Nondenominational. 80 Trinity Park, Oak Bluffs. Year created: 1835.
☎ 508-693-0525

Trinity Park is adjacent to the dock in Oak Bluffs.

In 1835, a group of Methodist ministers chose the northeast edge of Martha's Vineyard for their camp meeting because the area was remote and unspoiled enough that their shouts of "Hallelujah!" would go relatively unnoticed by all but the sheep grazing nearby. These revivals were long (a week or more) and intense, with individuals praying and listening to fire-and-brimstone sermons from dawn until well past dusk. Souls were saved (sixty-five in the first year, a great success) and marvelous hymns sung in the campground's inspiring setting by the ocean.

An annual revival like the Martha's Vineyard camp meeting exerted a considerable social and spiritual pull on early nineteenth-century Methodists. Still a relative minority in 1835, they could join together with other Christians who shared their values (no alcohol, dancing, or card-playing) and abandon the temptations of the world. Their lives were strictly regulated; families awakened at 5:30 A.M., attended thrice-daily preaching services, held family devotionals in their tents at night, and retired by 10 P.M. Yet many thrived on the structure and the spiritual stimulation, and the revivals began to stretch past one week to two, then four. By the late nineteenth century, the camp meeting was nearly a summerlong affair. It had also become a leisure activity as much as a religious one. By 1855, attendees enjoyed "the benefit of the sea air and bathing" as well

EARLY METHODISM

When the Methodists began their camp meetings here in the early nineteenth century, Methodism was an upstart frontier religion, its doctrine of warmhearted piety having found an eager audience in the new republic. Whereas Congregational theology had emphasized predestination (the belief that only the "elect" of God would be saved from hell), Methodism encouraged ordinary folks to take charge of their own salvation. Everyone could make a decision to be saved; no intermediary in the form of priest or minister was required. Revivals and camp meetings were an important expression of this theological transformation, as the pious gathered to dedicate, or rededicate, their souls to God.

Classwise, Methodism was still not quite respectable in early nineteenth-century New England. John Wesley's earliest converts had been drawn from the English working classes, a pattern that held sway in the United States until roughly the Civil War. The "establishment" churches of New England—at that time, the Episcopalians, Congregationalists, and Presbyterians—were a bit suspicious of the raucous Methodists.

Pink gingerbread cottage, Martha's Vineyard Camp Meeting Association

as "the pleasant social and select society that are accustomed to gather there."

The increasing sophistication of the Martha's Vineyard Camp Meeting Association reflects, in a microcosmic way, the changes that happened in American Methodism as the nineteenth century wore into the twentieth, and Methodism became the most populous and powerful Protestant denomination in America. For example, the early years of the revival saw attendees laying straw mats on the ground to sleep on, and packing food for the entire revival week before they left home. As the years passed, their humble tents were raised on platforms, which gave the tents a semipermanent feel. By 1860, the campground was drawing more than 12,000 people and had 500 tents. From the 1860s to the 1880s, those tents morphed into the more elaborate gingerbread cottages seen today, reflecting Methodism's new role as a leader of Victorian American culture. In its heyday in the late nineteenth century, this camp meeting (and others like it, such as Ocean Grove on the Jersey shore) featured prominent lecturers, preachers, and activists in an atmosphere of "wholesome" leisure. Other buildings followed; **Trinity Methodist Church**, which sits on the green, was constructed in 1878, and the next year saw the erection of the camp meeting's impressive iron tabernacle that can seat more than three thousand people.

The architecture of the cottages reflects some of the religious expression of the camp meeting; they are American Carpenter's Gothic, meaning that they exhibit Gothic decoration but were not built according to medieval construction principles. In keeping with late-nineteenth-century ideas about the home being a sanctuary, or sacred place, some of the cottages are constructed to resemble tiny chapels. A few even have, or once had, stained-glass cathedral windows. Today, the diminutive gingerbread cottages that surround the tabernacle have shot up in value to nearly a quarter of a million dollars apiece.

The Martha's Vineyard Camp Meeting reflects some of the Methodist Church's interesting racial history. American Methodists, particularly in the North, were counted among the nation's first abolitionists. There is historical evidence of at least a dozen leases to African American cottagers in the nineteenth century, though racial conflict did occasionally occur. One early twentieth-century dispute resulted in an African American woman, Mrs. Anthony Smith, removing her cottage to another site. She enlarged it and opened a boarding house for African American visitors to Martha's Vineyard. This house can still be seen on Circuit Street in Oak Bluffs, though it is not open to the public.

Throughout the summer, the Camp Meeting Association sponsors lectures, concerts, hymn sings and worship services that are open to the public. Many of the Sunday worship services feature some of the finest theologians and religion scholars in the New England region. Regular Wednesday evening community sings are held, with special hymn evenings celebrating "Christmas in July" and "Easter in August."

NEARBY

➡ While at the campground, don't miss the **Cottage Museum**, a former cottage that was donated to the association to educate the public. An informative tour guide, a cottager himself, is happy to answer all questions pertaining to the campground's history and the details of present-day life there. Among the exhibits downstairs are a family history chart showing six generations of a family owning the same cottage on the island. Be sure to ascend the steep steps to the cottage's second floor, which features two tiny bedrooms and various nineteenth-century objects for display. On the first floor, a gift shop sells local-interest books and knickknacks. *1 Trinity Park. Open 10 A.M. to 4 P.M. Monday through Saturday from mid-June to mid-September.*

A Nondenominational Summer Church
UNION CHAPEL
Kennebec Avenue, Oak Bluffs. Architect: Samuel F. Pratt. Year founded: 1872. ☎ 508-693-5350 (693-2426 in summer)

Union Chapel is located at the southern end of Kennebec Avenue. Sunday services are held in July and August at 10 A.M.

In the 1860s, members of the increasingly popular Methodist camp meeting (see above) took steps to separate themselves from the island's other vacationers, many of whom did not share their religious views. Other Protestant Christians who vacationed on the island were left without a church. To meet their needs, Union Chapel was established in 1872 as a nondenominational Christian house of worship (hence the "Union" part of the name). The chapel has been more than a church—it has also been a community center. It was the site of the town meetings that led to Oak Bluffs's secession from Edgartown, and more recently hosted a 1998 exhibit on nineteenth-century African American images in *Harper's Weekly*.

From the beginning, the church had close ties to the island's African American community, and has always been interracial. It is a summer church, serving the needs of vacationers, and has gained a reputation for excellent concert music. H. T. Burleigh (1866–1949), who arranged the Negro spirituals "Deep River" and "Swing Low, Sweet Chariot," was a regular soloist here in the early twentieth century. The opera singer Lillian Norton (granddaughter of the camp meeting revivalist preacher John Allen) also sang here. Today, Union's weekly services take advantage of the chapel's fabulous acoustics and Austin pipe organ, and regular musical events are held throughout the summer.

"The People of the Dawn"
WAMPANOAG SITES IN GAY HEAD/AQUINNAH
☎ 508-645-9265 🖥 www.wampanoagtribe.net

The town of Gay Head (Aquinnah) is located at the southwestern tip of Martha's Vineyard. Do not try to reach it on foot. There are regular buses that course through the island; call Island Transport at 508-627-TOUR (www.mvislandtransport.com) for fares and schedules.

The Wampanoag (and earlier indigenous peoples) have inhabited the island of Martha's Vineyard for at least 10,000 years, and today are concentrated most heavily in the western area around Aquinnah. The town's very name reflects something of the Wampanoag influence on the area: Aquinnah is a Wampanoag word, but English settlers changed the town's name to Gay Head. Nowadays, the community is still officially referred to as Gay Head, but as appreciation for indigenous history has increased, locals and visitors alike have returned to calling it "Aquinnah." When the federal government's Bureau of Indian Affairs officially recognized this community in 1987, the tribe took the name the "Wampanoag Tribe of Gay Head (Aquinnah)."

Gay Head/Aquinnah's remoteness helped the colonial-era Wampanoag retain their independence and even their very lives; this isolated area was far less ravaged by European diseases and wars than Wampanoag territories on the mainland. The Wampanoag trust lands span approximately 485 acres, with some designated for private and some for common use. The common lands include the Gay Head Cliffs, Herring Creek, and Lobsterville (and yes, the English dreamed up that name too). The **Gay Head Cliffs** reach heights of 145 feet and are believed to date back more than 100 million years. The cliffs are composed of layers of clay and gravel, resulting in multicolored strata that are lovely to behold. The different colors, now tightly compressed, speak to eons of history: of forests

THE DIVINE CREATION OF NOEPE

Centuries before the English settled on Martha's Vineyard, the Wampanoag passed down oral traditions about the origins of the island, which they called Noepe. In their creation myth, a giant named Moshup created Noepe and its neighboring islands, and taught the Wampanoag people to support themselves by fishing. In particular, Moshup instructed the Wampanoag in the art of catching whales. (Moshup would sit atop the Gay Head Cliffs and watch for the whales; a crater at the top of the cliffs was said to be his favorite seat.) According to legend, the Wampanoag were deeply grateful for the tips on whale hunting, so they gave Moshup an entire year's crop of tobacco to thank him. Moshup smoked the whole lot in one great pipe, then dumped the ashes into the ocean—forming the smaller island of Nantucket.

Each August, the Wampanoag of Gay Head (Aquinnah) hold a Moshup Pageant to reenact the story of Moshup's life through music, dance, and drama.

once resplendent, of desert, of ocean floors all crushed together by glaciation. The cliffs contain fossils of prehistoric animals, including whales. Legend has it that the English came up with the name "Gay Head" because they thought that the brightly colored cliffs seemed riotously happy. They have a point. Another interesting site is **Gay Head Lighthouse**, the oldest (1799) and most famous lighthouse on the island. It is open for tours during the summer season.

Mashpee (Cape Cod)

South of Sandwich on Route 130 is the town of Mashpee, which features into Cape Cod history as a site of great importance for the Wampanoag Indians. This is one of the last two remaining centers of Wampanoag culture (the other being Gay Head/Aquinnah on Martha's Vineyard; see above). The tribe has about 500 members here. In 1665, the Massachusetts colonial legislature set aside approximately twenty-five square miles for the Wampanoag; of a fashion, this was the first Native American "reservation" in America. Today, it is incorporated into the town of Mashpee.

In the 1970s, the Wampanoag of Mashpee sued the government to reestablish their ownership of tribal lands in and around the town. They were denied this claim because—in a gross and ironic injustice—it was ruled that they no longer had the population or infrastructure to maintain status as a tribe.

The Nation's Oldest Surviving "Indian" Church
THE OLD INDIAN MEETING HOUSE
Route 28. Year consecrated: 1684. ☎ 508-477-0208

Located just north of Massachusetts 28, one mile past the turnoff to the Village of Mashpee. The Museum is open on Wednesdays from 10 A.M. to 4 P.M., Fridays from 10 A.M. to 3 P.M., and by appointment on weekends from June to October. Donation requested.

Considered to be the oldest Christian meetinghouse still standing on the Cape, the Old Indian Meeting House was constructed in 1684 to meet the needs of the so-called "praying Indians" who had converted to Christianity (see sidebar). It was moved to this location in 1717,

*The Old Indian
Meeting House,
Mashpee*

and is now open by appointment as a museum. It is a typically unadorned
Puritan-era meetinghouse, with box pews and an organ gallery. Most interestingly, the church's burying ground is the final resting place of many
eighteenth-century members of the congregation. The Wampanoag of
Mashpee still use this building for occasional meetings, social events, and
worship services.

THE FATE OF THE
"PRAYING INDIANS"

Scholars ascribe mixed motivations to the attempts of English settlers to Christianize the Indians in New England. It is probably
true that they were driven by a great religious zeal to spread the
gospel, but it is also true that missionary efforts allowed the English to
exert an imperialistic control over native ways of life.

In 1640, as English migration stepped up in volume and the English began to outnumber native residents, John Eliot (1604–90) and a
few other Puritans began to teach Christianity to the Indians. Eliot
translated portions of the Bible into Algonquin (the first Bible to be
printed in North America) and took time to learn something about
native languages and customs.

But Eliot's evangelizing efforts did not stop with faith; rather,
Christian faith was to be the "civilizing" influence that transformed

native customs, dress, and family life. To remove new Christian converts from the supposedly baleful influence of their native homes, the
Puritans created "praying towns" in several locations in Massachusetts, including Natick (just west of Boston) and other villages. In the
praying towns, Indians were expected to dress like the English, speak
the English language, attend church, and abandon all native religious
traditions. By 1674, there were fourteen different praying towns
throughout New England, and a few Native Americans had been
ordained as missionaries to their tribes.

Unfortunately, the English remained suspicious of the native
Christians. Some Praying Indians served as spies for the English before
and during King Philip's War in 1675 and 1676, when the Wampanoag
and Narragansett attacked many white settlements in southern New
England. The English responded by devastating Native American
communities, killing all tribal leaders and many civilians. During the
war, the Praying Indians were caught in the middle, with sympathies
for both sides. Some Indians fled the praying towns or joined King
Philip's forces against the English. The roughly 500 Praying Indians
who remained were not treated well by those who had introduced
them to Christianity, but exiled to the outer islands of Boston Harbor
(especially Deer Island). They lacked provisions, and many did not
survive the winter.

A Museum of Wampanoag History and Culture
WAMPANOAG INDIAN MUSEUM
Route 130, opposite the Flume Restaurant. ☎ 508-477-1536

*Open Monday through Friday, 10 A.M. to 2 P.M., and Saturday by
appointment. Donations accepted.*

This small but fascinating museum offers exhibits on past and present-
day Wampanoag life. It is located in the former home of Richard Bourne,
an early minister who evangelized the area's Wampanoag Indians. In the
1793 building, visitors can see native crafts such as baskets, examples of
traditional dress, and arrowheads. The highlight of the museum is a reconstructed wigwam, showing a diorama of Wampanoag home life.

PRIVATE RITUALS

There are several powwows that the Wampanoag and Pequot tribes hold each year. These are great festive events, where Native Americans of various tribes offer glimpses of their cultural traditions and history through food, dance, music, and storytelling. However, many other indigenous gatherings take place throughout New England each year that are not open to the public. The Wampanoag, for example, "reinforce old values through ceremonies which reflect the old traditions of our ancestors." At these gatherings, "the people express their native spirituality" through ritual and ceremony. These sacred gatherings are strictly private, and are not photographed or recorded by participants.

Nantucket

In Algonquin, the name *Nantucket* means something like "island far out at sea." (It's actually only twenty-eight miles off the Cape, but requires a two-hour ferry ride to get there.) Herman Melville once called it "an anthill in the sea," but it became an anthill to reckon with when it gained its reputation as a whaling community.

The English settlers learned their whaling techniques in the eighteenth century from the Wampanoag, who have been called "the first whalemen of Nantucket." But it was the English, not the Wampanoag, who reaped great financial reward from depleting the waters of their whales. Selling their prized sperm oil and whalebone to London and beyond, they became extremely prosperous. However, since many of the island's English settlers were Quakers, they eschewed the fine mansions of Salem and other affluent seafaring towns in favor of simple, gray colonial homes, many of which have survived.

Today, of course, another sea-tied industry—tourism—has replaced whaling as the island's chief enterprise. In summer, Nantucket's population increases more than fivefold, and tourists pack the cobblestone streets of Nantucket Town. (If you plan to stay overnight during high season, it's usually necessary to make reservations several months in advance.)

"Old Meets New": A Congregational Church and a Puritan Meetinghouse

FIRST CONGREGATIONAL CHURCH

62 Centre Street. Year consecrated: 1834 (congregation dates to 1725, as does the Old North Vestry). ☎ 508-228-0950

> *Located on the outskirts of Nantucket town, on Centre Street. Open mid-June to mid-October, Monday to Saturday, from 10 A.M. to 4 P.M. Admission fee.*

This imposing Congregational Church on the outskirts of town, with its ornate Gothic-style design, was built to impress. Its 600-pound brass chandelier, trompe l'oeil wall paintings, and striking tower all testify to the success of the town's whaling industry. The artisan for the trompe l'oeil paintings was brought over from Italy and no expense was spared. As with other early nineteenth-century Congregational churches, it is fascinating to compare these developments to the stark simplicity that marked earlier Puritan meetinghouses. Here in Nantucket, visitors have the advantage of being able to see the difference firsthand; the congregation's older building, called the **Old North Vestry** (1725), was not destroyed when this Gothic church went up in 1834. It sits behind the grand church and serves the congregation as a smaller worship center. It is considered to be the oldest religious building still standing on Nantucket.

In 1968, a helicopter swooped over the newer church, dangling a thirty-foot, 2,600-pound steeple for placement atop the church's tower. The steeple is topped by a weathervane, crafted in England. (In a nod to local industry, the weathervane depicts not the usual rooster, but a whale.) Visitors can pay a small fee to climb the tower, which affords a magnificent view of the town.

> "The Nantucketer, he alone resides and riots on the sea; he alone in Bible language, goes down to the sea in ships; to and fro plowing it as his own special plantation. . . ."
>
> Herman Melville, *Moby Dick*

One of the Nation's Most Historic African American Buildings
THE AFRICAN MEETING HOUSE
29 York Street. Year consecrated: 1825. ☎ 508-228-9833
🖥 www.afroammuseum.org/afmnantucket.htm

Open in July and August, Tuesday through Saturday, 11 A.M. to 3 P.M.
and Sunday 1 P.M. to 3 P.M. Donations appreciated.

By 1820, 275 free blacks were listed on the Nantucket census, and this community grew even more during the whaling industry's most prosperous decade, the 1830s. Most of Nantucket's African American men were involved in the whaling or fishing industries. Nantucket Town was strictly segregated at that time, so African Americans crowded together in a single neighborhood near Pleasant and York Streets called "New Guinea." Some of the neighborhood's residents were of Cape Verdean heritage, and spoke Portuguese.

This meetinghouse is believed to be the second-oldest structure in the nation that was built by and for free African Americans in the early nineteenth century. (The 1806 African Meetinghouse in Boston is the oldest, and the two buildings are now administered as museums by the same organization; see page 82.) This small wooden meetinghouse, built in 1825, served as a church, a school for African American children, and a community center. The Nantucket *Inquirer* noted in 1825 that an "African Church" had been erected "for the purpose of accommodating the colored population" of Nantucket. The congregation had a loose affiliation with the Baptist denomination and had been meeting nearby since 1821.

When the island's economy collapsed in the 1850s because of the decline of the whaling industry, many of the meetinghouse's congregants left for the mainland in search of better work opportunities, and the building fell into disrepair. In the 1970s, concerned citizens fought to preserve the meetinghouse as a museum. It is the only structure remaining on Nantucket that was of central importance to the island's nineteenth-century African American community.

NEARBY
➥ The simple design of the **Friends Meeting House**, with its 12-over-12 windows and rectangular gray exterior, speaks eloquently of Quaker ideals. This mid-nineteenth-century building is the last remaining Quaker meetinghouse on an island that once granted refuge to so many members of the Society of Friends. *11 Fair Street.* ☎ 508-228-0136

QUAKER ARCHITECTURE
ON NANTUCKET

Old-time whalers called Nantucket the "little gray lady," referring to the fact that the island's shape resembles a gray whale. But gray is also the dominant color on Nantucket's architectural landscape; its stark, spare colonial buildings of weathered shingles remind visitors of the simplicity of the Quakers who once lived here. The typical Quaker home was a saltbox colonial with four or five windows in the upper story, and very little ornamentation. Examples include the Walter Folger house at 8 Pleasant Street or the Nathaniel Macy House (Christian House) on Walnut Lane, built in 1723.

Around 1830, more lavish and opulent styles supplanted the austere Quaker aesthetic. Nantucket is home to some grand examples of Federal architecture, with roof walks (or "widows' walks") that enabled wives to watch the harbor for sign of their long-absent seafaring husbands. Georgian houses such as the famous identical "Three Bricks" mansions on Main Street compete with heady examples of Greek Revival architecture. These were built to dazzle the eye: one of the two William Hadwen Greek Revival homes on Main Street had a second-floor ballroom and a retractable rooftop dome, so that guests could stargaze while dancing.

All of these architectural treasures, from the sober gray Quaker saltboxes to the showiest mansions on Main Street, are objects of historical preservation. Because of the tourist industry boom, with its accompanying real estate developments around the island, Nantucket was named in 2000 as one of the eleven "most endangered historic places" in the nation by the National Trust for Historic Preservation.

Orleans (Cape Cod)

A Contemporary Basilica and Center for Sacred Arts
THE COMMUNITY OF JESUS/THE CHURCH
OF THE TRANSFIGURATION
Ecumenical Christian. Year consecrated: 2000 (community dates to 1958). Architects: William Rawn Associates, Inc. ☎ 508-255-1904
💻 www.cofj.net

From the Mid-Cape Highway, take Exit 12 (Orleans and Brewster). At the end of the exit ramp, turn right onto Route 6A. Go straight through the first traffic light. At the next light, turn left onto Rock Harbor Road. After approximately one mile you will reach a T junction; turn left toward Rock Harbor. The first driveway on the left is the Community of Jesus.

On a blistering day in June 2000, more than 900 people gathered in the lovely Cape Cod town of Orleans to witness the dedication of the Church of the Transfiguration, an impressive basilica-style church modeled after the early liturgical churches of Europe. Community of Jesus member Father Martin Shannon, a doctoral candidate in liturgical studies at the Catholic University of America in Washington, D.C., knew from the early planning stages in 1994 that this church had a particular mission. "One principle was predominant," he wrote. "The building must *speak*. It must *teach* the gospel."

And teach it does. As visitors and worshipers move down the nave of the fifty-five-foot-tall building, they will notice that all of the artwork—frescoes, stained glass, stone carving, and mosaic—has been carefully plotted to depict the story of salvation. The fifteen-foot-tall bronze doors show Adam and Eve on the sixth day of creation; above them is a lintel depicting the Holy Spirit breaking through the chaos present at the beginning of creation. The creation theme carries over to the mosaic on the floor, beginning at the octagonally shaped baptismal font with a scene from the Great Flood (a symbol of the earth's baptism), and continuing along the nave. The mosaic culminates in a Tree of Life that bursts into bloom at the foot of the altar.

The upper levels depict another theme. Running along the north and south walls underneath the clerestory windows will be twelve frescoes with scenes from the life of Christ. Below, the spandrels (the bands in the triangular portion between each column) will contain Old Testament scenes that correspond to these twelve New Testament scenes. Finally, the stone capitals—the capstones for all of the columns in the church—will tie these scenes together with ancient Christian symbols and local flora and fauna (such as cod and lobster). The domed ceiling of the apse shows Christ's reign in glory, in a mosaic designed by Irish artist Helen McLean, the church's master designer. While the stone capitals and the bronze doors have been completed, the frescoes, stained glass, and mosaics are still in progress. The interior of the church should be finished by 2005.

*Processional of
the dedication
of the
Church of the
Transfiguration*

It is quite remarkable that the Community of Jesus, which numbers only 300-odd full members (see sidebar), has constructed this architectural marvel. Although some assistance has come from outside donors, the bulk of the funds has been raised within the community itself. The community hired artisans and craftspersons from the best workshops in Europe—a master mosaicist from Ravenna, Italy, for example, who was asked to train community members to assist her in doing the mosaics. The community has dedicated various members to learning the crafts of medieval Europe, believing that such specialized skills must be preserved in the Christian community and that the creation of fine art is a form of worship.

The community welcomes personal retreatants at any time of year. Spiritual counseling can be arranged. Several times a year, the community also hosts guided retreats for groups. Most individual retreatants stay in **Bethany Retreat House**, with five guest rooms, although there are remote cottages dotted across the compound for those who desire more solitude. Bethany House is lovely, with a tranquil air that has offered peace to many a weary soul. Retreatants take their meals in a semicircular dining room with bow windows overlooking Rock Harbor, where fishermen and -women put out early each morning for the day's catch.

Hospitality is a Benedictine tradition, and various regular outreach events are open to the public. Each Friday during the summer, guests can

THE COMMUNITY OF JESUS

The Community of Jesus is not a large organization—just over three hundred in number, including children. Approximately ninety-five of the members are celibate sisters and brothers, living in the convent and the friary, while others live with their families. Most of the noncelibate adults work at jobs both within and outside the community. "We are ordinary people, called to live beyond the ordinary," says the community's Rule. One unusual feature of community life is that several families often live together in a single house.

The community has evolved a great deal since its beginnings in 1958, when Cay Andersen and Judy Sorensen, two Episcopal laywomen, began a small ministry of prayer and healing in Orleans. Officially constituted in 1970, the community has become increasingly committed to living the values of the Benedictine monastic tradition. Today, the Church of the Transfiguration hosts four daily services in which members chant the daily offices (the "Liturgy of the Hours"), as Benedictine monasteries have done for centuries. The community is dedicated to ecumenical dialogue and is composed of members from across the spectrum of Protestant and Catholic traditions. The community's commitment to ecumenism is reflected in the form of the Church of the Transfiguration itself: a contemporary expression of a fourth-century basilica design was chosen because it predates all of the divisions that have plagued Christianity.

gobble a delicious "harborside tea" accompanied by live chamber music on the patio of Bethany House, overlooking Rock Harbor. In July or August, the **Abbey Arts Festival** offers a good introduction to the community's musical and theatrical groups, including the Spirit of America band (ranked in 2000 as the best marching show band in the United States, and second internationally). Visitors can listen to choral Evensong with the Gloriae Dei Cantores, the community's award-winning vocal group, or hear the perfectly-timed bell choir, the Gloriae Dei Ringers. Tapestry Dance, the liturgical dance group, also performs during the weekend, as does the Stages Theatre Company, which specializes in liturgical drama. As if that weren't enough, the community also features ensembles for brass, winds, and chamber music.

THE DIVINE OFFICE

The Divine Office can be a bit confusing for neophytes, though it is ultimately a deeply spiritual experience to chant the psalms that have sustained religious life for thousands of years. The services are mostly in Latin, with much standing and sitting, occasional bowing, kneeling, and making the sign of the cross. It can be difficult to follow the chant book, which features colored ribbons pointing to the various segments of the service, and requires the worshiper to switch repeatedly from one section of the book to another. If you have never participated in this type of service, it would be wise to arrive ten or fifteen minutes early. Enter the church through the side door on the left, and someone from the community will hand you a prayer book. A hospitality person is available in the vestibule prior to services, to familiarize guests with the order of service and with the prayer book.

Plymouth

About forty-five miles south of Boston is the site where it allegedly all began: Plymouth Rock, the Pilgrims' landing site. However, as the informative guides of this tourist haven will tell you, it didn't exactly happen according to the schooltext script. For starters, the Pilgrims were hardly the first Europeans to set foot upon Massachusetts's shores. When those weary souls docked in 1620, they discovered Wampanoag Indians who already spoke some English and possessed metal kettles, iron tools, and wool, obtained through trade with earlier Europeans who had already visited, decided there was no real treasure to be had, and moved on. Some European explorers had also fished for cod here; Virginia's Captain John Smith had given the area the name "Plymouth" when he explored it in 1614. One of Smith's companions, Thomas Hunt, was fishing for something else: Hunt lured a Wampanoag Indian named Squanto into a trap and brought him to Europe, where he was sold into slavery.

It should be noted that the Pilgrims did not intend to settle in this area, but in "Virginia," which at the time did technically include New England. They would have probably done better to have made it further south to Jamestown, because exactly half of the *Mayflower* company (51 out of 102) died in the first year. Because the *Mayflower* was delayed in its voyage, the Pilgrims arrived in the New World much later than they had originally hoped—just in time, unfortunately, to endure a particularly harsh New England winter with dwindling provisions.

The Nation's Most Famous, Uh, Rock
PLYMOUTH ROCK
Water Street. ☎ 508-866-2580
🖥️ www.state.ma.us/dem/parks/plgm.htm

Take Route 3 South to Route 44. Follow Route 44 East to the waterfront. Open daily during daylight hours. No admission fee.

The first of the Plymouth sites that most tourists flock to is undoubtedly Plymouth Rock, which is a shame because the rock itself is a bit of a disappointment. Through the years, when it was unprotected, many visitors felt entitled to "get a piece of the rock" and helped themselves to souvenirs with chisels and the like. Today, the rock is a petite shadow of its former self, but it is encased in a heavy canopy as protection against the elements and the more ruthless segment of tourists.

While the rock is a bit of a letdown, it is the only one of the three major Plymouth sites that is free, so by all means go and see it. The area surrounding it is one of the nation's smallest national parks, and is staffed by very well-informed guides.

"This rock has become an object of veneration in the United States. I have seen bits of it carefully preserved in several towns in the Union. Does this sufficiently show that all human power and greatness is in the soul of man? Here is a stone which the feet of a few outcasts pressed for an instant; and the stone becomes famous; it is treasured by a great nation; its very dust is shared as a relic."
—Alexis de Tocqueville, *Democracy in America,* 1835

A Living History Museum
PLIMOTH PLANTATION
Route 3A/Main Street. Year established: 1947. ☎ 508-746-1622
🖥️ www.plimoth.org

From Boston, take Route 3 South to Exit 4 South (Plimoth Plantation Highway) and follow the signs. From Cape Cod, take Route 3 North to Exit 5, pass under the highway, head south on Route 3, and follow directions above. Open daily from 9 A.M. to 5 P.M. from April until early December. Admission fee.

Although the Pilgrims and Puritans were fastidious about many things, spelling was certainly not one of them, which explains the many variations on the name "Plymouth" at the area's historic sites. "Plimoth" is a more authentic seventeenth-century rendition, demonstrating how closely the folks at Plimoth Plantation strive for historical accuracy.

Plimoth Plantation is one of the nation's most famous outdoor living-history museums. Although it began in the 1940s as a traditional museum complete with costumed mannequins, carefully curated plaques, and meticulously tended gardens, something about the waves of change of the 1960s affected this place. In 1969, the museum was entirely revamped, with the identifying markers swept away and nagging anachronisms (such as belt buckles on the black-clad Pilgrims or implausibly pretty home decor) removed. Not every visitor was impressed with the plantation's drive for historical accuracy; one woman called it "run down and shabby." (Well, responded the historians, Pilgrim life *was* dirty.) Today, the plantation strives to achieve historical exactitude in every detail, to the point of reverse breeding some livestock to seventeenth-century specifications. Visitors can see these new/old breeds in the Nye Barn, erected in 1995.

Plimoth Plantation

Be sure that while you are walking in and out of the dark, sparse Pilgrim cabins, you really engage the actors in conversation. In the village, all of the actors appear in the colorful costumes of seventeenth-century peasant life, and will speak in rough working-class tones of their exile in Holland, of the difficult months crossing the Atlantic, and the desperate tasks of taming the wilderness. For them, it is the year 1627. These actors are simply brilliant at what they do, and will not break character for all the tea in England. Feel free to ask them any questions (and be prepared to answer their questions in return: "Were ye on a passenger boat or a provisions boat? Are ye of the Reformed Church?"). The actors are happy to expound upon their devout Protestant beliefs. "We wish to purify the church of all the inventions of man," says one young mother.

The Pilgrim village includes numerous reconstructed houses, including the cabins of John Alden, Myles Standish, and Governor William Bradford. There is also a fort, an elevated structure erected in 1622 for defense purposes. It doubled as the town's meetinghouse, or place of worship, where the Pilgrims would gather twice each Sabbath.

Plimoth Plantation has added exhibits over the years to remind visitors

THOSE FUN-LOVIN' PURITANS

In our popular imagination, the word *Puritan* is almost synonymous with "killjoy." We tend to depict the Puritans as dour-faced people who look like they just canceled Christmas. (Actually, the Puritans *did* cancel Christmas—they banned its celebration in 1659 because of its pagan origins as a winter solstice festival.) Puritan theocracy made for some inflexible rules: Church attendance was required; the crime of adultery was punishable by death; theatricals of any kind were forbidden. But those Puritans still knew how to have a good time. Although they rejected drunkenness, they did drink alcohol—and quite a lot of it, since clean drinking water was rather hard to come by in early America. They had parties, and they wrote rather earthily of sexual relations (of the marital variety, of course). And although American schoolchildren only use black construction paper when they create cut-out Puritans to decorate the Thanksgiving centerpiece, the truth is that Puritans wore every color of the rainbow. In the eighteenth century, they decorated their houses with brilliant paints and dyed their fabrics in vibrant colors.

that before the area was called Plimoth or Plymouth, it was Patuxet, populated by the Wampanoag Indians who once dominated what are now
southern Massachusetts and Rhode Island. The Wampanoag had suffered a
terrible epidemic just a few years before the Pilgrims arrived, and had
mostly left the immediate area by 1620. In the 1620s, apart from a small
plot inhabited by one Wampanoag and his family (see below), the closest
Wampanoag community was at least fifteen miles from the Pilgrims.

The Wampanoag section of the Plantation, established in its present
form in 1990, works a little differently than the Pilgrim Village; here,
the guides do not affect a seventeenth-century demeanor. Those who are
descended from the Wampanoag wear traditional dress, and non-
Wampanoag guides do not. They speak freely of Wampanoag history and
the present-day tribe of which many are a part. They discuss modern con-
veniences.

The Wampanoag area is not a village; it is a reconstructed home site of
one family. The man who once lived here, Hobbamock, worked as a liaison between the Wampanoag and the Pilgrims, smoothing the troubles
created by wandering livestock and the like. He was a counselor to Massasoit, the sachem (chief) of the Pokanoket in what is now Rhode Island.
Hobbamock's extended family may have included ten to twenty people at
a time, living on-site. Around the clearing, visitors can learn about
Wampanoag techniques for bead making, cooking, and tool construction.
Questions on Wampanoag religious practices, however, elicit some blank
looks. "I don't really know anything about their beliefs," says one guide, a
Wampanoag descendent. "I think that the English never thought that was
important enough to write down."

A Reconstructed Pilgrim Vessel
THE MAYFLOWER II
State Pier, Plymouth Harbor. Year opened: 1958. ☎ 508-746-1622
🖳 www.plimoth.org

*From Plimoth Plantation, take the northerly exit out of the main parking
lot and turn left onto Warren Avenue, at the foot of the entrance drive.
Go two miles to downtown Plymouth, turning right on Water Street at the
bottom of the hill just past the Town Green (on the right). Follow Water
Street past Plymouth Rock, where Mayflower II is moored. Open daily
from April to early December. Admission fee (tickets purchased at
Plimoth Plantation).*

Visitors' first comments upon seeing the reconstructed *Mayflower* are often similar to their initial remarks about nearby Plymouth Rock: "It's so *small!*" And indeed, it is tiny—slightly more than a hundred feet from bow to stern. It is difficult for Americans of the SUV era to even imagine that 102 people could spend sixty-six days in the cramped quarters of the *Mayflower*, with livestock, human beings, and a year's provisions crammed into every nook and cranny of the little vessel.

The tour is given by modern-dress guides, though costumed actors will occasionally be on hand to discuss their travel travails. And since the *Mayflower* was not originally constructed to carry passengers, but cargo such as wine and fish, there were many travails.

THANKSGIVING: FROM PILGRIM FEAST TO ALL-AMERICAN HOLIDAY

More legends than facts exist regarding the 1621 "harvest feast" with the Pilgrims and Indians that evolved into the present-day celebration of Thanksgiving. After that dread first winter of 1620–21, the fall of 1621 seemed downright prosperous by comparison, with Governor John Winthrop writing that the colony was "all so recovered in health and strength and had all things in good plenty." After the harvest was gathered, the Pilgrims held a feast and invited the Indians.

What did they eat? Turkey or another wild fowl, probably. Although the turkey was a bird indigenous to North America, it was no stranger to the English when they arrived in 1620. This was because Spanish explorers had brought turkeys back to Europe nearly a century before and traded them with the English. So, turkey was familiar fowl to the colonists and may well have graced the first harvest table. While cranberry sauce is a staple of New England, it was probably not present at that early feast, since sugar was extremely scarce. The Wampanoag contributions probably included cod, corn meal, and fresh venison.

While this first-harvest-feast-with-the-Indians did actually happen (though not as late in the year as we celebrate it today), it's not quite the case that Thanksgiving immediately sprang into fame as a new American holiday. The 1621 harvest feast was not so much a religious celebration as a secular one, whereas "days of thanksgiving" became recurring religious feast days for later Puritans. Throughout the seventeenth century, days of thanksgiving were relatively common and spontaneous, not fixed annual events. Puritan ministers would call for such days to celebrate God's providence in community life. The days would be marked with community-wide celebration, just as Puritan fast days featured entire towns fasting and praying for a community's perceived sins.

In the late eighteenth century, George Washington tried to institute Thanksgiving as a late-November American holiday, but Thomas Jefferson thought this smacked of "kingly" arrogance and abolished the official practice when he became president. By the nineteenth century Thanksgiving had become an annual autumn observance that was the pride of New England. But this celebration remained almost wholly a regional holiday until the 1850s, when the editor of *Godey's Magazine and Lady's Book* gave the holiday terrific press in the hopes of uniting the increasingly splintered nation with a shared Thanksgiving tradition. During the Civil War, Abraham Lincoln thought along similar lines, seeking some sort of observance that could unite the Blue and the Grey in a common identity. He hit upon Thanksgiving. And although it took a while before the South caught on to this Yankee festival, it eventually became just what Lincoln had hoped: an all-American holiday.

Two Thanksgiving celebrations are observed in Plymouth today, reflecting tensions about the holiday and its history. The most well-known features a parade of fifty-one local residents, dressed in seventeenth-century attire, who represent the fifty-one survivors of the first harsh winter the Pilgrims endured. The other observance is not a celebration, but a National Day of Mourning. It is organized by area Wampanoag who, in the words of historian Diana Eck, "resist this picture-perfect rendition of a history that has remembered by name all of the survivors of the colony and forgotten the victims of the colonization." One 1998 speaker summarized the protestors' passion. "We will not give thanks for the invasion of our country; we will not celebrate the theft of our lands and the genocide of our people; we will not sing and dance to please the tourist who come here seeking a Disneyland version of our history."

NEARBY

➥ **Our Lady's Chapel** in **New Bedford** contains a shrine to Our Lady of Good Voyage, commemorating the miraculous appearance of Mary to three lost sailors in a deadly storm. Each September, the church hosts the Feast of Our Lady of Good Voyage, remembering those who have lost their lives on the sea and praying for the safety of all mariners. *600 Pleasant Street, New Bedford. The church is located in the historic district by the wharf, opposite City Hall.* ☎ 508-996-8274

➥ Directly across the street from the New Bedford Whaling Museum is **The Seamen's Bethel**, a simple church that was built in 1832. The church features into Herman Melville's novel *Moby Dick*, where it is called "The Whaleman's Chapel." The narrator, Ishmael, visits it just before shipping out on a dangerous sea voyage. Ishmael is unnerved by the black-bordered marble tablets that are set into the walls on either side of the pulpit— cenotaphs commemorating other mariners who lost their lives at sea. "It needs scarcely to be told, with what feelings, on the even of a Nantucket voyage, I regarded those marble tablets, and by the murky light of that darkened, doleful day read the fate of the whalemen who had gone before me," he recounts. There is a marker on the pew where Melville sat when he visited the chapel in 1840. *15 Johnny Cake Hill, New Bedford. Open daily from May to October from 10 A.M. to 5 P.M. From Columbus Day through April, the chapel is open on weekdays from 11 A.M. to 1 P.M., Saturday from 10 A.M. to 5 P.M., and Sunday from 1 P.M. to 5 P.M. Donation requested.* ☎ 508-992-3295

Provincetown (Cape Cod)

Provincetown has been through many dramatic transformations: When the Pilgrims stopped here in 1620, it was a barren outpost; two centuries later, it had achieved central importance as one of the premier fishing ports of North America. Today it is a haven for gay and lesbian vacationers, who are accepted enough in the area that Provincetown is one of the few places east of San Francisco where same-sex couples can comfortably hold hands in public. The community is well known for its ties to the arts (the Cape Cod School of Art was founded here in 1899) and its sleek restaurants.

Before Plymouth Rock . . .

PILGRIM MONUMENT AND PROVINCETOWN MUSEUM

High Pole Hill Road. Year created: 1910. ☎ 508-487-1310
💻 www.pilgrim-monument.org

From Route 6, take the Shankpainter Road Exit. Take the first left and then the next right, following signs for the monument and museum. Open April through June and September through November from 9 A.M. to 5 P.M.; open until 7 P.M. in July and August. Admission fee.

Provincetown, as the tip of the Cape, has an interesting religious history, though some of it is left up to the imagination since the original sites and buildings have not survived. Here is where the *Mayflower's* Pilgrims first docked on November 11, 1620. This is where the party signed the famous Mayflower Compact. If the area had been more conducive to agriculture, this could have been the site of the Pilgrims' first stronghold. As it was, the Pilgrims chose to move on, but at this site there is a striking granite monument (with a can't-miss observation area at the top) and a Pilgrim museum to commemorate what might have been.

Pilgrim Monument, dedicated in 1910, is the tallest solid granite monument in the United States—just over 252 feet tall, to be exact. The top of the monument is 353 feet above sea level, and the spectacular panoramic view makes the walk up to the tower well worth the effort. The committee that designed the tower scoured England and Holland for some example of a seventeenth-century "Puritan tower"; this search was of course in vain because the Puritans had wanted nothing of towers and

Detail from the Pilgrim Monument, Provincetown

turrets to adorn their plain-style meetinghouses. Instead of authenticity, the Provincetown committee settled for grandeur, modeling the tower after the Torre del Mangia in Siena, Italy. The Puritans may have condemned the final result as "Popish," but modern visitors are usually impressed by the slim, imperial monument that towers over Provincetown. The bottom floors are given over to a museum, with shipwreck salvages, whaling instruments, and a diorama of the *Mayflower*.

Stunning Trompe L'oeil Interior Design
UNITARIAN-UNIVERSALIST MEETING HOUSE
236 Commercial Street. Year consecrated: 1847 (congregation dates to around 1820). Architect: attributed to Benjamin Hallet.
☎ 508-487-9344 🖳 www.uumh.org

> *Take Route 6 into Provincetown. Turn left at the traffic light at Conwell Street, then right onto Bradford Street at the stop sign. Sunday services are offered at 11 A.M. year-round.*

Universalism was, quite literally, washed ashore into Provincetown. In 1820, two little girls were playing on the beach nearby when they discovered a waterlogged book—*The Life of Rev. John Murray, Preacher of Universalist Salvation*—in the sand. They took it home, dried it off, and read its message of God's love and acceptance. They passed it to adults, who passed it to friends. And so Universalism took root on the tip of Cape Cod. In short order, a congregation was formed and a church was built in 1829. It was quickly outgrown, however, and so in 1846–47 the congregation erected this handsome Greek Revival church. Rather unusually, the sanctuary is located on the second floor; the church's renovations have recently unearthed the reason for this. It seems that the church sits on just a few feet of sand over a high water table. Therefore, the first floor constitutes the vestry and serves as the foundation for the sanctuary above.

The church's most impressive feature is its trompe l'oeil paintings, which cover much of the walls, ceiling, and pilasters of the interior. These paintings come very close to achieving their purpose of "fooling the eye," making the sanctuary seem much larger and more grand than it is. A young German artist, Carl Wendte, painted the trompe l'oeil interior in the mid–nineteenth century, creating illusions of three-dimensional alcoves and wall panels.

NEARBY

➥ Provincetown boasts the Cape's "**Oldest Cemetery,**" which contains numerous eighteenth-century markers and a special plaque honoring those four *Mayflower* unfortunates who perished while the ship was docked in Provincetown's harbor. Listed as a National Historic Cemetery, the twenty-three-acre burying ground's oldest stone dates to 1637. *Cemetery Road.*

➥ In **Wellfleet,** the **Chapel of St. James the Fisherman** ministers each summer to the Episcopalian vacationers who frequent the Cape. Architect Olav Hammarstrom fashioned the 1958 wooden chapel to appear completely at home in its environment, surrounded by pine trees. *2317 Route 6, Wellfleet.* ☎ 508-349-2188

THE CAPE COD
NATIONAL SEASHORE

Although John F. Kennedy was only a summer resident on the Cape, locals are as proud of him as they would be of any native son— and for good reason. One of the most delightful things he did as president was to enact laws protecting a fifty-mile stretch on the eastern shore of Cape Cod from development. Established in 1961, the **Cape Cod National Seashore** stretches from Chatham to Provincetown, encompassing 43,000 acres of land (including offshore land). Most of it is public, although about six hundred private homes remain, which were standing before the law went into effect. More than five million visitors come to the seashore preserve each year, enticed by its eleven nature trails, six beaches, eight lighthouses, and three biking paths.

This is some of the most stunning oceanfront in the United States. When Henry David Thoreau walked the shores of Cape Cod, he called this long stretch of sand "an exceedingly desolate landscape," with "no house from shore to shore for several miles." The area is certainly not as isolated as in Thoreau's day; despite the lovely beaches, the crowds of people and distant condominiums are unerring reminders that "civilization" is but a few miles off. (Also, the land on which Thoreau walked has long since washed to sea, since the Cape shoreline is gradually eroding.) Still, the National Seashore is a national treasure and is not to be missed.

Sandwich (Cape Cod)

Many visitors bypass this quaint historic town not far from the entrance to Cape Cod. (Cape Codders refer to this eastern region as the Upper Cape.) But it would be a mistake to pass over Sandwich, with its rich spiritual history and artistic traditions. The oldest permanently established town on the Cape (settled in 1637), Sandwich is best known for its leadership in glassmaking in the nineteenth century. Today, the Sandwich Glass Museum chronicles the rise and fall of the town's glassmaking industry, while several upscale boutique shops in town still ply the trade.

The Oldest Church Bell in America
FIRST CHURCH OF CHRIST
Congregational/United Church of Christ. 136 Main Street. Year consecrated: 1847 (congregation dates to 1638). Architect: Whittemore Peterson. ☎ 508-888-0434
🖳 www.vsc.cape.com/~barnucc/church/sandwich/html

From the Mid-Cape Highway, take Exit 2 North, which is Route 130 for approximately one mile. The church is at the junction of Routes 130 and Main Street, across from the Town Hall on the right side. Tours are available in July and August, Monday through Friday from 10 A.M. to 4 P.M.

Many New England churches claim various "firsts," but this one can genuinely boast the oldest church bell anywhere in the country. Cast in 1675, the First Church's brass bell is now housed in an 1847 spire, constructed in the style of Christopher Wren's London churches.

This congregation, with its history of splits and mergers, reflects something of the schismatic history of New England Protestantism. When the great "Unitarian departure" divided many Congregational churches down the middle in the beginning of the nineteenth century, this church was no exception. The minister and most of the members toed the Reformed party line and called themselves "the Calvinist Congregational Church," demonstrating their rejection of Unitarian beliefs and staunch embrace of traditional Trinitarian Christianity. It was the Calvinists who built this church structure. A smaller group turned Unitarian, adopting the name "First Parish Society."

In 1918, the two churches (along with a Methodist congregation)

Old Town Cemetery and First Church of Christ, Sandwich

agreed to federate—meaning that they would worship in one building (this one) and use the same minister, yet maintain separate denominational identities. In 1965, the Unitarian and Congregational members joined in creating the First Church of Christ, which is affiliated with the United Churches of Christ and contributes to the social welfare programs of the Unitarian-Universalist Association. (The Methodists dropped out in 1965.) The rifts of the past have now been healed, and the church continues in its historic tradition as a leading congregation of the Cape.

NEARBY

➥ Slightly away from the center of town, tucked behind Route 6A, is the **Sandwich Friends Meetinghouse**. This rambling gray-shingled building is the quintessence of nineteenth-century Quaker architecture. Constructed in 1810, this is the third meetinghouse to rest on this site; the congregation, established in 1657, is the oldest continuous Quaker meeting in

Friends Meetinghouse, Sandwich

North America. Quakers did not have an easy time of it in early Sandwich, as elsewhere in Massachusetts, and it was not until the early eighteenth century that they enjoyed true freedom of worship in the colony. *6 Quaker Road. Sunday meeting is held at 10 A.M.* ☎ 508-888-4181

➡ **Heritage Plantation.** When many New Englanders hear the word rhododendron, they immediately think of this seventy-six-acre estate, which flourishes each June with thousands of rhododendrons in at least 125 varieties. In late July, the gardens' featured flower is the daylily, with over 500 varieties on display. *67 Grove Street. From Route 6, take Exit 2. Go north on Route 130 into Sandwich. Turn left on Grove Street to get to the museum. Admission fee. Open from Mother's Day through mid-October, 10 A.M. to 5 P.M. daily.* ☎ 508-888-3300 ▦ www.heritageplantation.org

West Barnstable (Cape Cod)

A Church Cut in Half
WEST PARISH MEETINGHOUSE
Congregational/Puritan. 2049 Meetinghouse Road. Year consecrated: 1719 (congregation dates to 1616). ☎ 508-362-4445
▦ www.westparish.org

Take Exit 5 off the Mid-Cape Highway (toward West Barnstable/ Marstons Mills). After the ramp, turn left onto Prospect Street/ Meetinghouse Way. The meetinghouse is .4 miles ahead.

This lovely meetinghouse may perhaps boast the longest history of any Protestant congregation in the country: The building dates to 1719, making it the second-longest-standing Congregational meetinghouse on the Cape. ("First" honors go to the Old Indian Meeting House in Mashpee, established in 1684; see page 210.) But the congregation dates a full century before that—to 1616, when Puritans in Southwark, London, removed themselves from the Church of England and formed their own meeting. The dissidents worshiped together in private homes in England for nearly twenty years, enduring persecution and the imprisonment of forty-two members for holding unlawful religious gatherings. After their release (negotiated with the understanding that their minister would thereafter be exiled from England), the Southwark Puritans braved the rocky waves of the Atlantic in 1634. Following a brief stint in Scituate,

West Parish Meetinghouse, West Barnstable

the congregation established itself in 1639 in West Barnstable, a very new outpost of the New World.

The rapid growth of the congregation and the community necessitated a larger, more commodious meetinghouse by the beginning of the eighteenth century. In 1717, work began on the present building, which was consecrated in 1719. But the Puritans had underestimated their own needs: Just four years later, the building was deemed too small for its growing membership. Rather than razing it in favor of a larger structure, the meetinghouse was cut exactly in half. The sides were extended outwards, with eighteen feet added to the center of the building. The congregation also added a bell tower, which later housed a bell cast by silversmith Paul Revere, still in use today. The gilded weathervane cock, which dates to 1723, still crowns the bell tower.

But history has a way of coming full circle. From 1950 through 1956 the congregation ordered a complete restoration and refurbishment of the aging building. Believe it or not, that restoration included the removal of the eighteen-foot addition that was added in 1723—so the meetinghouse you see today is quite true to the original structure (with the addition of the bell tower).

Woods Hole (Cape Cod)

The Nation's First Public Mary Garden
GARDEN OF OUR LADY
33 Millfield Street. Roman Catholic. Year created: 1932.
☎ 508-548-0990 💻 www.mgardens.org

> *Coming from West Falmouth on Route 28 South, bear right on Locust Street. After .3 miles, Locust turns into Woods Hole Road. After 1.3 miles, turn right onto Quissett Harbor Road. After .1 miles, turn left onto Quissett Avenue. After 1.6 miles, turn right onto Millfield.*

Woods Hole is most famous for its international leadership in the field of marine biology, having created the first major institutions for marine research in the United States. The town boasts another first as well. In 1932, the first public Mary garden in the United States was created on the lawn of St. Joseph's Church in Woods Hole. It has a connection to the famous Marine Biological Laboratory, located just across Eel Pond: The garden's founder, Frances Crane Lillie, was the wife of the laboratory's president in the 1920s and '30s. Mrs. Lillie, an enthusiastic convert to Catholicism, conceived of the Mary garden as a witness to the researchers and students at the marine laboratory, a reminder of the presence of Mary in the natural world they were studying.

A "Mary garden," as conceived in Renaissance times, generally incorporates two distinct elements: statuary or art depicting the Blessed Virgin Mary, and flowers and herbs that have Mary in their names or are otherwise associated with the Mother of Jesus. Hence, the Garden of Our Lady contains fifty such plants, including rosemary, Madonna Lily, Eyes of Mary, Cross Flower, Mary's Gold (marigolds), Ladder to Heaven (lily of the valley), and Assumption Lily, among other flowers. The garden recalls a time when flowers were seen as religious symbols (the rosary, for example, was once considered an "enclosed garden" of roses to be offered in prayer). In the Middle Ages faithful Christians saw the goodness of Mary reflected in the beauty of nature: Lilies recalled her purity, roses suggested her glory and sorrow, and violets symbolized her humility.

This garden contains a specially commissioned concrete sculpture of the Virgin created by artist V. M. S. Hannell. The sculpture, the focal point of the garden, is set in a cross-shaped bed of flowers and depicts Mary as she might have looked at the moment of the annunciation. Two large iron bells, cast in England and housed in a tall stone tower in the garden, delight residents and visitors by ringing three times each day in Mary's honor. The bells are inscribed with the names of two Catholic leaders in the fields of genetics and biology: Gregor Mendel and Louis Pasteur. "I will teach you of life and the life eternal," reads an inscription on one of the bells, a fitting summation of Lillie's desire to promote harmony between the worlds of religion and natural science. Mary is seen as the connection: By becoming a human vessel of the divine, she "opened up all natural life to the supernatural life of God."

NEARBY

➥ A sanctuary is a holy place, a site of both worship and refuge. In **East Falmouth**, visitors to the **Ashumet Holly and Wildlife Sanctuary** may feel closer to the realm of the spirit while taking in the beautiful plants and animals that have been protected here. This forty-nine-acre Massachusetts Audubon Society property specializes in holly, with more than 1,000 plants of 70 varieties, collected from all over the world. It also provides sanctuary for endangered species of turtles, birds, and frogs, who can be seen on the estate's well-marked walking trails. *286 Ashumet Road, East Falmouth. Admission fee (free to Audubon Society members).*
☎ 508-563-6390

THOREAU'S FINAL WORD ON CAPE COD

"The time must come when this coast will be a place of resort for those New-Englanders who really wish to visit the sea-side. . . . But this shore will never be more attractive than it is now. . . . A man may stand there and put all America behind him."

—Henry David Thoreau, *Cape Cod* (1864)

$\mathscr{R}$hode Island

RHODE ISLAND IS A DREAM destination for lovers of nature and of history. It has 400-odd miles of coastline and quite a few of the country's national historical landmarks—this despite the fact that the state is 200 times smaller than Texas. Specifically, Rhode Island packs more *religious* history per square mile than any other state in America, due to its unique, and early, policy of religious toleration.

"The State of Rhode Island and Providence Plantations," as it is officially called, was founded by a religious exile, Roger Williams (see page 257), whose unorthodox views earned him banishment from Puritan Massachusetts in 1635. After walking to Narragansett Bay in 1636, Williams created a small settlement called "Providence," which was the first town in New England to extend religious toleration to all residents. Puritan minister Cotton Mather, based in neighboring Massachusetts, called Williams's experiment "a sewer" of undesirable religious traditions—by which Mather presumably meant anything that was not Puritan. Although it was the first, Providence was not the only settlement to offer religious toleration: In 1638 Anne Hutchinson (another Puritan dissident, see page 254) sought refuge in a new village called Portsmouth, on the northern side of Aquidneck Island. A year later, the town of Newport was founded on Aquidneck's southern end. These towns became loosely federated as "Rhode Island colony." Providence's early policy of religious toleration was extended throughout all the colony's towns and was eventually codified in the colony's official charter. Persecuted Quakers such as Mary Dyer (see page 255) sought asylum in Rhode Island, as did Huguenots (French

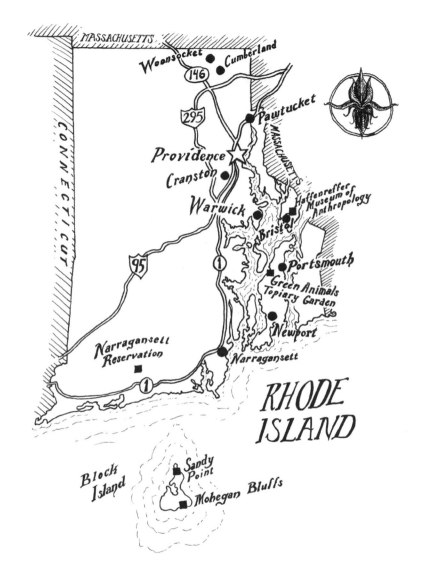

Protestants) and Roman Catholics, who were harassed in the other English colonies. Rhode Island also offered shelter to some of America's first Jews, Sephardim (of Spanish and Portuguese heritage) who built a synagogue in Newport in 1658. And of course, Rhode Island was home to Native American groups, such as the Narragansett and Wampanoag, who had occupied the region for centuries. Among the New England colonies, the best record for treatment of Native Americans belongs to Rhode

Island, which adopted Roger Williams's example in forging cordial and respectful relations.

Providence boasts the nation's oldest Baptist congregation, which dates to 1638 and was established by Williams. Its church building, completed in 1775, is widely regarded as one of the jewels of Georgian architecture in America. The city is also home to Brown University, the first educational institution in America to dispense with religious orthodoxy requirements for all students. Statistically, Providence is the nation's most heavily Catholic city, an identity that is proclaimed by the flying buttresses and Gothic Revival towers of the Cathedral of Saints Peter and Paul. Providence is also home to members of other faiths, including Zen Buddhists, who operate the only residential Zen center in the state. The Providence Zen Center (which is actually located in Cumberland, north of Providence) is the flagship institution of the Kwan Um School of Zen, which has more than sixty branches worldwide.

Block Island

"Nature's Treasure on the Sea"
Block Island is located twelve miles off the coast of Rhode Island, in Long Island Sound. ☎ Tourist Council: 401-466-5200
🖥 www.blockisland.com

> Block Island is accessible by ferry and plane. Interstate Navigation (401-783-4613) operates out of Port Judith year-round and offers summer service from Providence, Newport, New London (Connecticut), and Montauk Point (New York). Air service is also available from many airports throughout New England.

Twelve miles off Rhode Island's shore in Long Island Sound is one of the state's natural treasures, a largely unspoiled island that is a mere eleven square miles. Formed by glaciers thousands of years ago, Block Island is renowned for its grasslands, beaches, sand dunes, scrubland, salt ponds, and various wetland ecosystems. The island's wildlife includes more than forty species that are classified as rare or endangered.

Because it offers such marvelous examples of environmental variety, Block Island has become a popular spot for vacationers, and has had to fend off some of the more aggressive forms of development that have characterized other New England islands such as Nantucket and Martha's Vineyard. Block Island was a popular resort community in the late nineteenth century, in the days when it was a stopover on steamship routes. After the demise of steamship travel, the year-round islanders returned to quiet lives of farming and fishing; in the 1960s, however, vacationers discovered Block Island anew. Rather than submit to pervasive condominiums and new development, the islanders reopened many of the Victorian cottages and hotels that had been dormant for more than half a century. As a result, the island retains a quiet Victorian sensibility, mixed with a stubborn and forward-thinking commitment to environmental conservation.

At the southeastern edge of Block Island are the **Mohegan Bluffs**, a stunning array of cliffs with red and pink hues. The multicolored strata in the cliffs are the result of thousands of years of glaciation. From the cliffs, visitors have a perfect vantage point for watching ships as they pass along the shore.

A Beacon of Preservation
BLOCK ISLAND SOUTHEAST LIGHT
Mohegan Bluffs. Year built: 1875 (moved to present location in 1993).
☎ 401-466-5009

Bicycles, mopeds, and cars are available for rental on Block Island, near the ferry dock. The Mohegan Bluffs are on the southeastern tip of the island.

Block Island may be a vacationer's dream, but in days past it could be a sailor's nightmare: This small island was once nicknamed "stumbling block island" because so many ships ran aground here, costing hundreds of lives. Between 1819 and 1838, for example, no less than fifty-nine vessels were wrecked on Block Island's rocky shoals. Some of these shipwrecks are now open to scuba divers for exploration.

In 1875, Block Island Southeast Light was built atop Mohegan Bluffs, making it the highest light in New England. The brick building with its octagonal tower was then located over three hundred feet from the edge of the bluff, but decades of erosion took a dangerous toll. In 1990, when the building was only fifty-five feet from the brink, the Coast Guard deactivated the lighthouse, transferring its flashing green light to an automatic beacon on a nearby steel tower. In 1993, the 2,000-ton lighthouse was moved away from the eroding cliffs.

NEARBY

➡ On the north side of the island is **Sandy Point**, which has been preserved as a haven for birds and other wildlife. The area's 143 acres contain beach grass, sand dunes, and wild roses. At Sandy Point is **Old North Light**, a granite lighthouse that was built in 1867, the fourth to stand on its site. Although the lighthouse was deactivated in 1973, it is open to the public as the North Light Interpretive Center and offers exhibits about Block Island's maritime history. *Open weekends Memorial Day to Columbus Day, 10 A.M. to 5 P.M., and daily from June 20 to mid-September. Admission fee.* ☎ 401-466-3200

Bristol

The Largest Sequoia Tree East of the Rocky Mountains
BLITHEWOLD MANSION, GARDENS AND ARBORETUM

101 Ferry Road. Year created: 1907. Landscape architect: John DeWolf. ☎ 401-253-2707 🖳 www.blithewold.org

> *Bristol is located approximately fifteen miles north of Newport. Take Route 114 North across the Mt. Hope Bridge, bearing left onto Ferry Road (Route 114). Blithewold is one-eighth of a mile on the left. The mansion is open mid-April to mid-October, Wednesday to Sunday from 10 A.M. to 4 P.M. Gardens are open year-round, daily from 10 A.M. to 5 P.M. Admission fee.*

Blithewold is an old English term meaning "happy woodlands." It's an appropriate moniker for this 33-acre seaside garden, a product of Rhode Island's days as a summer haven for wealthy urbanites. In 1907, a forty-five-room manor house was constructed on the seashore for the Van Wickle family of Pennsylvania, who had made a fortune in mining. The Van Wickles hired landscape architect John DeWolf (who helped to execute Frederick Law Olmsted's design for Brooklyn's Prospect Park) to create a series of lush gardens for the estate. One of the highlights of Blithewold is a sequoia tree (*sequoiadendron giganteum*) that once grew in DeWolf's own Brooklyn greenhouse; it was transplanted here when it outgrew its city environment. Now a majestic eighty-five feet tall, it is the largest sequoia tree east of the Rocky Mountains. There are also twelve smaller sequoias on the grounds.

Blithewold offers several gardens of note, including a rose garden just outside the mansion, a Japanese rock garden along the shoreline, a bamboo grove, and a "water garden" where two small ponds are joined together by a picturesque stone bridge. In spring and summer, the gardens display vividly colored roses, daffodils, cherry blossoms, and other flowers. Blithewold also contains a small arboretum with ash, linden, maple, willow, and other varieties of trees. In all, there are more than 1,500 trees and shrubs.

NEARBY
➥ Like Harvard University's Peabody Museum (see page 118), Brown University's **Haffenreffer Museum of Anthropology** has a particularly strong collection in Native American history and cultures. Artifacts include baskets, feather headdresses, pottery, blankets and textiles, wooden bowls, and other objects from many different indigenous cultures, from Alaska to Peru. *300 Tower Street. The museum is located east of the town of Bristol. From Providence, take Route 195 East to MA Exit 2 (Route 136) South. Go south on 136 for 7.5 miles. Turn left at the museum sign onto Tower Street. The museum is 1.4 miles from Route 136. Admission fee. From June to August, the museum is open daily every day except Monday from 11* A.M. *to 5* P.M. *During the academic year it is open Saturday and Sunday from 11* A.M. *to 5* P.M. ☎ 401-253-8388 🖥 www.brown.edu/Facilities/Haffenreffer/

Cumberland

The "Head Temple" of the Kwan Um School of Zen Buddhism
PROVIDENCE ZEN CENTER
99 Pound Road. Year founded: 1972. ☎ 401-658-1464
🖥 www.kwanumzen.com/pzc

> *From Providence, take Route 146 North to I-295 North. From 295, take Exit 10 (Route 122) and turn right at the end of the ramp. Go 1.5 miles north on Route 122. After you pass under a footbridge, take the next right onto Pound Road. PZC is located about three-quarters of a mile up Pound Road on the right side.*

The Providence Zen Center, located fifteen miles north of Providence, is Rhode Island's only residential Zen center. Residents and guests practice in the Kwan Um Zen tradition, which originated in Korea (as an offshoot of Chinese Rinzai Buddhism) and was brought to the United States by Zen

Master Seung Sahn (1927–present). He founded PZC in 1972, the first school of its kind in the United States. It is the "international head temple" of the Kwan Um School of Zen, which has sixty affiliate institutions around the world.

Here, Buddhists ranging in level from neophyte to master live under one roof, learning from one another and supporting each other in meditation and practice. Although Buddhism is often perceived as a solitary spiritual path, Seung Sahn sees great benefit in mutual cooperation. Working together means eliminating divisiveness from the practitioners' midst. Those who live here agree to abide by the center's guidelines, which stipulate that personal opinions must be jettisoned in favor of community. ("Put away all your opinions. This is true Buddhism," declares one of the center's Temple Rules.)

Long-term residents are not the only occupants of the center; there are also retreats here lasting as little as one day or as many as ninety days. During multiday Yong Maeng Jong Jin retreats, the daily schedule includes ten hours of Zen practice, work and rest periods, vegetarian meals, and private interviews with the retreat leader. The Zen practice includes periods of chanting, sitting, and prostration.

Set apart from the Zen Center but also on the property is the **Diamond Hill Zen Monastery**, where serious students receive more extensive training in the Kwan Um tradition. The monastery's low, pagoda-shaped building with its fluted roofline hosts the center's semiannual Kyol Che retreats. These silent retreats are four weeks long in summer or three months in winter (though arrangements can be made for guests to participate in Kyol Che for shorter time periods, such as a week). Kyol Che retreats are modeled after the intensive winter and summer retreats in the mountain temples of Korea. The only reading materials permitted are the works of Zen Master Seung Sahn; there is no communication with the "outside" world by mail or telephone. Retreatants may not keep a diary or journal, and they practice Zen from 4:45 A.M. to 9:45 P.M. each day.

Narragansett

Spiritual Direction
OUR LADY OF PEACE
SPIRITUAL LIFE CENTER
Roman Catholic. 333 Ocean Road. Year founded: 1952.
☎ 401-783-2871

> *From the north, take I-95 to Exit 9 (on your left) to Route 4 to Route 1.*
> *Exit at Pont Judith in Scarborough. Cross Route 1. Go straight through*
> *the traffic light at South Pier Road to the T at Ocean Road. Turn right.*
> *The Spiritual Life Center is a half mile ahead, on your right.*

Our Lady of Peace Spiritual Life Center, opened by the Roman Catholic Diocese of Providence in 1952, offers year-round retreats for men and women. The center is located on a forty-acre estate with fifty-two private guest rooms. The retreat house is set back in a wooded, tranquil area, with the ocean nearby. Individual retreats can be arranged for a weekend or a longer period, and spiritual direction is available for a small added fee. "Hermitage stays" (more reclusive solitary retreats) are also offered, and there are occasional group training sessions for Christian leadership.

Retreatants who would like to do more than obtain spiritual direction for themselves can receive training here to *become* spiritual directors. The center offers a three-year certificate program in the art and practice of spiritual direction.

NEARBY
➥ Built in 1707, **Old Narragansett Church** in **Wickford** (North Kingstown) is one of the first Episcopal churches in New England. The church was originally located five miles to the southwest and was moved here in 1800 to accommodate the growing village of Wickford. The famous portrait painter Gilbert Stuart was baptized here in 1756. In 1848, Old Narragansett was abandoned because of its small size, and the congregation

Old
Narragansett
Church,
Wickford

moved worship services into the newly consecrated St. Paul's Church less than a block away. The historic Narragansett Church was not forgotten, however; the church conducted extensive repairs to it in the early twentieth century, and it is in excellent condition. The church still possesses a silver communion service that was a gift from Queen Anne in 1708. *Church Lane. Take Route 95 South and bear left on Route 4. After approximately 6.5 miles, take the Wickford Exit (102E) and proceed on 102E into the town of Wickford (approximately 3 miles). At a three-way intersection with a stop sign, turn left onto Brown Street. At the end of Brown, turn right onto Main Street. A greenway leads to the church from St. Paul's Parish House, 76 Main Street. Open for tours on weekend days in July and August from 11 A.M. to 4 P.M.* ☎ 401-294-4357

Newport

Although most people imagine elaborate Gilded-Age mansions when they envision Newport, the town should rightly be just as famous for its preservation of seventeenth- and eighteenth-century Colonial buildings. When the Vanderbilts and the Astors built their extravagant palaces by the sea in the late nineteenth century, they virtually ignored Newport's downtown—and thank goodness they did. Because they focused their sights almost exclusively on the seashore, very little Colonial architecture in the town had to be destroyed to make way for the wealthy summer denizens. As a result, Newport has one of the most intact colonial communities in New England, and many of its fascinating sacred sites still stand.

The Nation's Oldest Extant Synagogue
TOURO SYNAGOGUE
(CONGREGATION YESHUAT ISRAEL)
Jewish (Orthodox). 85 Touro Street. Year built: 1763 (congregation dates to 1658). Architect: Peter Harrison. ☎ 401-847-4794
🖳 www.tourosynagogue.com

From the south, take I-95 North to Route 138 East (Exit 3). Follow signs for the Jamestown and Newport Bridges. Take the first exit off the Newport Bridge, then turn right at the end of the ramp onto Farewell Street. Go straight through a stoplight; bear right at the next set of lights. At the second set of lights, turn left onto Marlborough Street. At the first

stop sign, turn right onto Thames Street. Turn left onto Touro Street after
the next set of lights. From July 1 to around Labor Day, tours are offered
Sunday through Friday from 10 A.M. to 5 P.M., with more limited hours
during the rest of the year. Tours are offered on the half hour, with no tours
on Saturdays or Jewish holidays. Men will need to wear yarmulkes, which
are provided. Men and women are seated separately in services.

Tucked away in colonial Newport is one of the nation's most important
sacred sites: the oldest existing synagogue in America. Its story reflects
much about the intersections of faith and freedom in American history.
The congregation began when a small party of fifteen Jewish families
arrived in Newport in the spring of 1658, possibly from Barbados or
Curaçao. They received a hospitable welcome. A few years later in 1663,
Rhode Island's royal charter formalized the religious toleration already
practiced in the colony, assuring Jews and all other persons "a full liberty in
religious concernments."

This was welcome information to Newport's Jews, who were establishing themselves as a vital part of the community and thriving in the import/
export business. For over a century after their arrival, the small group of
Jews held their services and holiday celebrations in people's homes. But
they grew in number, and in 1759 began drawing plans for this synagogue,
which they named after Isaac Touro, an esteemed member of the congregation. The building was dedicated on the first night of Hanukkah in
December, 1763. This was symbolically appropriate, since the members
felt that they, like the Maccabees who are celebrated in the Hanukkah
holiday, had endured oppression because of their faith, and could now celebrate their victory.

The building was designed by Peter Harrison (1716–75), one of the
most famous architects working in America in the eighteenth century; he
also designed King's Chapel in Boston (see page 77) and Christ Church in
Cambridge, Massachusetts (see page 119). Harrison had never seen a synagogue before, so he based the design on sketches the congregation showed
him of the Portuguese Synagogue in Amsterdam. There is no record that
Harrison accepted payment for his work, so many historians believe that
the final design was his gift to the congregation.

The synagogue's interior arrangement revolves around the symbolism
of the number twelve, reflecting the biblical promise that the twelve tribes
of Israel will eventually reunite, ushering in an era of world peace. Twelve
pillars support the gallery, and the building's twelve windows are each

Touro Synagogue and the Newport Historical Society, Newport

divided into twelve panes. The lovely Spanish chandelier has twelve branches, and twelve wooden torches stand above the Holy Ark. (The chandelier also depicts four monks, and no one knows precisely why; one theory is that it was brought from Spain by *conversos*—Jews who were forcibly converted to Christianity.)

In 1781 General George Washington visited the synagogue. Washington had learned something about Judaism from one of his advisors, Haym Salomon, a Philadelphia banker who gave more money to the Revolutionary cause than any other individual. Washington promised that if he ever attained a position of leadership he would make certain that Jews could practice their religion freely—not just in Rhode Island, but throughout the new nation. And he was one politician who kept his promises: Nine years later, Washington presented the Touro Synagogue with a document of religious freedom. Borrowing his wording from Touro Synagogue's own warden, Washington promised that the government of the United States would "give to bigotry no sanction, to persecution no assistance." This document pledged to extend religious freedom to all citizens—a year before the Bill of Rights guaranteed the right to free exercise of religion. The synagogue still owns the Washington document, but it is kept in the Library of Congress. Visitors can see a facsimile on the west wall of the building.

In part because of Washington's moral courage, the congregation offers prayers for the United States government every Saturday morning during Shabbat services. The synagogue has remained a focal point for cordial relations between religion and the government, having been visited by

Presidents Eisenhower and Kennedy, among others. In 1982 Touro was even featured on a postage stamp—the only American synagogue to be so honored.

Despite its prominence in the eighteenth and twentieth centuries, Touro synagogue weathered some dark times in the nineteenth. Not long after Washington's 1790 visit, Newport's Jewish community dwindled and scattered. From the 1820s to 1883, when eastern European immigration revitalized Newport's Jewish community, the synagogue was opened only for occasional special services. Some visitors reported seeing bats in the decaying building. Yet tradition states that even in its decline the synagogue, whose congregants had once endured bitter persecution for their faith, remained a symbol of freedom. Many legends assert that the building became a stop on the Underground Railroad. There is a trapdoor under the synagogue's reading desk in the center of the main gallery, leading to a basement where hundreds of slaves are said to have hidden in the years leading up to the Civil War.

Today, Touro Synagogue is a thriving Sephardic Orthodox congregation. The Society of Friends of Touro Synagogue helps to raise funds for the building's preservation and also sponsors lectures and symposia about Jewish history. There are daily services each morning and evening, and the rabbi stresses that "people of every religion come to pray here." Thus the synagogue extends the same kind reception its congregants enjoyed centuries ago in Rhode Island, welcoming people of all faiths.

Dissenting Baptists
THE NEWPORT HISTORICAL SOCIETY AND THE SEVENTH DAY BAPTIST MEETINGHOUSE
82 Touro Street. Year meetinghouse built: 1730 (congregation dates to 1671). Architect: Richard Munday. ☎ 401-846-0813
💻 www.newporthistorical.com

The center is open Tuesday through Friday from 9:30 A.M. to 4:30 P.M., and Saturday from 9:30 A.M. to noon.

In addition to its extensive library and museum, the Newport Historical Society has a unique exhibit: Appended on to the back of the building is the town's Seventh Day Baptist Meetinghouse. Erected in 1730, it is one of the oldest religious buildings in Newport. Its congregation, which had been meeting locally since around 1671, called themselves Seventh Day

Baptists (or Sabbath-Keepers, or Sabbatarian Baptists, or—whew!—the Church of Christ Observing the Seventh Day Sabbath). These various denominational titles all boiled down to one bone of contention: Some Baptists believed that Christians were supposed to worship God on the Jewish Sabbath, which was Saturday, not Sunday.

For a time, the contrarian Baptists flourished in Rhode Island, and this well-preserved example of a chapel reflects the stark beauty of their theology. The building is believed to be the design of Richard Munday, who was also responsible for Newport's Trinity Church (see below). Although most New England Protestants had, by the eighteenth century, relaxed many of their proscriptions on elaborate design and were favoring more elegant longitudinal architectural styles, the Seventh Day Baptists desired a return to simplicity. The building is almost square, which was typical of the meetinghouses a century earlier.

Although the exterior was spartan, the interior revealed many of the design embellishments of the day. The centerpiece of the sanctuary is a majestic pulpit, demonstrating the importance attached to the preaching of the sermon in Baptist churches. The pulpit was reached by ascending seven rather imposing stairs and was decorated with richly carved balusters. Many believe that it was designed by the same person who created Trinity Church's elaborate pulpit.

The congregation dissipated in the nineteenth century, and the building was occupied during the late 1860s by Shiloh Baptist church, an African American congregation. Shiloh eventually abandoned the building, which was purchased as a museum by the local historical society in 1884.

Rhode Island's Oldest Episcopal Parish
TRINITY CHURCH
Anglican/Episcopal. Queen Anne Square (off Spring Street). Year built: 1726 (congregation dates to 1698). Architect: Richard Munday.
☎ 401-846-0660 🖳 www.trinitynewport.org

The church is open for self-guided tours daily during the summer season, and more limited hours in the off-season. Services are offered on Sunday at 8 A.M. and 10 A.M., and Wednesday at noon.

Welcome to the oldest Anglican (Episcopal) parish in Rhode Island. It was erected in 1726, replacing a smaller church that had served Newport's

Trinity Church, Newport

Anglican and Huguenot communities since 1698. Richard Munday's design was loosely inspired by Christopher Wren and probably directly modeled after Old North Church (now Christ Church) in Boston (see page 86). Its 150-foot spire towers over Newport and has been used for nearly three centuries as a navigational aid by ships approaching the harbor.

The interior is marked by a clean, classical Colonial design, with some Victorian elements (such as two Tiffany stained-glass windows) tastefully interspersed. The sanctuary's most arresting embellishment is the elaborate "triple-decked" freestanding pulpit, considered to be the only such pulpit remaining in America today. It dominates the center of the church. The smallest deck was used for the reading of the Psalms, the middle pulpit for other biblical readings, and the hexagonal "wineglass" top pulpit for the preaching of sermons. What is unique about this arrangement is that the pulpit almost entirely eclipses the altar behind the chancel-rail, a very unusual configuration for a non-Reformed, liturgical congregation. (Typically, "high church" traditions such as Anglicanism have emphasized the sacraments, which are blessed and given at the altar, over the preaching of a sermon; see page 58.)

Because of its close ties with England before (and after) the Revolution, Trinity Church has some interesting connections with British history. As you walk down the center aisle, be sure to stop by Pew 81 on your right, where General George Washington once worshiped. Queen Elizabeth sat here in 1976 during a service for the bicentennial celebration, accompanied by the archbishop of Canterbury. Note the kneeling cushions marked with her majesty's seal. Other famous Church of England members who have sat in this pew have included Prince Andrew (1983), Archbishop Desmond Tutu (1984), and Princess Margaret (1988).

As with many New England churches, Trinity's pews used to be rented, and the right to lease them passed down through families. (In this congregation, the practice persisted until after World War II.) Because church services could be all-day affairs in colonial times, congregants needed to stay warm and comfortable—hence the high pew backs and doors to keep drafts out, and the warm coals and bricks placed at worshipers' feet. But if they became *too* warm and comfortable, drifting off into sleep, their punishment was a swift prod from the "nodding rod"—a gold-tipped staff that wardens used to keep parishioners alert. You can see examples of the nodding rod at the end of the wardens' pews.

The church is in splendid condition, thanks to an extensive $3 million restoration project in 1987–88. Its grounds are also pristine—partly because although the **Goelet Garden** to the south of the church appears to be an original complement to the church, it is a 1979 addition.

Newport's Oldest House of Worship
NEWPORT FRIENDS MEETINGHOUSE
Quaker. 21 Farewell Street. Year built: 1699. ☎ 401-846-0813

Tours by appointment only.

At the corner of Farewell and Marlborough Streets is Newport's oldest house of worship. This simple but large building was erected in 1699 to house the colony's growing Quaker population. Because of Rhode Island's policy of religious toleration, many Quakers who faced persecution in England and Massachusetts settled here. (Because they were active missionaries who sought to win converts to their cause, some slipped back into forbidden areas such as Massachusetts on proselytizing trips, angering the Puritans in these neighboring colonies to no end. See sidebar on Mary Dyer, page 255.) The spacious building, which was nicknamed the "Great Friends Meeting House" by Newport residents, was home to the New England Yearly Meeting in addition to its local congregation. Thousands of New England Quakers convened here regularly to discuss their beliefs and their plans for action on social issues such as slavery.

The colony's founder, Roger Williams, was not exactly enamored of the Quakers. At one point, Williams actually rowed himself thirty miles, at the age of sixty-nine, from Providence to Newport to engage in a heated debate with a group of them. He was disturbed by their theological teachings that the "inner light" of Christ dwelt in every person and by their unorthodox practices—such as staging parades of naked Quaker women through the streets of Newport to remind passers-by of the plight of the poor. It is true that Williams despised Quakers, yet he never once suggested that they be banished or punished for their beliefs. Quakers always

Friends Meetinghouse, Newport

enjoyed a safe haven in his colony. Their numbers declined in the mid-nineteenth century, and this building was abandoned in 1905. In the twentieth century, it became an important community center for Newport's African Americans, who founded a social agency called the Martin Luther King Center here. (It has since moved to another location.) In the 1970s, Newport residents restored the building and presented it to the Newport Historical Society.

NEARBY

➡ Newport's **Second Congregational Church** was built in 1735 because of dissatisfaction with the minister of First Church, Nathaniel Clapp. Although its architecture testified to Congregational simplicity, this church is now known for its opulence—it was converted into elegant, pricey condominiums in 1984. Second Congregational's most famous minister was Ezra Stiles (1727–95), who came to Newport in 1755. He stayed until the British occupied the town during the Revolution, when he, like most local patriots, fled. He never returned to his position in Newport, instead accepting the presidency of Yale College. Under his wing, Yale became a much stronger academic institution and came to rival Harvard as America's best college for ministers. Ezra Stiles's Georgian-style manse is directly across the street at 14 Clarke (now a home for aged men). Stiles was an early ecumenist, maintaining ties with Newport's small but active Jewish community. He attended the Touro Synagogue dedication in 1763 and spent the next fifteen years studying Hebrew with the rabbi. Those lessons bore good fruit. When Stiles was Yale's president, he required every student to learn Hebrew—no exceptions—and stipulated that the 1778 Yale valedictorian give his speech in Hebrew. Stiles also chose the enduring insignia of Yale, the light-and-truth symbol of the Jewish high priest. *15 Clarke Street.*

➽ At 49 Division Street (between Mary and Church Streets) is the Gothic Revival building of the **Union Congregational Church**, the town's first free black church, established in 1871. (Another congregation, Fourth Baptist, had previously occupied a different building on the site.) This church was the seed from which three other black churches were planted in Newport. On the church itself, a plaque boasts that the congregation was established in 1834 and was the first free black church in America. Not quite. That honor belongs to Bethel Church in Philadelphia, dedicated on July 29, 1794. Bethel is considered the "mother church" of the African Methodist Episcopal denomination, which now numbers more than 2.5 million members. Still, Union Congregational was an important regional pioneer as the first black church in Rhode Island. *49 Division Street.*

➽ On School Street is the **building where William Ellery Channing** (1780–1842) **was born.** Channing went on to become famous as a leader of the Unitarian movement in Boston, pastoring its flagship church at Arlington Street (see page 97). While in Newport, the Channing family owned a slave named Charity "Duchess" Quamino, who had allegedly descended from African royalty. In 1769 Charity married a slave named Quamino who, the story goes, was also of royal lineage. His father had sent him to Rhode Island to study, but Quamino was captured en route and sold into slavery. In 1773, he purchased his freedom with the proceeds of a lottery win and brought another slave with him to study at Princeton while Charity was still in Newport. They planned to return to Africa as Christian missionaries, but the Revolution made that impossible. Quamino was killed in action in 1779 on a privateer's ship. Duchess eventually purchased her freedom from the Channing family, likely through her well-known talents as a pastry chef. She is buried in "God's Acre," an African American section of the burying ground on Farewell Street. *24 School Street.*

➽ Garden lovers will not wish to miss the **Newport Mansion Gardens** at such palatial estates as **The Breakers** and **The Elms.** *For an overview of the area's mansions and gardens, see* www.newportmansions.org

➽ Tourists flock to the Gothic Revival **St. Mary's Church,** where John F. Kennedy married Jacqueline Bouvier on September 12, 1953. But even apart from its connection to Camelot, this 1852 Newport church, designed by Brooklyn architect Patrick Keely, commands historic interest as the home of the oldest Catholic parish in Rhode Island. *Spring Street and Memorial Boulevard. Mass is said Monday through Friday at 7:30 A.M., Saturday at 5 P.M., and Sunday at 8, 9:30, and 11 A.M.* ☎ 401-847-0475 💻 www.rc.net/providence/stmary/

Portsmouth

Portsmouth is where the controversial Puritan matriarch Anne Hutchinson (1591–1643) settled after she was excommunicated and banished from Massachusetts Bay colony in 1637. Hutchinson was accused of religious heresy, as Puritan leaders in Boston became uncomfortable with the amount of authority she wielded. Beginning with a small group of women who met in Hutchinson's Boston home to discuss the weekly Sunday sermon, Hutchinson's following grew to include large, mixed groups of both men and women. Her lively preaching was beloved by her adherents but considered dangerous by the Puritan hierarchy, who challenged her Quaker-like claims of "immediate revelation" and her immoderate presumption to teach men as well as women. Such activity, the court told Hutchinson, is "not fitting for your sex." When the court required her to explain her practice of teaching men, she retorted that if it was not lawful for women to teach men, then she should not have to answer the question and thereby "teach the court."

Hutchinson today is remembered as a courageous woman of faith, at least two centuries ahead of her time. After she and her large family (despite all of the religious controversy swirling around her, Hutchinson found time to bear fourteen children) fled to Rhode Island, they joined with a "covenanted" Christian community already settled in Portsmouth. But it soon disbanded when another member began preaching an even more radical Christian faith than Hutchinson had. The Hutchinsons moved to Long Island where, tragically, Anne Hutchinson and five of her children were slain by Native American raiders.

There is just one site relating to Hutchinson in Portsmouth today: a 1996 memorial plaque at **Founders Brook Park**, bolted to a rock. The plaque honors Hutchinson as "wife, mother, midwife, visionary, spiritual leader and original settler." Planted around the rock are medicinal herbs, to commemorate Anne Hutchinson's career serving women as a midwife and nurse. Buried under the rock is a scroll signed by 150 local

MARY DYER

Anne Hutchinson is not the only strong woman of faith who sought refuge in Rhode Island. A good friend of hers, the Quaker convert Mary Dyer, is widely regarded as a martyr for the Quaker cause because she was hanged in Boston Common in 1660. Dyer is held up as an example of Puritan intolerance and judgmentalism. But to be fair to the Puritans, it should be remembered that Dyer was amply warned about the consequences of preaching her message in Massachusetts. Exiled to Rhode Island upon threat of death if she returned to Boston, she dared to come back. The Puritans went through a vast show of placing a noose around her neck in a public execution ceremony, but did not actually execute her. She fled once again to Rhode Island, but decided to return to Boston, determined to "look the bloody laws in the face." The third time proved to be the charm— Dyer was rewarded with her long-wished-for martyrdom in May of 1660 and has gone down in history as a woman of tremendous courage. Contemporary Americans often forget the radical nature of the message she preached, remembering only that she died for her beliefs.

women and dedicated "to the memory of Anne Marbury Hutchinson from the women who won't forget." *Founders Brook Park is located just off Boyd's Lane (Route 138) in Portsmouth. Open daily from dawn to dusk.*

Lions and Tigers and Bears—Oh My!
GREEN ANIMALS TOPIARY GARDEN
380 Cory's Lane. Year created: 1872. Garden designer: Joseph Carreiro.
☎ 401-683-1267

Located just off Highway 114 in Portsmouth; turn at the stoplight at Cory's Lane. Green Animals is located a half mile ahead on the left. Open daily from 10 A.M. to 5 P.M., May to October. Admission fee.

Be careful if you accept a bear hug from the adorable, life-size bear that adorns the Green Animals Garden. It is, in a manner of speaking, alive. Like the other animals in this whimsical fantasy garden, the bear is a topiary—a bush that is carefully shorn to represent certain shapes. The garden contains dozens of evergreen animals, some of which are more than eighty years old. The privet, boxwood, and yew bushes that are used for the topiaries can take many years to grow. The bear, for example, took a full decade to reach its life-size height. Other favorites include the elephant, camel, lion, and giraffe. (The giraffe has a shorter neck than it used to, due to an unfortunate decapitation during a hurricane. Restoration has been slow but steady.)

Joseph Carreiro, a mill worker from the Azores, is responsible for beginning the fanciful garden with its animal forms. He worked as the gardener here for more than forty years, and his descendents have carried on the tradition. The garden has been used for decades for the functions of high society (Jacqueline Bouvier Kennedy Onassis had her debutante ball here) and remains a popular site for weddings, children's parties, and other events. All of the topiaries are trimmed and shaped every few weeks by hand.

NEARBY

➥ Men who desire a retreat in the Benedictine tradition will enjoy **Portsmouth Abbey (of Saint Gregory the Great)**, which is located on five hundred acres in Narragansett Bay. Since 1918, the monks have operated the abbey as well as its attached preparatory boarding school. Retreats are self-directed and conducted mostly in silence. There are no accommodations for female guests. *285 Cory's Lane.* ☎ 401-683-2000

Providence

Rhode Island's Champion of Religious Liberty
ROGER WILLIAMS NATIONAL MEMORIAL
North Main Street at Smith Street. Year dedicated: 1985.
☎ 401-521-7266 ▦ www.nps.gov/rowi/

From I-95 North, take Exit 23 toward the State Offices. Turn left at the stoplight on Orms Street, then right at Charles Street. Continue straight through one light; the memorial's parking lot will then be on your left. The memorial is open daily from 9:30 A.M. to 4:30 P.M. No admission fee.

It's taken a long time for Rhode Island's most famous iconoclast to get his due. Although a national memorial honoring Roger Williams (see also pages 14 and 237) was authorized by Congress in 1965, it was a full twenty years before the place opened to the public. This memorial occupies four and a half acres in Providence's downtown area, including some of the land Williams once owned. (His house was burned to the ground during King Philip's War in 1675–76, but it is thought to have been situated across from this site. A plaque marks the spot.)

The memorial is staffed by knowledgeable National Park Service guides and offers several exhibits and videos to teach visitors about the legendary Williams. In 1996, the memorial inaugurated a permanent exhibit called "Liberty of Conscience . . . An American Ideal," which describes Williams's commitment to a "wall of separation" between religion and the state (see entry on First Baptist Church, below).

ROGER WILLIAMS, THE CHURCH, AND NATIVE AMERICAN RIGHTS

Roger Williams (ca. 1603–83), a thorn in the side of the Anglicans in London and then the Puritans in Massachusetts, may be remembered as a hero today, but in his own time he was regarded as a heretic and a dissenter. Williams was exiled from Puritan Massachusetts in 1635, because he espoused the radical ideas that (a) there should be no state religion and (b) Native Americans should be fully compensated for their lands. In his English homeland, the Church of England had been a state church ruled by a monarch, and—even more alarming—an ironclad marriage of church and state was being instituted in Massachusetts. Ever an outspoken iconoclast, Williams had scarcely stepped off the boat from England in 1631 before he began protesting the "state church" model in Massachusetts. In its place, Williams proclaimed a new message of "soul liberty," in which an individual's absolute freedom of conscience would be protected from state interference. Williams felt that any state involvement would taint "the garden of the church," which should remain pure.

When Williams arrived in what is now Rhode Island (after walking the whole way from Salem, Massachusetts, in the snow), the Wampanoag chief Massasoit helped him to settle in an area that Williams named "Providence," to acknowledge God's care in bringing him safely to Rhode Island. He purchased the land from the Narragansett tribe and set about establishing a colony dedicated to religious freedom.

Williams was ridiculed in his own day for the very thing he is lauded for today: his respectful treatment of Native Americans. In his spare time (when he wasn't trying to govern the colony or tend to his six children), he operated a trading post close to the principal Narragansett village. This post became a sort of retreat for him, where he served as an interpreter for the Indians and became fluent in the Narragansett language. He wrote a book, *A Key into the Language of America*, that has been used for over three centuries as a textbook of Narragansett, which is closely related to Algonquin dialects. He also penned a treatise called *Christenings Make Not Christians*, in which he decried the practice of forced baptism of Native Americans and argued that they possessed souls (a progressive view for the time period). While today's readers would consider Williams's stance toward the Native Americans paternalistic—he refused to sell them liquor, for example, and prayed mightily for their Christian conversion—he became a valuable and levelheaded liaison between the English and native tribes such as the Wampanoag and the Narragansett.

The First Baptist Congregation in America
FIRST BAPTIST CHURCH
75 North Main Street. Year built: 1775 (congregation dates to 1638).
Architect: Joseph Brown. ☎ 401-454-3418
🖳 www.firstbaptistchurchinamerica.com

Guided tours on Sunday at 12:15 P.M., following the 11 A.M. service of worship. Self-guided tours are available from October through May, with guided tours offered from June through September.

Most of the time, the term "First Church" means that a particular congregation was the first of its type in a local community—the First Congregational Church of Northampton, Massachusetts, for example, or the First Church of Christ, Scientist in New York City. But the First Baptist Church here in Providence is indeed the first Baptist congregation anywhere in the United States.

As noted above, Roger Williams founded this church because he was desperately concerned about the government's role in traditional state religions. Williams's idea for a complete separation of church and state had been anathema to the Puritan magistrates in Boston, but here in Providence he was free to create a church based on these principles. The first meetings of like-minded souls occurred in 1638, and soon all of these new members were rebaptized. (Adult baptism, not infant baptism, was required because of the Baptists' emphasis on the individual's decision to embrace Christianity; see page 14.) Williams was influenced by what he knew of the Baptist movement in England, and applied their principles of separation of church and state to the creation of the first Baptist church in America.

His congregation thrived, but Williams did not last long as its pastor. Ever the idealist, he came to believe that all organized religion stood as an unnecessary intermediary between human beings and God. He resigned from his position

First Baptist Church, Providence

just months after he had started, and commenced studying church history in earnest, becoming convinced that no earthly institution could be considered a true church of Christ. At the end of his life, Williams had retreated so far into his own religious world that he refused to take communion with anyone and did not associate with any church whatsoever.

This building, the third and most imposing meetinghouse of the Providence Baptists, was erected in 1774–75. Its architecture reflects the full flowering of the classical New England meetinghouse style, with an overlay of the English Georgian design that became so popular in the late eighteenth century. The sanctuary (called "the auditorium") is a square eighty feet by eighty feet, in the meetinghouse tradition, with white walls and clear glass windows. The pulpit stands in the center of the chancel, in the place where an altar would be in a more liturgical church. The carved pillars, Palladian windows, and interrupted triangular pediments over the doors, on the other hand, are all signs of Georgian design.

Like many New England churches, First Church has box pews. These were rented by members of the congregation until the Great Depression, with the prime "real estate" near the pulpit going for top dollar, and the balcony for nothing. (In the church's earliest days, the balcony was reserved for Native Americans, slaves, and freedmen, and was free to all.) The pews themselves have changed very little, except that taller walls and doors were used until 1832. There are small drawers underneath the pews, where families could stash their Bibles and reading glasses, and perhaps a few toys to keep unruly children occupied.

The building is home to an active congregation, affiliated with the American Baptist Churches in the U.S.A. Because the historic church has a seating capacity of 1,200, it is also an important site for some community functions. Brown University still holds its annual commencement here, as it has done since the late eighteenth century, although in 1947 the school changed its tradition somewhat to accommodate the growing size of graduating classes. All of the ceremony's orations are still delivered inside the church, but the students, their families, and friends are now seated outside on the green.

An Early Commitment to Ecumenism
BROWN UNIVERSITY
45 Prospect Street. Year founded: 1764. ☎ 401-863-1000
▤ www.brown.edu

> *Take I-95 to I-195 East, exiting at Downtown Providence (Exit 1). At the second light (College Street), turn right. Proceed through the next light (South Main Street) and up the hill. Turn right on College Street.*

The university, first called The College of Rhode Island, was founded in the nearby town of Warren in 1764 and moved to this lovely College Hill neighborhood in 1770. Brown reflects the colony's full-fledged commitment to religious freedom. While the college was the brainchild of the colony's Baptists, it was never intended to be merely a denominational school. In fact, its charter made clear that no student in "this liberal and catholic [universal] institution" would ever be subject to any litmus tests on religious orthodoxy, but that freedom of conscience would be extended to all. This was a fairly radical approach for the eighteenth century; Oxford and Cambridge, for example, did not adopt similar policies for another hundred years.

One campus building of note is **Manning Hall**, dedicated in 1835. Named after the college's first president, James Manning, the building is one of the best examples of Greek Revival architecture in Rhode Island. In the nineteenth century it housed the library on the first floor and the chapel above. In the early twentieth century, the chapel was removed, but was restored to this building again in 1958. It is now a multifaith house of worship and hosts Christian, Buddhist, Muslim, Hindu, and other services.

A Flagship Cathedral for America's Most Catholic City
CATHEDRAL OF SAINTS PETER AND PAUL
Cathedral Square. Year dedicated: 1889 (congregation dates to 1837).
☎ 401-331-2434

Mass is held on Saturday evening at 5 P.M. and Sunday at 10 A.M., 1 P.M., 5 P.M., and 7:30 P.M. Weekday mass is held at 7:30 A.M. and 12:05 P.M., Monday through Friday.

This elegant cathedral is the seat of the bishop of the Diocese of Providence (the diocese was created in 1872). By 1874, construction had begun on this cathedral, which was supervised by an Irish-born immigrant bishop, Thomas Hendricken. Hendricken lived to participate in the first mass held here in 1886; a distant dream of Rhode Island's Roman Catholic community came true when the cathedral was dedicated in 1889. The church was designed in the Gothic Revival style that was popular in Victorian New England, with flying buttresses and square towers on both sides of the entrance. The exterior is of brown limestone. The cathedral is known for its excellent acoustics and its Cassavant organ, which has 6,330 pipes.

THE MOST CATHOLIC CITY IN AMERICA

What American city boasts the highest percentage of Roman Catholics? If you answered El Paso or Los Angeles, you clearly don't have the luck of the Irish. Providence has the honor of being the most Catholic city in America, and Rhode Island is the most Catholic state, with Catholicism claiming approximately two-thirds of the population.

Although Rhode Island practiced religious toleration as early as the 1630s, the first permanent settlement of Catholics in the colony did not take place until the Revolutionary War, when pro-American French troops were stationed here. Some remained after the war and were soon joined by a trickle of Irish immigrants. By the mid–nineteenth century, that trickle had become a flood, as thousands of Irish sought refuge here from famine and English oppression. In the late nineteenth century, a steady wave of Italian immigrants added to the mosaic of Rhode Island Catholicism, alongside smaller groups of Poles, French Canadians, and Portuguese. Today, the ethnic character of the state's Catholic community is becoming even richer through Hispanic and Southeast Asian immigration.

CHAPTER EIGHT

Connecticut

CONNECTICUT SOMETIMES gets shortchanged as being the
state that is "in the way" when one is driving from Boston to New York.
Connecticut residents are quite vocal in their belief that if those drivers
would only stop and spend some time in the "Constitution state" (so
named because Connecticut was the first of the New England colonies to

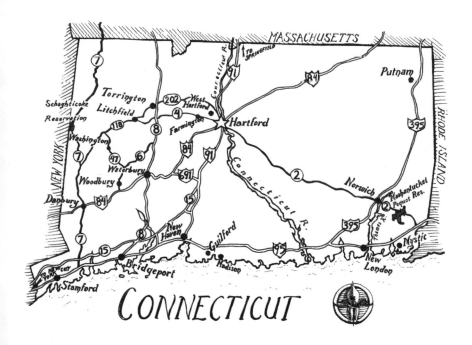

CONNECTICUT

draft a constitution), they would discover its riches. Connecticut is steeped in history and natural beauty. Although it is the third-smallest state in the nation, it packs quite a bit of punch into its few square miles.

Connecticut's sacred history has been, even more than other areas of New England, a bit of a one-trick pony. That is, when the English settled here in 1633, they established Congregationalism as the state religion—so, like Massachusetts, Connecticut has quite an allotment of Congregational churches. According to the colony's pattern of town development, every village had at least one, usually centrally located on "the green," the Connecticut equivalent of a common. Excellent examples of Congregational churches on the green can be seen in Litchfield, New Haven, Farmington, and other communities. Unlike Massachusetts, which has seen an explosion of religious diversity in the last forty years, Connecticut has remained predominately Christian (especially Roman Catholic), with a strong minority of Jews. A smattering of other faiths exist here, however, many clustered in the university town of New Haven and the southwestern counties that are close to New York City. In those areas the spiritual traveler will find thriving Buddhist, Muslim, and Jewish communities.

Connecticut is rich in Native American history and offers several museums, recreated villages, and burial sites to tempt the spiritual traveler. The name *quinnehtukqut* is roughly translated as "beside the long tidal river"—and the Connecticut River is where most indigenous groups still reside today. Entering the twenty-first century, tribes such as the Pequot are reclaiming their land and their heritage, revitalizing their reservations as they preserve their languages, traditions, and cultures.

Farmington

An Octagonal Sunken Garden
HILL-STEAD MUSEUM AND GARDEN
36 Mountain Road. Year built: 1901. Architects: Stanford White and Theodate Pope. ☎ 860-677-4787 ⌨ www.hillstead.org

From I-84, take Exit 39 to Route 4 West. Turn left onto Route 10 South. Turn left at the first light onto Mountain Road. The museum is a quarter mile up the hill on the left. Open Tuesday through Sunday from 10 A.M. to 5 P.M. from May until October and 11 A.M. to 4 P.M. from November to April. Admission fee for the museum (the grounds are free).

Hill-Stead Museum and Garden, Farmington

Just ten minutes from urban Hartford is this bucolic refuge, offering a host of Impressionist paintings and a sunken garden designed by the famed Beatrix Farrand. The 1901 house, a rambling Colonial Revival mansion, boasts thirty-six rooms and 33,000 square feet of space. Its design was a collaborative effort between established architect Stanford White and a young rising star, Theodate Pope. Pope, the daughter of a wealthy Cleveland industrialist, was educated at the swanky Miss Porter's School nearby, and took a shine to the area. Determined to be an architect, she persuaded her father to let her help design this as a retirement home for her parents, and went on to become one of the first licensed women architects in the United States. She left strict instructions that this home should be preserved as a museum, and it was opened to the public in 1946.

Like many nouveau riche Americans at the close of the nineteenth century, the Popes traveled across Europe on buying sprees, investing their new fortunes in furniture and art. The museum preserves the family's exceptional collections of Chinese porcelain, Japanese prints, and European furniture, as well as their outstanding examples of Impressionist paintings.

The property's 152 acres include a beautifully landscaped Sunken Garden, where a poetry festival occurs on alternate Wednesday evenings in the summer. (The setting's unusual, octagonal evergreen shape and lovely display of flowers surely inspire even the greatest poets to new heights.) The garden, which had disintegrated by midcentury, was restored to its Farrand-era glory in the 1980s by the Connecticut Valley Garden Club and the Garden Club of Hartford. The groups researched the original garden and reinstated approximately seventy-five kinds of plants, particularly perennials.

Visitors are welcome to venture beyond the sunken garden to the property's extensive walking trails, which wind through woods and meadows to a pond. Throughout the year, the museum offers special birdwatching and plant-identification programs for nature lovers.

Hartford

Not Exactly Roughing It: Mark Twain's Connecticut Mansion
MARK TWAIN HOUSE
351 Farmington Avenue. Year built: 1873–74. ☎ 860-247-0998
🖥 www.MarkTwainHouse.org

> *From I-84, take Exit 46 (Sisson Avenue). At the traffic light, turn right onto Sisson. Go four blocks, then turn right at the traffic light, onto Farmington Avenue. The parking lot entrance will be three blocks down on the right, just before the house itself. The house is open for tours daily from May through October and again in December; it is closed on Tuesdays all other months. Hours are 9:30 A.M. to 5 P.M., Monday through Saturday, and 12 P.M. to 5 P.M. on Sundays. The last 45-minute tour departs at 4 P.M. Admission fee.*

One of the greatest wits of the age, Mark Twain (born Samuel Clemens) did not suffer fools gladly, particularly when he felt that they were leading others astray in the name of religion. He once wrote a scathing biography of fellow New Englander Mary Baker Eddy, and his attacks on spiritualism (the religious movement that centered around séances and purported communications with the dead) were legendary. "I wish there were something in that miserable spiritualism," he once wrote. In 1871, he wrote *Roughing It*, a hilarious account of his rail journey to the American West, with biting critiques of the Mormons he found there.

Twain, then, was not exactly a friend to organized religion, especially of the experimental varieties. But he wrestled with spiritual questions throughout his writing, whether in the Christian ethics of *The Adventures of Huckleberry Finn* or the more cutting remarks of his humor pieces. He positioned himself as a good-natured skeptic. "I have long ago lost my belief in immortality—also my interest in it," he explained.

"I believe that our Heavenly Father invented man because he was disappointed in the monkey."

—Mark Twain (Samuel Clemens)

Although the one-time riverboat pilot had gotten his literary start on the Mississippi, he wrote some of the best books of his career from this nineteen-room home in Connecticut, now open as a museum. Twain moved to the Nook Farm neighborhood of Hartford in 1871, impressed by the depth of its literary community. Harriet Beecher Stowe, who wrote the best-selling antislavery novel *Uncle Tom's Cabin*, lived in a more modest home just a few steps away (see below), and Twain's own editor resided nearby, too.

Visitors to Twain's impressive Victorian estate will learn much about the man, his family, his work, and his tastes. Those tastes were expensive; this house was designed to impress. However, he made some rather short-sighted investments (including a huge sum in the "page compositor" on display where you purchase your tickets), and his family was forced to move from this house in 1891. He did extensive book tours in Europe to turn the family's fortunes around, since they missed their Connecticut home immeasurably. "How ugly, tasteless, repulsive, are all the domestic interiors I have ever seen in Europe compared with the perfect taste of this ground floor," Twain wrote in 1892, lauding his home's "all-pervading spirit of peace and serenity and deep contentments." Tragically, daughter Susie Clemens became ill and passed away while they were abroad, and the family did not have the heart to return to this memory-filled house when they could afford to do so. Twain moved to Reading, Connecticut, where he died in 1910 at the age of seventy-four.

"The Little Lady Who Made This Big War"
HARRIET BEECHER STOWE CENTER
77 Forest Street. ☎ 860-522-9258 🖳 www.hartnet.org/stowe

Follow driving directions to the Mark Twain home, described above. The museum is open Tuesday through Saturday, 9:30 A.M. to 4:30 P.M., and from noon to 4:30 P.M. on Sundays. It is open on Mondays from Memorial Day to Columbus Day, and in the month of December. The last tour leaves at 4 P.M. Admission fee.

Harriet Beecher Stowe's Hartford home

In 1863, Abraham Lincoln called her "the little lady who made this big war." The woman in question was Harriet Beecher Stowe, and the war in question, of course, was the Civil War. The reason Stowe took some measure of responsibility for the great conflagration was the impact of her famous 1851 book, *Uncle Tom's Cabin.* More than a host of antislavery political speeches and church sermons, that novel helped to persuade hundreds of thousands of American readers that slavery was wrong. Stowe wrote much of the novel by lamplight, after exhausting days of tending to her many children. She wrote from a deep spiritual conviction. "I wrote what I did because as a woman, as a mother, I was oppressed and brokenhearted with the sorrows and injustice I saw, because as a Christian I felt the dishonor to Christianity—because as a lover of my country, I trembled at the coming day of wrath," she later explained.

This Hartford home, just steps away from Mark Twain's house, is *not* where Stowe wrote her famous book; she wrote it in Brunswick, Maine (see page 354). She moved here in 1873 and remained until her death in 1896. In this home she continued her outstanding career of Christian activism, laboring for such causes as education and women's rights (though she was never as strident on the latter subject as one of her sisters, Isabella Beecher Hooker, who also lived in the Nook Farm neighborhood). The restored home is a fine example of Victorian furnishing and décor, which is not surprising when one discovers that Stowe coauthored a book on the subject (*The American Woman's Home,* 1869) with another sister, Catharine Beecher. In particular, the kitchen reflects the sisters' ideas that

HARTFORD HOUSES OF WORSHIP

Hartford, Connecticut's capital city, has some of the state's finest houses of worship. Spiritual travelers could begin by visiting the following:

Christ Church Cathedral, the Episcopal cathedral serving the Diocese of Hartford, was designed by Ithiel Towne in 1828 in the Gothic Revival style. The church was elevated to the status of cathedral in 1919. *45 Church Street.* ☎ 203-527-7231 💻 www.cccathedral.org

The **Metropolitan AME Zion Church**, also in the Gothic Revival style, dates to 1874. It is a central component of Hartford's African American community. *2051 Main Street.* ☎ 860-278-6290

Temple Beth Israel, built in 1876, is Connecticut's oldest standing synagogue, one of several Romanesque Revival synagogues throughout New England. The building is now home to the Charter Oak Cultural Center, which offers programs on Jewish heritage and multiculturalism. The COCC has recently begun an ambitious restoration project to return the building to its original condition. *21 Charter Oak Avenue.* ☎ 860-249-1207

Saints Cyril and Methodius Roman Catholic Church is an unusual blend of Romanesque Revival, with its round arches, and the Wren-Gibbs style, with its single tower. It was dedicated in 1916. *55 Charter Oak Avenue.* ☎ 860-522-9157

The **Guru Harkrishan Ashram** is one of five Sikh *gurdwaras* (temples) in Connecticut. *41 Thomson Road.* ☎ 860-521-0517

The Roman Catholic **Cathedral of St. Joseph**, built in 1962, is renowned for its stained-glass windows, designed by French glass artist Gabriel Loire, who also created the stained glass at First Presbyterian Church in Stamford (see page 286). *140 Farmington Ave.* ☎ 860-249-8431

Just outside of the city in **Windsor**, the **Islamic Center** was completed in 1993. This *masjid* (mosque) houses Connecticut's first full-time Islamic school, the Madina Academy. *1 Madina Drive, Windsor.* ☎ 860-249-0112 the home should be a place of convenience and comfort for women—a rather startling idea in the nineteenth century.

The Stowe Center features a world-class library for nineteenth-century American studies. It is particularly strong in African American history, Connecticut history, women's studies, and the decorative arts.

> "The way to be great lies through books, now, and not through battles . . . there is more done with pens than swords."
>
> —Harriet Beecher Stowe

Litchfield

Connecticut's Most Photographed Church
FIRST CONGREGATIONAL CHURCH
United Church of Christ (formerly Puritan/Congregational). 21 Torrington Road. Year consecrated: 1829 (congregation dates to 1721).
☎ 860-567-8705   🖳 www.fcclitchfield.hypermart.net

> *The church is located at the intersection of Route 118 and Route 202, on the Litchfield Green. It is open most days until 5:30 P.M. Sunday worship is held at 10:30 A.M. (9:30 A.M. in summer).*

This lovely shuttered church is possibly the most photographed house of worship in all of Connecticut. There is something universally appealing about its clean lines, black-and-white painted exterior, and simple meetinghouse style. Its congregation did not always feel that way, however. In 1873, the members of First Church decided that this 1829 building, which was in need of repair, was out of date. Henry Ward Beecher (1813–87), the famous Brooklyn preacher who was the son of First Church's former minister Lyman Beecher and brother of abolitionist novelist Harriet Beecher Stowe, voiced the opinion of the majority. "There is not a single line or feature in the old building suggesting taste or beauty," he declared. To keep up with the times, the congregation moved this building a short distance down Torrington Road, opting to use it as a social hall (it was later even used as a movie theater). In its stead, they erected a Victorian Gothic wooden church with stained-glass windows and dark wooden pews.

ORT

CONNECTICUT ～ 271

SIX SIMILAR CHURCHES

Although First Congregational in **Litchfield** is picture-perfect, its architecture is not wholly original. It is part of a set of nearly identical Congregational churches from the 1820s and early 1830s; the others can be found in **Old Lyme** (1817), **Milford** (1823), **Cheshire** (1827), **Southington** (1830), and **Guilford** (1830). Some are attributed to architect David Hoadley (1774–1838); for others, such as Litchfield's First Congregational, the architect is unknown. The six churches have identical spires, with two octagons narrowing into a cone-shaped top. The weathervanes may have actually been cast from the same mold. The windows in all six churches are double-hung, with twenty-over-twenty panes, and the front doors are all of the same height and width. All have the Greek Revival touch of a front portico with four fluted columns.

In the early nineteenth century, Litchfield was easily a two days' journey from Southington, and the range of all six churches stretches across sixty miles. No one knows exactly how the churches were designed so identically, except that some of the construction elements may have been prefabricated.

Tastes in architecture and design are sometimes fickle, however. The congregation changed its mind once again in the 1920s, perhaps influenced by the winds of the Colonial Revival movement. In 1929 the members razed the 1873 Victorian church, moved this building back to its original site, and began extensive repairs. The church's restored interior, designed by Richard Henry Dana, is a paragon of New England meeting-house design, with its clear glass windows, box pews, and symmetrical style. The walls are painted soft pink with white trim, accentuated by a rose-colored carpet. A gallery running around three-quarters of the building surrounds the nave. The glorious pulpit, which is a reproduction of the original, is a half story tall, accessible by twin spiral staircases on either side of the lectern.

Our Lady of Litchfield
LOURDES IN LITCHFIELD
Roman Catholic (Montfort Missionaries). Route 118. Year consecrated: 1958. ☎ 860-567-1041
🖥 www.montfortmissionaries.com/lourdes.phtml

From the Litchfield Green, take Route 118 East for one-half mile. The entrance to Lourdes in Litchfield will be on your left. The shrine grounds are open year-round from dawn to dusk. From May though October, mass is celebrated at the Grotto at 11:30 A.M. each day except Monday.

While millions are familiar with the famous grotto located in Lourdes, France, not quite as many realize that there is a very close replica in Litchfield. "Lourdes in Litchfield" welcomes more than 100,000 visitors each year, who are attracted by its devotion to Our Lady of Lourdes and its wooded, peaceful locale. The story of Lourdes begins with Bernadette Soubirous, a French peasant girl who claimed to have had a vision of the Virgin Mary in 1858. According to Bernadette, the mother of God spoke to her of peace and reconciliation among humankind.

In 1958, exactly a century after Bernadette's vision, Montfort Missionaries dedicated this replica of the Lourdes grotto to honor Mary. From May through October, the open-air grotto comes to life in daily masses and other special services. Visitors can also walk the path of the stations of the cross, which begins with Jesus' condemnation and culminates with his resurrection, or spend time at shrines tucked in the woods that are devoted to St. Joseph, St. Jude, St. Michael, and St. Louis de Montfort.

Lourdes in Litchfield is often so quiet that, apart from the distant rumble of cars on Route 118, the only sounds are the caw of wild birds and the babble of a stream. But on the third Sunday of May, the place explodes with the roar of motorcycles. About twenty years ago, it began hosting a "Blessing of the Motorcycles," a tradition that attracts as many as 500 bikers each spring. They line up, receive their blessing, and then actually drive through the grotto. The Montfort Missionaries see this as a valuable outreach to many people who may not otherwise get to experience the blessings of Mary.

Lourdes in Litchfield

An Interfaith Retreat
WISDOM HOUSE RETREAT AND CONFERENCE CENTER

Administered by the Daughters of Wisdom (Roman Catholic). 229 East Litchfield Road. ☎ 860-567-3163 💻 www.wisdomhouse.org

From Litchfield, take Route 118 for 2.75 miles. Turn right onto Clark Road. Wisdom House is one-tenth of a mile down on the left side.

Once a convent for the Roman Catholic order of the Daughters of Wisdom, Wisdom House now functions as a spiritual retreat and conference center. Beautifully situated on fifty-four acres of Connecticut woods and meadows, it is still run by the Daughters of Wisdom, who offer spiritual refuge and hospitality to people of all faiths.

The center welcomes up to 145 retreatants at a time and is a particular favorite of artists and writers (author Julia Cameron and actor Richard Gere, for example, both applaud Wisdom House as a haven for spiritual creativity). Special retreats are held periodically for artists and writers, who revel in the center's peaceful atmosphere and supportive crew. More than 100 retreatants may stay in dormitory-like rooms in a brick Colonial-

LABYRINTH

As the ancient practice of labyrinth walking makes its way into the spiritual heart of American life, all sorts of labyrinths—both moveable and permanent—are being constructed across New England. Wisdom House offers one of the most stunning permanent labyrinths in the region, based on a pattern found on ancient coins from Crete. Surrounded by aged trees and flowering shrubs, visitors walk the seven-circuit path of brick and stone in a slow, meditative manner. Wisdom House recommends that individuals enter the labyrinth in silence, concentrating their attention on the path ahead. Walking at a moderate pace, the goal is to let go of distracting thoughts and to reflect upon the activity of walking, giving mindful attentiveness to the here and now. In leaving the labyrinth, visitors do not cross over the labyrinth's paths, but carefully and prayerfully retrace the steps they have already taken.

style building; a circa-1770 farmhouse accommodates an additional twenty-three guests. Meals are cooked on-site by a chef who also offers delectable desserts and baked goods.

Wisdom House is a very active retreat center with a variety of ongoing programs. The Marie Louise Trichet Art Gallery offers revolving exhibits on spirituality and art; one recent show was "Painting as a Form of Prayer." Book and film groups meet twice a month, discussing classic spiritual thinkers like Hildegard of Bingen as well as twentieth-century writers such as Thomas Merton and Dietrich Bonhoeffer. Many special retreats focus on the mind-body-spirit connection, utilizing techniques such as walking meditation, viniyoga, Chi Gong, and Reiki to maximize spiritual well-being and physical health.

NEARBY

➧ On the western border of Connecticut in the town of **Kent** is the **Schaghticoke Reservation**, one of the smallest Native American reservations in the United States. The Schaghticoke tribal nation, which has been recognized by Connecticut since colonial times, is currently lobbying for recognition by the federal government, as well as a return of tribal lands. On the 400-acre reservation is a small cemetery. *From Route 7, go through the covered bridge at Bulls Bridge and bear right on Schaghticoke Road.* ☎ 203-736-0782 🖳 www.schaghticoke.com

Madison

A Seaside Retreat
MERCY CENTER AT MADISON
Interfaith (administered by the Sisters of Mercy). 167 Neck Road. Year opened: 1973. ☎ 203-245-0401 🖳 www.mercyctrmadison.com

Madison is located on the Connecticut shore of Long Island Sound, approximately fifteen miles west of New Haven. From I-95 North, take Exit 59. Turn right at the exit, then left at the light onto Route 1. Travel two miles along Route 1 and turn right onto Neck Road. Mercy Center is .5 miles down on the left side.

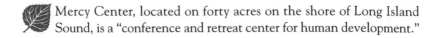

Mercy Center, located on forty acres on the shore of Long Island Sound, is a "conference and retreat center for human development."

The grounds, which include more than a thousand feet of gorgeous beach-front, are breathtaking; the estate first belonged to the Hotchkiss prep school and then was a summer playground of the magnate W. T. Grant. In the 1950s, the Sisters of Mercy acquired the property and dedicated it to human growth and spiritual renewal. It opened as an ecumenical retreat center in 1973. Accommodations are dormitory style in single and double rooms. Meals are provided; the center is known for its culinary excellence and healthy food, and has its own cookbook.

Group and individual retreats are available. Special weekend retreats have focused on women's issues, death and dying, personality discovery, mindfulness meditation, "stress and serenity," forgiveness, and art journaling, among other topics. Directed individual retreats last a week and are spent in silent prayer and meditation. Each year, Mercy Center holds a special directed retreat for Holy Week.

If a weekend or week-long retreat isn't enough to soothe the ruffled feathers of your soul, Mercy Center offers a unique "Seaside Sabbatical" program for one to eight months from September through May.

NEARBY

➥ In **Guilford**, just west of Madison, is **The Henry Whitfield State Museum**, which displays artifacts from colonial times. Built in 1639, it is the oldest stone dwelling in New England. *Old Whitfield Street, Guilford. From I-95, take Route 77 past Route 1 to the Guilford Green stop sign. Go right on Broad Street, then left on Whitfield Street. Bear left at the fork (just after the green) onto Old Whitfield Street. Take an immediate left onto Stone House Lane. The museum is on the left. Open daily from February to mid-December from 10 A.M. to 4:30 P.M. Admission fee.* ☎ 203-453-2457

Mashantucket

New England's Largest Museum of Native American History and Culture
MASHANTUCKET PEQUOT MUSEUM
110 Pequot Trail. Year opened: 1998. ☎ 800-411-9671
🖳 www.mashantucket.com

From I-95, take Exit 92 (Route 2) and follow signs for the museum (1.5 miles from Foxwoods Casino). The museum is open daily except

Tuesday from 10 A.M. to 6 P.M. (summer hours are extended until 7 P.M.). Admission fee.

This museum, which opened in 1998, is a must-see destination for anyone interested in Native American history. Great care and deliberation went into its creation—even the architecture itself expresses the legacy and spirit of the Mashantucket Pequot Tribal Nation. The entryway of the 85,000-square-foot museum features a wall of curving glass, designed to appear like an upturned canoe. Directly outside the windows is a row of tall trees, blurring the distinction between indoor and outdoor space. The windows face the east and thus the rising sun. Seashells are built into the terrazzo tile floors, a reminder of the importance of fishing in the tribe's history. And the cedarwood slats that appear throughout the building represent the cedar trees that have sustained the tribe for thousands of years.

The museum's exhibits are interactive, which is a hit not only with the thousands of schoolchildren who comprise a large portion of the museum's 300,000 annual visitors. Apart from the opening room, which chronicles recent Pequot history and the revitalization of the tribe, the exhibits are arranged chronologically. As visitors descend an escalator to the Ice Age exhibit, the temperature cools by several degrees, and faux glaciers appear on all sides. One of the highlights of the Ice Age section is a life-size diorama of a caribou hunt from 9,000 B.C.E.

Spiritual travelers will not want to miss the short films that run continuously in the museum's "Arrivals Theater." Through storytelling and beautiful cinematography, visitors learn ancient tribal myths about creation, some of which feature sea monsters and a great flood. Each creation story is presented in a different native tongue, with English subtitles.

Another highlight is the half-acre Pequot Village, a reconstructed community that provides a snapshot of Pequot life 400 years ago, just prior to contact with Europeans. It is like entering another world: The Passamaquoddy language is spoken, and the sounds of birds and animals accentuate the natural forest setting. There are twelve wigwams, twenty-five animal species, dugout canoes, a sweat lodge, and period weapons and tools. The exhibit's fifty-one lifelike, full-size wax figures are engaged in activities such as hunting, fishing, bead making, gardening, drying fish, and nursing babies. In one scene, a shaman attempts to heal a man who has fallen ill with a fever; another captures the joy two men express when they return home after a highly successful fishing expedition; a third shows a sweat-lodge ritual. Some of the recreated wigwams allow visitors to walk through their interior spaces.

Later exhibit rooms chronicle the arrival of European settlers and explain the disintegration of the Pequot tribe through smallpox, influenza and war with the English. If you have time, try to see *The Witness*, a thirty-minute, 70MM film about the 1637 massacre of the Pequot at Mystic, Connecticut. Approximately 600 Pequot died.

THE HISTORY OF THE MASHANTUCKET PEQUOT TRIBAL NATION

For more than 10,000 years, indigenous peoples have occupied this land in southeastern Connecticut. Before European contact, it is estimated that more than 8,000 Pequot lived here, but the ravages of smallpox in 1633–34, just a few years after the English had arrived, killed thousands of tribe members. That was not the end of the devastation. The surviving Pequot were engaged in a war with the English from 1636 through 1638 that decimated their numbers still further. After the war, the suspicious colonists forced the Pequot off their land and placed them under the control of other Indian nations. Today's Pequot are descendants of the Mashantucket, or western, Pequot.

The eighteenth and nineteenth centuries were an era of great trial for the Pequot. In 1761, the Connecticut colony reduced the Pequot reservation land from nearly 3,000 acres to 989. A 1774 colonial census counted only 151 Pequot in residence on those 989 acres; economic necessity forced many to seek work elsewhere. In 1856 the State of Connecticut reduced the tribal lands still further, to only 213 acres. By 1935, only forty-two Pequot lived on the denuded reservation, with the other members of the tribe scattered to the winds.

Elizabeth George, one of the few remaining Mashantucket Pequot living on the reservation, urged the tribe to reunite and find means to be self-sustaining. George died in 1973, but her grandson, Richard Hayward, carried on her legacy and sued for a return of tribal lands. The Pequot began to slowly return to the reservation, supporting themselves through hydroponic gardening, maple syrup cultivation, and raising pigs. These ventures were moderately successful, but not enough to fuel tribal growth and renewal. (The Pequot discovered, for example, that they couldn't kill the pigs for meat. "They never went to market," says Charlene Jones, a great-granddaughter of Elizabeth George. "Eventually they all had names. They became pets.")

In 1983, the Pequot achieved federal recognition as a tribe and invested in a local restaurant. In 1986, they obtained permission to open a bingo hall. This venture proved to be wildly successful, enabling more Pequot to move back to the reservation, where they could now find jobs and have good housing. In 1992, the Mashantucket Pequot opened Foxwoods, a world-class casino that brought the tribe economic security on a large scale. In addition to building new roads and additional housing, the Pequot have used the proceeds from Foxwoods Casino to further the cause of Native American pride. They opened the Mashantucket Pequot Museum and Research Center in 1998 and have also donated $10 million to build the National Museum of the American Indian in Washington, D.C.

Today, there are 655 Mashantucket Pequot enrolled in the tribe, and the reservation has expanded to 1,250 acres. It is among the oldest continuously occupied native reservations in North America. The tribe seeks to balance its recent development and growth with its traditional emphasis on ecology, and has set aside large chunks of reservation land for preservation.

Mystic

An Island Retreat for Roman Catholics
SAINT EDMUND'S RETREAT
Enders Island. Roman Catholic (Society of Saint Edmund).
☎ 860-536-0565 💻 www.newspringtime.org

Take I-95 to Exit 90 (Mystic). Go south on Route 27, past the Seaport, to Route 1. Turn left onto Route 1. At the first light, turn right onto Mason's Island Road. Bear left at all forks and follow signs for Enders Island.

This tiny island retreat is the perfect place to truly get away from it all. Although located just a few miles off shore from busy Mystic Seaport, the twelve acres of Enders Island feel like another world. Here, visitors can roam through the lovely Garden of Two Hearts (dedicated to the Sacred Heart and the Immaculate Heart of Mary) and enjoy many vistas of the Fisher's Island Sound. A seaside chapel welcomes retreatants for quiet meditation, accompanied only by the waves lapping on the shore. Run by the Roman Catholic Society of St. Edmund, an order of priests and brothers who seek to promote evangelization, renewal, and social justice, this center offers retreats, adult education, and programs in sacred art.

Most of the day-long or weekend retreats are Catholic in theme, organized around topics such as the catechism, the mass, apologetics, and vocations. Other weekend retreats seek to help married couples, women, recovering alcoholics, and other groups. Six-day retreats are available for individuals, featuring daily conferences with a spiritual director.

Saint Edmund's also includes the **Saint Michael Institute of Sacred Art**, which seeks to revive sacred art forms and create art dedicated to God's glory. Hands-on instruction is offered in sculpture, fresco, woodcarving, egg painting, iconography, manuscript illumination, stained glass, painting, drama, Gregorian chant, poetry, and the culinary arts. The weeklong classes are limited to fifteen participants, who enjoy approximately forty hours of studio time. All of the materials are included with the registration fee. Like Saint Edmund's Retreat, the institute is a religious center. Each day begins with prayer; mass is said each afternoon; and the day closes with the adoration and benediction of the Blessed Sacrament.

NEARBY

➤ **Mystic Seaport Museum** is one of Connecticut's top tourist attractions, highlighting Mystic's famous maritime history. The museum boasts the world's largest collection of boats and nautical photography, and features a recreated nineteenth-century port village, with wooden ships and historic homes and shops. *75 Greenmanville Avenue. Take I-95 to Exit 90, and drive one mile south on Route 27. Admission fee.* ☎ 1-888-9SEAPORT 🖳 www.mysticseaport.org

➤ **Mystic Aquarium** has more than 3,500 sea creatures from many types of marine environments. The "Alaska Coast" exhibit offers close encounters (through glass) with beluga whales and seals, and the "Challenge of the Deep" interactive exhibit lets you explore shipwrecks and encounter deep-sea creatures. *Located at Exit 90 off I-95.* ☎ 860-572-5955 🖳 www.mysticaquarium.org

➤ **St. James Church** in **New London** is a fine example of the Gothic Revival style that made architect Richard Upjohn (1802–78) so famous. Built in 1850, the church features six Tiffany stained-glass windows. The congregation dates to 1725, making it one of the oldest Anglican (Episcopal) congregations in Connecticut. *76 Federal Street (the corner of Federal and Huntington Streets), New London.* ☎ 860-443-4989 💻 www.interactdesigns.com/stjames/

New Haven

New Haven's Green, like Boston Common (see page 67), was the site of recreation and business, lighthearted frivolity, and public executions. As late as 1825, slave auctions were still occurring in New Haven. On March 8, 1825, Center Church's young minister Leonard Bacon witnessed a slave auction on the Green, and was shocked. Just twenty-three years old and fresh out of seminary, Bacon preached an antislavery message at Center Church with courage and conviction. He went on to become a leading abolitionist whose 1846 book *The Evils of Slavery* helped influence Abraham Lincoln's views.

The Green in New Haven is dominated by three churches, all standing side by side. The southernmost of them is an Episcopal church designed by Ithiel Towne, while the other two are Congregational churches (one of which was also designed by Towne). Although the Green was once used as New Haven's central burying ground, it is now simply an open park.

The Green in New Haven (from left to right: Trinity Episcopal Church, Center Church, United Church)

Tiffany Windows and Gothic Revival Architecture
TRINITY EPISCOPAL CHURCH ON THE GREEN
At the corner of Temple and Chapel Streets. Year consecrated: 1816
(congregation dates to 1752). Architect: Ithiel Towne. ☎ 203-624-3101
💻 www.trinitynewhaven.org

> *From I-95 North, get on I-91 North (Hartford) and take Exit 3 (Trum-*
> *bull Street). At the end of the ramp go straight to the third traffic light*
> *(including the light at the ramp). Turn left onto Temple Street and continue*
> *straight through two more lights. The New Haven Green, with its three*
> *churches, will be on your right. Trinity is the southernmost of the three.*

Trinity Church, built in the Gothic Revival style, is the oddball of the
three churches on the Green, but what a glorious oddball it is. It was constructed in 1816 by Connecticut architect Ithiel Towne, who had also
designed its Federal-style next-door neighbor, Center Church, two years
earlier. He obviously was a master of many styles. Trinity was one of the
first Gothic Revival churches in America, made from 50,000 cubic feet of
rough-hewn local sandstone. It is a far more imposing edifice than the congregation's first building, a simple wooden structure (no longer standing).
This present building suggests the Episcopal journey from a suspect minority to a prosperous, accepted American denomination, while simultane-
ously paying homage to the architectural legacy of the Church of England.

The church's interior is known for its string of Tiffany windows, all
installed around the turn of the twentieth century. They are relatively
unusual among the Tiffany oeuvre for their overtly biblical themes, appropriate for a High-Church setting (see page 58). In true Tiffany style, these
are done in opalescent glass, with luminous figures and a range of muted
colors. In direct contrast to this, Trinity Church also has more traditional
stained-glass windows designed by the Philadelphia firm of D'Ascenzo,
the twentieth-century artist who patterned painted glass in the style of the
medieval glassmakers. (More examples of D'Ascenzo's work can be seen in
Yale University's Dwight Chapel; see page 286.)

This church is famous for music, music, music—and its magnificent
organ is perfectly suited for this purpose. Built by the Aeolian Skinner
Company in 1935, it features more than 4,600 pipes. Trinity's extensive
music program features its Choir of Men and Boys, founded in 1885, one of
the oldest in the country. As early as the American Revolution, Trinity
was incorporating vocal music into its worship services, a rather daring
innovation at that time.

A New Light Church of the Great Awakening
UNITED CHURCH ON THE GREEN
United Church of Christ (formerly Puritan, or Congregational). 311 Temple Street (at the corner of Temple and Elm). Year consecrated: 1815 (congregation dates to 1742). Architect: Attributed to David Hoadley.
☎ 203-787-4195 🖳 www.newlights.org

Follow directions for Trinity Episcopal Church (see page 281).

Like Trinity, United Church on the Green occupies a proud corner lot. The Federal-style brick church was probably designed by architect David Hoadley, though there is some dispute on this point. What is not disputed is this church's important role in U.S. history.

When Connecticut and the surrounding colonies were caught up in the enthusiastic revivals of the Great Awakening in the early 1740s (see page 185), many people began to question the traditions of Puritanism. "New Light" Congregationalists called for a more warmhearted religion, based on a true conversion experience and an openness to the idea that God could work mighty wonders through revival. These "awakened" New Lights became dissatisfied with the cold forms of their churches, and many sought to separate from established Congregationalism. United Church on the Green, formed in 1742, was one of the first churches to emerge from the New Light split. Its members set up shop literally a stone's throw from their former church home, now called Center Church (see below). They cut themselves off from state support (the taxes that made Congregationalism the colony's established religion) and challenged the Puritan theocracy that united church and state.

New Lights preached a rather radical Protestant theology, teaching that each person had the ability to be awakened in spirit and discover God's truth. But as has happened many times in American religious history, a group that so heavily emphasized the individual suffered from the syndrome of "too many cooks." With each church member capable of discerning God's voice, the church was divided in many different directions—with the inevitable result of schism. This congregation split many times in the eighteenth and nineteenth centuries, as various leaders stressed divergent aspects of Congregational doctrine and practice. Happily, many of the factions remerged in 1884, giving this church its "United" identification.

Throughout its history, United Church has stood on the side of oppressed peoples, advocating social justice long before it was popular to do so. In 1839, a number of Africans were captured and placed on a slave ship bound for Cuba. En route, they overcame their captors and ordered the remaining crewmen to sail them home. The navigators disobeyed and took the ship to Long Island instead. This is the famous story of the *Amistad* and its human cargo, who spent the winter of 1839 to '40 imprisoned in New Haven awaiting trial. While the courts debated the issues of piracy, slavery, and property, members of the congregations that later formed United Church joined with other New Haven residents in assisting the Africans. Plans were laid to transport them back home if the courts should not decide in their favor. As the nation awaited the verdict, a ship cruised around Long Island Sound, ready to spirit the prisoners away if the U.S. Supreme Court ruled that they were still considered slaves. Fortunately, the court ruled to free the Africans and return them to their homes, so the daring rescue was not necessary.

In 1997, the church installed a plaque commemorating the abolition movement by its front doors, in honor of the many church members who fought bravely to end slavery. United Church has continued its fight for social justice, carrying on a mission that has guided the church since its founding in 1742. Members have been active in crusades for civil rights, peace, environmental healing, and the struggle to end poverty. As an "open and affirming" church, United is a leader in ministries to gays and lesbians.

New Haven's First Congregation
CENTER CHURCH ON THE GREEN
United Church of Christ (formerly Puritan, or Congregational). 311 Temple Street. Year consecrated: 1814 (congregation dates to 1638). Architect: Ithiel Towne. ☎ 207-787-0121

Between Trinity Episcopal Church and United Church; follow directions for Trinity Episcopal Church (page 281).

It's not difficult to see how Center Church got its name—as folks in New Haven will explain, "It's the one in the middle." That's true geographically, since Center Church sits between the two other stately churches on New Haven's Green, but it has also been true theologically. In the mid–eighteenth century, when the region's Anglicans on the one hand held fast to the Church of England, and the New Light Congregationalists, on the other hand, were challenging the foundations of Puritan theology (see previous entry), Center Church rode out the controversy by firmly, comfortably, adopting a middle way. It retained its century-old Puritan traditions and rejected the most dramatic manifestations of the Great Awakening, holding true to its own heritage.

Founded in 1638 by a group of Boston Puritans, this congregation is by far the oldest in New Haven. In fact, it was the only game in town for its first 100 years, when a faction of revival-oriented Congregationalists founded another church (see previous entry). For that first century, Center Church (known then as a meetinghouse) thrived as the town's established church, supported by public taxes. Even after other denominations entered the scene, this Congregational church continued to be supported by taxes levied on all citizens, until Connecticut disestablished the Congregational Church in 1818.

The current Federal-style brick edifice, consecrated in 1814, is the congregation's fourth house of worship to stand on or near this site. The first meetinghouse had been a functional, squat, square building; by this fourth incarnation the meetinghouse had come to resemble a more traditional church, with a tall spire and graceful bell tower. In fact, some old-school Puritans thought that the decorations were a bit popish: If you look closely at the frieze above the church's portico, you will see ornamental ox skulls at intervals. Although no one is exactly sure why designer Ithiel Towne chose ox skulls to adorn the church, it is most likely that he simply copied them from the building that inspired Center Church's overall architectural style: St. Martin-in-the-Fields in London.

The church's interior is refreshingly simple and filled with light. Plain-glass windows adorn both sides of the nave, with one magnificent stained-glass window taking pride of place above the altar. It was designed by Joseph Lauber of Tiffany Studios in 1890, and contains 2,320 separate pieces of glass. The window depicts a portion of New England's own sacred history: the first Sabbath the Puritans spent in Connecticut, when their minister, John Davenport, preached about their New Jerusalem under a mighty oak tree. The text? "Then Jesus was led up of the Spirit into the wilderness." Those words must have seemed like fresh balm to a group of religious dissenters who had fled England for the "wilderness" of southern Connecticut in order to pursue their religious and social vision.

A Colonial Burying Ground
THE CENTER CHURCH CRYPT
Below Center Church on the Green. Year consecrated: 1687 or earlier.
☎ 207-787-0121

Tours are offered by appointment, or after Sunday worship in the winter months.

New England is replete with remarkable historic cemeteries, but Center Church Crypt is unique. In the eighteenth century, much of the Green was simply covered with tombstones. Center Church was built in 1814 on top of one corner of that burial ground, and the 137 stones that remain in its basement crypt probably represent only a fraction of the people who are actually interred here. Archaeologists estimate that this small plot of land may be the final resting place of nearly 2,000 people. Many of the Green's other tombstones were moved in the 1810s to Grove Street Cemetery. (Some were used for building projects at Yale University, and one infamous tombstone was employed as the stone foundation for a local baker's oven. New Haven residents would bring their bread home and discover a poor chap's epitaph faintly imprinted on their crusts.)

Walking through the windowless crypt, with its ceiling only slightly higher than six feet, it is difficult to imagine that this enclosed space once enjoyed the copious sunlight and open air of the Green. The oldest stone here, dating back to 1687, is for Sarah Trowbridge; luminaries buried in the crypt include the hero-turned-traitor Benedict Arnold's first wife Margaret, who died in 1775 at the age of thirty-one. President Rutherford B. Hayes's grandparents are here, and the esteemed statesman paid a visit to their graves in 1880. The church offers a brochure listing all of those interred in the crypt, and a useful map of the tombstones.

"And this our life, exempt from public haunt,
Finds tongues in trees, books in the running brooks,
Sermons in stones, and good in every thing."
—William Shakespeare, *As You Like It*

A Meditation Center in the Kwan Um Tradition
THE NEW HAVEN ZEN CENTER
193 Mansfield Street. ☎ 203-787-0912 🖳 www.newhavenzen.org

> From I-91, take Exit 3 (Trumbull Street). At the fourth light (Prospect Street), turn right and go one block. At the next light (Sachem Street) turn left, then take the first right onto Mansfield Street. The Zen Center is a three-story blue house on the right.

Located on the edge of Yale's campus in an elegant Victorian house, the New Haven Zen Center is affiliated with the Kwan Um School of Korean Zen Buddhism. It was founded by Korean Zen Master Seung Sahn (see page 123), author of *The Compass of Zen* and *The Whole World Is a Single Flower*. Beginners are welcome to drop in for meditation. On Wednesday evenings at 6:30 P.M., an orientation is provided to teach basic meditation techniques; this is followed by a sitting meditation session at 7:30 P.M. Retreats include multiday silent retreats called *Yong Maeng Jong Jin*, work retreats, and innovative Christian-Buddhist retreats that emphasize the contemplative strains in both traditions.

NEARBY
➡ **Dwight Chapel** on Yale University's Old Campus is a fine example of the height of Gothic Revival architecture, with soaring buttresses, pointed archways, and D'Ascenzo stained glass. Completed in 1842, it was originally intended for use as Yale's library. Today, in addition to worship services, the building houses many of Yale's student-run outreach programs such as Adopt-A-Grandparent, Big Siblings, Habitat for Humanity, and Students Against Sweatshops. The chapel is taller than it is wide, giving the long, dark narrow room a confined sense that is mitigated only by the soaring stained-glass windows that draw the eyes upward. *67 High Street.* ☎ 203-432-1128 🖳 www.yale.edu/chaplain/home.html

Stamford
....

"The Fish Church"
FIRST PRESBYTERIAN CHURCH
1101 Bedford Street. Year consecrated: 1958 (congregation dates to 1854). Architect: Wallace Harrison. ☎ 203-324-9522 🖳 www.fishchurch.org

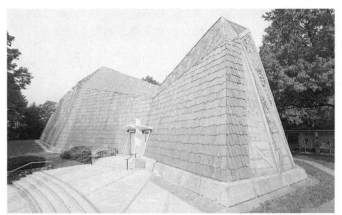

*First
Presbyterian
Church,
Stamford*

*From I-95 South, take the Elm Street Exit (8). Turn right onto Elm
Street, which becomes Grove Street. After approximately a half mile,
turn left onto Hoyt Street. After .2 miles, bear right onto Bedford Street.
Sunday worship is at 10 A.M.*

"Is that—is that a *fish?*" visitors sometimes ask, when they see First
Presbyterian Church for the first time. The building is, in fact, loosely
shaped like a fish, earning the church its nickname. But there's nothing
fishy going on here—the fish is simply one of the most ancient symbols of
the Christian faith. When Roman persecutions made it dangerous to
declare Christian faith by using the familiar symbol of the cross, Christians
communicated their identity to one another secretly by using the fish. So
too does this 1958 building communicate its Christian ideals. Considered
one of the most architecturally innovative modern houses of worship in
New England, First Presbyterian Church is particularly known for its
stained-glass windows. More than 20,000 pieces of faceted glass make for
multiple prisms on the interior of the church. Although they are abstract
and not representational, the windows symbolize the crucifixion and resurrection of Christ. They were designed in the 1950s by French glass master
Gabriel Loire, who also did the windows for the Cathedral of Saint Joseph
in Hartford, Connecticut (see page 269).

NEARBY
➡ **Temple Beth El** in Stamford began in 1920, when a small group of
local Jews decided to form a congregation. Today this Conservative synagogue serves over 650 families and occupies its third building, dedicated in

1973. *350 Roxbury Road. From Route 15, take Exit 33 (Den Road) and go south for .3 miles. Turn right, and then left on Roxbury Road.*
☎ 203-322-6901 🖳 www.tbe.org

➡ On nine acres overlooking Long Island Sound, the **Convent of St. Birgitta** in **Darien** promises quiet spiritual retreats for visitors. The nuns who live here do not lead directed retreats, but open the home for individuals and groups (up to twelve at a time) who wish to plan their own retreat programming. Mass and four prayer services are offered each day, and all guests are invited to participate. *4 Runkenhage Road, Darien.*
☎ 203-655-1068

West Hartford

Elizabeth Park and Rose Garden, West Hartford

The Nation's Oldest Municipal Rose Garden
ELIZABETH PARK AND ROSE GARDEN
Prospect and Asylum Avenues. Year established: 1904. ☎ 860-722-6541
🖳 www.elizabethpark.org

On the border between Hartford and West Hartford. From I-84 take Exit 44 (Prospect Avenue) and travel north on Prospect Avenue. The entrance to the gardens is three-quarters of a mile on your left. No admission fee.

With more than 800 varieties of roses and a mind-boggling 15,000 plants, this two-and-a-half-acre rose garden is one of the nation's largest. Strolling through it, visitors are treated to archways covered with climbing roses and flower beds profuse with roses in every possible color.

The rose garden occupies only a small fraction of the entire Elizabeth Park, which encompasses about 100 acres and was designed by the landscape firm of Olmsted and Son. The park offers an array of fields, meadows, and ponds, as well as serene walking paths.

The park's annual spring flower show is held the last two weeks of March (capped off by a plant sale), and a summer rose festival takes place in late June. If your visit does not coincide with New England's short and fickle growing season, never fear. In wintertime, you can get an indoor "sneak preview" of the plants that will be transferred to the park come spring. The 100-year-old greenhouses are open to the public each day and feature displays of poinsettias, palm trees, birds of paradise, cacti, and a Ponderosa Lemon tree.

NEARBY

➡ One of Connecticut's oldest houses of worship is **First Church of Christ, Congregational** in **Farmington**, completed in 1772. Built in the Wren-Gibbs style, the building's exterior is of white clapboard, with an octagonal belfry and 150-foot spire. The church is listed on the National Register of Historic Places for its role in helping the refugees from the slave ship *Amistad* in 1839. Church members provided housing, clothing, and education for the *Amistad* refugees (see page 283). *75 Main Street, Farmington.* ☎ 203-677-2601

Woodbury

The Birthplace of the "Episcopal" Church in America
THE GLEBE HOUSE MUSEUM AND THE GERTRUDE JEKYLL GARDEN
Hollow Road. Year house was built: 1750. Year museum opened: 1925.
☎ 203-263-2855

Between Route 6 and Route 317. From I-84, take Exit 15 and go east on Route 6. Drive five miles to Woodbury and turn left at the stoplight onto Route 317. Bear left when the road forks. The Glebe House will then be across the street from the stop sign. The museum is open from 1 P.M. to 4 P.M. Wednesday through Sunday, April through November. The museum has expanded summer hours (10 A.M. to 4 P.M.) on Saturdays from June through August. From December through March, open by appointment. Admission fee.

This museum is considered to be the birthplace of the Episcopal Church in America. During the Revolutionary War, an Anglican minister named John Marshall lived in this farmhouse with his wife, Sarah, and their nine children; it was a touchy time for American clergymen whose sympathies lay with England. In 1782, a group of them who could see the writing on the wall realized that in order to be perceived as patriots, they had better divest themselves quickly from the Church of England. They met in Reverend Marshall's house and elected their own bishop, one Samuel Seabury (1729–96), a loyalist who had served as a chaplain with the British armed forces during the war. Seabury actually had to travel to Britain for his ordination, since no other ranking clergy existed in the new American nation with the authority to ordain a bishop. But he waited in England for a full year, and still no one would ordain the upstart minister from the colonies. Undeterred, he journeyed to Scotland, where the ecclesiastical hierarchy was not quite so finicky. Seabury returned to America in 1784 as its first "Episcopal" bishop. The church's form of governance by bishops gave it its new American name: the Episcopal Church. (In Greek, *episkopos* means "bishop.")

The museum, which opened in 1925 as a historic site, is decorated with eighteenth-century period furnishings. But its garden is the real highlight. In 1926, the curators of this new small museum asked Gertrude Jekyll, one of England's most famous horticulturists, to design an authentic period garden for the site. She sent an extensive list of appropriate plants and flowers, but the garden was not installed until 1990. Although it was one of three that Jekyll designed in the United States, it is the only one that still survives. It includes a perennial border that is approximately 300 feet long and twelve feet deep, containing lilies, delphinium, hollyhock, and other plants. There is a small rose garden and a kitchen herb garden.

"GLEBE" LANDS

"Glebe" (pronounced "gleeb") lands were properties granted by the Anglican Church for the upkeep of the local parish and its minister. They are not very common in New England, since colonial-era Anglicans never held extensive political power in this Puritan-dominated region. But contemporary travelers to Virginia and the Carolinas, where Anglicanism was an established religion, will often see evidence of the Anglican presence in the form of streets and roads named "Glebe." These roads often bordered the glebe lands that were set aside for church use.

NEARBY

➥ **The Institute for American Indian Studies** in **Washington** offers a museum, a replicated Indian village and archaeological site, and a gift shop featuring native crafts. There are walking trails through nineteen acres of forest. *38 Curtis Road, Washington. Take I-84 West to Exit 15, then take Route 67 North to Route 199, then turn onto Curtis Road.* ☎ 860-868-0518

CHAPTER NINE

⟶ ❦ ⟵

$\mathscr{V}$ermont

AH, VERMONT. The "Green Mountain state" stands today as a reminder of what all of New England used to be at one time: rural farmland. It is, in fact, the nation's most rural state. With maple syrup as its most famous product, it retains its age-old agrarian character. Its largest cities are really just small towns (even its capital, Montpelier, is the nation's smallest, with fewer than 9,000 people). Today, this bucolic paradise invites more tourists each year than the state's resident population of just over half a million people; visitors are attracted by the area's wonderful skiing, beautiful nature reserves, and vital sense of history. Spiritual travelers who are interested in visiting some of the region's top gardens need look no further than Shelburne Farms, the gardens at the Shelburne Museum, or Hildene, Robert Todd Lincoln's summer estate. Those with a passion for ecospirituality should visit Spirit in Nature, an innovative outdoor sanctuary that encourages readers to reflect upon what the world's major religions have to say about the environment.

Dotted amidst the mountains and meadows of Vermont are some of the nation's oldest churches, many reflecting the state's seventeenth-century French Catholic heritage. (The name "Vermont" is French for "green mountain.") On Isle La Motte, where French explorers held mass in 1609, is a shrine to St. Anne. French heritage is also evident at Burlington's St. Joseph Co-cathedral, which was founded in the mid–nineteenth century. Vermont of course has its share of Congregational churches, though the first of these were founded later than Congregational churches in southern New England. Vermont's first Congregational church was established in 1762 in Bennington; in 1805 the congregation erected a lovely

VERMONT

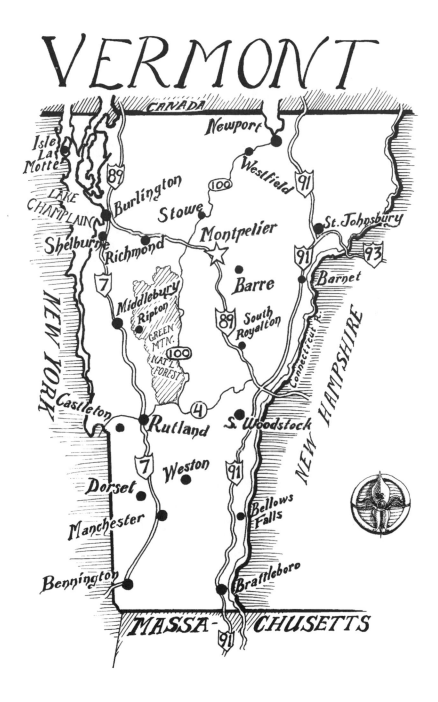

CANADA

Newport

Isle
La
Motte

89

Westfield

91

100

LAKE
CHAMPLAIN

Burlington

Stowe

Montpelier

St. Johnsbury

Shelburne

Richmond

91

93

Barnet

7

Barre

Middlebury
Ripton

89

South
Royalton

GREEN
MTN.
NAT'L
FOREST

100

Connecticut R.

NEW YORK

NEW HAMPSHIRE

Castleton

4

Rutland

S. Woodstock

7

Weston

91

Dorset

Bellows
Falls

Manchester

Bennington

Brattleboro

MASSA- CHUSETTS

91

church that has been designated by the Vermont legislature as the state's "Colonial Shrine." Unlike Massachusetts and Connecticut, colonial Vermont never passed legislation requiring an "established" (tax-supported) Congregational presence in the colony, though a few communities chose to levy taxes to support their local Congregational churches. By the early nineteenth century Congregationalism was the Protestant denomination of choice, though Methodists, Baptists, Presbyterians, Unitarians, and Universalists were also present. In the village of Richmond, several of these Protestant denominations united to build the Old Round Church in 1812, a circular house of worship where all members would feel equal, despite denominational differences.

Vermont was the birthplace of Joseph Smith, Jr., the founder of the Church of Jesus Christ of Latter-day Saints, and the site is a popular destination for tourists. In the last thirty years, Eastern religions have gained a foothold in the Green Mountains. Karmê-Chöling in Barnet is a world-famous Buddhist retreat center in the Vajrayana traditions of Tibet, while the Green Mountain Dharma Center in South Woodstock promotes the teachings of Vietnamese Zen Master Thich Nhat Hanh.

THE VILLAGES OF VERMONT

In Vermont, inspiring settings are the rule rather than the exception. Spiritual travelers might consider a leisurely tour of such charming southern Vermont villages as Weston, Newfane, Townshend, Chester, Grafton, Ludlow, Dorset, and Castleton. (In summer, be sure to catch a summer stock theater production at the Dorset or Weston Playhouses.) In northern Vermont, the villages of Cabot, Marshfield, Groton, Walden, Plainfield, St. Johnsbury, Barnet, and Peacham participate each autumn in the Northeast Kingdom Foliage Festival. The festival, which typically begins during the last week of September, runs for ten days and offers craft shows, church suppers, historical tours, and the like, all against a backdrop of fantastic foliage.
☎ 802-563-2472 🖥 www.vermontnekchamber.org

Barnet

Vajrayana in Vermont

KARMÊ-CHÖLING (TAIL OF THE TIGER)

369 Patneaude Lane. Year founded: 1970. ☎ 802-633-2384

💻 www.kcl.shambhala.org

> *Karmê-Chöling is located in north-central Vermont, approximately one hour north of White River Junction. From I-91, take Exit 18 (Barnet-Peacham) and go one-half mile west to the second driveway on your right, Patneaude Lane. The office is open daily from 1:30 P.M. to 5:30 P.M., including weekends, but is closed on staff retreat days.*

Karmê-Chöling, or "Tail of the Tiger," was one of the first Tibetan Buddhist meditation centers to open in the United States. It was founded in 1970 by Vidyadhara the Venerable Chögyam Trungpa Rinpoche, a Tibetan Buddhist meditation master in the Vajrayana (esoteric) tradition. Vajrayana Buddhism is characterized by a graduated hierarchy of teachings, from the most basic and public to the more tantric, or secret. As with ancient Jewish proscriptions that restricted the study of Kabbalah to persons of a certain age, Vajrayana Buddhists believe that the highest, most

Karmê-Chöling, Barnet

difficult teachings can actually do harm to those who study them before they are mentally and emotionally ready. To determine readiness and to teach the difficult texts, they rely upon a guru. More than other Buddhist traditions, Vajrayana Buddhists—particularly in Tibet—tend to emphasize guru devotion, though this has been downplayed in Vajrayana's transplant to the West.

Despite its Vajrayana origins, Buddhists of all varieties are welcome at Karmê-Chöling. Devotees of meditation could hardly hope for a lovelier spot. The complex is situated on 540 acres of Vermont woods and fields; great care was taken to ensure that the Tibetan-style meditation center, which seats 200 people, would blend in naturally with its New England surroundings. Despite its Tibetan roots, Karmê-Chöling reflects the American melting pot: Japanese Zen Buddhism has a place here too, particularly in the practice of Kyudo (Zen archery). The grounds feature one of the only outdoor target ranges (*azuchi*) in New England for the practice of Kyudo. A steep hiking trail leads past numerous small shrines and "concealed hermitages" (small, rustic cabins for secluded retreats) to a large outdoor shrine in a hilltop field.

As with other Buddhist retreat centers in America, instruction is available for every level, from the beginner to the adept. Novices can try their hand at meditation during introductory group retreats, usually over a weekend. A *dathun*, or month-long intensive meditation retreat, is available for more advanced practitioners. These retreatants follow a daily schedule with five hours of meditation, a three-and-a-half-hour work period, and evening classes. For the Kyudo practitioner, special retreats offer instruction, equipment, and use of the *azuchi*.

NEARBY

➥ One of New England's only Benedictine communities for women is the **Monastery of the Immaculate Heart of Mary**, located in the northeastern section of Vermont near Westfield. Women guests are welcome at the small retreat house, which has four bedrooms. The nuns gather several times a day in the chapel to chant the liturgies of the Divine Office; the evening vespers service is said in Latin. *4103 Vermont Route 100. From I-95 or I-89, take Route 100 into Westfield.* ☎ 802-744-6525

Bennington

A Poet's Final Rest
"OLD FIRST CHURCH" AND ROBERT FROST GRAVESITE

Congregational. Monument Avenue. Year built: 1805 (congregation dates to 1762). Architect: Lavius Fillmore. ☎ 802-447-1223

> *Drive west from Bennington on Route 9 for a half mile. The church will be on your left. Tours are available from July to mid-October, 10 A.M. to 4 P.M. Sunday worship is at 11 A.M.*

This white New England church, which the Vermont state legislature officially recognized in 1935 as "Vermont's Colonial Shrine," was constructed in 1805. But the congregation had gathered a half century earlier, in 1762, making it the first Protestant congregation in Vermont. The founding of this Congregational Church was markedly different from the new churches of Massachusetts and Connecticut: it was not paid for by mandatory local taxes, but commissioned by the congregation.

By the early nineteenth century, the congregation had outgrown its small pine meetinghouse and wished to erect a new, larger church. The builder of the 1805 church was a New Englander with the name of Lavius Fillmore (a second cousin of President Millard Fillmore). Fillmore adopted

Old First Church, Bennington

a Federalist style, modifying it slightly by adding Palladian windows and a belfry. He had no training as an architect, but his achievements here have garnered high praise; the book *Great New England Churches* calls this "perhaps the most beautiful meetinghouse in all of New England." The church has been restored several times, not always perceptively; little remains of the original interior except the old pews in the gallery (and the graffiti carved into them).

When "Old First Church" was restored in 1937, the poet Robert Frost (1874–1963) helped to pay the expenses; Frost and his family are buried in the church cemetery, which is the oldest cemetery in Vermont. Frost's ashes were interred here on June 16, 1963, five months after he died in a Boston hospital. The epithet he chose for his headstone was simply, "I had a lover's quarrel with the world."

The cemetery also contains the graves of approximately seventy-five Revolutionary War soldiers fighting on the American side, as well as British and Hessian soldiers who fell during the Battle of Bennington.

COVERED BRIDGES IN THE BENNINGTON AREA

Vermont, with its harsh snowy winters and commitment to historical preservation, is covered bridge country. There are more than a hundred covered bridges throughout the state, most of which date to the nineteenth century, called "America's golden age of woodworking." Wooden bridges were coverd in order to keep the wood dry and avoid rot. In *Covered Bridges of Vermont*, Ed Barna notes that Vermont's covered bridges are often "wounded survivors" because they were not built to withstand the loads of heavy motor vehicles. Thankfully, most of Vermont's bridges are on the National Register of Historic Places, and Vermont residents are committed to their preservation.

There are several covered bridges clustered around Bennington. The **Silk Bridge**, which dates to the 1840s, crosses the Walloomsac River at Silk Road. Also along the Walloomsac is **Henry Bridge**, which crosses the river at Murphy Road. Henry Bridge was constructed in 1840—but dismantled in 1989 because its timbers were bent. The current Henry Bridge is a replica of the original. One of Vermont's most photographed bridges is **West Arlington Bridge**, which crosses the Battenkill River. Built in 1852, this red painted bridge retains its authentic construction materials.

NEARBY

⇢ Life begins at seventy. Or so was the motto of Anna Mary Robertson Moses (1860–1961), otherwise known as "Grandma" Moses, who did not pick up a paintbrush until she was threescore and ten. Her paintings can be viewed at the **Bennington Museum**, which has the largest collection of Moses's work in the nation. Also on the grounds of the museum is the **Grandma Moses Schoolhouse**; the school she attended as a child now offers an exhibit on her life and work. *West Main Street. Open daily, 9 A.M. to 5 P.M. (until 6 P.M. June through October). Admission fee.*
☎ 802-447-1571 🖳 www.benningtonmuseum.com

⇢ Forty miles east of Bennington in **Brattleboro** is **Solar Hill Labyrinth**, a permanent, seven-path classical labyrinth marked with stones. Tucked away in the woods behind the Solar Hill Yoga Center, the labyrinth was completed in 1997 and has welcomed many visitors since then, eager to gain spiritual insight by walking its path. *229/231 Western Avenue, Brattleboro.* ☎ 802-254-6990

⇢ The town of **Bellows Falls**, twenty miles north of Brattleboro, was settled by the English in the 1780s, but Native Americans who had lived here centuries earlier left a marker of their presence. Right below the Vilas Memorial Bridge, **stone carvings** (petroglyphs) can be seen on some of the rock walls of the banks of the Connecticut River. The petroglyphs depict primitive human faces and were most likely created by Pennacook Indians who once fished here. It is unclear what the scene represents; various theories have proposed that it depicts a celebration, a successful fish catch, or a battle. Look for the petroglyphs from the bridge's southside pedestrian walk. They are marked by fairly faded yellow lines painted on the rocks.

Burlington

French Catholic Heritage
ST. JOSEPH CO-CATHEDRAL
85 Elmwood Avenue. Year consecrated: 1887. Architect: Father Joseph Michaud. ☎ 802-863-2388

> *Mass is said Saturday at 8 A.M. and 4 P.M.; Sunday at 9 A.M. and 11 A.M.; Monday, Wednesday, and Friday at 4:45 P.M.; and Tuesday and Thursday at 8 A.M.*

Burlington's position in northwestern Vermont, not far from the Quebec border, provides it with a rich French Catholic heritage, a heritage that is well-preserved in St. Joseph Church. The parish was established in 1850 when a French Canadian priest began holding mass here, making this the first French Canadian Catholic parish in New England. French-speaking people from all over Vermont began coming to St. Joseph's, and so in 1887, bolstered by strong parish growth, the church built and consecrated its current house of worship, which is the largest church in Vermont. The church's French roots are reflected in the cock that adorns the cross on the church's roof—cock symbols, which recall how St. Peter denied Christ three times before the cock crowed, are common in village churches throughout Quebec.

Many of today's more than 2,200 parishioners are descendants of the early Francophone pioneers. (The church secretary will mention proudly that her great-grandfather was the master carpenter of the church, which was built entirely by voluntary labor.) St. Joseph Church is currently engaged in a large restoration project to return the building to its original condition. Great care is being taken with the interior, with intricate gold-leaf designs being redone by hand. The thriving parish was designated as "St. Joseph Co-cathedral" in 2000 by the local bishop, recognizing its extensive seating capacity for important masses and events. (It thereby joined the Cathedral of the Immaculate Conception, on Pine Street, as the official seat of the bishop of Burlington.)

A Banner Church
FIRST UNITARIAN-UNIVERSALIST CHURCH
152 Pearl Street. Year built: 1806. Architects: Peter Banner (possibly with Charles Bullfinch). ☎ 802-862-5630 ▣ www.together.net/~firstuu/

Church and Pearl Streets. Sunday worship at 11 A.M.; 9 A.M. in July and August.

This Unitarian Church was designed in 1805 by Peter Banner, who was also the architect of Boston's famous Park Street Church (see page 73). (This is an ironic twist, since Park Street Church was founded precisely to combat the Unitarian trend sweeping the Congregational Church in the early nineteenth century, and this church was established to promote it.) Banner's trademark—the twin porches on either side of the tower—is in full evidence here. This red brick edifice boasts a square steeple and a double octagonal spire. It stands at the head of Church Street, which is now a pedestrian-only commerce area with over 130 shops, cafes, and restaurants. In summer, numerous street fairs and crafts shows are held here.

This church has a history of controversy; in 1820, a female member was ousted after she had publicly accused the pastor of bribery and behaving in "an improper and unchristianlike manner." (Unfortunately, the details of this juicy dispute have been lost to history.) And the Unitarian emphasis on social justice has been in full sway here for a century and a half: in 1852, a pastor was asked to resign from his position after he declared his solidarity with the abolitionist John Brown.

NEARBY

➥ Although Gothic Revival architecture is usually associated with Christianity, that was the style chosen by members of the **Ahavath Gerim Synagogue** in Burlington when the congregation formed in 1885. (At that time, it was called Ohavi Zedek.) When the congregation built a new synagogue in 1952, a group of members continued holding services in this red brick Gothic Revival building. *168 Archibald Street.* ☎ 802-862-3001

Isle La Motte

A Shrine at Vermont's Oldest Settlement
ST. ANNE'S SHRINE
Roman Catholic (Edmundite Brothers). Isle La Motte. Year dedicated: 1893 (fort settlement dates to 1666). ☎ 802-928-3362
💻 www.sse.org/stanneshrine.htm

> *St. Anne's Shrine is located off Route 129 on West Shore Road on Isle La Motte. The shrine is open each day from mid-May to mid-October, 9 A.M. to 7 P.M.*

Isle La Motte, closer geographically to Quebec than to mainland Vermont, reflects the French Catholic heritage of the seventeenth-century Jesuits who settled here and converted many natives and immigrants to Roman Catholicism. One of the islands at the northern end of

Lake Champlain, Isle La Motte is the site of Vermont's first French settlement, Fort St. Anne, dating to 1666. It began as a military fort erected to ward off expected attacks from the Mohawk Indians. In 1609, this area had been discovered by French explorer Samuel de Champlain, who was present at the first mass held here. Mass is still said daily (weather permitting) in the shrine's open-air pavilion chapel.

The chapel is a peaceful place, located in a grove of trees near the island's shore. The first official pilgrimage to the shrine occurred on July 26, 1893, the feast day of Saint Anne, the mother of Mary, who is the patron saint of special favors. A few other simple outdoor shrines and grottos dot the grounds, as does a statue of St. Anne, in the shape of an "A." Here, the faithful light candles and leave written petitions for Anne.

Richmond

An 1812 Overture
OLD ROUND CHURCH
Nondenominational Christian. Bridge Street. Year built: 1812. Architect: William Rhodes. ☎ 802-434-4119

> Richmond is twelve miles east of Burlington. From I-89, take Exit 11 (Richmond) and then take Route 2 to the center of the town of Richmond. Turn right onto Bridge Street. The church is on your left, across from the Winooski River. It is open daily from 11 A.M. to 4 P.M. during July and August and some weekends throughout the year. No admission fee.

This unique church is not exactly round, though it does give that initial impression. It has sixteen sides, making it "hexkaidecagonal" in form, and is topped by an octagonal belfry. It was built in 1812–13 for an unusual sacred purpose: it was intended for use as both a multidenominational church and a community meeting place. Members of five different denominations worshiped here. They were Methodists, Congregationalists, Universalists, Baptists, and restorationist Christians—groups that in the early nineteenth century generally argued, if they spoke to one another at all. They formed one church because there were not enough members of any one denomination to sustain a full-time minister and erect a building. By pooling their resources and membership, they could achieve what one congregation working alone could not. As the town grew in the mid–nine-

Old Round Church, Richmond

teenth century, individual denominations began spinning off their own churches and leaving the Round Church communion; in 1879, the building was given over to civic functions such as town meetings.

There are ancient precedents for round churches; in the first millennium C.E., churches in Rome, Ravenna, and Aachen/Aix-la-Chapelle all adopted a round (often octagonal) design for liturgical purposes. It was later superseded throughout Europe, however, by different types of cruciform designs. Thus New England master builder William Rhodes had few examples to draw upon when he designed this church, and its sophisticated simplicity stands as testament to his creative ingenuity. As a house of worship, its unusual shape helped to underscore the fact that it was not tied to a particular denomination.

Ripton

"Green" Spirituality in the Green Mountain State
SPIRIT IN NATURE
Interfaith. Goshen Road. Year created: 1998. ☎ 802-388-7244
🖳 www.spiritinnature.com

*Heading south from Middlebury on Route 7, turn east onto Route 125.
Go 5.5 miles until you see a road sign for Spirit in Nature. Turn right on
Goshen Road; proceed for a half mile to Spirit in Nature. Open daily
(except during deer season) from dawn to dusk. A small donation is
requested.*

Tucked away in the forests of central Vermont is Spirit in Nature, a carefully plotted ring of spiritual walking paths that was created to be traversed in meditation and prayer. Paul Bortz, the founder of Spirit in Nature, is a Unitarian-Universalist minister who retired from parish ministry so that he could work full-time on environmental issues. "The ultimate goal of Spirit in Nature is to have people of faith connect their beliefs to the environment, and act to improve the environment," he explains.

The ten paths, which range from one-half mile to four miles in length, are laid out on seventy acres of land, with 6,000 feet of river frontage. Each of the paths traces a different religious tradition: Jewish, Hindu, Muslim, Unitarian Universalist, Christian, Pagan Sacred Earth, Friends/Quaker, Baha'i, Buddhist, and Interfaith. Each path offers signposts with sayings from its particular faith tradition, explaining how that tradition connects to nature. Benches are placed throughout to encourage meditation and a thoughtful, slow approach to walking the trails. Each path also offers "nature notes"— specific references to items of interest in nature (types of ferns, white pines, old stone walls, ground cover, or bear markings on trees). The land, which is leased from Middlebury College, offers walking bridges, an apple orchard, and a beaver pond.

Spirit in Nature, Ripton

"Nature is God's will and is its expression in and through the contingent world."

—Quoted on the Baha'i Path

All ten paths converge on a Sacred Circle, symbolizing the unity of all religions in nature. The Sacred Circle has benches-in-the-round to seat up to fifty people. Each Sunday afternoon during the summer, a worship service is held here for a different religious tradition. Monthly moonlight services are also conducted year-round. The circle area is home to many groups that meet regularly to discuss spirituality and nature, including a "voluntary simplicity" group and a creativity crew that produces nature drawings, poetry, and essays. Students from nearby Middlebury College also come here to practice their nature writing and drawing.

Currently, this is the only place of its kind in the world, but Paul Bortz and his wife lead training seminars regularly to teach others how to create similar venues in other parts of the country. Spirit in Nature receives a couple thousand visitors each year, and that number is growing. Most visit in the summer months, but the paths are also open during the winter to encourage meditative cross-country skiing and snowshoeing. Spirit in Nature's proximity to both the Vermont Robert Frost Trail and Vermont's Long Trail is a draw for many nature lovers.

"The high, the low, of all creation
God gives to humankind to use.
If this privilege is misused,
God's justice permits creation
to punish humanity."
—Hildegard of Bingen,
Quoted on the Christian path

NEARBY

➥ The tranquil town of **Middlebury** is home to **Middlebury College**, founded in 1800 and now one of New England's most prestigious liberal arts institutions. **Mead Chapel**, the 1914 white marble meetinghouse at the highest point on campus, blends a Greek Revival façade with Georgian doors, windows, and interior paneling. *From I-89, take Exit 1 (Queechee) to Route 4 West to Route 7 North to Middlebury.*
☎ 802-443-5000 🖥 www.middlebury.edu

The Middlebury **Congregational Church** is a fine example of New England meetinghouse design. Designed by Lavius Fillmore (see page 297) in 1809, this black-shuttered, white clapboard meetinghouse boasts a striking exterior. *On Main Street at the Green, Middlebury.* ☎ 802-388-7634

Lavius Fillmore also did the woodwork in Middlebury's **St. Stephen's Episcopal Church**, a Gothic Revival building completed in 1827. St. Stephen's is a relatively early example of the Gothic Revival style in New England. *3 Main Street, Middlebury.* ☎ 802-388-7200 💻 www.ststephensmidd.org

Sharon/South Royalton

Birthplace of the Founder of Mormonism
JOSEPH SMITH MEMORIAL BIRTHPLACE
357 LDS Lane. Year memorial created: 1905. ☎ 802-763-7742
💻 www.lds.org/basicbeliefs/placestovisit/1085.html

Coming from the south, take the Sharon Exit (Exit 2) off I-89 until you reach Route 14, where you will turn right. Drive four miles to Dairy Hill Road and turn right at the sign for the memorial. Follow this road for approximately two miles up a steep hill to the memorial's entrance on your right. The memorial is open Monday through Saturday from 9 A.M. until 5 P.M. from November through April, and 9 A.M. until 7 P.M. from May until October. The site opens at 1:30 on Sundays. No admission fee.

Jesus once said that "a prophet is not without honor, save in his own country." (Matthew 13:57) Nowhere is this more evident than in Sharon (now South Royalton), the hometown of Joseph Smith, Jr. (1805–44), the founder of the Church of Jesus Christ of Latter-day Saints (see page 19). The town has done little to call attention to its most famous son, although the 1937 Works Progress Administration guidebook to Vermont conceded that "more than any other Vermonter, Joseph Smith spread far-reaching influences, whose impact affected the lives of many thousands." Today, make that millions: The Church of Jesus Christ of Latter-day Saints has more than eleven million members around the world.

If the town has chosen not to call attention to its ties to Joseph Smith, the religious movement he founded has certainly done so. As the LDS

Joseph Smith Memorial Birthplace, Sharon/South Royalton

Church became larger and more influential, it purchased many sites and buildings relevant to its history, and engaged in painstaking restoration efforts. Here in South Royalton, the Church purchased a total of 283 acres from 1905 to 1907, so visitors could view the site where Joseph Smith, Jr., was born and lived for most of his first ten years. The highlight of the area is the 38.5-foot granite monument erected in Smith's memory on December 23, 1905, on the hundredth anniversary of his birth. On that occasion, his nephew, Joseph Fielding Smith, journeyed east from Utah for the dedication of the granite monolith, quarried from a single block in nearby Barre. Every foot on the monument denotes a year in the life of Joseph Smith, Jr., from his humble birth here to his well-publicized assassination in Carthage, Illinois, in June of 1844. Hauling the granite shaft up the mountain was a colossal task requiring twenty-two horses and two oxen.

 The Church has recently added more land to the site, making it a beautifully-maintained 360 acres. The original Smith family cabin has long since disappeared, but a small plaque marks the spot where it once stood, and its hearthstone can be seen in the Visitors' Center. The center is staffed by full-time LDS missionary guides, who are happy to answer questions about the Smith family, as well as about Mormon history and beliefs. During the Christmas season, the grounds are illuminated by over 130,000 lights.

For a special treat, you can take the hiking trail up to the original home site of Joseph Smith's maternal grandfather, Solomon Mack. Follow the path behind the memorial to the foundation ruins of Mack's home, located in a quiet clearing. Surrounded by a thicket of trees and lovely wildflowers, this area looks much as it might have during Smith's childhood.

THE IMPORTANCE OF
JOSEPH SMITH
IN MORMONISM

Many LDS families make pilgrimages to the Joseph Smith Memorial to understand more about the founder of their church, while non-Mormons come to enjoy the beautiful setting and learn a bit about the LDS faith. Joseph Smith holds a significant role in Mormonism—not just as the founder of a new church, but as a prophet of God. Mormons believe that when Smith was a young man, living in upstate New York (where his family moved when he was ten years old), he saw a vision of God the Father and Jesus Christ descending to him with a special spiritual message.

This was the first of many supernatural events; another famous incident involved an 1823 visitation from the Angel Moroni, said to be a resurrected man who had once lived on the American continent. According to Smith, Moroni told him about some golden plates that were buried in the ground, which recounted the history of an Israelite people who had come to the Americas several hundred years before Christ. Moroni showed Smith where the plates were buried, but told him he could not open them at that time; it was four more years before Smith was permitted to gather the plates and commence the arduous work of translating them. This took him several more years. The work was published in March 1830 under the title "The Book of Mormon," since Mormon was the name of the man who had edited the record together in the late fourth century C.E., before burying the plates to ensure their safe survival. After completion of the translation, Latter-day Saints believe, the golden plates were taken up to God; numerous nineteenth-century witnesses signed affidavits saying that they had seen the plates before their disappearance.

On April 6, 1830, Smith founded the Church of Christ (the name was later changed to its present name) with six members. In its earliest days, the Church's beliefs and practices were similar to mainline Protestantism, though the early 1840s saw Smith offering up new revelations that his followers believed came from God. (Some of these innovations, such as the practice of polygamy, were eventually abandoned.)

NEARBY

➥ The town of **Barre** is well known for its granite quarries, so it should come as no surprise that **Hope Cemetery** has some of the finest examples of carved granite headstones in New England. There are also intricately carved mausoleums, sculptures, columns, and entrance gates. The sixty-five-acre cemetery was established in 1895. *Merchant Street, Barre.*

➥ Although not as large as the Norman Rockwell Museum in Stockbridge, Massachusetts (see page 199), the **Norman Rockwell Museum of Vermont** offers chronological displays of more than 2,500 magazine covers, calendars, advertisements, and illustrations by one of the nation's best-loved twentieth-century artists. *654 Route 4 East, near Rutland. On Route 4 two miles east of Route 7. Open daily, year round from 9 A.M. to 5 P.M. Admission fee.* ☎ 802-773-6095 🖳 www.normanrockwellvt.com

➥ **St. Bridget's Roman Catholic Church** in **West Rutland** was designed by Patrick Keely, who was also responsible for the Roman Catholic cathedral in Boston (see page 103). Keely specialized in Gothic Revival design, a style that is in full evidence in this 1861 edifice, the first Vermont Catholic church to be built of stone. *28 Church Street, West Rutland.* ☎ 802-438-2490

Shelburne

Vermont's Largest Museum
SHELBURNE MUSEUM AND GARDEN
U.S. Route 7. Year established: 1947. ☎ 802-985-3346
🖳 www.shelburnemuseum.org

The museum is located on Route 7, seven miles south of Burlington. From I-89, take Exit 13 to Route 7 South. From March 31 to Memorial Day and October 15 to December 7, the museum is open from 1 P.M. to 4 P.M. daily. Only some of the buildings are open. From Memorial Day to mid-October, the museum is open daily from 10 A.M. to 5 P.M. Admission fee.

The word *museum* doesn't do justice to this complex of thirty-seven buildings with their collections of decorative arts, quilts, toys, weathervanes, dolls, and circus memorabilia. The museum is so large (spanning forty-five acres) that its maps are divided into quadrants. If there is a theme to the eclectic collection, it is "the art of the people." Museum founder Electra Havemeyer Webb spent a lifetime collecting and celebrating folk craftsmanship, whether in textiles, furniture, art, or architecture. The museum's buildings are chock-full of more than 80,000 examples of Americana, and many of the buildings themselves are historic: an 1800 blacksmithing shop, an 1845 double-lane covered bridge, an 1890 jail, an 1840 Greek Revival Methodist meetinghouse, an eighteenth-century Colonial house. There is a three-story round barn, constructed in 1901 after a style first popularized by the Shakers of Hancock, Massachusetts (see page 188), and an 1840s schoolhouse. Most of these buildings were moved to this site in the mid–twentieth century, as Webb was amassing her collection.

Lilac enthusiasts will not want to miss the gardens, which boast one of the nation's largest lilac displays. Hundreds of lilac bushes of more than ninety different varieties burst into spectacular color in mid- to late May.

> "Heart-leaves of lilac all over New England,
> Roots of lilac under all the soil of New England,
> Lilac in me because I am New England."
> —Amy Lowell (1874–1925), "Lilacs"

NEARBY

➥ Although it was built in 1887 as a one-family residence, the "Big House" that belonged to William Seward and Lila Vanderbilt Webb was renovated in 1985 to become a luxurious inn with twenty-four guest bedrooms. The 3,800-acre farm on which the inn sits was also owned by the Webbs, who had the foresight to hire Frederick Law Olmsted (see page 114) to supervise the layout of farmland, open fields, and wooded groves. Since 1972, **Shelburne Farms** has been a nonprofit organization dedicated to conservation education. It is still a working farm that can be enjoyed by visitors, who come by the thousands to walk the nature trails, learn about agricultural history, and take in the English cottage garden designed by Lila Vanderbilt Webb. *1611 Harbor Road. From Burlington, take Route 7 South and turn right at Bay Road. It will end at Shelburne Farms. Walking trails are open year-round, weather permitting, from 10 A.M. to 4 P.M. daily. Ninety-minute guided wagon tours of the farm are offered from mid-May to mid-October. Admission fee.* ☎ 802-985-8686
💻 www.shelburnefarms.org

➥ Founded in 1988, the **Vermont Zen Center** embraces the teachings of Roshi Philip Kapleau, who blends the Soto and Rinzai Zen traditions. The foundation of practice is *zazen* meditation, or sitting with single-minded concentration. The center sponsors weekly *teishos* (formal commentaries on Buddhist teachings or koans) each Sunday morning, as well as regular study groups. Silent retreats called *sesshins* last from one to seven days. Visitors may choose to meditate in the tranquil Jizo Garden, which has a lotus pond. *From the south, take Route 7 toward Shelburne. Just before entering the village, turn right at the traffic light at Marsett Road. Go straight until you cross a small bridge. Immediately turn right onto Thomas Road. The center is one-half mile down the road on the right.*
☎ 802-985-9746   💻 www.vzc.org

South Woodstock

A Satellite of Plum Village
GREEN MOUNTAIN DHARMA CENTER
Buddhist (Unified Buddhist Church). Year founded: 1998.
☎ 802-457-9442 or 436-1103   💻 www.plumvillage.org

From White River Junction, take I-91 South and go one exit to Exit 9 (Hartland). Turn right from the exit onto Route 5 North and follow signs for Green Mountain Dharma Center.

Vietnamese Zen master and best-selling author Thich Nhat Hanh founded this quiet dharma center in 1998 as a satellite of Plum Village, the Buddhist community he began in France in 1982. There are currently thirteen monks, twelve nuns, and two laywomen living in or near the GMDC. (A permanent monastery called Maple Forest is also under construction; when it is completed, the nuns and monks will live there, freeing the GMDC building for full use as a retreat and practice center for the teachings of Thich Nhat Hanh).

In keeping with Hanh's teachings on interfaith understanding, the monastery and retreat center emphasize respect for all religious traditions. Twice each year, monks and nuns from GMDC gather with the Benedictine monks from the Weston Priory (see below) for a day of interfaith discussion and meditation. At one such gathering held recently at the priory, the Zen Buddhist monks and nuns offered traditional chants during a midday prayer service and spoke with the Benedictine brothers about the challenges of living in community.

Retreats are currently available for individuals and small groups, who share simple meals and lodgings (retreatants sleep on the floor and should bring their own sleeping bags). In winter, a three-month extended retreat is offered, with the aim of integrating mindfulness training into daily activities—working, eating, walking, etc.—rather than only engaging in seated meditation.

During the last week of June and the first week of July, a summer retreat is open for families. The GMDC pledges that "this is a time for family and friends to practice joyfully together," and for children to be included in mindfulness practice. The summer retreat fills up early, so families are encouraged to place reservations far in advance.

If you have just one day to spend at the GMDC and would like to gain a taste of Zen Buddhist life, "Mindfulness Days" take place year-round on Thursdays (9 A.M. to 4 P.M.) and Sundays (9 A.M. to 4:30 P.M.). They include a time of walking meditation and a Dharma Talk, either a video of teachings from Plum Village or a live talk by a monastery resident. Thursday afternoons offer dharma discussions, while Sunday afternoons feature tea meditation or a ritual of touching the earth.

Weston

Ministries of Social Justice
WESTON PRIORY
Roman Catholic (Benedictine). 58 Priory Hill Road. Year founded: 1953.
☎ 802-824-5409 🖳 www.westonpriory.org

The priory is located four miles north of the town of Weston. From I-91, take Exit 6 to Route 103 to Route 11 West to Route 100 North. Continue through the town of Weston. After 3.5 miles, take Route 155 North for a quarter mile. The priory will be the first left.

Fourteen Benedictine monks live at the Weston Priory, a jewel of south-central Vermont. Since the priory's 500 acres are located just at the edge of the Green Mountain National Forest, nature is captivatingly pristine here.

Weston Priory

The priory was founded in 1953 by the late Abbot Leo Rudloff of Dormition Abbey in Jerusalem, Israel. It retains a bit of an international flavor, with a number of brothers coming from Mexico and Canada as well as the United States. In fact, the monastery has served as an official sanctuary for Central American refugees for nearly two decades, and has offered shelter to the same Guatemalan family since March 24, 1984—the fourth anniversary of the assassination of Archbishop Oscar Romero of El Salvador. The brothers have consistently adopted an activist stance in similar ministries of social justice, calling attention to human-rights abuses within and outside the United States. In the nearby town of Weston, the monastery sponsors the House of Sabbath, a center to serve the homeless and the poor.

"Let all who come be received as Christ himself, for he will say: 'I was a stranger and you welcomed me.'"   —Rule of Benedict, Chapter 53

As a Benedictine monastery, the Weston Priory follows the sixth-century Rule of St. Benedict—and in fact the document is read aloud every single morning to remind the brothers of their values and commitments. The community sustains itself by gardening, forestry, maple sugaring, tending the apple orchards, and selling recordings of its liturgical music. Be sure to

listen to the music playing at The Gallery gift shop, where you can purchase the brothers' handmade woodwork crafts, ceramics, and greeting
cards. The shop also features religious art from around the world, including
nativity scenes from Mexico, Brazil, and the Holy Land.

Individual retreatants, male and female, are welcome at the Weston
Priory. They are invited to participate in the daily offices of the Benedictine tradition (see page 191), beginning at 5 A.M. with Morning Vigil
(6 A.M. on Tuesdays and Thursdays) and ending with Compline. Unlike
many other Benedictine monasteries, however, the monks here embrace
contemporary forms of worship and utilize folk music in worship.

NEARBY

➥ Robert Todd Lincoln was the only son of Abraham and Mary Todd
Lincoln to survive to adulthood. **Hildene**, his twenty-four-room
Georgian Revival mansion and estate garden in **Manchester**, is
open to the public from May to October. The home contains many of the
Lincoln family's original furnishings, and the garden (designed in 1907 by
Abraham Lincoln's granddaughter Jessie Lincoln Beckwith) is inspired by
the tracery windows of Europe's Gothic cathedrals. *Historic Route 7A,
Manchester. Tours begin every half hour from 9:30 A.M. to 4 P.M. Admission
fee.* ☎ 802-362-1788 🖥 www.hildene.org

CHAPTER TEN

⁓

New Hampshire

"WE ALL KNOW that something is eternal," declares the narrator
in Thorton Wilder's Pulitzer Prize–winning play *Our Town*. "And it ain't
houses and it ain't names . . . that something has to do with human
beings." Wilder based the play's fictional setting of Grover's Corners on
Peterborough, New Hampshire—which, in the estimable way of many
New Hampshire towns, manages to seem like Anytown. It is quiet, yet also
bustles with the all-important activity of daily life. And it is rich in sacred
history. As Wilder pointed out, history is more than places and names; it is
the lived reality of human beings. New Hampshire is steeped in that.

Before the American Revolution, New Hampshire's religious history
was dominated by Congregationalism, with Congregational parishes present in almost every town. Some of these, like the church at Wilton Center
(now Unitarian), have something of a tragic history, while others, like the
Danville and Sandown meetinghouses, are renowned for their age and
architectural simplicity. The Quakers also forged a presence in New
Hampshire, attested by the history of their early persecutions in Dover.
Then, too, there were the Freewill Baptists and the Shakers, two dissenting Protestant groups that were highly successful on the New Hampshire
frontier. The Shakers founded large communities at Enfield and Canterbury Lake, with the Canterbury village active until 1992. The nineteenth
century brought Roman Catholicism, with churches and special shrines
throughout the state, and the early twentieth saw the founding of a Russian Orthodox church in the snowy hinterlands of the north. New Hampshire's religious diversity is steadily increasing, as the diverse student body
at Dartmouth College and the new popularity of Buddhism in the Granite

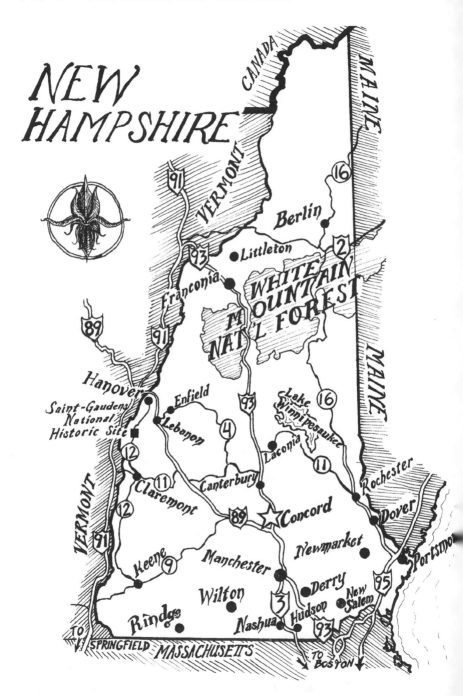

State both affirm. The Cathedral of the Pines offers itself as a multifaith sacred shrine to America's war dead, and "America's Stonehenge" asks visitors to ponder the mysteries of New Hampshire civilization from possibly thousands of years ago.

The Granite State is also known as the White Mountain State, featuring some of New England's highest elevations. The poet Ralph Waldo Emerson was so impressed when he ascended Mount Monadnock, in southern New Hampshire, that he wrote a poem about it; the thousands of visitors who hike its trails today would have to agree that they are some of the state's most sublime nature walks. New Hampshire provided inspiration to the poet Robert Frost and the sculptor Augustus Saint-Gaudens, both of whose homes are open for tours; and to the novelist Willa Cather, who is buried in a quiet church cemetery in Jaffrey. The state's covered bridges, public gardens, and hidden natural sanctuaries also offer respite to the spiritual traveler.

Berlin

White Russia in the White Mountains
HOLY RESURRECTION ORTHODOX CHURCH
20 Petrograd Street. Year consecrated: 1915. ☎ 603-752-2254

> *From the south, take Route 16 into Berlin. Turn left at the Berlin City Bank, then left at the traffic light. Turn right onto Mount Forist, cross the railroad tracks, then ascend a steep hill. Almost at the end of the street, turn left onto Russian Street. The service of Great Vespers is offered on Saturday at 6 P.M., and Divine Liturgy is offered on Sunday at 9 A.M.*

If the street name (Petrograd) doesn't give enough of a hint, the onion-shaped domes that grace Holy Resurrection Orthodox Church surely do. The Russian heritage of the congregation traces back to the lumber business that flourished in northern New Hampshire at the beginning of the twentieth century, when hundreds of Russian men, primarily from the towns of Minsk, Wolensk, and Gordensk, came to Berlin to earn a living in the lumber trade. Most of them had to leave their wives and families behind, and would send them money from the New World. This preponderance of lonely bachelors worried the newly consecrated Russian

Orthodox archbishop in Boston. He was concerned that the men might lose their way spiritually when they were so far from home and from the Mother Church. To this end, he dispatched a priest to the frontier of northern New Hampshire, with the charge of founding a church and a school there. The priest did this in an astoundingly short time; Holy Resurrection opened its doors a mere five months later, in 1915. Czar Nicholas II sent the icons that hang on the iconostasis (which separates the priest and the altar from the congregation), signaling the church's strong ties to Russia's state church and monarch.

Although 1915 was an auspicious beginning for this congregation, it was the beginning of the end for the czar—and for the church in Russia. A few years after the Russian Revolution of 1917, Holy Resurrection stopped receiving financial support from Russia, and priests were no longer sent to America and other missionary lands. In the United States, too, there were mill strikes, the Great Depression, and the Second World War to deal with, all events which pushed the congregation's original founders out of Berlin to find work or perform military service for their adopted country. In addition, the usual tensions immigrant churches encounter as they lose their first generation made the perfect recipe for a dwindling parish. In 1963, the church closed its doors. "The domes and crosses tarnished, the windows cracked, the paint chipped," the congregation's official history states. "But through this dark time, somehow the foundation held."

In 1974, a priest was once again assigned to the parish. Father Michael Westerberg reorganized the congregation, teaching the church's ancient doctrines to new followers, many of whom were the children or grandchildren of the church's founders. The church also opened itself to the larger community, welcoming not just Orthodox Christians of Russian descent but also those from Greek and other Orthodox traditions. Today, dedicated parishioners travel regularly to Berlin from throughout northern New England. Holy Resurrection, once an enclave of Russian culture as well as Russian Orthodoxy, has become a regional center for many different traditions of Orthodox Christianity.

NEARBY
➡ Fifty miles northwest of Berlin on the Connecticut River is the village of **Colebrook**, which offers the **Shrine of Our Lady of Grace**. The shrine was dedicated in 1948 to honor Mary, and features an eight-foot white marble statue of her. There are also more than fifty monuments and statues throughout the grounds. Each June, the shrine hosts the Great North Woods Ride-in Motorcycle Blessing, where motorcyclists from all across

the United States and Canada gather to have their bikes blessed. *Route 3, Colebrook. Open daily from May through October. No admission fee.*
☎ 603-237-5511 🖳 www.omiusa.org/ladyofgrace.htm
➥ In **Stark**, the **Union Church** and its adjacent **Covered Bridge**, both built in the early 1850s, epitomize many people's ideal of rural New England. (There's even a picket fence.) The bridge is listed on the National Register of Historic Places. *Located just off Route 110 (west of Milan and east of Groveton).*

Canterbury Lake

Two Centuries of Shaker Life
CANTERBURY SHAKER VILLAGE
288 Shaker Road. Year consecrated: 1792. Meetinghouse architect: Moses Johnson. ☎ 603-783-9511 🖳 www.shakers.org

From I-93, take Exit 18 and drive 6.7 miles to the village. Open from May through October, 10 A.M. to 5 P.M. Monday through Saturday, and noon to 5 P.M. on Sunday. In April, November, and December there are limited tours on the weekends. Admission fee.

Canterbury Shaker Village

There are no Shakers now at Canterbury Lake (the last sister died in 1992), but for two centuries this was one of the most important gathering places for the United Society of Believers in Christ's Second Appearing. Founded in 1792, the community reached its peak in the 1850s, when 300 Shakers lived here and had more than 100 buildings on 4,000 acres. Twenty-four buildings—several of which are part of an informative guided tour—remain on 694 acres.

In its heyday in the mid–nineteenth century, Canterbury was the printing center for every Shaker village in America, which meant that Shaker theologians and writers sometimes came here to produce periodicals and tracts on Shaker beliefs. The village was also a regional governing headquarters, or bishopric, so Canterbury's Shakers maintained close ties to the Central Ministry in New Lebanon, New York. As Shaker communities closed and consolidated in the twentieth century, Canterbury became *the* governing Shaker village, and in 1960 it replaced New Lebanon as the official headquarters for the Central Ministry. In 1972, the Shaker sisters here created a nonprofit corporation to manage the site and open it to the public. Their foresight ensured that Canterbury Village, the tourist destination, stayed true to the spirit of Canterbury Village, the home of the followers of Mother Ann (see page 189).

This community was once famous for the goods it produced. The "Shaker cloak," a plain gray outer cloak favored by Shaker sisters, became a fashion statement in 1893 when First Lady Frances Cleveland sported one at the Inaugural Ball. At Canterbury, visitors can see the Sisters' Shop, where the cloaks and many other items of clothing were cut and sewn. Also on the tour is the Carpenter Shop, where guides demonstrate Shaker techniques in dovetailing furniture and carving their famous oval boxes. The infirmary, which is part of the tour, contains a pharmacy lined with dozens of bottles of various Shaker remedies, believed to have salubrious effects on every ailment from heartburn to consumption. In particular, Canterbury enjoyed a reputation for the healing powers of Brother Thomas Corbett's Syrup of Sarsaparilla, an herbal remedy made from roots and berries grown by the Shakers.

The 1792 meetinghouse is a highlight of the tour. This was the first building that the Shakers constructed after founding this community, and its blue interior walls still seem to retain an echo of Shaker melodies and shuffling feet. The meetinghouse was constructed by Shaker brother Moses Johnson, who also created nine other Shaker houses of worship in New England and New York. Canterbury's is a white frame building in the Federal style, with a curved roof in the Dutch Colonial tradition. There are separate entrances for men and women.

One final word. You may wish to complete your visit with a delicious lunch at the Creamery, an on-site restaurant that serves meals in the Shaker tradition. The food is so good that you will have no trouble heeding Mother Ann's famous advice to "Shaker your plate" and not waste food. The Creamery is also open on weekend evenings for fixed-price, four-

SHAKER MEETINGHOUSES

Although they bear some similarities to Congregational meetinghouses, Shaker architecture remains distinct from its Puritanstyle cousin. As the spiritual center of Shaker life, meetinghouses were accorded pride of place in the physical world. They stood in the center of each Shaker community—although today, as outer buildings have been lost to history, they may not seem as centrally located as they once were. Whereas Puritan meetinghouses were often painted in bright colors (sometimes featuring several colors on the same building), the "Millennial Laws" (1821), which governed all Shaker communities, stipulated that meetinghouses be white and that they be the *only* white buildings in each community. This policy set the meetinghouses apart as sacred spaces. (As the decades wore on, however, the Shakers began creating other white buildings alongside their meetinghouses.)

The Millennial Laws also put forth a rather unusual decorating requirement: The interiors of meetinghouses had to be painted "of a bluish shade." This has resulted in some lovely variations; at Sabbathday Lake in Maine, for example, the trim is a colonial blue, contrasting with cream-colored walls and wood flooring. The significance of the color blue for the Shakers is uncertain; many believe that the color symbolized purity.

Like Puritan meetinghouses, Shaker meetinghouses were, above all, meant to be practical. For the Shakers, this meant that no supporting beams should interrupt the flow of movement in the building. The upper floors, where the elders and eldresses lived, were supported from above by a set of trusses. In this way, Shaker "labors" (dances) on the first floor could proceed apace without the worry of bumping into an obstacle while being caught up in the Spirit.

course candlelight dinners (and no, men and women do not have to sit separately).

NEARBY
➥ **Mary Baker Eddy**, the founder of Christian Science (see pages 100 and 135), was born on a farm in Bow, New Hampshire, approximately five miles south of Concord. She lived here until she was fifteen. The house burned down in 1910, but stones mark the **site** of the original foundation. *The property is open year-round for self-guided tours. On Route 3A, five miles south of Concord.* ☎ 617-566-3092 🖳 www.marybakereddylibrary.org

Cornish

Sculpting the Garden
SAINT-GAUDENS NATIONAL HISTORIC SITE
RR 3. Year created: 1885. ☎ 603-675-2175 🖳 www.sgnhs.org

From I-89, take Exit 20 and go south on Route 12A. From I-91, take Exit 8 to Route 131 East and turn left onto Route 12A North. Open from Memorial Day weekend to October 31 from 9 A.M. to 4:30 P.M. daily. From November 1 through May, the grounds only are open daily from 8 A.M. until dusk. Admission fee.

Saint-Gaudens National Historic Site, Cornish, New Hampshire

Cornish was the adopted home of sculptor Augustus Saint-Gaudens (1848–1907), who is famous for his statues of Civil War heroes and distinguished nineteenth-century Americans. Saint-Gaudens sculpted his most recognizable statue, a standing figure of Abraham Lincoln that is located in Chicago's Lincoln Park, here in Cornish. Another famous work by Saint-Gaudens is the Robert Gould Shaw and Massachusetts 54th Regiment Memorial at the edge of Boston Common (see page 84), a slightly different version of which is exhibited here in New Hampshire. Some of Saint-Gaudens's other sculptures hold pride of place in New York's Central Park, Chicago's Grant Park, and Boston's Trinity Church.

This site was Saint-Gaudens's summer studio from 1885 to 1897, and his year-round home from 1900 until his death in 1907. In summer, when the entire site is open for tours, visitors may see the sculptor's eighteenth-century home (called Aspet) and three exhibition galleries, as well as a studio where a sculptor-in-residence carries on the site's artistic legacy.

The 150-acre property is a work of sculpted art in itself, with a terraced perennial garden descending in three tiers from the house. A 6,000-square-foot "cutting garden" provides the lovely cut flowers and plants that can be seen throughout the galleries and in Aspet.

NEARBY

➡ **The Cornish-Windsor Bridge** is considered the longest covered bridge in the United States, at 460 feet. First built in 1866, it was reconstructed in 1989. *Two miles south of the Saint-Gaudens National Historic Site on Route 12A.*

Dover

Quakerism Born of Persecution
FRIENDS MEETINGHOUSE
141 Central Avenue. Year consecrated: 1768. ☎ 603-749-2302

From Portsmouth, go north on Route 1; this becomes Maplewood Avenue. After a mile, turn left onto Cutts Road, then bear right onto U.S. Bypass 1. After .7 miles, enter a rotary and take the first exit to U.S. 4W/NH 16N. After nine miles, take the Dover/Durham Exit. Bear right at the fork, merging onto Route 108. The meetinghouse is .2 miles ahead. Sunday worship is at 10:30 A.M.

Although there were once more than a dozen eighteenth-century Quaker meetinghouses throughout New Hampshire, the Dover Friends Meetinghouse is the last one remaining. The congregation (called a "meeting") was established in 1680, only eighteen years after three Quaker women who were evangelizing in Dover had been stripped to the waist and whipped as an example to the town. The women—Ann Coleman, Mary Tompkins, and Alice Ambrose—had been holding meetings in various homes throughout Dover for the previous six weeks, telling the people that the established Congregational church was in error. Needless to say, Reverend John Reyner, the Congregational minister, was none too pleased to have his flock listening to the preachings of "these vagabond Quakers," and circulated an angry petition among the residents of Dover. In the end it was decided that the women would be tied, half-naked, to a horse cart and publicly beaten. But it wasn't just Dover where the three women were to be whipped: the petition called for beatings in no less than eleven towns, requiring the women to travel over eighty miles in bitter winter cold so that all of New England could witness the dangers of embracing Quakerism.

"HOW THEY DROVE THE QUAKER WOMEN FROM DOVER"

The poet John Greenleaf Whittier, whose parents were married at this Friends meetinghouse, immortalized the women's 1662 sufferings in a poem:

> The tossing spray of Cocheco's falls
> Hardened to ice on its icy walls,
> As through Dover town, in the chill gray dawn,
> Three women passed, at the cart tail drawn,
> Bared to the waist, for the north wind's grip
> And keener sting of the constables whip
> The blood that followed each hissing blow
> Froze as it sprinkled the winter snow.
> Priest and ruler, boy and maiden
> Followed the dismal cavalcade;
> And from door and window, open thrown,
> Looked and wondered, gaffer and crone.

Happily for Dover, the Quaker women were undaunted by their persecution. They eventually returned to Dover and founded this meeting in
1680. The current building dates from 1768 and is the third meetinghouse
to stand on this site. Its architecture reflects some of Quakerism's principles: the equality of men and women can be seen in the building's separate
front entrances, while the interior shows a complete lack of liturgical symbolism. There is no pulpit, as the Quakers had no ordained clergy.

NEARBY

➡ Although it is not the oldest Congregational church in the United
States, **Newington Town Church** claims to be the oldest *continuously used*
Congregational church in the nation. The 1712 building has been in constant use for almost three centuries. Apparently the old adage about lightning never striking twice in the same place doesn't quite hold true;
lightning struck the spire of this church twice, which is why there is no
spire today. *316 Nimble Hill Road, Newington. From the Spalding Turnpike,
take Exit 4 South about 1.5 miles.* ☎ 603-431-8663

Enfield

The Great Stone Dwelling
THE ENFIELD SHAKER MUSEUM
24 Caleb Dyer Lane. Year consecrated: 1793. ☎ 603-632-4346
▣ www. shakermuseum.org

> *From I-89, take Exit 17. Bear right at the end of the ramp onto Route 4
> East. After approximately 1.5 miles, turn right onto Route 4-A at the
> blinking light. The museum is 3.5 miles down on Route 4-A. From
> Memorial Day through the end of October, the museum is open Monday
> through Saturday from 10 A.M. to 5 P.M. and Sunday from noon to 5 P.M.
> During the rest of the year, it is open on Saturday from 10 A.M. to 4 P.M.
> and Sunday from noon to 4 P.M. Admission fee.*

The most magnificent building at Enfield is the Great Stone Dwelling,
designed by Ammi B. Youngs and constructed between 1837 and 1841.
Youngs was not a Shaker; he was a professional architect who had also
designed the Vermont State House in Montpelier. His Great Stone Dwell-

ing is five stories tall, making it the largest Shaker building ever constructed. It was also the first Shaker house anywhere to be built of stone, which is why the Shakers hired an architect from "the world." The result is a marvelous edifice, which one visiting nineteenth-century Shaker elder called "a stone palace . . . one of the most stately, magnificent, and solid buildings I ever saw." The decision to use stone was an interesting one, since the Millennial Laws (1821), which governed every aspect of Shaker life, had stipulated that all dwellings be constructed of wood. But by the 1830s other Shaker communities were choosing brick instead of wood, so that aspect of the Millennial Laws had clearly been relaxed somewhat.

Since it was constructed later than many other Shaker buildings, the Great Stone Dwelling also shows the full flowering of Shaker community life. The dwellings served not only to house Shaker brothers and sisters, but also to preserve the separation between them; in this building visitors will see the separate entrances, stairways, and rooms that helped to maintain the segregation of the sexes.

In 1927, the Shakers sold the entire Enfield community to the LaSallette order of Roman Catholic priests, who established a seminary and lived here until 1985. The Enfield Shaker Village trustees are in the process of restoring the original Shaker village. Through the 1990s, the trustees set about acquiring some of the 200 buildings that were once a part of the village; thirteen of them are now open for a self-guided tour. In 1998, the highlight of the restoration was completed: The Great Stone Dwelling is now open as an inn for overnight guests. ☎ 603-632-7810 🖥 www.theshakerinn.com

The Great Stone Dwelling and the Mary Keane Chapel, Enfield

THE GLORY DAYS OF
SHAKER ARTIFACTS

"I almost expect to be remembered as a chair," quipped one late-twentieth-century Shaker sister. Her comment reflects two parallel trends: a widespread admiration for Shaker furniture, boxes, and architecture, coupled with a pervasive ignorance about the religious beliefs of the Shakers who made them. Stephen Stein, a historian of Shakerism, has written that America's "love affair with the Shakers can be explained in part by the American preference for 'things' rather than ideas." The Shakers' early religious ideas—which included celibacy, the sharing of all worldly goods and property, self-abnegation, ecstatic worship, and an almost unquestioning obedience to religious authority—are clearly out of step with the values of most contemporary Americans. But many of those same Americans are infatuated with a certain mythology about Shakerism that they attach to Shaker brooms, boxes, baskets, and chairs. Such everyday objects, says Stein, can become like sacramental icons to non-Shakers. "Artifacts are useful in their own right," he remarks. "Icons are treasured because they point to something beyond themselves." (Why else would Oprah Winfrey pay nearly a quarter of a million dollars for a Shaker work counter?)

NEARBY

➼ In 1927, the Shakers sold their Enfield village to the LaSallette order of Roman Catholic priests. **The Mary Keane Chapel** that the priests constructed in the 1930s sits between the Great Stone Dwelling and the Brothers' workshops, its full-fledged Greek Revival architecture and lavish interior bearing sharp contrast to the simplicity of the Shaker buildings. The bronze doors depict the fifteen mysteries of the rosary, while the stained-glass windows refer to the 1846 appearance of the Virgin Mary in LaSallette, France. The chapel was deconsecrated in 1985 and purchased by the Enfield Shaker Museum in 1997. 🖳 www.marykeanechapel.com

➼ A few hundred yards north of the Great Stone Dwelling, also on Route 4-A, is the **Shrine of Our Lady of LaSallette**, which opened in 1951. The landscaped hillside offers several spaces for prayer and meditation, including the Shrine Chapel, a number of gardens, the Rosary Pond, a peace walk, and the stations of the cross. The gift shop and a small retreat center are housed in one of the original Shaker buildings. *Open daily.*
☎ 603-632-7087

Hanover

From Indian Charity School to Multifaith College
DARTMOUTH COLLEGE
East Wheelock Street. Year established: 1769. ☎ 603-646-1110
💻 www.dartmouth.edu

> *From I-89, take Exit 18 (in Lebanon) onto Route 120. Bear right off the exit, heading north on 120 into Hanover. 4.1 miles from the exit, Route 120 forks at a traffic light. Bear right at the fork, following Route 120 .5 miles on South Park Street to the second traffic light. Turn left at the light, onto East Wheelock Street. Follow East Wheelock for .2 miles, when you will come to the Hopkins Center (left) and the Dartmouth Green (right).*

"As Your Lordship has been frequently mentioned with pleasure by the lovers of Christ in this wilderness," wrote New Hampshire Congregationalist Reverend Eleazar Wheelock to the Earl of Dartmouth in 1769, "I am now emboldened . . . to solicit your Lordship's favorable notice of, and friendship towards, a feeble attempt to save the swarms of Indian Natives in this land, from final and eternal ruin. . . ." And thus it was that Dartmouth got its charter. Wheelock had been running an Indian Charity School since 1754, but the patronage of the Earl of Dartmouth ensured that his efforts to evangelize the "swarms" (!) of Native Americans in northern New England would continue for many years to come.

Dartmouth was one of many educational institutions that arose during or immediately after the religious fervor of the Great Awakening (see page 185). (In his letter to the Earl, Wheelock even dropped the name of revivalist George Whitefield as a mutual friend.) During the 1740s and '50s, Princeton, Brown, Queen's (which became Rutgers after the Revolution), and Dartmouth were all founded by New Light clergymen—ministers who supported the Awakening. Part of the legacy of the revival was a desire to spread God's word to others, including Native Americans. Over time, however, Dartmouth's raison d'être shifted into a college for young Congregational men.

Dartmouth was still tied to the Congregational denomination when, in 1799, Eleazer Wheelock's son John became the college's president. He held very different views from his father's, and followed the example of

Jeffersonian education by severing the college's ties with the denomination. He was promptly fired by the all-Congregational board of trustees. The state legislature, which agreed with the young Wheelock that a small band of Congregationalists were controlling the interests of the institution, revoked Dartmouth's charter in retaliation. Thomas Jefferson himself sent a congratulatory note to the governor of New Hampshire, thanking him for taking on the old-guard Congregationalists.

The "Dartmouth College Case" went all the way to the Supreme Court in 1819, where Daniel Webster (Dartmouth class of 1801) argued that the government had no authority to tell a private, religious educational institution what to do. Chief Justice John Marshall agreed, and the court's landmark decision set a precedent for protecting religious and charitable corporations from the power of the state.

Dartmouth shed its Congregational affiliation long ago, and has taken its place as one of the premier liberal arts institutions in the nation. Today, its religious debates center on the same issues that have fostered discussion on other campuses: How can an American college or university that was founded as a Protestant institution become a multifaith campus in which all religions are recognized and supported? Dartmouth made great strides toward this goal in 2001 when it opened a new kosher-halal dining hall to accommodate the dietary needs of Jewish and Muslim students. Annual operating costs for the dining facility run in the six figures, demonstrating the institution's commitment to religious diversity. Truly, Dartmouth has come a long way from its original charter.

Hudson

Recovery Retreats and Other Programs
OBLATE RETREAT HOUSE
Roman Catholic (Missionary Oblates of Mary Immaculate). 200 Lowell Road. ☎ 603-882-8141 🖥 www.oblateretreathouse.org

From Route 3, take Exit 2. Cross the bridge and go left at the light. The Oblate Retreat House is .4 miles on the right. The gift shop is open Monday through Friday, 9 A.M. to noon and 12:30 P.M. to 5 P.M., and Saturday from 10 A.M. to 2 P.M.

In the woods of southern New Hampshire, a rustic retreat center offers visitors spiritual renewal weekends and programs in Christian formation. In particular, the Oblate Retreat House offers programs for those recovering from addiction—to alcohol, to food, to drugs. The Missionary Oblates of Mary Immaculate, founded in 1816 to evangelize and serve others, carries on its tradition here, as the priests, brothers, and lay leaders help those in recovery heal from their pasts.

Visitors may participate in guided weekend retreats on topics such as "The Eleventh Step," "Emotional Sobriety for Those in Recovery," and "Lighten Up Your Recovery." Other retreats offer instruction in everything from Tai Chi to Taizé.

Newmarket

Friends of the Western Buddhist Order
ARYALOKA BUDDHIST RETREAT CENTER
14 Heartwood Circle. ☎ 603-659-5456 💻 www.aryaloka.org

From the south, take I-95 North to Exit 2. Bear right onto Route 101 (toward Exeter). After the traffic light, take the exit onto Route 33/108 toward Portsmouth and Durham. After two miles, stay in the left lane at the rotary. Leave Route 33 and get onto Route 108, continuing for 2.5 miles. Cross a grid bridge. Turn left onto Ash Swamp Road and follow it for two miles until you reach a stop sign. Turn right here (Grant Road) and then take the next right onto Shady Lane. Shady Lane leads into Heartwood Circle. Go around the circle and turn right at the red mailbox and Aryaloka sign.

In the heart of Aryaloka's garden, a statuette of a meditating Bodhisattva sits atop a small heap of stones, surrounded by wildflowers. This summer scene encapsulates the spirit of this retreat center, an oasis of Buddhist meditation set in the natural beauty of southern New Hampshire.

Aryaloka ("noble world") is affiliated with the Friends of the Western Buddhist Order, an organization "devoted to re-expressing the essential truths of the Buddhist tradition in ways appropriate to the modern world."

The FWBO, founded in 1967, stresses the practical teachings of meditation to clarify the mind and rid the self of anxiety, bitterness, and confusion. The goal is to cultivate a calm, positive mentality and to learn the art of concentration. In particular, FWBO centers teach Mindfulness of Breathing techniques and the *Mettabhavana*, or Loving-Kindness meditation.

Aryaloka offers many retreats on its seventeen-acre campus, lasting from as little as a day ("meditation days" help to deepen personal meditation practice) to as long as a week. Some retreats are spent in silent meditation, while others offer lectures and workshops on various techniques, and still others are "study retreats" on a particular text or aspect of the dharma. Some are for women or men only. Because FWBO stresses the integration of Western traditions into Buddhist practice, some of the retreats reflect this interest.

NEARBY
➤ Consecrated in 1755, the clapboard **Danville (Hawke) Meeting House** is one of the earliest surviving meetinghouses in New Hampshire. It is a starkly simple two-and-a-half story box, with a steeply gabled roof and entrances on three of the church's four sides. In the nineteenth century the building was used for town meetings and social occasions (with pews removed to facilitate dancing—what would the founders have thought?). Preservation efforts have been carried out by the Old Meeting House Association. *Route 111A, 3.2 miles north of Route 111.*

New Durham

Birthplace of the Freewill Baptists
FIRST FREE WILL BAPTIST CHURCH
Depot Road. Year consecrated: 1819 (denomination founded in 1780).
☎ 603-859-6088

Just off Route 11.

Just as Providence, Rhode Island, is the birthplace of the Baptist movement, tiny New Durham (just southeast of Lake Winnipesaukee) is the birthplace of one Baptist sect in particular—the Freewill Baptists. Baptist founder Roger Williams (see page 14) was a Calvinist who embraced the doctrine of predestination. In contrast, the Freewill Baptists adopted all of the other tenets of the Baptist movement—including adult baptism and an emphasis on the separation of church and state—but rejected predestination in favor of "free will." In other words, they taught that God had endowed human beings with the ability to choose for themselves whether they wished to be saved. These Freewill Baptists could not believe that God would create people who, regardless of their own will to the contrary, were predestined to roast in hell for all eternity.

In 1779, a Baptist minister named Benjamin Randel (1749–1808; sometimes spelled Randall) was called to the New Durham pulpit. Nearly a decade earlier, Randel had become a believer after hearing the great revivalist George Whitefield preach in nearby Portsmouth. At first he dismissed the famous itinerant as "a worthless, noisy fellow," but a week later Randel changed his tune. The evangelist had died suddenly at Newburyport (just over the border in Massachusetts), and his death left Randel with an uncomfortable feeling in his soul. "Whitefield is now in heaven, while I am in the road to hell," he thought. He became convicted of his sins and gave his life over to God. In 1776 he was rebaptized as a Baptist, and became an itinerant preacher.

When the call came in 1779 to go to New Durham, which was an "Old Light" congregation (it supported traditional Calvinist doctrines and rejected the revivals of the Great Awakening), Randel admitted to the church's elders that he did not believe in, or even understand, the doctrine of predestination. They hired him anyway. He preached of God's "general provision"—the universal atonement of all in Christ—which offended some but attracted many others. In 1780, Randel held a series of week-long conferences in which he and like-minded Baptists ironed out the doctrines and practices that would define the "Freewill" churches. A new denomination was born, which was one of the most important Christian movements in northern New England in the late eighteenth and early nineteenth centuries.

This clapboard church, built in 1819 and remodeled in 1869, is considered the "mother church" of the denomination. However, the denomination officially merged in 1911 with the Northern (now American) Baptists, who had softened their once-rigid Calvinist stance and come to embrace the doctrines that the Freewill Baptists first preached so long ago on the New Hampshire frontier.

North Salem

New England's Ancient Ruins
"AMERICA'S STONEHENGE"
Haverhill Road. Year created: unknown. Opened to the public in 1958.
☎ 603-893-3300 💻 www.stonehengeusa.com

> *From I-93, take Exit 3. Take Route 111 East for about 4.5 miles. Turn right at the blue marker for "America's Stonehenge" (Haverhill Road). The site is 1.5 miles down on the right side. Open daily year round from 9 A.M. until 5 P.M. (until 7 P.M. from late June to Labor Day). Admission fee.*

Although it is fast evolving into a major tourist attraction, plenty of Americans still haven't heard about this possibly ancient granite ruin. Like its much more famous English counterpart, "America's Stonehenge" is shrouded in mystery—in fact, it was called "Mystery Hill" until 1982. Who created these standing stones, and for what purpose? Were they used for religious ceremonies? How old are they?

More questions than solid answers exist about "America's Stonehenge." In 1957, a man called (appropriately enough) Robert Stone purchased the property and undertook detailed archaeological research of the ruins. He

"America's Stonehenge," North Salem

discovered that the stones form an astronomical calendar. Like certain Mayan temples or the elusive Stonehenge in England, these stones become aligned during major astronomical occasions like the summer and winter solstices. Despite the displacement and wreckage of some stones over time, the site can still be used as an accurate calendar of solar and lunar events. From the Astronomical Viewing Platform, visitors can see the major alignment stones throughout the site; you can then hike the self-guided "Astronomical Trail" to see the stones up close.

Several theories exist about the origins of the stones, though little is known for certain. One archaeologist (Penn State professor emeritus Dr. Louis Winkler) believes that the site may be 4,000 years old, having been constructed during the Bronze Age. Like Winkler, most people believe that the site was designed by indigenous North Americans, who have lived in this region for thousands of years. A minority view is that the stones were placed by Celtic visitors; one early excavator of this site in the 1930s was Robert Goodwin, author of *The Ruins of Great Ireland in New England*. Goodwin believed that the etchings and notches on some of the stones came from the twenty-letter alphabet called "ogham" used by fifth- and sixth-century-C.E. Irish peoples. This would make the site much younger than 4,000 years. Still others believe that the site is even younger still— because although radiocarbon dating suggests that the stones themselves are ancient, there's little proof that they were indeed *arranged* by ancient peoples. Whatever the case, "America's Stonehenge" is a source of great delight—and puzzlement—to more than 30,000 visitors annually. Plan to spend an entire morning or afternoon here. In the Visitor's Center (remodeled in 1994), the short film *Puzzles in Stone* runs continuously; this is a fine introduction to the area.

The site, which is still being excavated, is initially not as visually impressive as the monolithic, vertical slabs of sarsen and bluestone at England's Stonehenge. (Although there is a saying that everything is bigger in America, in this case it's just not true.) Some of the chambers are in ruins, and few of them are tall enough to generate real excitement unless you know their fascinating history. And unfortunately, the family that lived here in the mid–nineteenth century carted off several tons of stones for various construction projects, so a certain amount of guesswork is involved in excavating the site. On the other hand, unlike Stonehenge in England, you can walk on, crawl through, and thoroughly investigate "America's Stonehenge." You don't have to take the word of the brochure that there's a "secret bed" in the sundeck chamber; you can crawl through the stone passageway and squeeze into the tiny compartment yourself.

STONE WALLS OF NEW ENGLAND

Robert Frost once wrote that "something there is that doesn't love a wall." But you'd never guess that New Englanders had any reservations about the rock walls that divide their landscapes, since they are so ubiquitous in the region. At Canterbury Shaker Village, for example, every orchard and field that composed the Shakers' 4,000 acres was surrounded by tidy stone walls. One nineteenth-century survey estimated that the state of Connecticut had more than 20,000 miles of stone, nearly enough to encircle the earth.

While stone fences are the most enduring of boundaries, it should not be assumed that they have "always" been a part of the New England landscape. When farmers cleared land to plant crops or graze animals, they usually erected wooden fences first, not stone ones. The reasons for this are clear. First, it has been estimated that two men could only lay about ten feet of stone wall each day, so creating a stone wall was a time-consuming, labor-intensive project. (Apart from labor, however, it was inexpensive, since the rocks themselves were so plentiful in most of New England. A popular saying in Maine is that its second most important crop is potatoes—after rocks.) Second, the rapid deforestation of New England in the seventeenth and eighteenth centuries created a relative shortage of wood for traditional fences, making the half century from 1775 to 1825 the most active burst of stone-wall building in American history.

New England's historic stone walls may not appear as though they are high enough to corral sheep or rein in cattle, but the passage of time has partially submerged many of the walls into the ground. As New England was transformed in the nineteenth century from an agricultural economy to an industrial one, the rock walls that defined the small family farm became something of an anachronism. But they remain a fixture on the landscape, a welcome physical reminder of the generations that have gone before.

NEARBY
➥ In **Manchester, St. Anselm Abbey** is a Benedictine monastery, where a community of about thirty-five monks gathers daily to chant the Liturgy of the Hours. Men are welcome for retreats, where they follow the daily routine of the monastic community. *100 St. Anselm Drive, Manchester.*
☎ 603-641-7000 💻 www.anselm.edu/abbey

ROBERT FROST COUNTRY

Before Robert Frost (1874–1963) became a successful poet, he was a New Hampshire farmer who had dropped out of both Harvard and Dartmouth and struggled with depression. From 1900 to 1909, he lived at **The Frost Farm** in southern New Hampshire, outside of **Derry** (just southeast of Manchester). At the farm, visitors can see the simple country house where the Frosts lived, which daughter Lesley Frost Ballantine has helped to restore to its early-twentieth-century appearance. On the property is the stone wall that must be the most famous in all of New England; in his poem "Mending Wall," Frost used the annual repair of the border between his property and his neighbor's as an opportunity to ruminate on boundaries. ("Before I built a wall I'd ask to know/What I was walling in or walling out.") *The Frost Farm is located at 172 Pembroke Road outside Derry. From I-93, take Exit 3. Take 111 East for one mile; turn left onto 28 North. The farm is five miles ahead. The farmhouse and barn are open from late June to Labor Day from 10 A.M. to 5 P.M. daily; limited hours at other times. Admission fee.* ☎ 603-432-3091 🖳 www.npu2.org/frostfarm/

When the Frost family returned to the United States from England at the start of World War I, the forty-year-old poet settled down in a white clapboard farmhouse in **Franconia**, now preserved as a

The Frost Farm, near Derry

museum called **The Frost Place**. Frost had published two books of poetry that were modestly successful in England, but it was in Franconia that the poet's career took off. From 1915 to 1920, Frost published several more books, each to greater acclaim, and won a Pulitzer Prize. The Frosts left this farm in 1920 when the now-famous poet was offered a specially created position as poet-in-residence at Amherst College. But he returned here each summer, finding inspiration for his work and refreshment for his spirit. Today, the Frost Place is a museum of the poet's memorabilia, as well as a cultural center for the encouragement of poetry and the arts. One special highlight of the Frost Place is the poetry trail that winds behind the house and through the property. Frost himself walked this path regularly, and snippets of his poetry are posted on wooden plaques along the trail. Two poems— "Evening in a Sugar Orchard" and "Goodby and Keep Cold"—are posted where Frost was sitting when he wrote them. *From I-93 North, take Exit 38. Go left off the ramp onto 116 South for just over a mile, following the signs for the Frost Place. The Frost Place is open in June on Saturday and Sunday from 1 P.M. to 5 P.M., and from July 1 to Columbus Day every afternoon from 1 P.M. to 5 P.M. Admission fee.*
☎ 603-823-5510 🖳 www.frostplace.com

Portsmouth

Three and a Half Centuries of "Living History"
STRAWBERY BANKE MUSEUM
Marcy Street. Year founded: 1958. ☎ 603-433-1100
🖳 www.strawberybanke.org

> *From I-95, take Exit 7. Follow the green signs for Strawbery Banke, which is 1.7 miles from Exit 7. Open daily from mid-April through October, 10 A.M. to 5 P.M. Guided ninety-minute walking tours are also available in winter. Admission fee.*

Portsmouth, New Hampshire's largest seaside town, offers a number of attractions in the form of shops, restaurants, and museums, including the innovative Strawbery Banke Museum. The unusual and whimsical name comes from a colonial legend; the story goes that a group of English settlers sailed up the Piscataqua River in 1630 looking for till-able land and fresh water. What they found were strawberries—thousands of them—which was apparently enticement enough to encourage a permanent settlement. In 1653, the town changed its name from Strawbery Banke to Portsmouth, reflecting its seafaring interests.

Like other "living history" museums in New England (including Plimoth Plantation in Massachusetts; see page 221), Strawbery Banke has costumed actors who portray life in a particular era. What's different about Strawbery Banke is that three centuries are represented here: Exhibits present daily life for the 1630 colonists as well as WWII–era residents of Portsmouth, and every era in between. Some actors are clothed in the garb of the Revolutionary War era; others sport early twentieth-century finery. There is a Victorian Garden and a Victory Garden. And somehow, it all works. Strawbery Banke has become a popular tourist destination, with more than 60,000 visitors a year. Its twin commitments—urban renewal and historic preservation—have served as a model to other communities.

Most of the museum's forty buildings stand on their original foundations, making Strawbery Banke a real neighborhood museum, demonstrating change over time in one small, ten-acre site. Many buildings are dedicated to a particular period, while others feature various epochs under the same roof. The eighteenth-century Drisco House on Puddle Lane features both "Shapley's Shop" (ca. 1790) and a 1950s parlor across the hall, where Dale Evans and Roy Rogers chatter happily from the room's focal point—a black and white television.

A century ago, this harborside neighborhood was home to Portsmouth's Jewish community. The museum includes an exhibit devoted to a Portsmouth immigrant family, the Shapiros, Jews who emigrated in the early twentieth century from Ukraine. As you enter the Shapiro home, a costumed actress playing Mrs. Shapiro greets you with "Shalom," and proceeds to tell you how she keeps kosher in America. She may discuss the tensions of raising a daughter with one foot in the Old World and one in the New; this daughter is worrying the Shapiros because she objects to speaking Yiddish at home. The house is furnished as it would have been when the Shapiros lived here (from 1909–28).

NEARBY
➧ Just across the street from Strawbery Banke, **Prescott Park** offers a harborside refuge that is famous for its flowers. At the turn of the century, two sisters donated the land and a generous endowment for its upkeep to the city of Portsmouth, dedicated for public enjoyment. The

five acres of the park feature a shady garden, with sparkling fountains and surrounded by a picket fence. *105 Marcy Street. Open daily from dawn to dusk.* ☎ 603-431-8748

➥ Built in 1773–74, the **Sandown Meetinghouse** was added to the National Register of Historic Places in 1978. Its pulpit is especially renowned: It is a full-fledged wineglass pulpit, half a story tall and illuminated by a plain-glass window just behind it. The church contains its original pews, including a separate seating area for slaves. *Located just north of the town of Sandown, on Fremont Road .3 miles from Route 121-A. Open by appointment only. Donations suggested.* ☎ 603-887-3453

➥ Nine miles south of Portsmouth, in **North Hampton**, is **Fuller Gardens**, on the estate that belonged to former Massachusetts governor Alvan Fuller. Arthur Shurtleff, who helped to design the gardens at Colonial Williamsburg in Virginia, was the chief landscape architect for this two-acre garden, which was created in 1927–28. The gardens feature a vibrant display of tulips in early May, followed by the flowering of the Japanese garden (which offers wisteria, rhododendrons, and azaleas) in early June. More than 2,000 rose bushes are in bloom in late June and early July, with some continuing as late as October. *10 Willow Avenue, North Hampton. Located 200 yards north of the intersection of Routes 111 and 1-A. Gardens are open daily from mid-May through mid-October, 10 A.M. to 6 P.M.* ☎ 603-964-5414 🖳 www.fullergardens.org

➥ The Isles of Shoals are divided almost exactly down the middle between Maine, which owns five (see page 357), and New Hampshire, which owns four, including the rocky **Star Island**. Since 1916, Star Island has been operated as a religious and educational conference center by a group of Unitarian Universalists and members of the United Church of Christ. Conferences are open to people of all faiths. Each evening, participants close out the day with a candlelight service in the stone chapel, which was built around 1800 on the island's highest point of land. *Ferry service is available from Portsmouth via the Isles of Shoals Steamship Company.* ☎ 603-430-6272 🖳 www.starisland.org

Rindge

A Shrine to America's Fallen Soldiers
CATHEDRAL OF THE PINES
Nondenominational. 75 Cathedral Entrance. Year consecrated: 1957
☎ 603-899-3300 🖳 www.cathedralpines.com

*Take Route 119 to Cathedral Road in Rindge, and follow the signs
approximately 1.5 miles to the Cathedral of the Pines, which is on the left.
The cathedral is open daily, May through October, from 9 A.M. to 5 P.M.
During July and August, outdoor organ meditations are scheduled Tuesday
through Thursday from 11 A.M. to 3:30 P.M., weather permitting.
Admission fee is for guided tours only.*

This hilltop land in southwestern New Hampshire was intended to
be the setting for a felicitous home: Lieutenant Sanderson Sloane
and his wife, Peggy, chose this site to build a house for the family they
hoped to start when he returned from World War II. Tragically, however,
his plane was shot down over Germany on February 22, 1944, and he
never came home. Sloane's parents honored his memory—and the sacrifices of all of the country's veterans—by dedicating this land to a shrine for
America's war dead. On the ground where the Sloanes had hoped their
grandchildren would run, the footsteps are not the playful scampering of
children but the hushed and measured gait of those who come here to
mourn, and to remember.

In 1957, by a unanimous vote, Congress recognized the cathedral's
"Altar of the Nation" as a national memorial to America's fallen soldiers.
The altar is composed of stones donated from every U.S. President since
Harry Truman, and from each of the fifty states and four territories of the
United States. On the grounds, there is also a Memorial Bell Tower, which
honors the women who have served in America's various conflicts, and
contains a museum with war memorabilia from 1775 to the present.

Cathedral of the Pines has always considered itself to be nondenominational, but its commitment to including *all* faiths was challenged in
1995, when a Wiccan priestess requested permission to conduct a hand-
fasting (marriage) ceremony here. The cathedral is a popular spot for weddings and other family festivities, so she was surprised when her request
was denied on the ground that Wicca was not a recognized religion. Nearly
two years of legal wrangling followed, and the New Hampshire Commission for Human Rights became involved. In 1997, the Cathedral of the
Pines issued a statement that it would be "a place where all people may
worship without regard to denomination . . . a place that celebrates the
values we all share in common, that allows us to accept differences and
that promotes a community whose members strive to understand and
respect one another." Moreover, the cathedral agreed to create a "memorial circle" on the property, to commemorate "Wiccans and Pagans as well

as followers of other Earth-centered spiritual paths who have stood in military service to their homelands."

Today, services of all faiths are conducted at the Cathedral of the Pines. Thus it would seem that those who gave their lives to make this a free country—where freedom of religious worship is honored for all spiritual traditions—did not die in vain. As spiritual travelers visit the cathedral, gazing up at the majestic pines that crown the hilltop, they might wish to give thanks for religious freedom, and for the sacrifices of those who fought to preserve it.

NEARBY

➥ On the grounds of the Cathedral of the Pines is **Cathedral House**, a year-round bed and breakfast in a refurbished 1850s farmhouse. In its bucolic setting, surrounded by meadows, gardens, and a fishing pond, this is an ideal resting place for the spiritual traveler. ☎ 603-899-6790 🖳 www.cathedralpines.com

➥ Made famous in Emerson's poem of the same name, **Mount Monadnock** is renowned for its forty miles of hiking trails and stunning scenery. Locals claim that the 3,165-foot peak is the most-climbed mountain in North America, and second in the world (after Japan's Mount Fuji). The western side of the mountain is a state park encompassing 900 acres. ☎ 603-532-8862

➥ In the valley down below Mount Monadnock is **Jaffrey Center**, whose **Old Meeting House** was built in 1775. Construction began on June 17,

Old Meeting House, Jaffrey Center

the very day that the Battle of Bunker Hill was fought. The church and its attached school were endowed by Amos Fortune (1710–1801), an African-born slave who bought his freedom and was very successful in the tannery business. The Amos Fortune Forum Series of lectures and performances occurs each Friday evening in July and August at the Meeting House. Fortune is interred in the **Old Burying Ground** behind the church. So is Willa Cather, who penned *Death Comes to the Archbishop* and *My Antonia* while staying at a nearby inn. *In Jaffrey Center, on the south side of Route 124, about two miles east of its junction with U.S. 202.*

Wilton Center

Blood, Sweat, Toil, and Tears
FIRST UNITARIAN
CONGREGATIONAL CHURCH
Unitarian Universalist (formerly Congregational). Isaac Frye Highway. Year consecrated: 1860 (congregation dates to 1763). ☎ 603-654-9518
🖥 www.wiltonunitarian.beliefnet.com

> *From Route 101, take the Isaac Frye Highway .7 miles to the church, which is on the left side. Sunday worship at 10:30 A.M.*

September 7, 1773, dawned clear and sunny in the village of Wilton, with no hint of the tragedy that was about to befall the town. Approximately 120 men had gathered to raise the town's first meetinghouse, making it a joyous and auspicious occasion. The grounds were also bustling with women, children, older men, and slaves, including one who entertained the crowd with a magic show. It was a festive day; the town ordered six barrels of rum to make hundreds of gallons of celebratory rum punch, and the townswomen set up long tables of food for the hungry workers. Later, after the raising, there would be wrestling matches, games with iron rings, and a competition of "goal" (a precursor of soccer). The town's celebrations were expected to last far into the night.

Except that it was not to be. In the midafternoon, as the assembly of men placed the third or fourth truss upright, a man named John Bradford noticed with horror that the tree trunk that was serving as a temporary support for the tie beam was beginning to crack. Whether it was because of

"On Tuesday se'ennight, as a great number of people were assisting in raising the frame of a new meeting house in Wilton, New-Hampshire, one of the large beams accidentally gave way, when the greatest part of the frame, with fifty-three persons that were upon it, fell to the ground, by which unhappy event, three men were instantly killed, and fifty wounded, two of whom have since died of their wounds. . . ."
—*Pennsylvania Gazette*, September 29, 1773

"Of the fifty-three that fell, not one escaped without broken bones, terrible bruises or wounds from the axes, &c. And as they were men picked up from that and neighboring towns, and many of them heads of families, the news of their catastrophe filled those places with weeping, lamentation and woe, and may fully mind us that 'Man knoweth not his time,' but 'at such an hour as we think not the son of Man cometh,' and it therefore concerns us to be always ready."
Extract of a letter to New-Ipswich, 13 September 1773

worms or decay is uncertain, but the tree was giving way under the immense weight of the partially completed structure. Bradford immediately brought this to the attention of Ephraim Barker, the master builder, who dismissed his worry and called him a coward. Barker derided Bradford by telling him to go home if he was afraid, so Bradford angrily followed the advice and took off on his horse for home.

He had not gone far before he heard a deafening crash, followed by screams that another witness claimed "rung in his ears for years after." The entire upper structure had collapsed, sending fifty-three men plunging down from a height of twenty-seven feet (three stories). With them fell their axes, hammers, planks, and giant crowbars. Every man was injured, five fatally. George Lancey, whose wife, Elizabeth, was at home pregnant with their fourth child, was killed instantly. Four others died in the succeeding hours and days; two more were paralyzed for life.

Just a few days later, the congregation began work again on the meetinghouse, which was dedicated in January of 1775. In the months after the horrible tragedy, residents of Wilton and the neighboring towns struggled to come to terms with the catastrophe's meaning. "At Wilton did Almity God His anger there Display," claimed one popular ballad that circulated around New England. Had God been displeased with the town's efforts to build a meetinghouse? Was the incident a visitation of God's wrath upon the town for some terrible sin? Although religious faith was not as centered on God's fierce and sovereign judgment as it had been a century before, such rationalizations continued to be popular in New England. Witnesses of the tragedy, and those who experienced it vicariously through word of mouth, focused on consummating their own relationships with God in case they, too, should be the victims of a fatal accident or sudden illness. "Let us be making peace with god/while we have life and breath/so that we may prepaired be/To meet a Sudden death," concluded the ballad.

Today, First Unitarian Congregational Church occupies an 1860 church that stands just adjacent to the site of the original meetinghouse, which burned to the ground in 1859. The location of the 1773 meetinghouse is now the newer church's parking lot, and the old meetinghouse's foundations are still intact beneath the layers of gravel. These foundations are not just literal: Although the congregation is now Unitarian, its spiritual touchstones remain Congregationalist. This church is the only "Christian Unitarian" congregation in the state of New Hampshire; it is a member of the Unitarian Universalist Association but has never adopted the humanism that characterizes the denomination as a whole. Services are fairly traditional, with scripture readings and the Lord's Prayer. Communion is observed twice a year, on Christmas and Maundy Thursday. The congregation "maintains the Puritan custom of no ornamentation in the meetinghouse," says the minister. "Most Congregationalists would not feel out of place in our service."

CHAPTER ELEVEN

························· ❧ ·························

$\mathscr{M}$aine

MAINE IS BY FAR the largest New England state; the other five would nearly fit inside its commodious boundaries. Yet with just over a million inhabitants, Maine is quite sparsely settled, particularly in its northern regions. Its capital, Augusta, has fewer than 25,000 residents, and the largest city, Portland, has just 65,000. This very tranquility has given Maine the nickname that graces its license plates: "Vacationland." In summer, tourists descend upon the seacoast in search of lobster, rocky shores and sailing adventures.

Maine is rightly known for its incredible coastline. As visitors wind their way "down east" (despite the "down" orientation, this entails going not south but northeast), they inevitably marvel at the rocky shores that become more wild and untamed the further north they travel. Along this shore is the famous Acadia National Park, a crown jewel of Maine's natural beauty, and the resort community of Bar Harbor, with its summer churches and other houses of worship.

While Maine's coast is delightful—and figures prominently in this chapter—it constitutes only ten percent of the state's total area. The interior of Maine is home to some of the loveliest countryside in New England, the more so because it is relatively unspoiled. Spiritual travelers may wish to take advantage of the beauty of the "backcountry" at retreat centers like the Notre Dame Spiritual Center in Alfred and the Living Water Spiritual Center in Winslow (near Waterville). And in the vast stretches of northern Maine, New England's spiritual heritage of Congregationalism blends with an equally important legacy of French Catholicism; the towns and

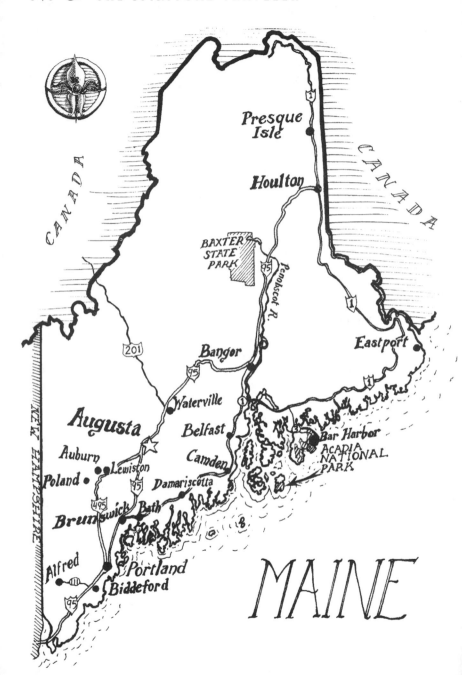

Presque Isle

Houlton

BAXTER STATE PARK

Penobscot R.

Eastport

Bangor

Waterville

Augusta

Belfast

Auburn

Poland

Lewiston

Camden

Bar Harbor

ACADIA NATIONAL PARK

Damariscotta

Brunswick

Bath

Alfred

Portland

Biddeford

MAINE

CANADA

NEW HAMPSHIRE

villages acquire an increasingly French character as you head north toward Quebec. Catholicism is a dominant force throughout the entire state; more than a third of Maine's population is Roman Catholic. Then again, membership numbers aren't everything: the world's last active Shaker community, located in New Gloucester, has just eight members, yet they carry on the traditions of one of New England's most historic faiths.

Alfred

A Roman Catholic Retreat in a Former Shaker Village
NOTRE DAME SPIRITUAL CENTER
Shaker Hill Road. Year founded: 1931 (Shaker community dated to 1791).
☎ 207-324-6160

> *From the Maine Turnpike (I-95), take Exit 2 (Wells-Sanford) and turn right on Route 109 West. Go about thirteen miles to the second traffic light, and turn right onto Route 202 East. Follow this through Alfred Village Square and continue for about one mile to Shaker Hill Road, across from Shaker Pond. Turn right. Follow the signs marked for the Brothers of Christian Instruction.*

This small monastery campus, located on 300 acres of woods, was once home to the Alfred Shaker Community, one of three Shaker villages in the state. In fact, the famous Shaker hymn "Simple Gifts" was composed on these grounds. In 1931, the village's last remaining Shakers moved to Sabbathday Lake (see page 364) and this campus was sold to the Brothers of Christian Instruction, who used it as a training school for future monks. Today, it is home to nearly two dozen brothers who have retired from "active service" yet remain committed to actively serving the community. Each winter, they tap into the monastery's hundreds of maple trees and make their own syrup, which they sell to the public (though there is never enough to meet demand). The brothers also own an apple orchard with over 3,000 trees. Visitors can pick their own apples each autumn, or buy them at the brothers' seasonal shop, which also sells hot apple cider.

A spiritual mainstay of this community is the Notre Dame Spiritual Center, which is housed in two buildings on the campus (one of which,

Eugene Hall, is one of the eight original Shaker buildings). Ninety guests can be accommodated in thirty-six private rooms. There are two lakes for swimming, fishing, and boating, as well as numerous hiking trails.

Bangor

Two Centuries of Training Protestant Leaders
BANGOR THEOLOGICAL SEMINARY
United Church of Christ (Congregational). 300 Union Street. Year founded: 1814. ☎ 207-942-6781 🖥 www.bts.edu

> *From I-95, take Exit 46 (Hammond Street). If you are coming from the south, turn left after the exit; if you are coming from the north, turn right. After .8 miles, turn left onto West Broadway. Take the second right onto Hayward Street. At the stop sign, proceed straight to the seminary parking lot.*

This seminary, perched on a hill overlooking the Penobscot River and the city of Bangor, emerged out of the optimism of the religious revivals of the early nineteenth century. Just as evangelical Protestants at Williams College in Massachusetts were praying about making a difference in their world through missionary work (see page 197), Christians in Bangor turned their thoughts to religious education. At that time, there was no seminary anywhere north of Massachusetts to train pastors, and Maine was feeling the need. Jonathan Fisher, one of the seminary's founding trustees, wrote in 1811 that he was "strongly adverse to an unlearned ministry," but that Maine was too remote to attract educated ministers from the likes of Boston. "If in this district we wait to be supplied from other institutions," he warned, "I am fully persuaded that the ground would be preoccupied by Sectarians, many of whom would not only be unlearned, but *very* unlearned." Other Mainers clearly agreed with Fisher that the prospect of a *very* unlearned ministry was dire indeed. The new theological seminary received its charter in 1814.

Now fully ecumenical (though still affiliated with the United Church of Christ), Bangor Theological Seminary remains the only accredited theological school in northern New England. In 1991 it expanded its operations to include campuses in nearby Portland and in Hanover, New

Hampshire. Today, it carries its mission of theological education to laity as well as clergy, and does so through a wide range of programs. The seminary has sponsored kayaking retreats in Penobscot Bay, for example, as well as continuing education courses that combine skiing with spiritual study.

NEARBY

➥ **Mount Hope Cemetery**, founded in 1834 and inspired by Mount Auburn Cemetery in Cambridge (1831), was Maine's first garden cemetery. Like other burial grounds of the period, Mount Hope is carefully landscaped with rolling hills, trees, ponds, and winding paths. As with Mount Auburn (see page 121), the cemetery's goal was to provide a respite from urban life, a bucolic and lovely setting in which the living could contemplate their Creator and remember their loved ones. The parklike cemetery encompasses nearly 300 acres of land on the banks of the Penobscot River. *1048 State Street.* ☎ 207-945-6589 🖳 www.mthopebgr.com

➥ After World War II, Torah scrolls and other artifacts that had been confiscated by the Nazis were redistributed to Jewish synagogues around the world. One recipient of a so-called "Holocaust Torah" was **Congregation Beth El**, Bangor's Reform congregation. The congregation's Torah dates to 1730s Moravia. *183 French Street.* ☎ 207-945-4578

➥ The **Silo 7 Bookstore** on Bomarc Road has a strong stock of spirituality titles, particularly for New Age, Eastern, and earth religions. Everything about this bookstore is interesting, including the name: This building was the seventh of twenty-eight warehouses that were used to house ground-to-air missiles during the Cold War. The foot-thick walls certainly make for quiet reading. *7 Bomarc Road.* ☎ 207-942-5590 🖳 www.silo7.com

➥ **Living Water Spiritual Center** offers directed and private retreats on a sixty-one-acre campus bordering the Sebasticook River in **Winslow**. Since 1994 this facility (formerly a novitiate for Roman Catholic nuns) has been operated by the Sisters of St. Joseph as a spiritual renewal center for people of all faiths. (Until 1999 it was called the Saint Joseph Christian Life Center, but the name was changed to reflect its focus on interfaith activity and ecospirituality.) Most retreats are conducted in silence; individuals who desire spiritual direction may arrange in advance to speak with an assigned director. In their free time, retreatants may take quiet walks along the groomed trails that wind along the riverbank, or swim in the center's outdoor pool. *93 Halifax Street, Winslow. From I-95*

North, take Exit 33 (Waterville-Oakland). Turn right onto Kennedy Memorial Drive at the end of the exit. Continue 1.5 miles for six lights, then turn right after Route 137 (to Route 201) over the bridge. Take the first left at the light, onto Route 201/100. Follow this for approximately one mile. Stay in the right lane when crossing the small bridge; take the first right onto Halifax Street and continue for about a half mile. The center will be on your right.
☎ 207-872-2370 💻 www.e-livingwater.org

Bath

Overcoming Anti-Catholic Prejudice
ST. MARY'S CHURCH
144 Lincoln Street. Year built: 1969 (congregation dates to 1849). Architect: Leo A. Whelan. ☎ 207-443-3423 💻 www.saintmarysbath.f2s.com

> The church is on Lincoln Street near the intersection with Green Street. From the south, take I-95 North. Take Exit 24 (the Coastal Connector exit). Turn right and continue straight through five sets of traffic lights. Follow the signs to Bath (approximately ten miles). Take the High Street exit (do not take the Historic Bath exit.) At the stop sign, turn left onto High Street. At the second stop sign, turn left and then take an immediate right onto Lincoln Street. Continue approximately a third of a mile and turn left into the St. Mary's driveway. Mass is held each weekday at 8 A.M.; Saturday at 5 P.M.; and Sunday at 8 A.M. and 10:30 A.M.

Since Roman Catholicism is, numerically, the dominant religious tradition in New England today, it's difficult to imagine that just 150 years ago, many residents regarded Catholics with deep suspicion. Catholicism was present in Maine in small numbers in the early nineteenth century, but the devastating blow of the potato famine in the 1840s and '50s brought thousands of Irish Catholics to northern New England. At first, relations between the Irish immigrants and the more established Protestant Mainers had been cordial, if a little distant; the Irish found work in the state's shipbuilding and ironworks industries, and they set about building their own infrastructure of churches, schools, and neighborhoods. But as their numbers grew, signs of ethnic and class prejudice began to rise among New Englanders. In 1854 the "Order of the Star Spangled Banner" formed chapters throughout Maine. This organization was dedicated to promoting the cause of "native" Americans, by which they meant not Indians but American-born white persons of western European descent. A related group called the "Sons of Uncle Sam" gained control of the city councils in Augusta and Portland.

In Bath, anti-Catholic rioters threatened and intimidated Catholic families. A group called the "Know-Nothing Party"—so called because they were secretive about their activities, claiming to "know nothing" of the violent acts of which they were accused—circulated petitions to the citizens of the town. "Is there a Catholic Church in your town? How many foreigners are in your town?" the flyers asked, urging Bath residents to be wary of the "popery" and foreign domination of the Roman Catholic Church. On July 6, 1854, an anti-Catholic mob, incensed by the nativists' allegations, descended upon the Old South Church in High Street, which the Catholic parish was leasing. Brandishing an American flag, the mob set fire to the building, which was utterly destroyed.

A sympathetic local resident allowed the Roman Catholics of Bath to meet in his home while they raised the funds needed to build a church. In 1856—after two more arson attempts—St. Mary's Church was dedicated. The building was used for just over a century before being razed in favor of the present red brick structure.

AWASII IN GOTHIC AND GREEK REVIVALISM

This small seafaring community, called "the City of Ships," is renowned for its role in the shipbuilding industry. It could also be famous for its Greek and Gothic Revival houses of worship, for Bath is home to some fine examples of nineteenth-century church architecture. The once-Congregational **Winter Street Church** is renowned for perfectly blending the Gothic and Greek revival styles into a cohesive whole. Built in 1843 by local builder Anthony Raymond, its central steeple towers over the town green. It is no longer used as a church, but preservation efforts in the 1970s saved the building from decay. Winter Street Church regularly hosts local cultural events and includes a studio theater. *Washington at Winter Street.*
☎ 207-443-2174

Another decommissioned Congregational house of worship that has become a center for the arts is **Chocolate Church**, so nicknamed because of the chocolate-colored exterior of the Greek Revival building. Originally called Central Church, the building was designed in 1846 by Boston architect Arthur Gilman, who intended it to resemble medieval English churches. Throughout the year, the Chocolate Church Arts Center sponsors an impressive calendar of musical and dramatic performances. *804 Washington Street.* ☎ 207-442-8455 🖥 www.chocolatechurcharts.org

An ancient Greek temple in southern Maine? Many first-time visitors gawk openly at the **Swedenborgian Church** on Middle Street, which appears in its proportions and architectural details to be a perfect example of a Greek temple. While it may appear a bit out of place in this quiet New England community, this 1843 church is one of the best examples of Greek Revival architecture in the state. The designer and builder, A. B. Farnham, was from Bath. The congregation is officially called **New Jerusalem Church**, in honor of the denomination's founder, Emmanuel Swedenborg (1688–1772), a Swedish visionary who taught others about his visions of the "New Jerusalem" of spiritual awakening. *887 Middle Street.* ☎ 207-443-6401

Guided walking tours of Bath's historic district are offered by Sagadahoc Preservation each Tuesday and Thursday from mid-June to early September. Copies of a self-guided walking-tour pamphlet are also available from the Bath Chamber of Commerce at 3 Front Street. ☎ 207-443-2174 🖥 www.sagadahocpreservation.org

NEARBY

➥ Nestled into the seaside community of Tenants Harbor is **Greenfire**, an interfaith women's retreat center in a 200-year-old farmhouse. Greenfire is located on fifty-nine acres of woods on the **St. George Peninsula**. Guests may borrow Greenfire's canoes or kayaks, or enjoy long walks by the seashore. Spiritual direction is available in the form of guided conversations with community members. *From I-95, take either Exit 22 (Brunswick) or Exit 24 (Topsham) to coastal Route 1 heading toward Bath. Stay on Route 1 until you have gone through Thomaston. Turn right onto Route 131 South. After 6.7 miles, go right at the fork onto Wallston Road and follow it for 1.9 miles. Greenfire is the blue farmhouse on the left.* ☎ 207-372-6442 🖥 www.greenfireretreat.org

Biddeford

A Retreat Center in a Converted Resort
MARIE JOSEPH SPIRITUAL CENTER
Roman Catholic (Sisters of the Presentation of Mary). RR 2. Year center founded: 1979. ☎ 207-284-5671
💻 www.presmarymethuen.org/mariejo.htm

> *From the Maine Turnpike, take Exit 4 (Biddeford). At the light after the toll booth, turn left onto Route 111 East. At the sixth set of lights, turn right onto Route 9/208 (Pool Street). Go 7.5 miles and take a left onto Route 208. Take this for .6 miles to a stop sign; turn left onto Mile Stretch Road, following Route 208 South and bearing right at the fork. After .3 miles, turn right at the sign for Marie Joseph. The center is closed for the first two weeks of June and September.*

The Marie Joseph Spiritual Center says that it is "a Sacred Space for persons seeking to encounter God in solitude and in stillness." It is difficult to imagine a more tranquil spot for such solitude. The retreat center occupies an imposing building that was once a luxurious seaside hotel; in 1948 the Sisters of the Presentation of Mary bought it and operated a girls' boarding school. In 1979 it was converted to a retreat center and can house up to seventy men and women.

Private retreatants are welcome to come and spend a few days in spiritual repose. There are also programmed retreats on various topics such as forgiveness, Celtic spirituality, holy days, the enneagram, or family worship.

NEARBY
➡ In 1915 Albanian Muslims who were employed in Biddeford's mills began holding religious meetings in the back room of a coffeehouse on Main Street. Although no evidence remains of the building, it is considered to have been one of the first mosques in the United States, and the first in Maine. Today, there is no mosque in Maine, though Friday midday prayers are held in several places, including the University of Southern Maine at Portland. The closest full-fledged Masjids are in Quincy and Cambridge, Massachusetts (see pages 150 and 124), but plans are underway to build one in Maine to accommodate the growing Muslim community. It will most likely be located in the Bangor area.

Brunswick

A Historic Literary Inn
STOWE HOUSE INN
63 Federal Street. Year built: 1807. ☎ 207-729-7869

> *From I-295, take the Brunswick Exit. Enter onto Pleasant Street;*
> *continue until Main Street. Turn right on Main, then left on Bath Road.*
> *Go for one block and take a left on Federal Street.*

This Federal-style house on Federal Street is where Harriet Beecher Stowe (see page 267) wrote the book that may have saved the federal government. In 1850 and '51, Stowe lived here with her husband, then serving as a professor at Bowdoin College, and a growing brood of children. These were difficult years for Stowe, who complained that the house was cold and crowded. Because there was a public dining room next door and a schoolroom upstairs, she could find little peace during the day. No wonder she did most of her writing at night; after the children were asleep, she devoted her energy to writing *Uncle Tom's Cabin*, the antislavery book that shocked the world.

In 1999, the house fetched $865,000 at auction; the new owners have opened it to the public as a restaurant and inn. Visitors can stay in the same rooms that such luminaries as Nathaniel Hawthorne and Henry Wadsworth Longfellow called home during their visits here. Twenty guest rooms and suites, five decorated with Maine authors in mind, offer respite for visitors in an inn that is conveniently located just two blocks from the Bowdoin campus. In December 2001 ownership of the inn was transferred to Bowdoin College.

NEARBY
➡ The **Bowdoin College Museum of Art** is one of the top collections in Maine, with over 14,000 works of art. The museum is particularly strong in American painting, and boasts an entire collection devoted to Winslow Homer. *From the south, take the Maine Turnpike to Exit 9 (95 to Coastal Route 1). Continue on 95 to Exit 22 (Brunswick). At the business district, turn right onto Maine Street, following signs to the college. The museum is housed in the Walker Art Building on the quadrangle. Open daily except Mondays.*
☎ 207-725-3275 🖳 www.bowdoin.edu/art museum/

RICHARD UPJOHN IN BRUNSWICK

Architect Richard Upjohn (1802–78) was responsible for some of the most memorable examples of Gothic Revival architecture in New England, and the town of Brunswick has no less than three of his houses of worship, all dating from the 1840s. **St. Paul's Episcopal Church** on Pleasant Street is one of the more simple churches Upjohn designed, with a cruciform pattern and board-and-batten construction. It dates to 1846. *27 Pleasant Street.* ☎ 207-725-5342 🖳 www.members.aol.com/stpaulsme/

Also in 1846, Upjohn designed **First Parish Church**, an elaborate Gothic Revival church. Although its gray appearance gives the impression that the exterior is stone, it is actually painted wood. The interior features an intricate, detailed system of trusswork in dark wood. A footnote of history: In 1851, Harriet Beecher Stowe was attending services in this building when she had what she called a "vision" of a slave being beaten to death. She incorporated it into *Uncle Tom's Cabin* as the scene where Tom is martyred. Today, the historic building houses Maine's largest United Church of Christ congregation, with about a thousand members. *9 Cleaveland Street.* ☎ 207-729-7331 🖳 www.firstparish.net

Finally, the **Bowdoin College Chapel** was also designed by Richard Upjohn, in a style that blends Gothic Revival and Romanesque Revival. There are free guided tours of the campus each day, beginning at the admissions office. *On the Bowdoin College campus.* ☎ 207-725-3100 🖳 www.bowdoin.edu

Damariscotta (Newcastle)

The Oldest Surviving Catholic Church in New England
ST. PATRICK'S CHURCH
380 Academy Hill Road. Year built: 1808 (congregation dates to 1798).
Architect: Nicholas Codd. ☎ 207-563-3240

The church is located 2.5 miles north of U.S. Route 1 on Highway 215. In summer, mass is offered on Saturday at 5 P.M. and Sunday at 8 A.M. and 10:30 A.M.; the rest of the year, mass occurs on Saturday at 4 P.M. and Sunday at 10:30 A.M.

St. Patrick's was not the first Catholic church in New England—French missionaries had established mission churches in what is now northern Vermont as early as the seventeenth century—but it is the oldest that is still standing. Designed by Irish architect Nicholas Codd, the church has brick walls that are a foot and a half thick. Like many New England churches, St. Patrick's has a bell cast by Paul Revere; it dates to 1818, the year he died. The church has recently been restored, and has its original altar, floors, stair rails, and a few pews.

After its founding in 1798, the congregation grew with the times. In 1818, Father Dennis Ryan came to Damariscotta as the first resident Catholic priest in Maine. The parish was ready to receive a large influx of Irish Catholic immigrants, beginning in the 1820s and continuing through the middle of the nineteenth century. But unlike many other Roman Catholic churches, St. Patrick's continued to grow throughout the twentieth century, and the parish greeted the new millennium with plans for an elaborate addition to the church.

 Adjacent to the church is one of the oldest cemeteries in the state, surrounded by a forest.

NEARBY

➡ **Monhegan Island**, situated about twelve miles off the Maine coast, is definitely worth a visit. Only a third of the island is developed, while the rest is natural woods and forest, with seventeen miles of hiking trails. There is no electricity on the undeveloped portion of the island, an ironic fact considering that one of Monhegan's chief landowners in the mid–twentieth century was Theodore Edison, son of the famous inventor Thomas Edison. No cars are permitted on Monhegan, and there are no paved roads. In the summer, the island is host to an artist colony (Jamie Wyeth and Edward Hopper once painted here), but during the rest of the year there are fewer than a hundred residents. The **Cathedral Woods** are renowned for their dense canopy of fir and spruce trees. Local lore suggests that "fairy houses" are hidden under the moss-covered forest floor. Some artists have responded to this whimsical legend by creating actual playhouses for the fairies, a few of which are quite elaborate. Conservationists oppose the practice, since some builders have pulled moss from the forest floor, thereby killing it. *Ferry service to the island runs from Damariscotta and Booth Bay. A daily mail boat from Port Clyde also accepts passengers. There are several inns on Monhegan Island, including The Island Inn* (☎ 207-596-0371 🖥 www.islandinnmonhegan.com) *and Shining Sails Bed and Breakfast* (☎ 207-596-0041 🖥 www.shiningsails.com).

Eastport

Maine's Largest Native American Reservation and Museum
PLEASANT POINT RESERVATION/
WAPONAHKI MUSEUM
Pleasant Point. Year established: 1987. ☎ 207-853-4001 or 853-2551
🖳 www.wabanaki.com

> *On the north side of Route 190 at Pleasant Point. Open weekdays from*
> *8 A.M. to 11 A.M. and 1 P.M. to 3 P.M., or by appointment.*

The tiny town of Eastport (population 2,500) is, true to its name, the easternmost port in the United States; the sun rises first here. This area is also home to a proud Native American legacy. Before the Europeans came to Maine in the sixteenth century (and perhaps earlier), Passamaquoddy Indians inhabited this land, ranging from southern Maine into New Brunswick, Canada. They lived by hunting in winter and fishing in summer (*Passamaquoddy* means "people who fish for pollack"). In 1866, the tribe was restricted to occupying this 100-acre reservation, where more than 700 descendants live today. Some still speak the Passamaquoddy language, and there are efforts to teach it in schools.

The museum collection includes photographs, baskets, tools, and other artifacts documenting Passamaquoddy life before and after European contact. Mannequins display traditional Passamaquoddy dress. A highlight of the exhibit is a century–old birchbark canoe.

Isles of Shoals

An Island Garden
CELIA THAXTER'S GARDEN
Appledore Island. Year garden created: 1893. ☎ 607-254-2900 for information; ☎ 607-255-3717 for reservations. 🖳 www.sml.cornell.edu

> *Appledore Island can be reached by ferry from Portsmouth, New Hampshire; call the Isles of Shoals Steamship Company at 800-441-4620*
> *(www.islesofshoals.com) for schedules and fares. Note that there are no*

longer any hotels on the islands; unless you are a guest at the Star Island Religious and Educational Conference Center (see page 339), it is not possible to stay overnight. Because of the fragility of the island's environment, access to Appledore Island is carefully regulated by the Shoals Marine Laboratory. Celia Thaxter's garden is open to the public on Wednesdays only from late June to late August. Reservations for garden tours must be made in advance; the steamship company will permit only preapproved visitors to board the ferry to Appledore. There are no restaurants on the island, but visitors are welcome to pack a picnic lunch or purchase food on the ferry. Visitors to the garden should be in reasonably good physical shape, because a visit requires a quarter-mile walk over rocky terrain from the dock.

Maine owns five of the nine Isles of Shoals (see page 339), including Appledore Island, which in the nineteenth century was the vacation home of an illustrious colony of artists. One hotelier named Celia Thaxter (1835–1894) hosted well-known musicians, writers, and painters of the era at Appledore House, a wooden seaside hotel. Among the greats who visited was the artist Childe Hassam, whose 400-odd watercolors and drawings of Appledore are considered among his best work. Thaxter herself was an established poet and artist, lavishing her own illustrations on her books of poems. Her 1893 book called *An Island Garden*, about the garden she created on Appledore Island, is still in print today.

It was through this garden that Celia Thaxter achieved true immortality. It is now owned and operated by the Shoals Marine Laboratory of Cornell University, and the lab's volunteers have taken great pains to restore the garden to its original condition, based on Thaxter's notes and Hassam's paintings. Thaxter based her plan on a traditional English cottage garden, with vivid color and heavy fragrance. The garden is especially known for its many varieties of poppies.

"Of all the wonderful things in the wonderful universe of God, nothing seems to me more surprising than the planting of a seed in the blank earth and the result thereof. . . . You may watch this marvel from beginning to end in a few weeks' time, and if you realize how great a marvel it is, you can but be lost in 'wonder, love, and praise.'"
—Celia Thaxter, *An Island Garden*, 1893

NEARBY

➥ Just a mile south of the highly trafficked Route 9 in **Wells** is the **Rachel Carson National Wildlife Refuge**, a salt marsh haven for Maine's wildlife. A mile-long hiking trail winds around the marsh, where visitors can see more than 250 species of birds, as well as the occasional moose, black bear, river otter, and deer. A map of the trail is available from the U.S. Fish and Wildlife Service. *321 Port Road, Wells.* ☎ 207-646-9226

Mount Desert Island

Mount Desert Island, a popular resort destination, is one of the treasures of Maine. Locals can't agree on much about the island, including how *Desert* should be pronounced. Some feel that it should sound like *dessert*— and this is appropriate, given that M.D.I. is such a pleasurable treat. The island's two most famous attractions are Bar Harbor, a resort community that became popular among the well-to-do in the nineteenth century, and Acadia National Park, one of the loveliest spots in New England.

The First National Park East of the Mississippi
ACADIA NATIONAL PARK
Route 3. Year established: 1916. ☎ 207-288-3338
🖳 www.nps.gov/acad/anp.html

Take Route 1 North along the coast to Ellsworth, and then take Route 3 South to the Hulls Cove park entrance. Admission fee.

Acadia, on Mount Desert Island, is the second most visited national park in the United States, and once you catch a glimpse of its coastline you will know why. Beneath tall cliffs of sheer granite, craggy shoreline meets the crashing waves of the Atlantic. Acadia is home to many varieties of animals (including the endangered peregrine falcon) and plants. The park's thousands of acres of woods and coastline afford innumerable opportunities for observing the splendors of nature. It's not surprising that this land has given inspiration to some of America's best artists, including Thomas Cole and Frederic Church of the Hudson River school.

This area became home to wealthy vacationers in the middle of the

Acadia National Park

nineteenth century. As they built their elaborate seaside "cottages" (read: "mansions"), discussions began about the degree to which Mount Desert Island's natural state should be preserved. At the turn of the century, John D. Rockefeller, one of the summer residents, assisted with financing the purchase of the land that would become Acadia National Park. In 1916, it was opened to the public, the first national park to be created east of the Mississippi River. Rockefeller also created nearly fifty miles of stone "carriage roads" to access the park's remote interior. Visitors can walk, cycle, or ride horses along these roads, but cars are not permitted.

Other portions of the park are accessible by car. In fact, an automobile tour is available on audiocassette; this can be a good introduction to the highlights of the park, especially for travelers who are not physically able to hike in the park. The twenty-mile drive hits the major points on Park Loop Road—not exactly off the beaten track, but with some spectacular vistas. Park Loop Road was designed in part by landscape architect Frederick Law Olmsted, Jr., who wished to create "a pleasing landscape experience for motorists." Highlights include the **Wild Gardens of Acadia**, which feature labeled samples of the flowers, trees, and plants on the island; **Beaver Dam Pond**, a great place to see nature's engineers in action; and the famous **Otter Cliffs**, with some of the highest headlands anywhere on the Atlantic coast. And don't miss the stunning ocean view from the top of **Cadillac Mountain**, a 1,530-foot summit.

NEARBY

➥ Horticultural enthusiasts will enjoy the **Asticou Azalea Garden**, designed by Charles Savage. Particularly noteworthy is Savage's blending of Eastern and Western traditions; parts of the garden exhibit Japanese Zen influences. The two-and-a-half-acre garden is open daily from April to October, and the azaleas reach their peak in the last few weeks of June. *Seal Harbor and Peabody Drive, Northeast Harbor. The garden is located 100 yards north of the intersection of Routes 3 and 198. No admission fee.* ☎ 207-276-5130

➥ This region is known for its abundance of white cedars (*thuya occidentalis*), giving rise to the name of one of the area's most famous gardens. **Thuya Garden** was created by Boston landscape architect Joseph Henry Curtis and adapted for the coastal Maine environment by Beatrix Farrand. It is an English-style, semiformal garden, its carefully cultivated flowerbeds flanked by alpine woods. *Follow directions for the Asticou Azalea Garden.* ☎ 207-276-5130

St. Katharine Drexel's Summer Parish
HOLY REDEEMER CHURCH
Roman Catholic. 21 Ledgelawn Avenue, Bar Harbor. Year built: 1907 (congregation dates to the late nineteenth century). ☎ 207-288-3535

Holy Redeemer Church, Bar Harbor

In October 2000, members of Holy Redeemer Church flew to Rome on a special pilgrimage to the Vatican. The occasion was the official canonization of Mother Katharine Drexel (1858–1955), who had personal ties to this parish: her half-sister, Louise Drexel Morrell, was a member here. Mother Drexel was a regular summer visitor to Bar Harbor and to this parish, and many senior members still remember her. The Morrells built Saint Edward's School and Convent, where Katharine Drexel sometimes occupied a room on the second floor.

This church, built in 1907 to resemble Irish country churches, replaced an earlier parish building from the nineteenth century. At the turn of the century, the membership consisted largely of domestic staff of Irish descent who served the owners of the summer "cottages" of the Bar Harbor area. Although there were some wealthier members, as the presence of the Morrells would attest, this church had something of an "upstairs-downstairs" relationship with Saint Saviour's Episcopal Church a block away (see below).

Today, the year-round membership is relatively small (about 150 families), but attendance blossoms to about 1,400 per service in the summer

SAINT KATHARINE DREXEL
(1858–1955)

When millionairess Katharine Drexel had a special audience with the pope in the late nineteenth century, she asked him point-blank why the Roman Catholic Church wasn't sending more missionaries to Native Americans and African Americans. He replied that if she had prayed about it and determined that such a mission was God's will, she should start one herself. And that is just what Drexel, the daughter of a Philadelphia bank mogul, set out to do. She founded the Sisters of the Blessed Sacrament for Indians and Colored People, as well as 145 missions, twelve schools for Native Americans, and fifty schools for African Americans (including Louisiana's Xavier University). It is estimated that she contributed more than $20 million to fund these missionary efforts.

Drexel died in 1955, but her spirit lives on in the philanthropic institutions she founded. She was beatified in 1988, receiving the title of "Blessed." On October 1, 2000, Pope John Paul II canonized her as an official saint of the Catholic Church.

months. With its granite stone exterior, 1912 pipe organ, and capacious nave, Holy Redeemer is also a popular wedding destination.

A Feast of Tiffany Stained Glass
ST. SAVIOUR'S EPISCOPAL CHURCH
41 Mount Desert Street, Bar Harbor. Year built: 1878 (congregation dates to 1876). ☎ 207-288-4215 ⬛ www.ellsworthme.org/ssaviour/

During July and August, there are free tours of the church at 11 A.M. on Wednesday and 3 P.M. Monday, Wednesday, Thursday, and Friday.

With forty-two stained-glass windows, ranging in date from 1886 to 1992, St. Saviour's is one of the most frequently visited churches on Mount Desert Island. Ten of those windows were designed by the studios of Louis Comfort Tiffany, more than in any other church in Maine. (Several of these are endangered and under repair; a Windows Restoration Fund has been founded to ensure the windows' preservation for generations to come.)

This congregation, though Episcopalian, takes its name from the early seventeenth-century Roman Catholic mission. When French Jesuits landed on Mount Desert Island in 1613, they named their outpost "Saint Sauveur," and this parish took its name from that pioneering effort. The church was completed in 1878, but it only seated 325 people. This soon proved to be a problem, because summer congregations often exceeded 1,000 worshipers. In 1885 and '86, the original church building became the transept of a larger edifice, whose apse was sixteen feet in diameter.

NEARBY
➡ **Our Lady Star of the Sea**, erected in 1942, serves the community of Islesford on Little Cranberry Island. The island is a bit remote; one area resident can vividly recall rowing a dory with her family on Christmas Eve to attend midnight mass, in those days a five-hour trip each way. The chapel's cobalt stained-glass windows are thought to originate from Europe and are among the best examples of stained glass in the Acadia region. *The chapel is accessible by a scheduled mail boat departing from Northeast Harbor for Great and Little Cranberry Islands. In July and August, mass is offered on Sundays at 11:30 A.M.; during the rest of the year, mass is said on the first Tuesday of the month at 10 A.M.* ☎ 207-288-3535

New Gloucester Area

The World's Only Community of Living Shakers
SABBATHDAY LAKE
707 Shaker Road. Year founded: 1783 (meetinghouse dates to 1794).
☎ 207-926-4597 🖳 www.shaker.lib.me.us

> *The Shaker village is located on Route 26, approximately eight miles north of Exit 11 on the Maine Turnpike. Guided tours are offered Memorial Day through Columbus Day, Monday through Saturday from 10 A.M. to 4:30 P.M. every hour on the half hour; the last tour leaves at 3:15 P.M. Admission fee. Meeting for worship is held each Sunday at 10 A.M. and is open to the public. There is a small guesthouse for researchers who are using the library, but no other accommodations are available for visitors.*

This relatively small and remote village, once considered "the least of Mother's children in the East," is now last and not least. This is the only Shaker village that is still home to an active community of covenanted Shakers. Eight men and women live the faith that was founded by Mother Ann Lee (see page 189) in the eighteenth century.

Brother Arnold Hadd, a fit and forty-something Shaker, is the elder of this community. He converted in 1978 at the age of twenty-one, and signed the covenant as a full member five years later. He says that while many have explored the possibility of joining the Shakers, "not one in five ever stays." The lifestyle is just too demanding. "What we're trying to do is live the life of Christ—the celibacy, the community of goods, the pacifism, the equality," says Brother Arnold. And then, there is the hard work. Everyone has multiple tasks and "needs to be multitalented" to sustain the Shaker community's life and worship. "When I came, I was a city boy. And the first job I was given was tending the sheep," he laughs.

In his chino pants and dark green polo, Brother Arnold looks more like the men of "the world" than the hat-clad Shakers of yesteryear. Only the archaic habit of answering questions by "yea" or "nay" sets him apart. He says that the most common misconception of the Shakers "is that we still live in the nineteenth century." Shakers have always been known for their embrace of useful technologies; they were, for example, the first people in the town of New Gloucester to install electricity. Today's Sabbathday Lake community is no different. The Shakers watch television, use microwave ovens, and subscribe to two daily newspapers. They are fully engaged in the world, whether by lecturing about Shakerism to interested audiences around New England or taking their music on the road (they have even performed at Carnegie Hall). The Sabbathday Lake Shakers vote and pay property taxes—though they could qualify for exemption as a religious group.

The community owns 1,800 acres of land, mostly forest, which is a lot of work for a small group. The Shakers lease the orchard with its 10,000 apple trees, but they continue their ventures in publishing, crafts, keeping sheep for wool, creating oval boxes, and making foods for sale. They also produce musical CDs, including albums called *Simple Gifts* and *Early Shaker Spirituals*. On the first Saturday of December, the village hosts a special Christmas fair that is very popular with Maine residents. In 2000, there were 700 people waiting to get into the village when it opened. "Mostly, they come for the food," says Brother Arnold. "We bake and bake and bake." There are also Christmas crafts.

Tours of the village begin in the boys' shop (which offers a very interesting exhibit on children's lives among the Shakers) and winds its way through other buildings. One highlight is the meetinghouse, which still has its original interior blue paint (pigmented with blueberry skins—how authentically Maine is that?). Before 1900, there were no pews in the meetinghouse; the floor was open to allow for the active Shaker worship practices of dancing and marching. The separate doors for men and women are still used by the community, which observes separation of the sexes during worship and at meals. Sunday morning worship is open to the public and features scripture reading, Shaker songs, and "the work" (testimony time). While on weekdays their dress is casual, at worship, Shakers wear traditional dress (black trousers, white shirts, and black vests for the men, and long, colored dresses for the women).

Near the end of her life, Mother Ann predicted that a time would one day come when the Believers would have dwindled down to a mere handful. That time seems to have arrived, but the Sabbathday Lake Shakers persevere with faith and determination. "Survival is the underlying challenge," says Brother Arnold. "At least, somewhere in the back of our minds, it's there."

NEARBY
➥ Built in 1912, **All Souls Chapel** originally served as a house of worship for the employees and guests of the Poland Spring resort. Architect G. Henri Desmond, of Boston, designed it in an early Norman style, with sug-

All Souls Chapel, Poland Spring

gestions of Gothic Revival. With its handcrafted stained-glass windows, the stone chapel is now a very popular site for weddings and other events. *Preservation Way. Go north on Route 26 past the Shaker Village and turn right on Preservation Way. The chapel is located behind the Poland Springs Inn. Open six days a week (except for Friday); closed in winter.* ☎ 207-998-4981

Portland

Portland, Maine's largest city, is replete with historic houses of worship. Here is a selection of historic churches:

One of only a handful of buildings to survive Portland's Great Fire of 1866, **First Parish Church** is the oldest house of worship in the city. Its Federal-style building was consecrated in 1826, replacing "Old Jerusalem" (1740), the first Congregational parish in the area. The constitution of the State of Maine was drafted on this site in 1819. The congregation has been Unitarian (now Unitarian-Universalist) since 1809. *425 Congress Street.* ☎ 207-773-5747 🖥, www.firstparishportland.org

In 1828, African Americans in Portland built the "Abyssinian meetinghouse" (**Fourth Congregational Church**), the oldest African American house of worship in Maine. Before the Civil War, the church performed double duty as Portland's only school for African American children. It was also a stop on the Underground Railroad. It closed in 1917, and Portland residents are currently raising funds for its preservation. *73-75 Newbury Street.*

Like the Roman Catholic cathedral in Boston (see page 103), the **Cathedral of the Immaculate Conception** was designed by the architect Patrick Keely. The cathedral's early years were plagued by some bad luck; the first edifice was destroyed in 1866 by Portland's Great Fire, and on the day when the current building was consecrated in September 1869, a terrible storm blew the steeple all the way across the street. Undeterred, the congregation replaced the steeple within a month. The 1910 stained-glass windows were designed by the Franz Mayer studio of Munich, Germany. *307 Congress Street.* ☎ 207-773-7746

St. Luke's Cathedral, an 1868 stone church in the Gothic Revival style, features Emmanuel Chapel with "the American Madonna," an altar painting by John La Farge. The cathedral serves the Episcopal Diocese of Maine. *135 State Street.* ☎ 207-772-5434 🖳 www.diomaine.org

GLOSSARY

Altar (or **communion table**): Article of furnishing from which the sacrament of the Eucharist, or the Lord's Supper, is shared.

Ambulatory: In churches, a place to walk around behind the altar.

American Renaissance: A late-nineteenth-century American art and architecture style characterized by collaboration among several artists.

Apse: A semicircular area terminating a space.

Arch: A curved structure for spanning an opening. Semicircular **round arches**, also called **Roman arches**, usually characterize Romanesque (and Romanesque Revival) architecture. **Pointed arches** generally characterize Gothic (and Gothic Revival) architecture. **Moorish arches**, also called **horseshoe arches**, widen up from their bases, then narrow toward their tops.

Ark: In a synagogue, a receptacle containing the Torah scrolls.

Attributes (or **emblems**): Symbolic objects used to identify individual saints.

Baptistery: Corner, room, or separate building for the baptismal font.

Basilica: As a style, a basilica is a rectangular building with the entrance on one of the short sides (at one end), and, in churches, the altar and pulpit at the other end. *Basilica* is also a special designation awarded by the pope to Roman Catholic churches of special historical or religious merit.

Beaux-Arts: When used as a descriptive term, usually reserved for late-nineteenth-century buildings of a particularly lush classicism, almost baroque in character. These buildings, including, typically, museums and courthouses, boast large stone bases, grand stairways, paired columns on bases, monumental attics, grand arched openings, medallions, and sculptural figures.

Bimah: In a synagogue, a platform with a lectern from which the Torah is read.

Buttress: Structure built against a wall for support.

Byzantine Revival style: A particularly ornate form of Romanesque Revival architecture characterized by complex vaulting, large open spaces, and lavish decoration with precious marbles, mosaics, and gilding.

Campanile: A freestanding bell tower.

Cantor: The synagogue official who sings liturgical solos.

Cast iron: A hard, brittle, and nonmalleable alloy of iron that is shaped by being poured into molds. It was used in building from the late eighteenth century until superseded by steel in the mid–nineteenth century.

Cathedral: The church in which a bishop keeps his *cathedra* (throne).

Chancel: In churches, the area in which the clergy performing a service move or sit.

Choir chancel: The area where the choir sits, but separate from the sanctuary, where the altar is.

Classical: Any style that revives the art of the classical periods of history (the Greek, Roman, or Renaissance), especially as taught at Paris's École des Beaux-Arts.

Clerestory (clear story): A portion of an interior—usually the center aisle—that rises above the adjacent roof—usually over lower side aisles—and has windows allowing light into the interior.

Colonial Revival style: Name given to the Wren-Gibbs and Georgian classical styles when they were revived in the United States in the late nineteenth and twentieth centuries.

Crossing: The area where the transept intersects the body of a cruciform church.

Crucifix: A cross with an image of the crucified Christ on it.

Cruciform: In the form of a cross. A **Latin cross** has a long staff and two short crossing arms; a **Greek cross** has four arms of equal length.

Diocese: The territory of jurisdiction of a bishop.

Flying buttress: A freestanding pier that extends an arm against a wall to support it.

Font: The source of water for the sacrament of baptism.

Garbhagriha: The womb-chamber of a Hindu temple, where the principal deity resides.

Georgian style: A style popular during the reigns of England's first three Georges (1714–1820). It is classical, imitating northern Italian late-Renaissance architecture, particularly that of Andrea Palladio. Characteristics include a formal dignity and symmetry, solid proportions, ornate frames around doorways, stone quoins, and Palladian windows.

Gothic Revival style: A style characterized by pointed arches, buttresses, stained-glass windows, tracery, large rose windows, and sculpture with medieval inspiration. The original Gothic style predominated in Europe from about the twelfth century until the sixteenth century. **Carpenter's Gothic,** which exhibits Gothic decoration but is not actually built according to medieval Gothic stone construction principles, is often differentiated from **Stonemason's Gothic,** which is built according to these historic Gothic construction principles. A type of late-nineteenth-century Gothic Revival style called **High Victorian Gothic** is usually characterized by the use of stones in contrasting colors.

Greek Cross plan: Church architectural style in which all arms radiating from the crossing are of equal length.

Greek Revival style: A style imitating the buildings of ancient Greece. It is usually characterized by a portico across the front, and a roof ridge running from front to back. Doors and windows are built with posts and beams and are, therefore, rectangular, and glass windows are clear. The five classical styles of columns are: Doric, Ionic, Corinthian, Tuscan, and Composite.

Gurdwara: A Sikh temple; no particular style is prescribed.

High Church: A church that favors ceremony, formality, and elements of mystery, ornate vestments, candles and incense, artistic and symbolic decorations, including crosses and crucifixes.

Iconography: The study of symbols and symbolic decorations.

Iconostasis: A screen covered with icons (sacred images) dividing the nave from the chancel in an Orthodox or Armenian church.

Italianate: Italian in character, in architecture usually referring to classical Roman- or Renaissance-style designs.

Kursi: A small pulpit (or large lectern) in a mosque.

Lantern: A structure on top of a roof or dome having windows to let in light.

Lectern: In churches, a Bible-stand.

Low Church: A church that forgoes decoration and ceremony but expresses piety in plain and simple furnishings and ceremonies.

Magen David: A six-pointed star symbolizing Judaism.

Meetinghouse style: A design for a rectangular church building that places the entrance in the middle of one of the long walls, and the pulpit in the middle of the other long side.

Menorah: A candelabrum.

Mihrab: A shallow apse in a mosque that identifies the direction of Mecca.

Minaret: A tall slender tower at a mosque used to call the people to prayer.

Minbar: The tall pulpit in a mosque, usually incorporating a steep staircase.

Minyan: The minimum number of men necessarily present (ten) to have a Jewish religious service.

Narthex: An enclosed porch or vestibule at the entrance to the building.

Natmandir: The main sanctuary in a Hindu temple.

Nave: The part of a house of worship where the congregation stands or sits.

Ner Tamid: A continuously burning lamp in front of the ark in a synagogue.

Nonritual or nonliturgical church: A church in which the most important part of the service consists of listening to the Word, so church design usually focuses on the pulpit.

Pagoda: An Eastern-style tower with rooflines that curve upward; may be used as a temple or memorial.

Palladian window: A large round-arched central window flanked by lower rectangular windows.

Pediment: A wide low-pitched gable on top of a colonnade or division of a façade.

Portico: A porch with a roof supported by columns, usually in front of a doorway.

Pulpit: The speaking platform from which the pastor delivers the sermon.

Qibla: In a mosque, the wall in the direction of Mecca.

Quoins: Blocks used to reinforce or decorate at a building's corners.

Reliquary: An object displaying a relic of a saint.

Renaissance Revival style: Architecture based on the styles of the Italian Renaissance.

Reredos (or **retable** or **altar screen**): A large decorative screen behind the altar drawing attention to it.

Richardsonian Romanesque style: Architecture following the style of American architect Henry Hobson Richardson (1838–86), characterized by stone construction, round arches framing deeply recessed windows and doors, rough textures, and a horizontal heaviness.

Rimmonim: Tiny caps on the tops of Torah scrolls, often of precious metal.

Ritual or liturgical church: A church that focuses worship on the altar as the site of the ritual sacrifice of the Eucharist. Ritual churches also usually need space for processions and for the clergy.

Romanesque Revival style: Architecture usually characterized by round arches, apsidal chancels, a dome, clear glass, a bell tower, and, often, wheel windows. The original Romanesque style predominated in Europe roughly from the sixth century until the twelfth century.

Rose window: A circular window with tracery. Characteristic of Gothic and Gothic Revival architecture.

Sacristy: A room near the chancel where the robes and altar vessels are stored and where the clergy vest themselves for services.

Shrine: In churches, a special chapel dedicated to the worship of a particular saint.

Stations of the cross: Fourteen specific scenes from Jesus' trial and crucifixion.

Stupa: Any mound or tower serving as a Buddhist shrine; often, but not always, dome-shaped.

Tabernacle: In churches, an object containing portions of Reserved Sacrament between services.

Tebah: Sephardic for *bimah*.

Terra-cotta: "Baked earth" in Italian; a hard-fired clay, reddish brown in color, used for architectural ornaments, tiles, pottery, and for covering steel to fireproof it.

Torah: A scroll of parchment containing the first five books of the Hebrew scriptures (Genesis, Exodus, Leviticus, Numbers, Deuteronomy).

Trabeated: Built with posts and beams; all openings are, therefore, rectangular.

Tracery: Curvilinear openwork shapes creating a pattern within openings.

Transept: The arms of the cross in a cruciform church, crossing the nave.

Transubstantiation: The belief that in the act of consecration of the host, an ordained priest is the instrument for transforming bread and wine into the actual human flesh and human blood of Christ.

Triforium: An arcaded passageway along the nave high in the wall but below any clerestory windows.

Trumeau: The column in the center of the main door of a building. Often used for medieval church portals.

Truss: A structural frame stiffened by triangular forms.

Tympanum: The carved and decorated space above the main door of a building. Often used for medieval church portals.

Vault: An arched structure forming a ceiling or roof.

Vigil light (or **sanctuary lamp**): A light hanging beside the tabernacle and burning if the tabernacle contains Reserved Sacrament.

Wheel window: A large round window having distinctly radiating spokes. Characteristic of Romanesque and Romanesque Revival architecture.

Wren-Gibbs style: A style usually characterized by the combination of a classical portico or porch with a tower and steeple. The tower is often centered on the façade with the principal entrance at its base.

—*Glossary by Edward F. Bergman*

ADDITIONAL READING

Ahlstrom, Sydney E. *A Religious History of the American People*. New Haven: Yale University Press, 1972.

Alcott, Louisa May. *Transcendental Wild Oats: And Excerpts from the Fruitlands Diary*. Boston: The Harvard Common Press, 1981.

Anderson, William C. and Eloise. *Guide to Mormon History Travel*. Provo, Utah: Bushman Press, 1991.

Balmer, Randall. *Religion in Twentieth Century America*. New York: Oxford University Press, 2001.

Barna, Ed. *Covered Bridges of Vermont*. Woodstock, Vermont: The Countryman Press, 1996.

Bushman, Richard, ed. *The Great Awakening: Documents of the Revival of Religion, 1740–1745*. Chapel Hill: University of North Carolina Press, 1969.

Chiat, Marilyn J. *America's Religious Architecture: Sacred Places for Every Community*. New York: John Wiley & Sons, 1997.

Clark, Charles E. *The Meetinghouse Tragedy: An Episode in the Life of a New England Town*. Hanover, New Hampshire: University Press of New England, 1998.

Coleman, James William. *The New Buddhism: The Western Transformation of an Ancient Tradition*. New York: Oxford University Press, 2000.

Copp, Jay. *The Liguori Guide to Catholic USA: A Treasury of Churches, Schools, Monuments, Shrines and Monasteries*. Liguori, Missouri: Liguori Publications, 1999.

Curry, Helen. *The Way of the Labyrinth: A Powerful Meditation for Everyday Life*. New York: Penguin Compass, 2000.

Czarnopys, Theresa Santa, and Reverend Thomas M. Santa. *Marian Shrines of the United States: A Pilgrim's Travel Guide*. Liguori, Missouri: Liguori Publications, 1998.

Daniélou, Alain. *The Hindu Temple: Deification of Eroticism*. Rochester, Vermont: Inner Traditions, 2001.

Deloria, Vine, Jr. *For This Land: Writings on Religion in America*. New York: Routledge, 1999.

Demos, John. *The Unredeemed Captive: A Family Story from Early America*. New York: Vintage Books, 1994.

Donahue, Brian. *Reclaiming the Commons: Community Farms and Forests in a New England Town*. New Haven: Yale University Press, 2001.

Donnelly, Marian Card. *The New England Meeting Houses of the Seventeenth Century.* Middletown, Connecticut: Wesleyan University Press, 1968.

Eck, Diana L. *A New Religious America: How a "Christian Country" Has Now Become the World's Most Religiously Diverse Nation.* San Francisco: Harper San Francisco, 2001.

———. *On Common Ground: World Religions in America.* New York: Columbia University Press, 1997.

Eisler, Kim Isaac. *Revenge of the Pequots: How a Small Native American Tribe Created the World's Most Profitable Casino.* New York: Simon & Schuster, 2001.

Faison, S. Lane, Jr. *The Art Museums of New England: Connecticut & Rhode Island.* Boston: David R. Godine, 1982.

———. *The Art Museums of New England: New Hampshire, Vermont & Maine.* Boston: David R. Godine, 1982.

Fisher, James T. *Catholics in America.* New York: Oxford University Press, 2000.

Francis, Richard. *Ann the Word: The Story of Ann Lee, Female Messiah, Mother of the Shakers, The Woman Clothed with the Sun.* New York: Arcade Publishing, 2001.

Gaustad, Edwin Scott. *Liberty of Conscience: Roger Williams in America.* Valley Forge, Pennsylvania: Judson Press, 1999.

———. *A Religious History of America: New Revised Edition.* San Francisco: Harper San Francisco, 1990.

Gaustad, Edwin Scott, and Philip L. Barlow. *New Historical Atlas of Religion in America.* New York: Oxford University Press, 2001.

Gurek, Gerald and Patricia. *Visiting Utopian Communities: A Guide to the Shakers, Moravians, and Others.* Columbia: University of South Carolina Press, 1998.

Handy, Robert T. *A History of the Churches in the United States and Canada.* New York: Oxford University Press, 1976.

Harris, John. *The Boston Globe Historic Walks in Old Boston.* Second edition. Chester, Connecticut: The Globe Pequot Press, 1989.

Hawkins, Chad S. *The First 100 Temples.* Salt Lake City: Eagle Gate, 2001.

Hayden, Robert C. and Karen E. *African-Americans on Martha's Vineyard & Nantucket: A History of People, Places & Events.* Boston: Select Publications, 1999.

Jenkins, Mary Zuazua. *National Geographic Guide to America's Public Gardens: Three Hundred of the Best Gardens to Visit in the U.S. and Canada.* Washington, D.C.: National Geographic Society, 1998.

Joselit, Jenna Weissman. *Immigration and American Religion.* New York: Oxford University Press, 2001.

Kalvelage, David A. *Cathedrals of the Episcopal Church in the U.S.A.* Cincinnati: Forward Movement, 1993.

Kelly, Jack and Marcia. *Sanctuaries: The Complete United States: A Guide to Lodgings in Monasteries, Abbeys, and Retreats.* New York: Bell Tower, 1996.

Kennedy, Roger G. *American Churches.* New York: Stewart, Tabori & Chang, 1982.

Kirk, John T. *The Shaker World: Art, Life, Belief.* New York: Henry T. Abrams, 1997.

Lee, Laura. *Arlo, Alice, & Anglicans: The Lives of a New England Church*. Lee, Mass.: Berkshire House, 2000.

Linder, Eileen W., ed. *Yearbook of American & Canadian Churches 2001*. Sixty-ninth edition. Nashville: Abingdon Press, 2001.

Marini, Stephen A. *Radical Sects of Revolutionary New England*. Cambridge, Massachusetts: Harvard University Press, 1982.

Martin, Joel. *The Land Looks After Us: A History of Native American Religion*. New York: Oxford University Press, 2001.

Matlins, Stuart, and Arthur Magida, eds. *How to Be A Perfect Stranger: A Guide to Etiquette in Other People's Religious Ceremonies*. 2 vols. Woodstock, Vermont: SkyLight Paths, 1999.

Morrison, Dorothy. *The Craft: A Witch's Book of Shadows*. St. Paul, Minnesota: Llewellyn Publications, 2001.

"The Mosque in America." Report of the Hartford Institute for Religious Research, 2001.

Murray, Stuart. *Shaker Heritage Guidebook: Exploring the Historic Sites, Museums & Collections*. Spencertown, New York: Golden Hill Press, 1994.

Mutrux, Robert H. *Great New England Churches: Sixty-five Houses of Worship That Changed Our Lives*. Chester, Connecticut. The Globe Pequot Press, 1982.

Nicoletta, Julie. *The Architecture of the Shakers*. Woodstock, Vermont: Countryman Press, 2000.

Raboteau, Albert. *Canaan Land: A Religious History of African Americans*. New York: Oxford University Press, 2001.

Roberts, Bruce, and Ray Jones. *New England Lighthouses: Bay of Fundy to Long Island Sound*. Old Saybrook, Connecticut: Globe Pequot Press, 1996.

Ross, Michael A. *The Jewish Friendship Trail: Guidebook to Jewish Historic Sites of Boston, 1841–1926*. Belmont, Massachusetts: BostonWalks, 2000.

Ruether, Rosemary Radford, and Rosemary Skinner Keller. *In Our Own Voices: Four Centuries of Women's Religious Writings*. Louisville, Kentucky: Westminster John Knox Press, 2000.

Sadleir, Steven. *Looking for God: A Seeker's Guide to Religious and Spiritual Groups of the World*. New York: Perigee, 2000.

Seager, Richard Hughes. *Buddhism in America*. Columbia Contemporary American Religion Series. New York: Columbia University Press, 1999.

Sedgwick, Mark J. *Sufism: The Essentials*. Cairo: American University of Cairo Press, 2000.

Simmons, William S. *Spirit of the New England Tribes: Indian History and Folklore*. Hanover, New Hampshire: University Press of New England, 1986.

Smith, G. E. Kidder. *The Beacon Guide to New England Houses of Worship: An Architectural Companion*. Boston: Beacon Press, 1989.

Stein, Stephen J. *The Shaker Experience in America*. New Haven: Yale University Press, 1992.

Thoreau, Henry David. *Cape Cod*. Hyannis, Massachusetts: Parnassus Imprints, 1984.

Whitmire, Catherine. *Plain Living: A Quaker Path to Simplicity*. Notre Dame, Indiana: Sorin Books, 2001.

Williams, Peter W. *Houses of God: Region, Religion and Architecture in the United States*. Urbana: University of Illinois Press, 1997.

Wuthnow, Robert. *After Heaven: Spirituality in America Since the 1950s*. Berkeley: University of California Press, 1997.

INDEX

Numbers in **bold** indicate illustrations.

ABOUT HISTORIC BOSTON

Historic Boston Incorporated, founded in 1960, is a private, nonprofit organization that puts people and resources together to preserve endangered historic sites in the city of Boston. It gives priority to projects which will leverage additional public and private commitments, embody thoughtful restoration standards, catalyze neighborhood renewal, and protect cultural resources. To accomplish these objectives, Historic Boston engages in a variety of entrepreneurial activities which include buying property, making grants, providing technical assistance, lending money, building the capacity of other organizations with similar goals, and conducting feasibility studies. In addition, Historic Boston periodically publishes historic property casebooks to focus attention on endangered properties important to the social and architectural fabric of Boston and its neighborhoods.

Historic Boston's Steeples Project is the only program of its kind in Massachusetts, providing competitive matching grants to historic religious property owners of all denominations throughout Boston. Established in 1993, Historic Boston has raised over $1 million to provide matching grants for major repairs, technical assistance, and exterior illumination. These funds have leveraged close to $8 million in total project costs to preserve some of Boston's most treasured historic sites. Historic Boston also conducts educational seminars on preservation of religious buildings and provides technical assistance to congregations.

For additional information, contact: Historic Boston Incorporated, 3 School Street, Boston, Mass. 02108 Phone: 617-227-4679; Fax: 617-742-7431; Web site: www.historicboston.org

PICTURE CREDITS

Permission to use copyright material is gratefully acknowledged to the following. While every effort has been made to trace all copyright holders, the publisher apologizes to any holders possibly not acknowledged.

Christian Charisius: 68, 76, 85, 87, 90, 93, 96, 103, 110, 142, 144, 150, 165, 174, 181, 196, 211, 232 top, 232 bottom, 234, 244, 247, 250, 252, 265, 272, 280, 287, 288, 333, 336, 341

The First Church of Christ, Scientist: 136

Jean Donohue: 147

Judson H. Flower, Jr.: 307

Jan-Erik Guerth: 171, 188, 222, 295, 303, 313, 322, 326, 360

Mama Guerth: 138, 228, 297

Historic Boston Incorporated: 52, 62, 106

Susan Humphrey: 304

Jana Riess: 158, 192, 206, 218, 259, 268, 319, 361, 366

Four-color insert
Christian Charisius: all photos on page A; page B, top left and bottom; page C, bottom; page D, top and center
Jan-Erik Guerth: page B, center; page D, bottom
Jana Riess: page B, top right
The First Church of Christ, Scientist: page C, top